Play, Learn, and Grow™

Advisers

Marcella F. Anderson
Patient/Family Librarian
Rainbow Babies and Childrens Hospital
Cleveland, Ohio

Carolyn S. Brodie
Assistant Professor
School of Library and Information Science
Kent State University
Kent, Ohio

Kathleen Deerr
Head
Children's & Parents' Services
Mastics-Moriches-Shirley Community Library
Shirley, New York

Carol A. Doll
Assistant Professor
Graduate School of Library & Information
Science
University of Washington
Seattle, Washington

Frances Smardo Dowd
Associate Professor
School of Library and Information Studies
Texas Woman's University
Denton, Texas

Jeannine Laughlin-Porter
Associate Professor
School of Library Science
University of Southern Mississippi
Hattiesburg, Mississippi

Ruth K. MacDonald
Professor of English and Head,
Department of English and Philosophy
Purdue University—Calumet
Hammond, Indiana

Ellen Mahoney
Children's Librarian
San Francisco Public Library
San Francisco, California

Rita G. Newman
Principal
Amelia Earhart Learning Center
Dallas Independent School District
Dallas, Texas

Mary M. Schumacher
Head
Children's Programming & Early Childhood
Services
Middle Country Public Library
Centereach, New York

Betty Kay Seibt
Doctoral Candidate
Department of English
Texas Woman's University
Denton, Texas

Maureen White
Assistant Professor
Library and Information Sciences
The University of Houston at Clear Lake
Houston, Texas

Kathy Woodrell
Reference Specialist
Humanities and Social Services Division
Library of Congress
Washington, District of Columbia

Play, Learn, and Grow ™

An Annotated Guide to the Best Books and Materials for Very Young Children

James L. Thomas

R. R. BOWKER ®
A Reed Reference Publishing Company
New Providence, New Jersey

Published by R. R. Bowker, a Reed Reference Publishing Company
Copyright © 1992 by Reed Publishing (USA) Inc.
All rights reserved
Printed and bound in the United States of America
Bowker is a registered trademark of Reed Publishing (USA) Inc.

Library of Congress Cataloging-in-Publication Data

Thomas, James L., 1945–
    Play, learn, and grow : an annotated guide to the best books and
    materials for very young children / by James L. Thomas.
          p.   cm.
    Includes bibliographical references and index.
    ISBN: 978-0-8352-3019-3

    1. Bibliography—Best books—Children's literature.   2. Preschool
children—Books and reading.   3. Children's literature—
Bibliography.   4. Audio-visual materials—Catalogs.   I. Title
Z1037.T46   1992
[PN1009.A1]
028.1'62—dc20   92–15458
                                                      CIP

Contents

Reviewers

Susan Allison
Dallas, Texas

Karen Altstaetter
Arlington, Texas

Marcella F. Anderson
Pepper Pike, Ohio

Jeanie Athens
San Diego, California

Judith Baggett
Coppell, Texas

Ann Bailey
Austin, Texas

Cheryl Barry
Allen, Texas

Linda Batchler
Ferris, Texas

Nonie Bliss
Dallas, Texas

Carolyn S. Brodie
Kent, Ohio

Mary Louise Budd
Cincinnati, Ohio

Beth Conaway
De Soto, Texas

Claudia Cooper
Fort Stockton, Texas

Cindy Davenport
McKinney, Texas

Dorothy Davidson
Abilene, Texas

Kathleen Deerr
Shirley, New York

Carol Doll
Seattle, Washington

Deborah Dudash
Lewisville, Texas

Marianne Farner
Dallas, Texas

Judith Gloyer
Milwaukee, Wisconsin

Anna Biagioni Hart
Alexandria, Virginia

Karen Hill
Inman, South Carolina

Nancy Howland
Hannibal, Missouri

Celia A. Huffman
Brook Park, Ohio

Debby Jennings
Fort Worth, Texas

Virginia Jeschelnig
Mentor, Ohio

Betty Jean Kennedy
Carrollton, Texas

Nancy Krueger
Hurst, Texas

Starr LaTronica
Berkeley, California

Jeannine Laughlin-Porter
Hattiesburg, Mississippi

Carolyn Lucas
North Richland Hills, Texas

Ruth K. MacDonald
Hammond, Indiana

Ellen Mahoney
San Francisco, California

Elaine Markley
Euless, Texas

Nancy Mitchell-Tapping
Dallas, Texas

Virginia Hammond Mundt
Farmers Branch, Texas

Rita G. Newman
Dallas, Texas

Carolyn Noah
Worcester, Massachusetts

Deborah Perez
Dallas, Texas

Heide Piehler
Shorewood, Wisconsin

Karen K. Radtke
Milwaukee, Wisconsin

Bill Raley
Garland, Texas

Deanna Robertson
Dallas, Texas

JoAnn Rogers
Fort Worth, Texas

Jane Ross
Coppell, Texas

Connie Ryle
Denver, Colorado

Belinda Sakowski
Sherman, Texas

Jane Saliers
Decatur, Georgia

Mary M. Schumacher
Centereach, New York

Betty Kay Seibt
Sanger, Texas

Janice D. Smuda
Parma, Ohio

Barbara Spencer
Dallas, Texas

Evelyn Squillari
Las Vegas, Nevada

Robin Switzer
Henderson, Texas

Judith A. Thomas
Abilene, Texas

Pat Vera
Crowley, Texas

Chris Vinsonhaler
Hattiesburg, Mississippi

Tim Wadham
Grand Prairie, Texas

Dona Weisman
Garland, Texas

Peggy Wheeler
Mentor, Ohio

Maureen White
Abilene, Texas

Gloria Willingham
Irving, Texas

Kathy Woodrell
Alexandria, Virginia

Jackie Writz
Calgary, Alberta
Canada

Foreword
The Adult's Role in the Emergent Literacy Process

by Frances Smardo Dowd

LITERACY, THE ABILITY TO READ AND WRITE one's native language, is the foundation for achievement both in school and in the world of work (Kulleseid and Strickland, 1989). Adults, parents, grandparents, early childhood teachers, librarians and child-care providers can play a vital role in helping young children achieve "a set toward literacy" and look upon reading as a pleasurable lifelong experience (Holdaway, 1976 and 1979).

The significant role of adults in facilitating literacy in preschoolers is evident from recent research findings about the beginning reading process. These findings have resulted in a shift of thinking from the concept of "reading readiness" to "emergent literacy." The traditional belief in "reading readiness," which implied that age six is a magic point in development or sudden period of transformation when children are ready to begin to learn to read via systematic instruction in and accumulation of isolated prereading and prewriting skills, has been discredited as incorrect for several reasons (Strickland and Morrow, 1988 and 1989 A).

First, we now know that children's knowledge and skills about reading emerge continually from infancy, with exposure to and active engagement with oral and written language, books, and stories (Strickland and Morrow, 1989 A). Second, contrary to the "reading readiness" perspective, reading and writing develop concurrently and interrelatedly with oral language. For example, children as young as two may recognize and try to say the names of all the sugar-laden cereals in the grocery store, and even three-year-olds often want to "write" and "read" their own shopping lists (Strickland and Morrow, 1988). Early readers also like to make marks on paper, and consequently have been identified as "pencil and paper kids" (Clark, 1976; Durkin, 1966). Third, in that literacy develops slowly through countless experiences with books, writing tools, and conversations with others, it is a social process, not just a cognitive skill (Silvern and Silvern, 1989; Strickland and Morrow, 1989 A). Fourth, another major difference between the concept of "reading readiness" and that of "emergent literacy" is that the latter emphasizes children's ongoing development of skills in reading and writing rather than the accumulation of a set of isolated prerequisite subskills (Strickland and Morrow, 1988). Fifth, young children learn to read and write by active use, or by reading and writing, just as they learn to talk by talking (Walton, 1989). Lastly, literacy is goal-directed or functional. Preschoolers pretending to read a recipe when "baking" and pretending to write a message to a parent are illustrating the fact that print is meaningful to them and serves an important function (Teale and Sulzby, 1989).

The crucial role adults can play in facilitating the beginning reading process, or emergent literacy, of young children is also apparent from the findings of a large body of research. Four factors are repeatedly present in the homes and learning environments of children who learn to read at an early age: (1) an availability and range of printed materials in the environment; (2) reading "done" in the environment both by the adult for the child and by the adult for himself or herself; (3) facilitation and encouragement of the child to use pencil and paper; and (4) adult responsiveness to children's attempts to read or ask questions about printed material and stories heard (Teale, 1978).

What implications do the "emergent literacy" perspective and related research hold for adults interested in the literacy of young children? Or, in other words, how can adults aid the emergent literacy process in young children? They can and should talk and listen to children, answer their questions about print, regularly read books aloud to them for sheer pleasure, and model reading and writing for them so that they learn to value and enjoy books. Reading road signs, store signs, and package labels is important, too (Mavrogenes, 1990). Adults can and should take young children to the public library to obtain a library card. Allow children to make their own selection of books they want to hear or browse through, as this opportunity seems to be extremely important in establishing their orientation to literacy (Kulleseid and Strickland, 1989). Reward children's attempts to read and write with praise (Mavrogenes, 1990). By providing opportunities for young children to participate in dramatic play activities, by encouraging them to take risks in and experiment with "reading" and "writing," and by creating environments rich in functional, meaningful, and holistic experiences with print, adults can help children become literate (Teale and Martinez, 1988; Walton, 1989).

But the single most important activity, and the one essential for building the knowledge required for eventual success in reading, is reading aloud regularly to children. Reading aloud is especially valuable during the preschool years and when children are active participants in discussing the meaning of stories and words (Anderson, et al., 1985). For years, educators have known that children who come from homes and environments in which storybook reading takes place regularly have an educational advantage over those who do not. The benefit is that those children are more likely to learn to read before being given any formal instruction in first grade and are more likely to become proficient readers (Smith, 1989; Strickland and Taylor, 1989). Neither race, ethnicity, socioeconomic level, nor IQ distinguish readers from non-readers. Differences lie solely in access to print, being read to, valuing education/ reading, and early writing (Cullinan, 1989).

Why exactly is reading aloud to young children so influential in literacy? It is because reading aloud specifically increases young children's listening, writing, and speaking ability; vocabulary; letter and symbol recognition; ability to use more complex sentences; literal and inferential comprehension skills; ability to match spoken words with print; positive attitudes toward reading; and tendency to view reading as a valued activity (Jalongo, 1988). Shared book experiences help preschoolers better understand the concept of authorship; what a book is for and how to handle a book (e.g., turning the pages correctly from front to back); directionality of print (i.e., knowing that reading is from left to right); the concept of words, letters, and punctuation; the idiomatic forms of language; and the meaning of the story in "book language," which is more formal than ordinary conversation (Jalongo, 1988; Strickland and Morrow, 1989 C).

Through interaction with an adult that is centered around books, young children learn modeling of the reading they are exposed to; similarities and differences between spoken and written language; the basic form and structure of written language and literary conventions; the function of print (i.e., that marks on paper have sounds and meaning); a "sense of story" (i.e., that a story has a beginning, a middle, and an end); and the concept that what is spoken can be written (Kontos, 1986; Mavrogenes, 1990). In addition, the social activity of reading aloud to preschoolers helps them learn to predict what will happen next in stories, and causes them to associate reading with pleasure (Strickland and Morrow, 1989 C). Stories broaden children's experiences, help them develop rich imaginations, and increase their listening skills (Smardo and Curry, 1982). Still further, children who are read to on a regular basis are better able to narrate events, describe scenes, follow instructions, and invent stories based on illustrations (Wells, 1986).

How should adults share storybooks with young children? Before reading, show children the cover of the book, encourage predictions of content, let children discuss their own experiences related to the topic of the story, and introduce the main characters. During the reading encourage children to react to and comment about the story and illustrations, to voice their own interpretations, to elaborate on the text when appropriate, and to participate or "help" in reading the story by repeating various phrases. After reading the story, help children participate in a follow-up activity (in art, music, language, science, etc.) that requires thinking about the book, and discuss motives of characters or a possible different ending (Mason, Peterman, and Kerr, 1989).

Sharing books with young children both on a one-to-one basis and in small groups of four or five children is beneficial to their emergent literacy growth. Reading books aloud to a child one-to-one is a "celebration of family life" and an "intimate occasion which can not be staged" (Strickland and Taylor, 1989). These home lap-reading situations appear to have a powerful impact on preschool literacy development (Kulleseid and Strickland, 1989). On the other hand, reading books to preschoolers in small groups seems to offer as much interaction as one-to-one readings; and, perhaps because literacy is such a social activity, it has been found to result in greater comprehension than one-to-one readings (Morrow and Smith, 1990).

Do not hesitate to read the same favorite storybook again and again, if children request this. Although this may be boring for adults, it is very valuable to young children. Not only does listening to rereadings fulfill children's emotional need for security and stability, but, more importantly, hearing the same book repeatedly permits young children the opportunity to explore a variety of features of the story (Teale and Martinez, 1988). Research indicates that the books that are read to young children repeatedly are also those that they select to "read" on their own to themselves or to others before they have learned to read in the conventional sense (Martinez and Teale, 1988).

These "emergent storybook readings" or "independent reenactments" of books are young children's first approximations at reading. They follow a developmental pattern, gradually sounding more like the text of the actual book (Cullinan, Greene, and Jaggar, 1990; Sulzby, 1985).

For example, children's initial attempts to "read" are governed solely by the pictures in the book, with no attention given to the print. That is, children first label, or point to an object in the book and name it. This is followed by commenting, or giving information about the labeled object. Interestingly enough, it seems that the old adage of "a little knowledge is a dangerous thing," or, conversely, that "ignorance is bliss," holds true and is at work in the emergent reading process (Sulzby, 1985). After children progress through the solely picture-governed to the print-governed attempts to "read" a book, but before they actually read in the conventional sense, they often are reluctant to "read," and may even refuse to try, as they realize they must attend to the print instead of the pictures to understand the story. This reluctance stems from their awareness that they don't yet know many of the words on the page. Giving preschoolers opportunities for emergent storybook readings to adults, to their dolls and stuffed animals, and to their peers, is important as it helps them learn to read by allowing time to practice and model what they experience when adults read aloud to them.

Parents, early childhood teachers, librarians, child-care providers, and other adults can enhance the literacy development of young children by creating a library corner full of reading materials, a writing center with an abundant supply of implements for writing, and a dramatic play area with simple props to stimulate oral language (Strickland and Morrow, 1989 B). A library corner assures that children have convenient access to books. Its design has been found to increase children's interest in and use of books (Morrow, 1982; Morrow and Weinstein, 1982). For example, children are more likely to interact with books if the classroom library is a focal point of the room; is partitioned off from the rest of the room and distraction free; is large enough for four or five children at once; and contains comfortable pillows, open-faced shelves for books to be displayed, and a wide variety of trade books, literature-oriented displays, and props (Morrow, 1982; Morrow and Weinstein, 1982).

A writing center should include an assortment of different writing implements (e.g., pens, pencils, computers, markers, typewriters, magnetic letters, chalk, and crayons) for children to explore writing and print and to collaborate with others (Teale and Sulzby, 1989). Also include paper (e.g., note pads, forms, greeting cards, lined paper, and envelopes) for children to write "messages," letters, grocery lists, telephone numbers, and the like.

Praise young children's attempts at writing and encourage their "invented spellings," which are their first approximations of conventional writing (Mavrogenes, 1990). Often this consists of only the beginning letter of a word and of the invented spelling of sounds children hear. Invented spelling is developmental, not random or incorrect (Cullinan and Strickland, 1986; Schickedanz, 1986). Children who are encouraged to draw and scribble stories at an early age will later learn to compose more easily, more effectively, and with greater confidence than children who do not have this encouragement (U.S. Department of Education, 1986).

The early childhood environment should also provide opportunities for dramatic play as this is a powerful vehicle for oral language development, allows young children to rehearse the dramas of life, and helps them use language in lifelike but play settings (Glazer, 1989). Children use dramatic play to try on language and to practice their developing understanding of the function of print and language (Vukelich, 1990). Of course, a prerequisite to dramatic play is young children's exposure to the real world environment, in order that they can incorporate their actual experiences into their role playing and dialogue (Vukelich, 1990).

When literacy props are included in the early childhood environment, when aspects of the environment are labeled, and when the play area is sharply defined (such as a specific place designated as a library, kitchen, grocery store or post office) and set apart from noisier areas, there are added advantages in terms of emergent literacy enhancement. Under these conditions, young children use reading and writing in more purposeful and complex ways, increase the amount of literacy activities in their play, and behave more interactively with their peers rather than in a solitary way (Neuman and Roskos, 1990). Props in the dramatic play area, such as stuffed animals, hand puppets, and old real telephones, provide points of departure for children to use oral language (Glazer, 1989).

As print is an integral part of real life situations, literacy materials can be easily integrated into the dramatic play setting. Immerse children in an environment with a range of printed materials including, in addition to books, displays of children's art and writing, calendars, magazines, newspapers, telephone directories, store catalogs, greeting cards, letters, food coupons, stationery, letters, junk mail, and functional labels for the contents of cabinets. Research indicates that when these items are added to the play environment, their presence seems to encourage young children to incorporate more literacy activities into their behavior (Vukelich, 1990).

The role of the adult in this dramatic play is to assemble and display literacy materials and props in the environment and to permit and guide young children to play independently and informally with them (Vukelich, 1990). For example, to promote literacy, a "bakery" in the dramatic play area would require the following props: a baker's hat and apron, cookie cutters, rolling pin, measuring cup, bowls, spoons, pans, and trays, as well as printed recipes, cookbooks, an order pad with pencil, a telephone, a cash register, printed receipts, name tags for employees, and a list of prices next to the various names of baked items sold (Morrow, 1989). Literacy props should be: (1) appropriate (used naturally and safely by young children); (2) authentic (real rather than pretend or made up); and (3) utilitarian (serving a particular function young children may be familiar with in their everyday life) (Neuman and Roskos, 1990).

In summary, adults have a remarkable opportunity to impact the extent of young children's emerging literacy. Charlotte Huck, children's literature specialist, states that adults do not help children achieve literacy and then give them literature, but rather children achieve literacy through literature and the love of good books (Huck, 1979). Huck further states that, since learning to read and to enjoy books begins so early in life, parents (and librarians and teachers) are primarily responsible for developing this love of reading (Huck, 1987). Stated another way, the "single most important ingredient in exciting children about good literature is an adult committed to these books" (Silvey, 1988). *Play, Learn, and Grow: An Annotated Guide to the Best Books and Materials for Very Young Children* can enable parents, caregivers, teachers, and librarians to identify appropriate quality titles to share with infants, toddlers, preschoolers, and kindergartners. Once favorite selections are made, the titles can be enjoyed together, and adults can provide the best gift for young children—a love of books and reading. Those who wish to extend their readers' capabilities can also utilize the criteria for selection and apply it to newer titles on the market.

References

ANDERSON, R. C., ET AL. *Becoming a Nation of Readers: The Report of the Commission on Reading.* Washington, D.C.: National Institute of Education, 1985.

CLARK, MARGARET. *Young Fluent Readers.* Portsmouth, N.H.: Heinemann, 1976.

CULLINAN, BERNICE. "Literature for Young Children." In Dorothy Strickland and Lesley Morrow (eds.). *Emerging Literacy: Young Children Learn to Read and Write.* Newark, Del.: International Reading Association, 1989.

CULLINAN, BERNICE, ELLIN GREENE, AND ANGELA JAGGAR. "Books, Babies and Libraries: The Librarians' Role in Literacy Development." *Language Arts* 67(1990): 750–755.

CULLINAN, BERNICE, AND DOROTHY STRICKLAND. "The Early Years: Language, Literature, and Literacy in Classroom Research." *The Reading Teacher* 39, #8(1986): 798–806.

DURKIN, DOLORES. *Children Who Read Early: Two Longitudinal Studies.* New York: Teachers College Press, 1966.

GLAZER, SUSAN. "Oral Language and Literacy Development." In Dorothy Strickland and Lesley Morrow (eds.). *Emerging Literacy: Young Children Learn to Read and Write.* Newark, Del.: International Reading Association, 1989.

HOLDAWAY, R. D. *The Foundations of Literacy.* Sydney: Ashton Scholastic, 1979.

HOLDAWAY, R. D. "The Oral Dimensions of Literacy." In D. B. Doake and B. T. O'Rourke (eds.). *New Dimensions for Reading.* Wellington: New Zealand Educational Institute, 1976.

HUCK, CHARLOTTE. *Children's Literature in the Elementary School.* 4th edition. New York: Holt, Rinehart and Winston, 1987.

HUCK, CHARLOTTE. "No Wider than the Heart Is Wide." In J. E. Shapiro (ed.). *Using Literature and Poetry Affectively.* Newark, Del.: International Reading Association, 1979.

JALONGO, MARY. *Young Children and Picture Books: Literature from Infancy to Six.* Washington, D.C.: National Association for the Education of Young Children, 1988.

KONTOS, SUSAN. "Research in Review: What Preschool Children Know about Reading and How They Learn It." *Young Children* 42, #1(1986): 58–66.

KULLESEID, ELEANOR, AND DOROTHY STRICKLAND. *Literature, Literacy, and Learning: Classroom Teachers, Library Media Specialists, and the Literature-Based Curriculum.* Chicago: American Library Association, 1989.

MARTINEZ, MIRIAM, AND WILLIAM TEALE. "Reading in a Kindergarten Classroom Library." *The Reading Teacher* 41, #6(1988): 568–572.

MASON, JANA, CAROL PETERMAN, AND BONNIE KERR. "Reading to Kindergarten Children." In Dorothy Strickland and Lesley Morrow (eds.). *Emerging Literacy: Young Children Learn to Read and Write*. Newark, Del.: International Reading Association, 1989.

MAVROGENES, NANCY. "Helping Parents Help Their Children Become Literate." *Young Children 45*, #4(1990): 4-9.

MORROW, LESLEY. "Designing the Classroom to Promote Literacy Development." In Dorothy Strickland and Lesley Morrow (eds.). *Emerging Literacy: Young Children Learn to Read and Write*. Newark, Del.: International Reading Association, 1989.

MORROW, LESLEY. "Relationships between Literature Programs, Library Corner Designs, and Children's Use of Literature." *Journal of Educational Research 75*, #5(1982): 339-344.

MORROW, LESLEY, AND JEFFREY SMITH. "The Effects of Group Size on Interactive Storybook Reading." *Reading Research Quarterly 25*, #3(1990): 213-231.

MORROW, LESLEY, AND C. S. WEINSTEIN. "Increasing Children's Use of Literature through Programs and Physical Design Changes." *Elementary School Journal 83*, #2(1982): 131-137.

NEUMAN, SUSAN, AND KATHY ROSKOS. "Play, Print and Purpose: Enriching Play Environments for Literacy Development." *The Reading Teacher 44*, #3(1990): 214-221.

SCHICKEDANZ, JUDITH. *More than the ABC's: The Early Stages of Reading and Writing*. Washington, D.C.: National Association for the Education of Young Children, 1986.

SILVERN, STEVEN, AND LINDA SILVERN. *Beginning Literacy and Your Child*. Newark, Del.: International Reading Association, 1989.

SILVEY, A. "Editorial: The Love of Reading." *The Horn Book 64*, #4(1988): 422.

SMARDO, FRANCES, AND JOHN CURRY. *What Research Tells Us About Storyhours and Receptive Language*. Denton, Tex.: North Texas State University, 1982.

SMITH, CARL. "Reading Aloud: An Experience for Sharing." *The Reading Teacher 42*, #4(1989): 320-321.

STRICKLAND, DOROTHY, AND LESLEY MORROW (EDS.). *Emerging Literacy: Young Children Learn to Read and Write*. Newark, Del.: International Reading Association, 1989. A.

STRICKLAND, DOROTHY, AND LESLEY MORROW. "Environments Rich in Print Promote Literacy Behavior During Play." *The Reading Teacher 43*, #2(1989): 178-179. B.

STRICKLAND, DOROTHY, AND LESLEY MORROW. "Interactive Experience with Storybook Reading." *The Reading Teacher* 42, #4(1989): 322. C.

STRICKLAND, DOROTHY, AND LESLEY MORROW. "New Perspectives on Young Children Learning to Read and Write." *The Reading Teacher* 42, #1(1988): 70-71.

STRICKLAND, DOROTHY, AND DENNY TAYLOR. "Family Storybook Reading: Implications for Children, Families, and Curriculum." In Dorothy Strickland and Lesley Morrow (eds.). *Emerging Literacy: Young Children Learn to Read and Write.* Newark, Del.: International Reading Association, 1989.

SULZBY, ELIZABETH. "Children's Emergent Reading of Favorite Storybooks: A Developmental Study." *Reading Research Quarterly* 20, #4(1985): 458-481.

TEALE, WILLIAM. "Positive Environments for Learning to Read: What Studies of Early Readers Tell Us." *Language Arts* 55, #8(1978): 922-932.

TEALE, WILLIAM, AND MIRIAM MARTINEZ. "Getting on the Right Road to Reading: Bringing Books and Young Children Together in the Classroom." *Young Children* 44, #1(1988): 10-14.

TEALE, WILLIAM, AND ELIZABETH SULZBY. "Emergent Literacy: New Perspectives." In Dorothy Strickland and Lesley Morrow (eds.). *Emerging Literacy: Young Children Learn to Read and Write.* Newark, Del.: International Reading Association, 1989.

UNITED STATES DEPARTMENT OF EDUCATION. *What Works: Research About Teaching and Learning.* Washington, D.C.: Government Printing Office, 1986.

VUKELICH, CAROL. "Where's the Paper? Literacy during Dramatic Play." *Childhood Education* 66, #4(1990): 205-209.

WALTON, SHERRY. "Katy Learns to Read and Write." *Young Children* 44, #4(1989): 52-57.

WELLS, GORDON. *The Meaning Makers: Children Learning Language and Using Language to Learn.* Portsmouth, N.H.: Heinemann, 1986.

Introduction

WITH THE INCREASED EMPHASIS on day care and programs for preschoolers, the practitioners—day-care providers, teachers, and librarians—are being bombarded by publishers with materials designated "appropriate for this age group." To date, there has been no single work that provides guidance for the selection of exemplary media (print and nonprint) for use with or by these youngest children and the professionals who serve them. *Play, Learn, and Grow: An Annotated Guide to the Best Books and Materials for Very Young Children* fills this gap.

Background

"Never before in our history have so many of our infants and young children been enrolled for extended periods in regular out-of-home programs" (Elkind, 1987, p. 5). If this be the case, and there is no reason to doubt it given the data that the experts cite repeatedly, what are the reasons for the proliferation of these programs and the enrollment of so many children?

As a result of legislation being passed to provide for our "youngest" children, ages birth to four, more and more state service agencies have identified funding for programs. Numerous states have seen that support for day care is essential for the well-being of the child as well as the adult, and have provided services such as designated funding packages, sliding-fee scales, head start programs for children identified "at risk" and clearinghouses for resource and referral services to clients, to name only a few.

With the increased availability of supportive monies from these agencies and the individual states, and with the resulting decrease in charges assessed families, mothers (the typical care provider for these young children) are now able to either enter or return to the workforce. As reported by Lein (1986),

In the United States:
Almost 47% of mothers with children under one year of age were in the paid labor force.
Over 52% of mothers of children under six years of age were in the paid labor force in 1984.
By 1990, approximately 60% of all elementary school-age children will live in households where all resident parents are employed. (p. 1)

And as mentioned again in *Monthly Labor Review* (Hayghe, 1988, p. 38), "The potential demand for child care is immense. As of March 1987, there were 10.5 million children under the age of 6 whose mothers were in the labor force . . . ."

School systems are continuing to include and are increasing the number of head start programs for many of the disadvantaged children who desperately need and benefit from exposure to a well-managed, developmentally appropriate environment prior to entering kindergarten. In order to meet this influx of children, there has been a noted increase and interest in early childhood education bachelor's and master's programs among those entering the teaching profession throughout this country. Also, as a result of more highly educated individuals entering the field, quality of the curricula and programming possibilities have typically changed for the better. As one might expect, however, philosophical approaches vary widely. As discussed by Hendrick (1986), three perspectives with numerous offshoots presently exist: "the behavioristic learning theory approach, the Piagetian cognitive-interaction approach, and the developmental-interaction approach" (p. 7).

Another major influence that has helped to determine the direction of quality day care, funding, resource acquisition, etc., is national and international professional organizations, such as the Association for Childhood Education International and the National Association for the Education of Young Children, to name only two. These groups continue to have a major impact on all aspects of this field since their constituency comprises parents and teachers genuinely interested in the ongoing growth and development of services for young children. As would be expected, pushing for legislation both federally and locally as well as providing continuing education possibilities are among the groups' major areas of emphasis.

The Importance of Exposure to Quality Materials

Most new parents want to provide the best, the most positive environment in which their children can grow and flourish. Concern for the physical well being of the newborn, once stabilized, quickly extends to other areas involving both the mental and emotional development of the child. Therefore, providing materials that will stimulate visual and auditory responses becomes a challenge for the parent who does not have an adequate background in children's materials. The same may be true of the day-care provider or the teacher who has never taken any formal course work in this subject area.

Before establishing how and where one locates the best materials to share with these younger children, perhaps it is appropriate at this point to examine briefly the role that parents and/or teachers/day-care providers play in developing a child's potential abilities. Individuals writing in this area have provided us with conclusive evidence on the difference adults can and do make in this process:

> ... what experiences in a child's life are most suited to promote his ability to find meaning in his life; to endow life in general with more meaning. . . . nothing is more important than the impact of parents and others who take care of the child . . . . (Bettelheim, 1976, p. 4)

and

> Parents are their children's first and most influential teacher. What parents do to help their children learn is more important to academic success than how well-off the family is. (Bennett, 1986, np)

Specifically in promoting a child's eventual love for reading and the benefits to be realized, the researchers point to the following:

> The love of reading is the foundation of literacy, and as such it will become the cornerstone of your child's intellectual and educational development. (Copperman, 1986, p. 9)
>
> Research has shown us that reading to preschool children should be more than an occasional activity . . . . Reading books to children can positively affect their language development, interest in books, academic readiness, success in learning to read, specific reading interests, and social attitudes and values. (McCormick, 1983, p. 7)
>
> Parents are their children's first and most important teachers. Children begin learning to read at an early age when parents first use words and images to describe and interpret their world. (Binkley et al., 1988, iii)

and finally,

> I believe that books should play a prominent part in children's lives from babyhood; that access to books, through parents and other adults, greatly increases a child's chances of becoming a happy and involved human being. (Butler, 1980, p. 9)

What we do for these young children in sharing materials clearly does make a difference. Since this is true, we must select the *best*, the *most appropriate* from that which is offered by a wide variety of publishers.

Speaking to this challenge, Betsy Hearne (1981) makes the following plea:

> Children deserve the best you give people you care for. It doesn't take an educational study to show that children do what you do, not what you tell them to do. If you like to read to yourself and your children, they will like reading to themselves and their children. Childhood is the time and children's books are the place for powerful emotions, powerful language, powerful art. (pp. 7–8)

In addition to using the annotated titles in *Play, Learn, and Grow* and surveying the materials listed in Appendix 1: Professional Resources, teachers and parents will want to consult frequently such periodicals as *Young Children, School Library Journal, Booklist, Reading Teacher, Childhood Education*

International, Horn Book, and Early Years for reviews of new materials. When visiting bookstores specializing in children's materials, one should ask the trained personnel for guidance in selection. This is far superior to browsing in a grocery store and selecting inferior titles that perhaps cost less but will not withstand repeated usage and are typically poorly written or unimaginatively illustrated. Talking with others in the profession, such as your school and/or public librarian, and forming partnerships to share resources and successes and failures with materials for preschoolers, is another avenue for improving and developing a collection. Also, if nonprint materials, such as audiotapes, videotapes, filmstrips, etc., are purchased, then an allotment must be made for equipment acquisition and maintenance. Finally, and perhaps most important in such a listing as this, is the process of field testing the materials presently available with the youngsters themselves. Seeking their reactions—likes and dislikes—is the best way to identify favorite themes and subjects appropriate for their particular age and stage of development. All of these suggestions will assist in keeping the collection current and meaningful for this young clientele.

References

BENNETT, WILLIAM J. What Works: Research About Teaching and Learning. U.S. Department of Education, 1986.

BETTELHEIM, BRUNO. The Uses of Enchantment: The Meaning and Importance of Fairy Tales. Knopf, 1976.

BINKLEY, MARILYN R., ET AL. Becoming a Nation of Readers: What Parents Can Do. Heath/Office of Educational Research and Improvement, 1988.

BUTLER, DOROTHY. Babies Need Books. Bodley, 1980.

COPPERMAN, PAUL. Taking Books to Heart. Addison-Wesley, 1986.

ELKIND, DAVID. Miseducation: Preschoolers at Risk. Knopf, 1987.

HAYGHE, HOWARD V. (1988) "Employers and Child Care: What Roles Do They Play?" Monthly Labor Review September 1988: 38–44.

HEARNE, BETSY. Choosing Books for Children: A Commonsense Guide. Delacorte, 1981.

HENDRICK, JOANNE. Total Learning: Curriculum for the Young Child. Merrill, 1986.

LEIN, LAURA. The Child Day Care Crisis in Texas: An Introduction to the Problem. United Way of Texas Child Care Working Group, 1986.

McCORMICK, SANDRA (1983) "Reading Aloud to Preschoolers Age 3–6: A Review of the Research." Reading Horizons 24: 7–12.

Matching Books to Young Children*

ADULTS WHO CHOOSE BOOKS to share with young children should have at least a basic understanding of child development. Although each child is unique and has individual needs, interests and abilities, most children have similar developmental characteristics at various ages and stages. Keeping in mind children's emotional, social, intellectual and physical abilities at each age level will help assure that only books that appropriately match their level of developmental maturity are shared. Information about developmental levels can tell us not only something about children, but can also indicate the type of literature that children are likely to enjoy and understand at a specific age.

The following chart summarizes and provides an overview of some characteristic growth patterns, suggests implications for selection and use of books, and provides examples of a few suitable titles for a particular stage of development.

Developmental Portrait of Young Children as a Guide to Book Selection

Age Characteristics	Implications	Sample Book Titles
INFANTS: BIRTH THROUGH 12 MONTHS		
Explores and learns through senses	Needs tactile, auditory, visual experiences	*Pat the Bunny* (Kunhardt) (cardboard and "toy" books)
Learns by hands-on approach, activity and manipulation	Needs opportunity for exploration	*Hand Rhymes* (Brown)
Responds to sounds of human voice, especially rhythmic patterns	Enjoys rhymes, songs, lullabies	*Hush, Little Baby* (Zemach); Mother Goose rhymes

*Compiled by Frances Smardo Dowd, Associate Professor, School of Library and Information Studies, Texas Woman's University.

Age Characteristics	Implications	Sample Book Titles
Learns basic language—associates objects with words, and plays with sounds	Enjoys finding and naming things	*Baby Around the Clock* (Slegers); *Crash! Bang! Boom!* (Spier)
Learns basic trust in human relationships	Needs love and affection from people and stories as well as dependable routines	*Goodnight Moon* (Brown)
Has a very limited attention span	Needs books with little to no story-line that can be shared one page at a time in any order	*My Day* (Rippon)

13 MONTHS THROUGH 2 YEARS

Has limited experiences so interests center on self; egotistical (doesn't play with others—parallel play)	Needs books that deal with self and immediate familiar activities/ environment	*Family* (Oxenbury); *My Hands Can* (Holzenthaler)
Learns autonomy and basic self-help skills and has pride in personal accomplishments	Enjoys stories of toddler accomplishments and growing independence	*What Do Toddlers Do?* (Slier)
Turns pages of a book one at a time—better fine motor coordination	Can begin to use/look at regular paper (non-cardboard) paged books	Any paper (non-cardboard) paged book
Has great deal of curiosity	Enjoys games and guessing	*The Saucepan Game* (Ormerod); *Where's Spot?* (Hill)
Wants to test limits of adults; assertive and argumentative	Enjoys books in which characters are in charge and in control of the situation	*When You Were a Baby* (Jonas); *Geraldine's Blanket* (Keller)
Doesn't share—possessive (may hoard!)	Relates to books about owning personal items	*Have You Seen My Cat?* (Carle)

3 THROUGH 4 YEARS

Begins to develop a sense of story	Needs simple, well structured plots	*Rosie's Walk* (Hutchins)

Age Characteristics	Implications	Sample Book Titles
Develops language skills rapidly	Enjoys rhymes, repetition, cumulative tales and simple folktales	*Goldilocks and the Three Bears* (Brett); *Brown Bear, Brown Bear, What Do You See?* (Martin)
Is curious about own world	Enjoys stories about pets, play, home, everyday experiences	*Sam* (Scott); *Can I Keep Him?* (Kellogg)
Builds concepts through many first-hand experiences	Needs books that extend and reinforce developing abstract, simple concepts	*Is It Rough?* (Hoban); *Trucks* (Gibbons)
Develops a sense of humor	Enjoys nonsense and laughable, preposterous situations	*Anno's Faces* (Anno)
Imitates and plays pretend; very imaginative	Enjoys make-believe stories	*Martin's Hats* (Blos); *Angelina Ballerina* (Holabird)
Often has imaginary worries	Needs books that reassure	*The Little Engine That Could* (Piper)

5 YEARS

Age Characteristics	Implications	Sample Book Titles
Expresses normal realistic fears	Needs books that address fearful and new situations	*Who's Afraid of the Dark?* (Bonsall)
Develops self identity	Enjoys stories about self-importance	*Big Sarah's Little Boots* (Bourgeois)
Develops powers of observation	Gives attention to detail	*Who's Counting?* (Tafuri)
Has little understanding of time concepts	Needs books that can help understand time sequence	*Spring Is Here* (Gomi); *Time to . . .* (McMillan)
Makes absolute judgments about right and wrong	Needs books that reward good behavior and punish "bad" behavior—poetic justice and happy endings	*Big Al* (Clements); *The Three Billy Goats' Gruff* (Galdone); *Androcles and the Lion* (Stevens)
Develops definite friendships with age mates; plays in a group	Enjoys books about friends	*We Are Best Friends* (Aliki)
Begins to develop concepts about print and recognize letters	Needs books that address print and reading	*Ready . . . Set . . . Read!* (Cole)

Age Characteristics	Implications	Sample Book Titles
Strives to accomplish skills expected of adults	Needs reassurance that everyone progresses at his/her own rate	Leo the Late Bloomer (Kraus)
Is curious about a wider range of topics	Needs a wide variety of books	Fish Is Fish (Lionni); Color Dance (Jonas)
Begins to develop empathy and understanding for others	Needs books that deal with a range of emotions	Now One Foot, Now the Other (dePaola); When a Pet Dies (Rogers)
Continues to seek independence from adults and to develop initiative	Enjoys stories about responsibility	If You Give a Mouse a Cookie (Numeroff)

Sources:

Cullinan, Bernice. *Literature and the Child*. Second Edition. Harcourt Brace Jovanovich, 1989.

Huck, Charlotte, Susan Helper, and Janet Hickman. *Children's Literature in the Elementary School*. Fourth Edition. Holt, Rinehart & Winston, 1987.

Lamme, Linda. *Raising Readers: Guide to Sharing Literature with Young Children*. National Council of Teachers of English. Walker & Co., 1980.

Sutherland, Zena, and May Hill Arbuthnot. *Children and Books*. Seventh Edition. Scott, Foresman, 1986.

How to Use This Guide

THIRTEEN MONTHS WERE SPENT compiling this guide and over 5,000 print and nonprint titles were examined by 64 reviewers. The resulting compilation represents some of the best on the market for very young children. An effort was made to identify those titles still in print; however, as any buyer of material knows, books and materials come and go too quickly to say that ALL are readily available. Also, the editor tried to achieve a balance between the well known or "classics" of children's materials and the newer, contemporary titles.

Selection Process

Individuals assisting in the evaluation of materials were selected from the areas of librarianship and early childhood education. The team of advisers is made up of experts in resources for preschool children recognized either for their work with children or because they are college or university instructors in library science or early childhood education.

Using standard bibliographies and other resource tools that include preschool materials, publishers were identified and contacted. They were requested to forward a copy of any recently published print or nonprint item as well as other retrospective materials still in print for evaluation and possible inclusion in the guide. Only those items selected and recommended by the advisory committee for purchase are listed. This book is a *highly selective, evaluative* collection development resource guide.

Not included in this book are evaluations of games and toys for preschoolers. Just recently a number of quality publications have been published that review both subjects. These are annotated in Appendix 1: Professional Resources.

Selection criteria for the materials included in this edition were developed by the committee. These cover both general and specific considerations to be made by the consumer when examining the media. A listing of items follows:

Criteria for the Selection of Materials

General

Is the content of the material appropriate to the developmental abilities, needs, and interests of a young child?

Does the content relate to familiar life experiences or provide opportunity for expanding a child's understanding of his/her world or the world of others?

Is the language natural, clear, and simple? Does it read aloud smoothly?

Do text and illustrations have unity and complement each other?

Is the subject matter discussed in the text adequately complemented by the accompanying illustrations?

Are the illustrations authentic in detail, realistic, and concrete? Or do they appeal to the child's imagination and sense of wonder?

Do the illustrations depict life as it is—cultural, ethnic, racial, sexual, and various age levels—without stereotyping?

Are the artistic aspects (medium, color, line, shape, and balance) of high quality and suitable for the young child?

Will the format (endpages, cover, illustrations, placement of print on pages, and size) be attractive to young children?

Specific Stories

Does the story progress to a satisfying conclusion? Are loose ends tied up? Or is a "hanging" ending artistically satisfying?

Is the plot easy to follow for the child?

If unusual elements exist, can they in some way be related to the young child's real world experiences?

Do illustrations help the story?

Informational

Are the concepts discussed within the child's framework of understanding?

Are they adequately covered for the young child's age level and abilities?

Do the subjects presented represent natural phenomena that young children encounter or would be interested in (e.g., weather, seasons, animals)?

Is the book logically arranged and easy to follow?

Is the information provided up-to-date and accurate?

Is the author qualified to write about the topic judging from information in the book or cover (if provided)?

Is the style of writing clear and direct? Does this style create a feeling of reader involvement?

Do the illustrations extend the text?

Is the medium used the most appropriate one for the topic?

Science

Is the content within the interest and comprehension range of the intended audience?

Do the text and illustrations avoid anthropomorphisms (attributing human characteristics to animals or things)?

Are generalizations supported by facts?

Do illustrations assist with explanations? Are they appropriate? If experiments are present, are they safe? Are pictures part of the instructions?

Is simplicity rather than complexity emphasized?

Math

Are basic numbers featured? For older preschoolers, does the text stop at 100?

Are objects to be counted discernibly represented?

Are objects recognizable to a young child?

Is a left to right counting progression possible?

Are math concepts accurately portrayed?

Are the concepts within the grasp of young children?

Other

In ABC, counting, concept, and wordless books, are objects recognizable and are items included to which the child can relate?

Are objects presented that depict the most common sounds, numbers, elements, or things for the very young child?

Nonprint

Is the medium appropriate for the designated age?

Is the content appropriate for young listeners/viewers?

Is the content accurate?

Are the audio and video quality good?

Does the speaker/singer speak clearly and slowly? Are voices well modulated and pleasing?

Are visuals clear and uncluttered?

If an adaptation of print, does it retain essentially the same mood and quality?

Technically, does it provide clarity, high quality with effective background music and sound effects that are balanced?

Periodicals

Is the periodical affordable for the intended usage?

Is the periodical appropriate for the interest of the age level of the child?

Will it withstand repeated use? Is it durable? Is the binding sturdy and safe for young children?

Is layout presented in an attractive format? Are page layouts simple and pleasing to the eye?

Are illustrations colorful and relevant to the contents?

Are advertisements suitable and few?

If activities are presented, are they appropriate for preschoolers' abilities? Can these be performed with little assistance from adults? Or do they promote positive interaction between the child and adult?

Does the periodical invite reader's works? art? poetry? etc.?

Professional Resources

Is the publication appropriate for its intended use of reference and guidance?

Is it within a cost range that merits purchase?

Is there an attempt within the contents to relate information to appropriate age levels?

What are the reputation and the credentials of the author(s)?

Is it easy to access information? Is there a table of contents? Are there appropriate author, title, and subject indexes? Is there a bibliography of sources cited as well as one for further reading?

Using these criteria for each category, the reviewers examined the material, wrote an evaluative annotation, and ranked the item as a first, second, or third purchase priority for the collection. Those items that would be most important or critical for any day-care center or preschool program to own were given a purchase priority number one (see sample entries). Those that would greatly enhance the basic collection were given purchase priority number two. And finally, those that round out or perhaps make the collection a model library for preschool children were numbered three. There are 396 items in the basic collection, an additional 444 are included in the second, and 234 in the third, for a total of 1,074.

Overview of Contents

This book places all preschool materials in one numbered listing called Annotated Titles. The numbered entries are arranged alphabetically by title. The user should note that nonprint is totally integrated within the print items by title since most children will want access and will enjoy having both formats available.

Following the Annotated Titles section are three appendixes. Appendix 1: Professional Resources lists titles recommended for building a professional collection. Included are titles that guide parents in their selections, examine the design of playgrounds, and list criteria for selecting safe toys for toddlers. Appendix 2: Print Publishers and Nonprint Suppliers lists the names and addresses of the publishers and distributors of materials included in this book. Appendix 3: Organizations lists organizations that supply guidance and assistance for parents.

Five indexes provide access to entries: Name, Subject, Age/Category, Age/Purchase Priority, and Format.

Description of Annotated Entries

Each item is listed alphabetically by title and has been assigned a unique number that is used to access the title from the numerous indexes at the back of the book. This is followed by basic bibliographic information and a general category designation similar to a genre type. The eight categories are: Concept/Counting/Alphabet; Folklore/Folktales/Fairy tales; Informational; Periodicals; Participation and manipulative; Poetry/Nursery rhymes/Songs; Story; and Wordless.

Some titles are recommended for one specific age, such as I for Infants, while others have a wider range, such as T-P-K, meaning the material is suitable for use with or by Toddlers, Preschoolers, and Kindergartners. A brief, evaluative annotation containing a descriptive overview of the item and possible uses follows. The purchase priority, other published review sources (when available), and awards are also noted. Sample print and nonprint entries are shown below.

Sample Print Entry

Entry #   Title   Author

190 *A Child's Garden of Verses.* Robert Louis Stevenson. {Pages

Publisher/ ——Chronicle Books, 1989. 121 pp. $15.95. (0-87701- {Price

Date   608-9).

ISBN

Category: Poetry/Nursery rhymes/Songs **Age:** P–K

A stunning edition of one of the best-loved collections of poetry in the world, lavishly illustrated by the most distinguished children's book artists of the late 19th and early 20th centuries, including Jesse Wilcox Smith, H. Wilebee le Mair,

Annotation and Bessie Collins Pease. The illustrations, brimming with color and lush detail, brilliantly capture the universal splendor of a child's imaginative world. Also available in other formats from the National Library for the Blind and Physically

Subject } Handicapped.   [1]

Listings } Imagination; Poetry

Rev: BKL 11/1/89

Review   **Awards:** Redbook's 1989 Top Ten Picture Books of the Year

Citations

Purchase Priority

Sample Nonprint Entry

Entry #   Title   Authors

191 *A Child's Gift of Lullabyes.* J. Aaron Brown and David R. {Producer

Contributor ——Lehman. Narrated by Tanya Goodman. A Child's Gift of {Date

Format }   Lullabyes, 1987. Dist. by J. Aaron Brown & Associates.

Run Time } ——Audiocassette. 60 min. $12.95.   Distributor

Price }   **Category:** Poetry/Nursery rhymes/Songs **Age:** I–T–P–K

A collection of nine contemporary, original lullabies, three of which are "Rock-a-Bye," "Lullaby and Goodnight," and "May All Your Dreams Come True." Side one features vocalist Tanya Goodman with a fully orchestrated background.

Annotation

Subject } Side two has only the instrumental background and can be used for listening or singing along. Lyrics are included. [1]

Listings } Lullabies; Songs

Rev: SLJ 4/89

Review   **Awards:** Grammy Award Nominee "Best Recording for Children"

Citations

Purchase Priority

Acknowledgments

Ann, Anna, Barbara, Belinda, Beth, Betty, Betty Jean, Betty Kay, Bill, Brooke, Carol, Carolyn, Celia, Cheryl, Chris, Claudia, Connie, Deanna, Debby, Deborah, Dee Dee, Dick, Dona, Dorothy, Elaine, Ellen, Ernest, Evelyn, Gloria, Heide, Jackie, Jane, Janel, Janice, Jeanie, Jeannine, JoAnn, Judi, Judith, Julia, June, Karen, Kathleen, Kathy, Linda, Marcella, Marianne, Mark, Mary, Mary Louise, Maureen, Nancy, Nonie, Pat, Peggy, Rita, Robin, Ruth, Starr, Susan, Tim, Toni, Virginia

.... THANKS!

You made this possible.

Special thanks go to two individuals of the Bowker staff: Marion Sader, publisher, for her expert guidance, and Roy Crego, production executive editor, for his endless patience.

Key to Abbreviations

Ages

I	Infant
T	Toddler
P	Preschool
K	Kindergarten

Review Sources

BBC	Bibliography of Books for Children/ACEI
BKL	Booklist
CBK	Choosing Books for Kids
CBY	Children's Books of the Year
CCL	Canadian Children's Literature
EL	Emergency Librarian
ESLC	Elementary School Library Collection
HB	Horn Book
NYT	New York Times Parent's Guide to the Best Books for Children
PP	Primaryplots
SLJ	School Library Journal

Annotated Titles

1   *A Apple Pie.* Tracey Campbell Pearson. Dial, 1986. Unp. $5.95. (0-8037-
0252-3).   **Category:** Concept/Counting/Alphabet   **Age:** P–K

What's 18 feet long and covers the misadventures of an apple pie in the hands
of mischievous children sitting at a very long table? Tracey Campbell Pearson
has adapted the 1671 traditional alphabet rhyme into the accordion-style book
that folds out to become a wall decoration or even a standing poster on a library shelf.   [3]
ALPHABET; FOOD
Rev: NYT

2   *A. B. C. of Fashionable Animals.* Cooper Edens, Alexandra Day, and Wel-
leran Poltarness. Illus. by Harry B. Neilson and others. Green Tiger Press,
1989. 64 pp. $12.95. (0-88138-122-5).
                                          Category: Concept/Counting/Alphabet   **Age:** P–K

This unusual ABC book features a compilation of many different artists' illustrations, dating from 1842 to 1938, of animals bedecked in human clothing and
engaged in various human endeavors. The book's simple format presents the
alphabet concept clearly. Large, full-color illustrations of the same animal, an
insightful introduction, and a list of picture credits provide useful information
for adults.   [3]
ALPHABET; ANIMALS

3   *A Is for Animals: 26 Pop-up Surprises.* David Pelham. Simon & Schuster,
1991. Unp. $14.95. (0-671-72495-9).
                                          Category: Participation and manipulative   **Age:** P–K

Each page contains two brightly colored square doors with contrasting colored
uppercase and lowercase alphabet letters. Open the doors and out pop appropriate exotic animals. Animals are bright, appealing, and realistically portrayed in their environment. Pop-ups are unique but somewhat delicate and
will require supervision.   [2]
ALPHABET; ANIMALS

4   *Aaron's Shirt.* Deborah Gould. Illus. by Cheryl Harness. Bradbury, 1989.
Unp. $12.95. (0-02-736351-1).   **Category:** Story   **Age:** T–P–K

A little boy has an attachment to a red and white striped T-shirt. Over the
course of time, Aaron and his favorite shirt have many good times together,
but inevitably the day comes when he outgrows it. His well-loved shirt seems
destined for the giveaway box, until his teddy bear inherits it. A satisfying
story about a common childhood experience.   [1]
CLOTHING
Rev: BKL 3/1/89; CBY-90

5   *ABC.* Rosalinda Kightley. Little, Brown & Co., 1986. 32 pp. Paper $6.95.
(0-316-49930-7).   **Category:** Concept/Counting/Alphabet   **Age:** P–K

A bright, cheerful alphabet book with bold illustrations. Each page includes
the letter of the alphabet featured in uppercase and lowercase and a large, simple illustration with a one-word text. There is an interesting mix of both familiar and unfamiliar objects to keep the child's interest (such as I for Igloo, W for
Wool). The simple and bright illustrations are especially appropriate for
young children.   [2]
ALPHABET
Rev: ESLC

6   *An ABC Bestiary.* Deborah Blackwell. Farrar, Straus & Giroux, 1989. Unp.
$13.95. (0-374-30005-4).
                        Category: Concept/Counting/Alphabet   **Age:** P–K

Starting with "Aardvark arranging art," one knows this is not the usual ABC
book. Using bold colors outlined with a heavy black line, Blackwell presents
the alphabet in uppercase and lowercase with an alliterative phrase and picture to match. These are not easy words but lip-smacking challenges with
some highly improbable constructions such as a "Jaguar juggling jellybeans"
and a "Newt nibbling noodles" in a diner.   [3]
ALPHABET; ANIMALS
Rev: BKL 1/15/90

7   *ABC Bunny.* Wanda Gag. Putnam, 1933. Unp. $6.99. (0-698-20000-4).
                        Category: Concept/Counting/Alphabet   **Age:** T–P–K

A longtime nursery favorite, the pencil drawings of the rabbit have stood the
test of time. The hand lettering, the music provided, and the careful weaving
of story line from an alphabet song show the crafting of a book designed not
only for the young reader but also for the adult. After all these years, the book
might feel like an antique, but it will continue to provide new fun for new
readers.   [3]
ALPHABET; RABBITS
Rev: ESLC

8   *The Accident.* Carol Carrick. Illus. by Donald Carrick. Clarion Books/
Houghton Mifflin, 1979. Unp. $13.95. (0-395-28774-X).
                                        Category: Story   **Age:** K

Christopher's dog, Bodger, is hit by a pickup truck and is killed. Christopher experiences a variety of emotions as he comes to accept the death of a loved pet and friend. Ideal for sharing before such an event happens in a child's life, or even out of necessity when a pet dies. [1]
ACCIDENTS; DEATH; DOGS
Rev: BBC

9   ***Across the Stream.*** Mirra Ginsburg. Illus. by Nancy Tafuri. Greenwillow Books, 1982. 24 pp. $12.88. (0-688-01206-X).

Category: Story   **Age:** P–K

Some chickens are plagued by bad dreams, and their worst nightmare comes to life: being chased by a fox. In this story, they are rescued by a duck family, who ferries them across a stream to safety. The dreamlike pictures with a close-up perspective extend to the edge of the page, emphasizing the vividness of the experience. The rhyme gives pacing and closure, providing an ending to the bad dream in family unity. [1]
CHICKENS; DREAMS; DUCKS; FOXES
Rev: BBC; ESLC

10   ***Addie Meets Max.*** Joan Robins. Illus. by Sue Truesdell. Harper & Row, 1985. 32 pp. $9.89. (0-06-025064-X).   **Category:** Story   **Age:** P–K

Addie is sure the new boy next door is nothing but trouble. He has a big, scary dog, and she blames him for a bicycle accident. Addie's mother does not take her complaints seriously and invites Max over for lunch. After a rocky beginning, Max, Addie, and even Ginger, the dog, become friends. Charmingly told with few words, while illustrations are filled with action and detail. [1]
FRIENDSHIP
Rev: CBK

11   ***Aesop's Fables.*** Aesop. Illus. by Charles Santore. Jellybean Press/Crown, 1988. 48 pp. $8.98. (0-517-64115-1).

Category: Folklore/Folktales/Fairy tales   **Age:** P–K

A wonderfully illustrated, oversized collection containing 24 fables, including many favorites: "The Wolf in Sheep's Clothing," "The Lion and the Mouse," and "The Fox and the Grapes." Each story is placed on one page in large print with realistic pictures of the animals. [1]
ANIMALS; FABLES; FOLK AND FAIRY TALES
Rev: BKL 1/1/89

12   After Dark. Teryl Euvremer. Crown, 1989. Unp. $13.95. (0-517-57104-8).
                                    Category: Poetry/Nursery rhymes/Songs   **Age:** P–K

A bevy of familiar evening rituals—bathing, brushing teeth, etc.—are combined with the nonsensical in a musical, unpredictable bedtime story. Softly but richly illustrated animals and insects sing lullabies, wish pleasant dreams, gaze at stars, and even fuss about bedtime. Although words like "beguiled," "jabot," and "lagoon" stretch young minds, cheerful, affectionate poetry makes this a favorite bedtime read-aloud.   [2]
ANIMALS; BEDTIME; POETRY
Rev: BKL 3/15/89

13   ahl belle cité/a beautiful city abc. Stephane Poulin. Tundra Books, 1985. Unp. $14.95. (0-88776-175-5).
                                    Category: Concept/Counting/Alphabet   **Age:** P–K

Poulin uses colorful scenes of Montreal to present the alphabet. Each letter of the alphabet is represented by both an English and a French word that have the same meaning as well as the same initial letter, such as l - lake, l - lac. The illustrations are clean, with strong colors that will attract and challenge the young child. A sense of humor is evident on each page.   [2]
ALPHABET; CITIES AND TOWNS
Rev: SLJ 4/86

14   Airmail to the Moon. Tom Birdseye. Illus. by Stephen Gammell. Holiday House, 1988. Unp. $13.95. (0-8234-0683-0).
                                    Category: Story   **Age:** K

Ora Mae is positive someone stole her tooth and vows that when she catches the culprit, she'll "send 'em airmail to the moon!" After a frustrating search, the tooth is found in her overalls pocket. The spunky girl's language is quite colorful, as in "embarrassed as a zebra without stripes" and "I was popcorn-in-the-pan excited." The writing style and quirky cartoonlike illustrations make this book fresh and fun.   [1]
MOON; TEETH
Rev: BKL 3/15/88

15   Airplanes. Byron Barton. Harper & Row, 1986. Unp. $11.89. (0-690-04532-8).   **Category:** Informational   **Age:** P–K

Various types of planes are introduced to children in their natural surroundings. The text is written in simple, descriptive sentences allowing for further discussion, if desired. The childlike pictures are printed in bold outlines around bright, exciting colors. This book can be used one-on-one or in a group situation. Appropriate for children with a short attention span. [1]

AIRPLANES

Rev: BBC; ESLC

16   *Albert's Play.* Leslie Tryon. Atheneum, 1992. Unp. $13.95. (0-689-31525-2). **Category:** Story **Age:** K

The production of Albert's play is illustrated from casting to curtain call including all the planning, preparation, practice, publicity, and performance.

PLAYS [2]

17   *Alexander and the Terrible, Horrible, No Good, Very Bad Day.* Judith Viorst. Illus. by Ray Cruz. Atheneum, 1972. 32 pp. $11.95. (0-689-30072-7). **Category:** Story **Age:** K

Alexander wakes up with gum in his hair, his lunch does not have a dessert in it, he falls in a mud puddle, and he gets into a fight. All day long, everything goes wrong, so he decides to run away to Australia. His mother helps him understand that some days are bad, even in Australia. [1]

BAD DAY; BOYS; FAMILY LIFE

Rev: BBC; ESLC

18   *Alexander and the Terrible, Horrible, No Good, Very Bad Day and Other Stories and Poems.* Judith Viorst. Read by Blythe Danner. Music composed and conducted by Don Heckman. Harper Audio, 1984. Audiocassette. 54 min. $9.95. **Category:** Story **Age:** K

Danner's readings of five stories (side 1) and short poems (side 2) will delight and amuse adults as much as youngsters. Viorst's stories are witty, nonsexist, and written from a young child's perspective on topics such as "plain ol'" bad days, the death of a pet, the difficulties of saving money, family life, and the meaning of friendship. Each is full of honesty, love, and humor. [2]

BAD DAY; DEATH; FAMILY LIFE; FRIENDSHIP

Rev: ESLC

19   *Alfie Gives a Hand.* Shirley Hughes. Morrow Jr. Books, 1983. Unp. $12.95. (0-688-02387-8). **Category:** Story **Age:** P–K

Alfie goes to his first birthday party with his security blanket. When the overexcited birthday boy and a tearful guest both want to hold Alfie's hand in the circle game, he bravely puts down his blanket to solve the problem. Children will identify with the colorful, appropriately rumpled multiethnic guests and —"The Blanket." [2]

BIRTHDAYS; BLANKET; FRIENDSHIP

Rev: CBY-87

20 **Alice and the Birthday Giant.** John F. Green. Illus. by Maryann Kovalski. Scholastic, 1989. 40 pp. $12.95. (0-590-43428-4).

Category: Story **Age:** P–K

Imaginative drawings and hilarious text. It was Alice's birthday, and she knew it would be an "extraordinary day" but to find a huge, lovable giant in her bed! This she would never have guessed. Alice cannot wish him home, or even hide him, so what to do? Ask the librarian, of course! [2]

BIRTHDAYS; GIANTS; LIBRARIES

Rev: BKL

21 **All about Hanukkah.** Judyth Groner and Madeline Wikler. Illus. by Rosalyn Schanzer. Kar-Ben Copies, 1988. Unp. $10.95. (0-930494-81-4).

Category: Informational **Age:** K

A sound history of the Jewish people that commemorates ancient and contemporary religious freedom and celebrates Hanukkah as it is known today. Including descriptions of candlelighting, recipes, and games, this observant account is illustrated with alternating black-and-white drawings. [3]

HANUKKAH

Rev: SLJ 10/88

22 **All Around Us.** Eric Carle. Picture Book Studio, 1986. Unp. $11.95. (0-88708-016-2). **Category:** Concept/Counting/Alphabet **Age:** T–P–K

Three sturdy cardboard friezes showing items in three geographical locations —"In the sky above us," "On earth's surface," and "Below the sea"—provide a variety of play experiences at a variety of levels. Each panel can be used for simple object identification or as a diorama for imaginative play, or the panels can be placed together showing the interrelationships of earth's ecostructures.

EARTH; SEA AND SEASHORE [1]

23 **All by Myself.** Anna G. Hines. Houghton Mifflin, 1985. Unp. $10.95. (0-89919-293-9). **Category:** Informational **Age:** T

The story depicts how a little girl named Josie goes to the bathroom one night by herself. A clearly written story for parents to read to their children while they are talking about use of the toilet. [2]
TODDLERS; TOILET TRAINING
Rev: NYT

24 *All Fit with Slim Goodbody.* Directed by Dana Calderwood and Lou Castelli. Agency for Instructional Technology, 1988. Videocassette. 15 min. $125 ea. **Category:** Informational **Age:** P–K

Promoting that all children should be physically fit to realize their full potential, Slim Goodbody, in this introductory video, supplies the viewer with simple exercises and health and fitness facts as a preface to the 15-part series. Emphasizes the importance of "personal space" while exercising and respect for healthy bodies. Teacher's guide accompanies the series. [1]
EXERCISE
Rev: BKL 9/1/89

25 *All Gone!* Sarah Garland. Viking Kestrel, 1990. 29 pp. $8.95. (0-670-83074-7). **Category:** Concept/Counting/Alphabet **Age:** T–P

Colorful illustrations and simple text combine to illustrate the concept of "all gone." Each two-page spread presents a different situation. The baby tosses its teddy bear into the air, and it disappears over the side of the crib. The baby holds a bright red balloon in its hands, and when the balloon pops, it is "all gone." Young children will enjoy this fun game of "now you see it, now you don't." [1]
BABIES; CONCEPTS
Rev: BKL 2/15/90; SLJ 5/90

26 *All I Am.* Eileen Roe. Illus. by Helen Cogancherry. Bradbury, 1990. Unp. $12.95. (0-02-777372-8). **Category:** Concept **Age:** P–K

Soft, nurturing paintings illustrate numerous positive and multi-faceted qualities of a child that help describe one as a friend, neighbor, artist, dancer, animal lover, daydreamer, listener, and thinker. An excellent source for building and developing self-image and self-esteem. [2]
SELF-CONCEPT

27 ***All of Us Will Shine.*** Tickle Tune Typhoon, 1987. Audiocassette. 44 min. $8.98. **Category:** Poetry/Nursery rhymes/Songs **Age:** K

A varied collection of entertaining songs, including folksongs—"We've Got the Whole World in Our Hands," funny songs—"Bicycle Cowboy," and instructional songs—"My Body Belongs to Me." Some are accompanied by a full orchestra. Lyric sheet included. [3]

SONGS

Rev: BKL 11/1/88 **Awards:** ALSC Notable Recording

28 ***All Shapes and Sizes.*** Shirley Hughes. Lothrop, Lee & Shepard, 1986. Unp. $4.95. (0-688-04205-8).

Category: Concept/Counting/Alphabet **Age:** P–K

Basic concepts are realistically illustrated and verbally described. For example, children are shown as tall and short, squeezing through narrow spaces and running through wide ones, and climbing up a ladder or sliding down a slide.

CONCEPTS; SHAPE; SIZE [1]

Rev: CBY-87

29 ***All Small.*** David McCord. Illus. by Madelaine G. Linden. Little, Brown & Co., 1986. Unp. Paper $4.95. (0-316-55520-7).

Category: Poetry/Nursery rhymes/Songs **Age:** I–T–P–K

All Small features 25 small, delightful poems on small, delightfully illustrated pages. While many of the works offer extended appeal to more mature minds, the lighthearted rhythm and rhyme offer auditory pleasure for the youngest audiences. This, in fact, is the sort of book a child could grow up with: first enjoying the melody of the lyrics and eventually coming to recognize the power in the lines. [2]

POETRY

Rev: BKL 1/1/88; NYT

30 ***Alligator Pie.*** Dennis Lee. Illus. by Frank Newfeld. Macmillan of Canada, 1974. 64 pp. $12.95. (0-7715-9591-3).

Category: Poetry/Nursery rhymes/Songs **Age:** T–P–K

Children of all ages will enjoy these poems first written for Lee's daughter. The rhyme and rhythm are sure to elicit a smile as the words are read aloud. Whether it is the fun of the cumulative poem "On Tuesdays I Polish My Uncle" or the challenge of "Tongue Twister," young children and their reader will share the fun, humor, or special warmth contained in each poem. [3]

POETRY

31   ***Allsorts.*** Tony Wells. Aladdin, 1988. 32 pp. Paper $4.95. (0-689-71185-9).
Category: Concept/Counting/Alphabet   **Age:** P–K

Numerous items, categories, and opportunities for naming and sorting everyday things. Double-page spreads show individual items such as blue things, soft things, and edible things on the left side; the right side of the page asks a question such as "How many blue things are in this picture?" Concepts move from simple to more complex. Answers are included on the last page. Entertaining as well as useful.   [2]
CONCEPTS; PUZZLES
Rev: BKL 5/1/88

32   ***Alphabatics.*** Suse MacDonald. Bradbury, 1986. 64 pp. $15.95. (0-02-761520-0).   **Category:** Concept/Counting/Alphabet   **Age:** P–K

Inanimate letters of the alphabet suddenly come to life as they roll across the page and magically become an object representing the letter. A becomes an ark, H a house, S a swan. The reader is struck by the author-illustrator's marvelous use of color and placement of letters as well as pictures on the page. This is an alphabet book that should be in every child's collection.   [1]
ALPHABET
Rev: CBY-87; ESLC; NYT   **Awards:** Caldecott Honor Book

33   ***Alphabatics.*** Suse MacDonald. Random House/Miller-Brody, 1988. Dist. by American School Publishers. Filmstrip. 16 min. $29.50.
Category: Concept/Counting/Alphabet   **Age:** T–P

Each letter of the alphabet "tilts, shrinks, expands" to become an appropriate object: A floats away as an ark, J springs into a jack-in-the-box, etc. Although the 16-minute time frame may seem tedious for very young viewers, the length devoted to the unusual perspectives allows imaginative anticipation of the object being created. A clever musical rendition of the Caldecott Honor winner (Bradbury, 1986). Accompanied with audiocassette.   [2]
ALPHABET
Rev: SLJ 4/89   **Awards:** ALSC Notable Filmstrip

34   ***Alphabears: An ABC Book.*** Kathleen Hague. Illus. by Michael Hague. Henry Holt & Co., 1984. Unp. $11.95. (0-8050-0841-1).
Category: Concept/Counting/Alphabet   **Age:** P–K

A treasure of an alphabet book. Michael Hague's superbly executed, richly detailed full-color paintings portray 26 irresistible teddy bears. Kathleen Hague's endearingly simple two-line rhymes, appearing below each illustration, will assuredly delight young ears. For example, "F is for Freedie, a big frightful mess; What he has been up to no one can guess." [2]

ALPHABET; RHYMING TEXT; TEDDY BEARS

Rev: CBK, ESLC, NYT

35 *Alphabet Puzzle.* Jill Downie. Lothrop, Lee & Shepard, 1988. Unp. $16.00. (0-688-08044-8).

Category: Concept/Counting/Alphabet   Age: P–K

An unusual alphabet book with window frames for every other letter, thus providing an opportunity for readers to predict what the letter stands for. Each page offers a partial visual clue to the next letter's puzzle picture as seen through the window frame. Uppercase and lowercase letters and large print add to the simplicity for younger children, but illustrations provide for usefulness with older children. [3]

ALPHABET; PUZZLES

Rev: BKL 9/1/88; CBY-89

36 *Alphabet Soup.* Kate Banks. Illus. by Peter Sis. Alfred A. Knopf, 1988. Unp. $12.95. (0-394-89151-1).   Category: Story   Age: P–K

A young boy's dissatisfaction with his alphabet soup lunch turns mealtime into a fantasy tabletop journey as each word he spells in his spoon becomes reality. Sis's distinguished illustrations add to the surreal quality of the tale—adventurous, yet never too far from the boy's familiar kitchen surroundings. Childpower in action! [2]

ALPHABET; IMAGINATION

Rev: BKL 11/1/88; CBY-90

37 *Always Gramma.* Vaunda Micheaux Nelson. Illus. by Kimanne Uhler. Putnam, 1988. Unp. $13.95. (0-399-21542-5).

Category: Story   Age: P–K

A loving grandchild remembers her grandma and the activities they shared: singing, walking barefoot in the creek, and baking yellow birthday cakes. Even though Gramma does not remember her family now, they continue to show love in countless ways. The impressionistic watercolor illustrations poignantly portray many emotions and add to the mood of the story. [3]

FAMILY LIFE; OLD AGE

Rev: BKL 10/15/88

38 *Amazing Animal Alphabet Book.* Roger Chouinard and Mariko Chouinard. Illus. by Roger Chouinard. Doubleday, 1988. Unp. $12.95. (0-385-24029-5). **Category:** Concept/Counting/Alphabet **Age:** P–K

Outrageous, colorful, framed illustrations depict imaginative, alliterative text sure to tie a reader's tongue. How about a "Frog feeling forlorn" or a "Gorilla getting into a girdle" or a "Yak on a yacht with a yoyo"? The large illustrations are ideal for large groups. The text is most fun for those who already know their alphabet. [2]

ALPHABET; ANIMALS

Rev: BKL 7/88

39 *The Amazing Bone.* William Steig. Narrated by John Lithgow. Weston Woods Studios, 1985. Videocassette. 11 min. $60.00.

Category: Story **Age:** P–K

When Pearl, a young pig, finds a bone with unusual powers, her life changes. Not only does the bone save her life, but it also comes to enrich the life of her family. Steig's visuals and Lithgow's narrative are bound to delight young audiences (Farrar, Straus, 1976). [1]

MUSIC; PIGS

Rev: BKL 5/1/89

40 *Amos Ahoy: A Couch Adventure on Land and Sea.* Susan Seligson. Illus. by Howie Schneider. Little, Brown & Co., 1990. Unp. $14.95. (0-316-77403-0). **Category:** Story **Age:** P–K

Although Amos is an old dog, the days spent on the family couch are anything but dull. With a flick of his paw, Amos propels the couch through the streets, upsetting the neighborhood bully, the dog catcher, the veterinary office, and the toll bridge operator and is finally credited with saving another Amos on the ferry. [2]

DOGS

41 *Amy Loves the Rain.* Julia Hoban. Illus. by Lillian Hoban. Harper & Row, 1989. Unp. $9.89. (0-06-022358-8). **Category:** Story **Age:** P–K

A simple story of Amy and her mother as they go to pick up Daddy is expanded to include the sights and sounds of the weather. Through the illustrations and language, readers can feel, hear, and see the rain. [2]

FAMILY LIFE; RAIN

Rev: BKL 4/15/89

42 *Androcles and the Lion.* Retold by Janet Stevens. Holiday House, 1989. Unp. $14.95. (0-8234-0768-3).

Category: Folklore/Folktales/Fairy tales   **Age:** K

A retelling of the Aesop fable. Androcles is a gentle, animal-loving slave who has escaped a cruel master and is hiding in a quiet forest. Awakened by loud groaning, he befriends a lion by pulling a painful thorn from the lion's paw. Later, when both are captured and thrown into the arena together, the good deed is repaid. Youngsters will enjoy the large, colorful illustrations ideal for sharing during a storytelling session. [2]

FABLES

Rev: BKL 11/1/89

43 *An Angel for Solomon Singer.* Cynthia Rylant. Illus. by Peter Catalanotto. Orchard Books, 1991. Unp. $14.99. (0-531-08578-3).

Category: Story   **Age:** K

Catalanotto's double-page watercolors bring to life this story of a man's loneliness in a new place far from his boyhood home and friendly memories. One night he meets Angel in a cafe where "all your dreams come true," and sure enough, as the days go by, he feels more and more at home with his new surroundings, sights, and sounds. [1]

LONELINESS; WISHING

44 *Angelina Ballerina.* Katharine Holabird. Illus. by Helen Craig. Clarkson N. Potter/Random House, 1983. Unp. $11.95. (0-517-55083-0).

Category: Story   **Age:** P–K

First in a series of books about Angelina, this one tells of a little girl mouse whose heart's desire is to be a ballerina. She gets her wish. Instead of doing what she is supposed to do, like setting the table for dinner, she dances. Finally, her parents decide to give her dance lessons, and from that day on she does everything she is asked to do. [1]

BALLET; MICE

Rev: BKL 1/1/88; CBY-90; ESLC; NYT

45 *Angelina Ballerina and Other Stories.* Katharine Holabird. Performed by Sally Struthers. Music composed by Don Heckman. Harper Audio, 1986. Audiocassette. 27 min. $9.95.   **Category:** Story   **Age:** P–K

Struthers' readings coupled with Heckman's musical compositions produce such an animated combination that this cassette could be used with or without

the books on which the stories are based. The short and lively productions of five stories are ideal for those in preschool through the early grades.   [2]
BALLET; FAMILY LIFE; GIRLS; MICE
Rev: ESLC

46   ***Angus Lost.*** Marjorie Flack. Phoenix BFA Films & Videos, 1982. Videocassette. 11 min. $175.00.   **Category:** Story   **Age:** K

Angus, a Scottish terrier, is awakened by the milkman making his morning deliveries. After chasing the cat and being banished from the house, Angus escapes from the yard through the open gate and experiences many exciting adventures. Although he loses his way and gets caught in a thunderstorm, he successfully finds his way back home by stowing away on the familiar milk truck (Doubleday, 1932).   [2]
DOGS
Rev: BKL 5/1/89

47   ***Animal Alphabet Songs.*** David S. Polansky. Great American Music, 1982. Audiocassette. 45 min. $11.95.   **Category:** Informational   **Age:** P–K

Reviewing the 26 letters of the alphabet has never been so much fun until children have had an opportunity to listen to these uplifting and clever musical arrangements. Animals sing their way through each letter, using various original melodies by this gifted composer.   [3]
ALPHABET; ANIMALS; SONGS
Rev: BKL 2/15/85   **Awards:** Artists' Foundation Fellowship Award

48   ***Animal Families: The Pig.*** Directed by Fred Ladd. Barr Films, 1989. Videocassette. 11 min. $195 ea.   **Category:** Informational   **Age:** K

A concise introduction to the world of pigs, showing their eating habits, basic anatomy, and the playfulness of young piglets. Other titles in the series of 12 are equally informative and include footage about mammals, mollusks, birds, bees, cats, sheep, and chickens.   [3]
PIGS; SCIENCE
Rev: BKL 1/1/90

49   ***Animal Sounds.*** Illus. by Aurelius Battaglia. Western, 1981. Unp. (0-307-12122-4).   **Category:** Concept/Counting/Alphabet   **Age:** I–T

This sturdy board book uses a question-and-answer format to present the distinctive sounds of various animals from the rooster's cock-a-doodle-doo to the

owl's who-o-o-o! Battaglia's illustrations are simple but lively as he works his way through pigs, ducks, frogs, and goats. [3]
Animals; Board books; Sounds
Rev: CBK

50   *Animals.* Valerie Greeley. Peter Bedrick, 1990. Unp. $5.95. (0-87226-435-1).   **Category:** Informational   **Age:** T

A board book that introduces the very young to the animal kingdom. The illustrations, portraying both tame and wild animals, are executed with finely drawn features and realistic colors. [1]
Animals; Board books
Rev: CBK

51   *Animals A to Z.* National Geographic Society, 1988. Dist. by Karol Media. Videocassette. 15 min. $59.95.   **Category:** Informational   **Age:** P–K

While teaching a child the letters of the alphabet, animals from anteater to zebra are shown and discussed in rhyme. Outstanding photography, typical of National Geographic presentations, will captivate the viewer. Teacher's guide included. [1]
Alphabet; Animals; Poetry

52   *Animals Should Definitely Not Wear Clothing.* Judi Barrett. Illus. by Ron Barrett. Atheneum, 1970. Unp. $13.95. (0-689-20592-9).
    Category: Story   **Age:** T–P–K

Children will not be able to keep a straight face as they see why it is not practical for animals to wear clothing. A camel might wear it in the wrong place, a snake would lose it, and it would be very messy for a pig. This hilarious look at a variety of animals shows even the youngest child why animals' clothing is perfect just as it is. Large, bold type and illustrations make this an easy read-aloud. [3]
Animals; Clothing
Rev: NYT

53   *Annabelle and the Big Slide.* Rita Pocock. Harcourt Brace Jovanovich, 1989. Unp. $10.95. (0-15-200407-6).   **Category:** Story   **Age:** T–P

Going to the park with Mom to play is one of a child's joys. In an appealing, nondramatic, yet sensitive way, the text deals with Annabelle's visit to the

park and her anxiety about going down the slide for the first time. Simple illustrations with an imaginative use of collages, patterns, and bright colors make this book very attractive for the younger child. [2]
PARKS; PLAY
Rev: BKL 1/1/90

54 *Anna's Secret Friend.* Yoriko Tsutsui. Illus. by Akiko Hayashi. Puffin Books, 1988. 32 pp. Paper $3.95. (0-14-050731-0).
Category: Story **Age:** P–K

Anna, excited about her new home near the mountains but lonesome for her old friends, ponders the mysterious appearance of flowers and a note. Cozy illustrations perfectly accompany the reassuring text and finally reveal Anna's new friend. [3]
FRIENDSHIP; MOVING
Rev: BKL 11/1/87; ESLC

55 *Annie and the Wild Animals.* Jan Brett. Houghton Mifflin, 1985. Unp. Paper $3.95. (0-395-51006-6). **Category:** Story **Age:** P–K

Set in a midwinter environment somewhere in the North country, this gentle story is frosted with a touch of fantasy. After her cat, Taffy, mysteriously disappears, the lonely Annie attempts to make friends with an odd assortment of woodland animals. Observant readers discover how Taffy's secret is gradually revealed in the intricately detailed border designs that frame the exquisite illustrations in Scandinavian style. [1]
CATS; FRIENDSHIP; LONELINESS
Rev: ESLC, NYT

56 *Annie's One to Ten.* Annie Owen. Alfred A. Knopf, 1988. Unp. $8.95. (0-394-82791-0). **Category:** Concept/Counting/Alphabet **Age:** T–P–K

One to 10 becomes a wonderful game for both beginners and old hands. Each two-page spread offers four groups of 10 finely detailed objects drawn from a theme such as the seashore, transportation, or birthday parties. In sequence, the groups are broken into subsets (1 moon/9 stars; 2 cookies/8 rolls, etc.), challenging the reader to discriminate among the smaller items. [2]
COUNTING
Rev: BKL 6/1/89

57 *Anno's Alphabet: An Adventure in Imagination.* Mitsumasa Anno. Harper & Row, 1975. Unp. $13.89. (0-690-00541-5).

Category: Concept/Counting/Alphabet   **Age:** K

Artistic and unusual, three-dimensional, oak capital letters with full-page pictures of an object beginning with each letter, as well as additional objects hidden in the border. Young children may have some trouble identifying the objects because many are antiques, yet the creative pictures encourage readers to use their imagination. A glossary at the end helps readers to identify the objects.   [1]

ALPHABET; IMAGINATION

Rev: NYT   **Awards:** NYT Best Illustrated Book

58 *Anno's Counting House.* Mitsumasa Anno. Philomel, 1982. Unp. $12.95. (0-399-20896-8).   **Category:** Concept/Counting/Alphabet   **Age:** P–K

Ten children move, one by one, from the house on the left page to fill the new house on the right. The cut out, exterior-scene page in the middle allows for learning concepts such as full/empty, part/whole, and above/below. Except for introductory and concluding notes, the book is wordless.   [2]

COUNTING; WORDLESS

Rev: BBC; BKL 6/1/83; ESLC

59 *Anno's Faces.* Mitsumasa Anno. Philomel, 1989. Unp. $10.95. (0-399-21711-8).   **Category:** Participation and manipulative   **Age:** P–K

Anno realistically illustrates 47 fruits and vegetables—some as exotic as the gingko nut and mangosteen—on white background. Accompanying transparent plastic bookmarks invite the child to overlay smiling or frowning faces. Designed for the prereading (and even preverbal) child, the book lets the child express preferences or imaginatively personify the objects.   [2]

CONCEPTS; FACES; VEGETABLES; WORDLESS

60 *Anno's Peekaboo.* Mitsumasa Anno. Philomel, 1987. Unp. $10.95. (0-399-21520-4).   **Category:** Participation and manipulative   **Age:** T–P

Daddy, Mother, lion, puppy, kitty, clown, and Santa peek from behind 3/4-page hand cutouts. Turn the hand page and surprise—a person or an animal is revealed. Adult supervision is necessary to prevent tearing the hand pages.

ANIMALS; GAMES; WORDLESS   [1]

Rev: BKL 5/1/88; SLJ 9/88

61 ***Apples and Pumpkins.*** Anne Rockwell. Illus. by Lizzy Rockwell. Macmillan, 1989. Unp. $12.95. (0-02-777270-5). **Category:** Story **Age:** P–K

The story of a young girl and her family as they go on their annual fall outing to pick apples and the perfect pumpkin for Halloween. Simply told with only one or two sentences on each page. The warm tone of the story and the brightly colored illustrations create feelings of joy and love between members of the family. The story of this secure, happy family will be enjoyed by young children. [1]

FAMILY LIFE; HALLOWEEN

Rev: BKL 9/15/89; SLJ 11/89

62 ***Arroz con Leche: Popular Songs and Rhymes from Latin America.*** Selected and illustrated by Lulu Delacre. Scholastic, 1989. 32 pp. $12.95. (0-590-41887-4). **Category:** Poetry/Nursery rhymes/Songs **Age:** P–K

Especially appreciated by child care centers and library preschool story hours serving a Hispanic clientele. The poetry can be used as an introduction to verse and songs as well as to English-Spanish translation. Typical activities and real places are enhanced by numerous illustrations of active children. Music scores appear in back of the book. [2]

SONGS; SPANISH LANGUAGE

Rev: BKL 4/1/89; CBY-90

63 ***Arthur.*** Lillian Hoban. Read by Suzanne Toren. Listening Library, 1987. Audiocassette. 67 min. $15.95. **Category:** Story **Age:** P–K

A pleasant female voice reads "Arthur's Honey Bear," "Arthur's Christmas Cookies," "Arthur's Prize Reader," and "Arthur's Funny Money." These four I Can Read books feature Arthur and his sister Violet, two monkeys, involved in typical childlike situations that are resolved satisfactorily by the characters. Designed for beginning readers, the stories, which come on two cassettes, will entice younger listeners. [2]

ADVENTURE; MONKEYS

64 ***Arthur Sets Sail.*** Libor Schaffer. Translated by Rosemary Lanning. Illus. by Agnes Mathieu. North-South Books, 1987. Unp. $13.95. (0-8050-0489-0). **Category:** Story **Age:** P–K

Arthur the aardvark sets sail for adventure, journeying to the land of the rosy-pink pigs. He is unhappy here because the pigs make fun of his different appearance. Later, Arthur admonishes his aardvark friends back at home when

they laugh at Rudolph, his pig friend, because of his different appearance. In both lands, the animals learn to accept the differences of others.   [3]
AARDVARKS; ANIMALS; PIGS
Rev: BKL 1/1/88

65   *Arthur's Eyes.* Marc Brown. Little, Brown & Co., 1979. 32 pp. $14.95. (0-316-11063-9).   **Category:** Story   **Age:** P–K

Arthur the aardvark learns that he needs to wear glasses. At school the children make fun of him, so he takes them off. However, he finds that he does much better with them on. After many trials, he learns to be satisfied with himself.   [1]
AARDVARKS; GLASSES; SELF-CONCEPT
Rev: CBY-87; NYT

66   *Arthur's Honey Bear.* Lillian Hoban. Harper & Row, 1974. 64 pp. $10.89. (0-06-022370-7).   **Category:** Story   **Age:** K

Arthur, a monkey, is outgrowing many of his old toys, so he decides to have a tag sale. Unfortunately, the only toy anyone wants to purchase is his Honey Bear. He finally sells the bear to his little sister and must reconcile himself to the fact that it is no longer his. Children will readily identify with Arthur and his problem.   [2]
EMOTIONS; GROWING UP; TOYS
Rev: NYT

67   *Arthur's Thanksgiving.* Marc Brown. Little, Brown & Co., 1983. 32 pp. $14.95. (0-316-11060-4).   **Category:** Story   **Age:** P–K

Arthur, an aardvark, is surprised but pleased when his teacher chooses him to direct the school's Thanksgiving play. The only problem he has is finding someone to play the turkey. For some reason, no one seems to want to be a turkey! But, as usual, Arthur finds a funny solution to his problem.   [3]
AARDVARKS; THANKSGIVING DAY
Rev: BBC

68   *Ask Mr. Bear.* Marjorie Flack. Macmillan, 1932. Unp. $10.95. (0-02-735390-7).   **Category:** Story   **Age:** P–K

In a delightful story of a young boy who wants to find a birthday present for his mother, Danny seeks advice from a variety of animals before Mr. Bear suggests the perfect gift. Young children have long loved this warm story, its use of repetition, and its happy ending. [2]

BEARS; BIRTHDAYS; CUMULATIVE TALES

Rev: CBK; ESLC

69 *At the Beach.* Anne Rockwell. Illus. by Harlow Rockwell. Macmillan, 1987. Unp. $12.95. (0-02-777940-8).

Category: Concept/Counting/Alphabet **Age:** T–P–K

A young girl finds there is much to do on a day at the beach. Using short, simple text, the author explores the world of the seashore through the eyes of the very young. Bold, colorful illustrations show the girl following sandpipers, gathering shells and seaweed, building a sand castle, and swimming. A perfect introduction to the seashore in science units or as a supplement to the study of safety. [3]

SEA AND SEASHORE

Rev: CBY-88; ESLC

70 *Autumn Story.* Jill Barklem. Putnam, 1980. Unp. $8.95. (0-399-20745-7).

Category: Story **Age:** K

Primrose, the young daughter in a tiny field mice family, wanders off while helping gather food for winter and gets lost. After a frightening time in the forest, she is found by her family and goes home to hot acorn coffee and a warm bed. Illustrations are reminiscent of Beatrix Potter with their rich color, background detail, and 19th-century period costumes. One of four seasonal titles. [2]

FALL; MICE; SEASONS

Rev: NYT

71 *Babar the King.* Jean De Brunhoff. Reprint. Random House, 1935. 48 pp. $9.95. (0-394-80580-1). **Category:** Story **Age:** K

In this oversize reprint, King Babar constructs a model city with houses and community services for all the elephants, naming it Celesteville in honor of the queen. All is perfect until sickness and fire strike the citizens of this utopian society, who conclude that hard work and cheerfulness will bring the return of good times. Primary colors reminiscent of comic strips enliven the scenes of team effort. [1]

ELEPHANTS; ROYALTY

Rev: CBY-87; ESLC

---

72   *Babes, Beasts and Birds.* Pat Carfra. Lullaby Lady Productions, n.d. Dist. by A & M Records. Audiocassette. 41 min. $8.50.
Category: Poetry/Nursery rhymes/Songs   **Age:** T

A full range of original and unusual tunes. Some of them ask for inventive participation; others entice and soothe in preparation for quiet time and bed. Songs from around the world add a multicultural flair to this unique audiocassette. [2]

BEDTIME; LULLABIES; SONGS

Rev: SLJ 4/88   **Awards:** ALSC Notable Recording

---

73   *Babies.* Gyo Fujikawa. Grosset & Dunlap, 1963. Unp. Paper $3.95. (0-448-03084-5).   **Category:** Concept/Counting/Alphabet   **Age:** I–T

Board book shows that babies are "very little...soft, warm and cuddly." The daily activities of a baby are presented with cheerful, colorful, active illustrations. The babies represent a multiethnic population. Siblings and pets are included, providing subjects familiar to the infant. [1]

BABIES; BOARD BOOKS; CONCEPTS

Rev: CBK

---

74   *Babies Love a Goodnight Hug.* Harold Roth. Putnam, 1986. 14 pp. Paper $2.50. (0-448-10677-9).   **Category:** Story   **Age:** T

Realistic photographs accompanied by a simple story line show the daily routine of a toddler playing with his daddy, putting toys away, "reading" a picture book, eating dinner, taking a bath, putting on pajamas, brushing teeth, and listening to Mommy read a goodnight story. Sturdy board book construction with rounded corners increases the likelihood of repeated usage. [2]

BABIES; BOARD BOOKS; LOVE

Rev: CBY-87

75 **Baby Around the Clock.** Guusje Slegers. Barron's Educational Series, 1987. Unp. $1.95. (0-8120-5804-6).   **Category:** Wordless **Age:** I–T

Follow the roly-poly cherub as he awakens, bathes, dresses, plays, and so on, round the clock until he sleeps again. The wordless, accordion-folded board book is brightly illustrated and has rounded edges for safety. A companion book to Baby Toys.   [3]
BABIES; BOARD BOOKS; WORDLESS

76 **Baby Bubbles.** Pam Adams. Child's Play, 1986. Unp. $4.95. (0-85953-265-8).

Category: Wordless **Age:** I

Many children are fearful of bath time. Sharing this title, which shows animals happily bathing, at bath time should help ease any anxieties and make the event fun.   [2]
BATHS; FEAR; WORDLESS

77 **Baby Can Too: Songs and Activities Babies Can Do.** Melody House, 1982. Record. 30 min. $9.95.

Category: Poetry/Nursery rhymes/Songs **Age:** I–T

A wonderful, age-appropriate record, each song inspires children to perform simple, creative activities. It includes some perennial favorites, such as "Twinkle, Twinkle Little Star" and "Rock-a-Bye Baby," as well as some lesser known but equally enjoyable songs. The album jacket lists activities to accompany the songs.   [1]
BABIES; SONGS

78 **A Baby for Max.** Kathryn Lasky and Maxwell B. Knight. Photos by Christopher G. Knight. Macmillan, 1984. 48 pp. $12.95. (0-684-18064-2).

Category: Informational **Age:** P–K

Five-year-old Max describes his mother's pregnancy, his preparations, the arrival of his new sister, and his feelings throughout the experience. Documented by the father's black-and-white photographs of the Knight family during those months, this is a realistic story that offers children the facts rather than the myths of pregnancy in appropriately simple terms.   [2]
BABIES; SIBLING RIVALRY
Rev: CBK; NYT

79   ***Baby in the Box.*** Frank Asch. Holiday House, 1989. Unp. $12.95. (0-8234-0725-X). **Category:** Story   **Age:** I–T

What's better than a box of blocks? Dumping them out, climbing in, and being joined by "friends." A playful, rhymed fantasy ideal for intimate sharing. BABIES; BLOCKS; BOXES [2]

Rev: BKL 12/1/89

80   ***Baby Inside.*** Neil Ricklen. Simon & Schuster, 1991. Unp. $4.95. (0-671-73878-X). **Category:** Informational   **Age:** I–T

Crisp photographs of infants and toddlers playing with objects and peers inside the home illustrate this board book. Actions and items are clearly identified with one or two words placed close to the activity. Heavy-duty construction lends to the appeal for the child to use alone, yet many of the pictures are ideal for adult-child sharing. Includes pictures of children from numerous ethnic backgrounds. Part of a series of 15 other titles. [1] BOARD BOOKS; FAMILY LIFE; PLAY

81   ***Baby Says.*** John Steptoe. Lothrop, Lee & Shepard, 1988. Unp. $11.95. (0-688-07423-5). **Category:** Story   **Age:** T

Big brother and baby learn from one another in this simple portrait of a sibling relationship. Large, clear, softly shaded illustrations in full color reflect the universally recognized expressions of mischief, patience, frustration, and love as these two Afro-American children interact. The sparse text accurately captures the interchange between a toddler and a child. [2] AFRO-AMERICANS; BABIES; BROTHERS

Rev: BKL 4/1/88; CBY-89; ESLC

82   ***A Baby Sister for Frances.*** Russell Hoban. Illus. by Lillian Hoban. Harper & Row, 1964. Unp. $12.89. (0-06-022336-7). **Category:** Story   **Age:** P–K

Frances, the delightful badger, has a new sister who seems to be taking all her parents' time and attention. Frances decides to run away but stays close enough to hear her parents talk about her importance to the family. The soft, warm pictures add to the warmth and tenderness of the story. [1] BADGERS; FAMILY LIFE; RUNNING AWAY

Rev: CBK

83 **Baby-Sit.** Anne Miranda. Illus. by Dorothy Stott. Little, Brown & Co., 1990. Unp. $9.95. (0-316-57454-6).

Category: Participation and manipulative **Age:** T–P

Lift-up tabs reveal all the fun children can have with their babysitter while Mom and Dad have a night out. With adult supervision, this sturdy book with reinforced pages might even be used with older infants to allay separation fears. [2]

BABY-SITTING; TOY AND MOVABLE BOOKS

84 **Baby Songs: A Collection of Songs for the Very Young.** Hap Palmer. Illus. by Susannah Ryan. Crown, 1990. 64 pp. $13.95. (0-517-57593-0).

Category: Poetry/Nursery rhymes/Songs **Age:** I–T–P

Twenty-one songs with simple piano accompaniment and guitar chords cover the baby's life from learning to share, to fears of separation, to boisterous play. A companion to the music videos "Baby Songs" and "More Baby Songs," the book is spiral bound and contains an index of titles and first lines. [1]

BABIES; SONGS

85 **Baby Songs by Hap and Martha Palmer.** Hap Palmer and Martha Palmer. Educational Activities, 1984. Audiocassette. 30 min. $9.95.

Category: Poetry/Nursery rhymes/Songs **Age:** I–T–P

A happy collection of 12 sensitive songs about a child's everyday experiences: "Sittin' in a High Chair," "Security (Don't Wash My Blanket)," for example. Lyrics reflect the universal emotions of very young children. The upbeat and soothing music will have parents and children singing along. [2]

BABIES; SONGS

Rev: SLJ 4/85 **Awards:** ALSC Notable Recording

86 **The Baby's Bedtime Book.** Kay Chorao. Dutton, 1989. Unp. $13.95. (0-525-44149-2). **Category:** Poetry/Nursery rhymes/Songs **Age:** I–T–P–K

Pictures of children asleep in bed or cradle set the scene for Chorao's excellent collection of children's poetry. Lullabies and nursery rhymes all touch on the theme of evening or bedtime. Each poem is framed in a soft, dusky-blue border and matched by a large, soft-colored illustration rich with detail and patterning. Poets such as Kipling, Tennyson, and Rosetti are included. [1]

BEDTIME; NURSERY RHYMES; SLEEP

Rev: BKL 1/1/88 & 1/15/90; CBK; NYT

87   ***Baby's Bedtime (Stories to Remember).*** Illus. by Daniel Ivanick. Joshua M. Greene for Lightyear Entertainment, 1989. Dist. by Media Home Entertainment. Videocassette. 27 min. $14.98.

Category: Poetry/Nursery rhymes/Songs   **Age:** I–T

An adaptation of Kay Chorao's *The Baby's Bedtime Book* (Dutton, 1989), Judy Collins sings 17 rhymes and poems as a background to the richly animated pictures of Daniel Ivanick. Children will enjoy viewing as well as just listening to the wide variety of selections ranging in theme from the security of a father's arms to an escape to a make-believe realm.   [1]
BEDTIME; POETRY; SONGS
Rev: BKL 12/1/89   **Awards:** Parent's Choice Award

88   ***The Baby's Book of Babies.*** Kathy Henderson. Photos by Anthea Sieveking. Dial, 1989. Unp. $9.95. (0-8037-0634-0).

Category: Informational   **Age:** I–T

Full-color photographs of multiethnic babies "squeaking, peeping, crawling, creeping" are sure to delight all ages. Photos are at the child's level—whether on the adults' shoulder or in strollers—and capture the exuberance of infants. Although the pages are not cardboard, they are sturdy and tear resistant. [1]
BABIES; CONCEPTS
Rev: BKL 3/1/89

89   ***Baby's Book of Lullabies & Cradle Songs.*** Yvonne Gilbert. Dial, 1990. Unp. $12.95. (0-8037-0794-0).

Category: Poetry/Nursery rhymes/Songs   **Age:** I–T–P

Sixteen traditional lullabies from various world cultures are richly illustrated. The melody and first verse of the song are given on each two-page spread, and the complete lyrics for all songs are listed at the book's end. Also useful for teaching differences in customs among different nationalities.   [3]
LULLABIES; SONGS
Rev: BKL 10/1/90; SLJ 2/91

90   ***The Baby's Catalogue.*** Janet Ahlberg and Allan Ahlberg. Little, Brown & Co., 1982. Unp. $14.95. (0-316-02037-0).

Category: Informational   **Age:** T–P

Here it is: the baby's "Sears Roebuck" filled with countless items important to little ones. Dads, moms, lunches, toys, and accidents are just a few of the items shown. Humor packed for the adult reader as well as for the child.   [1]
BABIES
Rev: BBC; ESLC; HB 4/83

91   *Baby's First Christmas.* Tomie dePaola. Putnam, 1988. Unp. $4.95. (0-399-21591-3).   **Category:** Informational   **Age:** I–T

For children beginning to recognize some of the symbols of Christmas, this sturdy board book is ideal. Simple, colorful illustrations capture the essence of the season: dePaola shows a wreath hanging on a door, a candle shining in a window, a manger scene on the mantle, etc. This is an appropriate book to share with infants in order to introduce them to the season and all its activities.   [1]

BOARD BOOKS; CHRISTMAS

Rev: BKL 10/15/88

92   *Baby's First Words.* Photos by Lars Wik. Random House, 1985. Unp. Paper $2.95. (0-394-86945-1).   **Category:** Concept/Counting/Alphabet   **Age:** I–T

An engaging board book in the Chunky Book series. This title is filled with color photographs of objects familiar to young children that are necessary for certain activities. For example, a bib and a spoon are needed before the blond toddler depicted is ready to eat. The small, sturdy format is designed for a baby's hands, and the content will stimulate vocabulary development.   [3]

BABIES; BOARD BOOKS; CONCEPTS; WORDS

Rev: CBK

93   *Baby's First Year.* Phyllis Hoffman. Illus. by Sarah Wilson. Harper & Row, 1988. Unp. $12.89. (0-06-022552-1).   **Category:** Informational   **Age:** I–T

Young listeners can follow the first year in a baby's life with bright pictures and few words. Baby's first chair, first tooth, and first birthday offer a good chance to reminisce about those same events with older youngsters.   [2]

BABIES; BIRTHDAYS; FAMILY LIFE

Rev: BKL 10/1/88

94   *The Baby's Story Book.* Kay Chorao. Dutton, 1989. 64 pp. $13.95. (0-525-44200-6).   **Category:** Folklore/Folktales/Fairy tales   **Age:** T–P–K

Anthology includes familiar stories such as "The Gingerbread Boy" and "The Three Little Pigs," combined with the less familiar "The Boy Who Turned Himself into a Peanut." Fables are "The Wind and the Sun" and "The Lion and the Mouse." Poetry choices are "The History of an Apple Pie" and "The House That Jack Built." Detailed, pastel illustrations add humor and variety. Text and length of stories are well suited to young children. Also available in other formats from the National Library for the Blind and Physically Handicapped. [3]

FABLES; FOLK AND FAIRY TALES

95 ***Baby's Storytime (Stories to Remember).*** Illus. by Kay Chorao. Produced by Joshua M. Greene. Lightyear Entertainment, 1989. Dist. by Media Home Entertainment. Videocassette. 28 min. $14.98.

Category: Folklore/Folktales/Fairy tales **Age:** T

Eleven favorite stories, among them "The Three Little Pigs," "Henny Penny," and "Little Red Riding Hood," are told by Arlo Guthrie. Based on Kay Chorao's *Baby's Storybook* (Dutton, 1985), the animation is true to the book illustrations. [1]

BEDTIME; FOLK AND FAIRY TALES

Rev: BKL 1/15/90

96 ***Baby's Words.*** Photographs selected by Deborah Slier. Checkerboard, 1988. Unp. Paper $2.95. (0-02-688751-7). Dist. by Macmillan.

Category: Informational **Age:** T

Simple photo layout on solid backgrounds provides an uncluttered environment while the single word per page text identifies familiar objects or "fun" photographs of puppies, cookies, etc. Small-sized and sturdy construction, the book is ideal for small hands. [2]

BABIES; WORDS

Rev: BKL 7/88

97 ***Baby's World: A First Picture Catalog.*** Photos by Stephen Shott. Dutton, 1990. 40 pp. $13.95. (0-525-44617-6).

Category: Informational **Age:** T–P

Forty pages pack virtually every conceivable object, activity, or concept impacting a baby's world into "a first picture catalog." Clean layout of brightly colored, clearly labeled photos and sturdy binding should provide many happy hours of browsing and identifying. Includes table of contents. [3]

BABIES; WORDS

Rev: BKL 1/15/91

98 ***Backwards Land.*** Performed by Hap Palmer. Educational Activities, 1987. Record. 30 min. $10.95.

Category: Poetry/Nursery rhymes/Songs **Age:** P–K

Fun and enjoyable music, these imaginative songs such as "If I Had Wings" coupled with educational verses such as "Amanda Schlupp Who Would Not Pick Her Toys Up," are written from a child's point of view. Issues of value are presented in the context of entertaining stories in song form. Children will learn not to be distressed when leaving a familiar place or frustrated when they do not get what they want.   [3]

FAMILY LIFE; SONGS

Rev: BKL 11/1/88

99   ***The Ball Bounced.*** Nancy Tafuri. Greenwillow Books, 1989. Unp. $11.95.
        (0-688-07872-9).   **Category:** Story   **Age:** T

A bouncing ball causes much excitement around the house as each brightly colored scene shows the consequences of a bouncing, rolling ball. It frightens a cat, bumps a table, splashes the fish bowl, and startles a dog and a bird before it comes to rest near a laughing baby. Simple, declarative sentences teach action words with visually exciting pictures.   [1]

BALLS

Rev: BKL 3/15/89; SLJ 7/89

100   ***A Balloon for Grandad.*** Nigel Gray. Illus. by Jane Ray. Orchard Books,
        1988. Unp. $13.99. (0-531-08355-1).   **Category:** Story   **Age:** P–K

Sam is distraught when his balloon floats out the back door. His Dad comforts him by suggesting the balloon is on its way to Grandpa Abdulla in North Africa. The two imagine a detailed journey over mountains, oceans and deserts, ending at Grandpa's little brown house built of mud. Grandpa welcomes the balloon, knowing it was sent by Sam. Primitive pictures in pure, clear colors add to this heartwarming tale.   [3]

BALLOONS; FAMILY LIFE; FOREIGN LANDS

Rev: BKL 12/1/88

101   ***Banana, Banana...Banana Slugs!*** Daniel Zata, 1988. Dist. by Bullfrog
        Films. Videocassette. 8 min. $145.00.
                                        Category: Informational   **Age:** P–K

As a group of young children become acquainted with "banana slugs" in their natural redwood forest habitat, initial revulsion changes to interest and acceptance. Child narration and pleasant folk music lyrics effectively describe the slug. This not only introduces an often overlooked lifeform, but also illustrates how understanding can change attitudes.   [3]

ECOLOGY; NATURE; SNAILS

Rev: BKL 5/1/89; SLJ 4/89   **Awards:** ALSC Notable Film/Video

102   *Barn Dance!* Bill Martin, Jr. and John Archambault. Illus. by Ted Rand. Henry Holt & Co., 1986. 32 pp. $12.95. (0-8050-0089-5).

Category: Story   **Age:** P–K

A full moon, the beckoning of an owl, and the sounds of a fiddle lure the curious, skinny kid out of bed and to the hoe-down. All do-si-do till morning to the calls of the scarecrow. As he slips back into bed, the kid still has "the wonders of the barn dance...dancin' in his head." The magic of lyrics and illustrations will lure you down to the barn, too!   [2]

DANCING

Rev: ESLC

103   *Barney Is Big.* Nicki Weiss. Greenwillow Books, 1988. 24 pp. $11.95. (0-688-07586-X).   **Category:** Story   **Age:** P

Barney can take a bath by himself, dress himself, and go to nursery school. He feels really big! But the joy of being big can still include being babied, as Barney and Mom both realize the night before his first day of nursery school.

BABIES; GROWTH   [2]

Rev: BKL 9/1/88

104   *Bear Hugs.* Kathleen Hague. Illus. by Michael Hague. Henry Holt & Co., 1989. Unp. $9.95. (0-8050-0512-9).

Category: Poetry/Nursery rhymes/Songs   **Age:** T–P

Nine delightful poems reflect the very special relationship of children and teddy bears. A good naptime or bedtime book with especially appealing illustrations, this is a companion book to the Hagues' other books.   [2]

POETRY; TEDDY BEARS; TOYS

Rev: SLJ 8/89

105   *Bear Shadow.* Frank Asch. Simon & Schuster, 1988. Paper $4.95. (0-671-66866-8).   **Category:** Story   **Age:** T–P

When his shadow frightens the fish he wants to catch, Bear tries several means to get rid of his shadow. His efforts provide a simple explanation of the relation of the sun to objects on earth and how shadows are formed. Also available in videocassette and filmstrip from Coronet/MTI Film & Video.   [3]

BEARS; SHADOWS

Rev: BBC; ESLC

106 *Bears, Bears, Bears: A Treasury of Stories, Songs, and Poems about Bears.* Compiled by Mary P. Osborne. Illus. by Karen L. Schmidt. Silver Press, 1990. 96 pp. $18.98. (0-671-69630-0).

Category: Poetry/Nursery rhymes/Songs **Age:** I–T–P–K

An extensive treasury to be shared and enjoyed by all ages, celebrating bears in stories, songs, poems, fables, and folktales. Different cultures are represented by, for example, an Alaskan tale, an African-American tale, and a Native American legend. Schmidt's whimsical illustrations provide a visual feast for young nonreaders. This collection should be a "bear" necessity for everyone! [1]

BEARS; POETRY; SONGS

Rev: CBK; ESLC

107 *Beauty and the Beast.* Retold and illustrated by Jan Brett. Houghton Mifflin, 1989. Unp. $14.95. (0-89919-497-4).

Category: Folklore/Folktales/Fairy tales **Age:** K

Brett's retelling of this classic fairy tale is based on the 1910 edition by Sir Arthur Quiller-Couch. The narrative has been shortened, but flows easily. The illustrations are colorful and detailed. The tapestries in the Beast's palace show the same scene that is taking place on the page. The book will delight all ages, but will require a mature reader to truly appreciate all the nuances of the illustrations. [2]

BEASTS; FOLK AND FAIRY TALES; LOVE

Rev: BKL 10/1/89

108 *Beauty & the Beast (Stories to Remember).* Narrated by Mia Farrow. Joshua M. Greene for Lightyear Entertainment, 1989. Dist. by Media Home Entertainment. Videocassette. 27 min. $14.98.

Category: Folklore/Folktales/Fairy tales **Age:** P–K

Actress Mia Farrow narrates Mordicai Gerstein's brilliantly animated version of *Beauty & the Beast* (Dutton, 1989). Young children might miss the lesson on the recognition and appreciation of genuine beauty, but they are bound to enjoy seeing and listening to the timeless tale of enchantment and romance.

BEASTS; FOLK AND FAIRY TALES; LOVE [1]

Rev: BKL 10/1/89 & 1/15/90; SLJ 5/90

Awards: Parents' Choice Award; Cine Golden Eagle Award

109 *Bedtime for Frances.* Russell Hoban. Illus. by Garth Williams. Harper & Row, 1960. Unp. $12.89. (0-06-022351-0).

Category: Story **Age:** P–K

In this first book of the series, Frances is in bed singing the alphabet until she reaches T for tiger and begins worrying about tigers in her room. Children can easily relate to this little badger as she tries one ploy after another to put off going to bed. Hoban is whimsically able to mirror the concerns of preschoolers. Illustrations are drawings in black, white, and green. Also available in other formats from the National Library for the Blind and Physically Handicapped. [1]

BADGERS; BEDTIME; FEAR
Rev: BBC; CBK; ESLC; NYT

110 *Bedtime Stories.* Weston Woods Studios, 1987. Videocassette. 18 min. $59.00. **Category:** Poetry/Nursery rhymes/Songs **Age:** I–T–P

Four classic tales are included in this endearing collection. "Hush Little Baby" (Aliki) is sung with the camera panning the book illustrations. "A Picture for Harold's Room" is simply animated, and Barbara Cooney's book illustrations are viewed for "The Owl and the Pussy-cat" and "Wynken, Blynken and Nod." The text is poetically spoken. [2]

BEDTIME; NURSERY RHYMES

111 *Bedtime Story.* Jim Erskine. Illus. by Ann Schweninger. Crown, 1982. 24 pp. $8.95. (0-517-54540-3). **Category:** Story **Age:** T–P

Pastel hues of blue, yellow, gray, and white in the watercolor illustrations complement the gentle text of this story within a story. A little boy is asked to listen for all the sounds and sights he might hear and see at night: the clock that chimes downstairs, the "moon man" smiling, the twinkling of the stars, or an old owl swooping into the air. This presents a soothing lullaby-type tale for bedtime. [2]

BEDTIME
Rev: CBK

112 *Ben's Baby.* Michael Foreman. Harper & Row, 1988. Unp. $14.89. (0-06-021844-4). **Category:** Story **Age:** P–K

Four-year-old Ben requests a baby for his birthday. Thus begins a chronicle of events surrounding the forthcoming baby. Foreman describes Ben's Christmas when he learns of his mother's pregnancy, a January trip with Mom to the hospital to view a sonogram of the baby, and then finally a visit to the hospital for the baby's birth. A wonderful way to introduce the older sibling to the arrival of a brother or sister. [2]

BABIES; FAMILY LIFE
Rev: BKL 5/1/88; CBY-89; ESLC

113 *The Berenstain Bears: Learn about Counting.* Britannica Software, 1990. Software (IBM, Tandy). $24.95.

Category: Concept/Counting/Alphabet **Age:** P–K

Enticed by the well-known characters from the Berenstain Bear family, youngsters will both benefit from and enjoy counting apples passed by Brother Bear to Sister Bear in "Apple Toss," one of the eight options for math practice and problem solving. Color graphics are particularly notable, and the flexibility to choose categories for varying abilities makes the program appropriate for a wide span of ages. The package includes four puppets and a guide.   [2]

BEARS; COUNTING

Rev: SJL 1/91

114 *Best Friends.* Selected by Lee Bennett Hopkins. Illus. by James Watts. Harper & Row, 1986. 48 pp. $11.89. (0-06-022562-9).

Category: Poetry/Nursery rhymes/Songs **Age:** P–K

The personalities, pleasures, and challenges of childhood friendships are noted by 18 contemporary poets. Cheerful, silly drawings accompany the short verses, which insist upon being read aloud. Hopkins is a noted anthologist with many poetry collections for children.   [2]

FRIENDSHIP; POETRY

Rev: PP

115 *Best Friends: Old Bear Tales.* Jane Hissey. Philomel, 1988. 76 pp. $16.95. (0-399-21674-X). **Category:** Story **Age:** P–K

A delightful read-aloud collection of 12 inventive tales revolving around Hissey's familiar nursery characters—Old Bear, Bramwell Brown, and Rabbit—and many new characters. Plots are simple and appealing. Incredibly realistic, soft colored-pencil drawings are the icing on the cake for this large format book.   [1]

FRIENDSHIP; TOYS

Rev: BKL 3/15/89; CBY-90

116 *Best Friends for Frances.* Russell Hoban. Illus. by Lillian Hoban. Harper & Row, 1969. 31 pp. $12.89. (0-06-022328-6).

Category: Story **Age:** P–K

Frances the badger learns that best friends can come in all sizes, shapes, and genders. Her problems with best friend Albert and baby sister Gloria are brought to life through the clever songs Frances makes up. Hoban's charcoal illustrations with two-color highlights are most entertaining.   [2]

BADGERS; FRIENDSHIP; SISTERS

Rev: CBK

117   ***Better Not Get Wet, Jesse Bear.*** Nancy White Carlstrom. Illus. by Bruce Degen. Macmillan, 1988. Unp. $13.95. (0-02-717280-5).

Category: Story   **Age:** P–K

Like most children, Jesse Bear loves playing in water, and children will love watching him take every opportunity to get wet: washing dishes, playing with his fish, making a puddle for a worm. Even though his parents often warn him not to, they finally agree that "Hey, Hey, getting wet is okay" and let him play in his very own pool.   [1]
BEARS; WATER
Rev: BKL 4/15/88

118   ***Big Al.*** Andrew Clements. Illus. by Yoshi. Picture Book Studio, 1988. Unp. $14.95. (0-88708-075-8).   **Category:** Story   **Age:** P–K

Big Al is a gentle, friendly fish, but because he is also very large and very ugly, none of the other fish ever get close enough to find out. Al is sad and lonely until the day he rescues the other fish from the net. Ironically, his appearance saves his own life: "those fishermen took one look at him, and threw him right back." Yoshi's brilliant batik illustrations add much to the appeal of this thought-provoking story.   [1]
FISH; FRIENDSHIP
Rev: SLJ 6/89

119   ***Big and Little.*** Ruth Krauss. Illus. by Mary Szilagyi. Scholastic, 1987. Unp. $12.95. (0-590-41707-X).   **Category:** Story   **Age:** I–T–P

Explores the value of little things in a big world. Beautifully etched in warm pastel colors are the things a boy finds all around him, in forests, fields, the seashore, cities, towns, and in his own home. A celebration of life and love, this story deserves to be shared with a little one on an adult's lap.   [1]
LOVE; VALUES
Rev: BKL 5/15/88

120   ***Big Brother.*** Charlotte Zolotow. Illus. by Mary Chalmers. Harper & Row, 1960. Unp. $12.89. (0-06-026921-9).   **Category:** Story   **Age:** P–K

Subtle pencil sketches with minimal color humorously illustrate the relationship between a big brother and his little sister, whom he teases. The text is simple, yet warm and inviting as the reader watches the little sister come to

understand her big brother's ways and use them to bring about their friendship. A wonderful book to use to help children with relationship building.
BROTHERS; SIBLINGS; SISTERS   [1]
Rev: CBK

121   *Big Jeremy.* Steven Kroll. Illus. by Donald Carrick. Holiday House, 1989. Unp. $13.95. (0-8234-0759-4).   **Category:** Story   **Age:** P–K

Big Jeremy is a warm, friendly giant who loves the enormous barn he lives in, helping his friends work in their apple orchard, and watching the sun set from his big elephant-sized arm chair. One night when the orchard catches fire and his clumsiness only causes problems, he decides to run away. After a long time, he is convinced by his friends that he is needed and returns home. Carrick's drawings show a gentle, loving giant.   [2]
FRIENDSHIP; GIANTS
Rev: BKL 11/1/89; SLJ 2/90

122   *Big Like Me.* Anna G. Hines. Greenwillow Books, 1989. Unp. $12.88. (0-688-08355-2).   **Category:** Concept/Counting/Alphabet   **Age:** T–P–K

"Big" brother exuberantly assumes the task of teaching his new baby sister "everything" she must learn in her first year in order to be "Big Like Me." Her development and their relationship are followed month by month with activities appropriate for development and the seasons. Warm close interaction of all family members—parents as well as the siblings—is reflected in the soft watercolor and colored pencil drawings.   [1]
BABIES; BROTHERS AND SISTERS; MONTHS OF THE YEAR
Rev: CBY-90; BKL 10/1/89

123   *Big Red Barn.* Margaret Wise Brown. Illus. by Felicia Bond. Harper & Row, 1989. Unp. $11.89. (0-06-020749-3).   **Category:** Story   **Age:** T–P

Familiar farm animals are introduced in this quiet, simple story of a day in the barnyard from daybreak to moon glow. The original rhythmic text has been coupled with new artwork featuring colors as fresh and inviting as country air. A good choice for a group read-aloud or a one-on-one sharing.   [1]
ANIMALS; FARMS
Rev: BKL 3/1/89; CBK; CBY-90

124   *Big Sarah's Little Boots.* Paulette Bourgeois. Illus. by Brenda Clark. Kids Can Press, 1987. Unp. $11.95. (0-590-42622-2).
Category: Story   **Age:** P–K

When Sarah discovers her beloved yellow rain boots no longer fit, she tries every means to make them "grow." Realizing that she is the one that has grown and needs new boots, Sarah is disconsolate, until her old boots are passed down to her little brother. When both go out to play, Sarah discovers all the "bigger" things she can do in her new boots because of her new-found maturity. [2]
BOOTS; BROTHERS AND SISTERS; GROWING UP
Rev: BKL 1/1/90; EL 3/23/88

125 *The Big Sneeze.* Ruth Brown. Lothrop, Lee & Shepard, 1985. 32 pp. $13.95. (0-688-04665-7). **Category:** Story **Age:** P–K

One afternoon, a farmer dozes in the barn along with the barnyard animals. When a fly lands on the farmer's nose, the farmer sneezes, causing a chain of startled reactions among the animals. Spiders, birds, cats, dogs, rats, hens, and a donkey all get into the act, leaving the barn in complete disarray and the farmer bewildered. Also available in other formats from the National Library for the Blind and Physically Handicapped. [2]
CUMULATIVE TALES; FARMS; HUMOR
Rev: ESLC

126 *Biggest Bear.* Lynd Ward. Houghton Mifflin, 1952. 88 pp. $13.95. (0-395-14806-5). **Category:** Story **Age:** P–K

When Johnny brings home a little bear cub, he does not foresee the problems his growing pet will cause. His bear grows and grows! Soon his father, at the neighbors' insistence, tells him that the bear must be shot. Some circus men come along just in time to give this wonderfully illustrated story a happy ending. [3]
BEARS
Rev: BBC **Awards:** Caldecott Medal

127 *The Biggest Nose.* Kathy Caple. Houghton Mifflin, 1985. 32 pp. $13.95. (0-395-36894-4). **Category:** Story **Age:** P–K

Ridiculed by her classmates because of her large nose, Eleanor, an elephant, tries desperately to shorten her trunk. Her attempts fail, and in an admirable display of courage, Eleanor reminds fellow students that they too have shortcomings. Caple employs humor in creating a work that promotes the acceptance of individual differences. [3]
ANIMALS; ELEPHANTS; NOSES
Rev: ESLC

128   *The Bionic Bunny Show.* Marc Brown and Laurene Krasny Brown. Illus. by Marc Brown. Little, Brown & Co., 1984. 32 pp. $14.95. (0-316-11120-1).   **Category:** Story   **Age:** P–K

Wilbur is an ordinary rabbit until he reaches the TV studio, where he dons a costume to become "Bionic Bunny." Readers are introduced to TV production and the idea that stars have real lives, too. Cheery, humorous illustrations cut between the frame of a television set and the larger forum of the real world. The tale is appropriate for individual or small group use.   [2]
RABBITS; TELEVISION
Rev: NYT   **Awards:** Reading Rainbow Book

129   *Birthday for Frances.* Russell Hoban. Illus. by Lillian Hoban. Harper & Row, 1968. 32 pp. $12.89. (0-06-022339-1).   **Category:** Story   **Age:** K

It is Gloria's birthday and Frances is typically jealous. Generosity does win out over sulking and imaginary friends in the end. Understanding parents assist in bringing this story to a happy conclusion. Also available in other formats from the National Library for the Blind and Physically Handicapped.   [2]
BADGERS; BIRTHDAYS; SIBLING RIVALRY
Rev: CBK

130   *Birthday Presents.* Cynthia Rylant. Illus. by Suçie Stevenson. Orchard Books, 1987. Unp. $13.95. (0-531-08305-5).

Category: Story   **Age:** P–K

A mother and father tell their daughter about her first six birthdays. Each birthday is chronicled, and the little girl's development can be followed from birth to five years of age. As her sixth birthday approaches, our heroine has grown up quite a bit and is interested in helping her parents celebrate their own birthdays. Pen and ink drawings are cartoonlike in quality, but also convey warmth and sensitivity.   [3]
BIRTHDAYS; GROWING UP
Rev: ESLC

131   *Black Is Brown Is Tan.* Arnold Adoff. Illus. by Emily McCully. Harper & Row, 1973. 32 pp. $13.89. (0-06-020084-7).   **Category:** Story   **Age:** K

Adoff has written a wonderful story in verse about an interracial family that is filled with love and everyday happenings. Daddy and Mommy play with their children, read to them, and occasionally "puff and yell [them] into bed." The illustrations are so well-drawn that the reader becomes involved in the bustle and the quiet times of this very real family.   [1]
FAMILY LIFE; POETRY
Rev: BBC; ESLC

132 *The Black Snowman.* Phil Mendez. Illus. by Carole Byard. Scholastic, 1989. Unp. $12.95. (0-590-40552-7). **Category:** Story **Age:** K

"I hate being black!" says Jacob, repeating the words he had heard others say. "Everything black is bad!" A threadbare kente cloth from Africa, its magic still powerful after many generations, makes the boy's snowman come alive. The cloth begins to change Jacob's negative feelings about himself in this poignant, urban fantasy. [1]

AFRO-AMERICANS; SELF-CONCEPT; SNOWMEN

Rev: BKL 10/1/89

133 *Blackberry Ink.* Eve Merriam. Illus. by Hans Wilhelm. Morrow, 1985. 40 pp. $11.88. (0-688-04151-5).
Category: Poetry/Nursery rhymes/Songs **Age:** P–K

A collection of 24 poems on such diverse subjects as vegetables, pizza, bugs, monsters, and laundry. Children will also enjoy keeping track of the bear who frolics throughout most of the accompanying watercolor illustrations. [2]

FRIENDSHIP; POETRY

Rev: CBK; PP

134 *Blackberry Ramble.* Thacher Hurd. Crown, 1989. 32 pp. $13.99. (0-517-57105-6). **Category:** Story **Age:** P–K

Bold strokes of color set the pace for Baby Mouse's mischievous springtime adventures. When she mistakes Becky the cow's tail for a rope, she is sent with a great swat sailing homeward to the tiny cottage. In a second encounter, the mouse takes possession of the family car on a picnic supper and lands in the blackberry pie. All ends happily, however, after a game of catch and an uneventful ride home as Baby Mouse falls asleep. [2]

MICE; SPRING

Rev: BKL 9/1/89

135 *Blackboard Bear.* Martha Alexander. Dial, 1969. Unp. $9.89. (0-8037-0651-0). **Category:** Story **Age:** P–K

A little boy wants to play with the bigger boys, but they don't like to play with little boys. With limited text and selective illustrations, the author shares the sadness of a small boy "not old enough" and the joy of finding a solution. A

small book format, difficult to share within a larger group, but the imaginativeness and warmth of the illustrations should not be missed. [2]
BEARS; FRIENDSHIP; WORDLESS
Rev: BBC; CBK

136   Blue Hat, Green Hat. Sandra Boynton. Simon & Schuster, 1984. Unp. Paper $3.95. (0-671-49320-5).   **Category:** Story   **Age:** T–P–K

This board book contains simple illustrations of three animals dressed in various articles of clothing. The fourth, a turkey, adds humor by wearing clothes incorrectly: the shirt as pants, the hat on his feet, etc. Finally, wearing clothes properly, he dives into the swimming pool. The rhythmic, patterned text offers the opportunity for the audience to "read along." Illustrations are in primary colors which add to the book's usefulness. [1]
BOARD BOOKS; CLOTHING
Rev: CBK

137   Blueberries for Sal. Robert McCloskey. Viking Penguin, 1948. 56 pp. $13.95. (0-670-17591-9).   **Category:** Story   **Age:** T–P–K

Little Sal and her mother go to pick blueberries on Blueberry Hill. Meanwhile, Little Bear and his mother go to the same hill to eat blueberries. During the day, Little Sal and Little Bear become confused, and each follows the other's mother for a time. The amusing mix-up is soon resolved, and each follows the right mother home. Also available in other formats from the National Library for the Blind and Physically Handicapped. [2]
BEARS
Rev: BBC; CBK; ESLC; NYT

138   Boats. Byron Barton. Harper & Row, 1986. Unp. $11.89. (0-690-04536-0).   **Category:** Story   **Age:** P–K

Simple, bold illustrations of boats are enhanced with simple text and clear settings. Basic concepts as size, shape, and color can be easily extended with discussion. [3]
BOATS
Rev: ESLC

139   Bones, Bones, Dinosaur Bones. Byron Barton. Thomas Y. Crowell, 1990. Unp. $12.89. (0-690-04827-0).   **Category:** Story   **Age:** P–K

This simple story shows the process of archeological exploration from dig site to museum and back. Bold colors and simple illustrations with large text make

this particularly suited for group participation. The book ends with a full display of all the dinosaurs shown. [1]
Dinosaurs

140 **The Book of Kid's Songs: A Holler-Along Handbook.** Nancy Cassidy and John Cassidy. Illus. by Jim M'Guinness. Klutz Press, 1986. 50 pp. $10.95. (0-932592-13-9).

Category: Poetry/Nursery rhymes/Songs **Age:** T–P–K

Twenty-two popular, traditional and contemporary classics are presented with music for piano and guitar on spiral-bound pages of heavy, glossy stock. Brief instructions for making four simple musical instruments and a 48-minute sing-along cassette are also provided. Sprightly pen and watercolor illustrations convey the spirit of the songs. [2]
Songs

141 **The Book of Pigericks.** Arnold Lobel. Harper & Row, 1983. 48 pp. $13.89. (0-06-023983-2). **Category:** Poetry/Nursery rhymes/Songs **Age:** P–K

Lobel, "an old pig with a pen," gives us 38 clever "pig" limericks delightfully illustrated "with brushes, some paints and his pen." A lighthearted approach to loosely disguised human foibles in a favorite form. [3]
Limericks; Pigs
Rev: BKL 1/1/88

142 **A Book of Seasons.** Alice Provensen and Martin Provensen. Random House, 1976. Unp. Paper $1.95. (0-394-83242-6).

Category: Concept/Counting/Alphabet **Age:** P–K

The cycle of the changing seasons is described with happy pictures and with activities associated with each. While not all children will relate to spring being "maple-syrup time," they will gain an appreciation for the promise that "Spring is the earth's birthday. It comes again and again and again." [3]
Concepts; Seasons
Rev: CBK

143 **Boot Weather.** Judith Vigna. Albert Whitman & Co., 1989. Unp. $12.95. (0-8075-0837-3). **Category:** Story **Age:** P–K

After Kim's father announces it is boot weather, Kim uses her imagination to take her to wild and exciting places. She climbs up a slide and imagines herself climbing a mountain. She leaps over rocks and pretends she is weightless on the moon. "In boot weather Kim can go anywhere at all...and still be home for lunch." [1]

IMAGINATION; SNOW; WEATHER

Rev: BKL 3/1/89

144 *The Box with Red Wheels.* Maud Petersham and Miska Petersham. Macmillan, 1949. Unp. $12.95. (0-02-771350-4).

Category: Story **Age:** T–P–K

This classic little mystery is the story of a strange-looking box with red wheels sitting under a tree in the garden. Each of the curious farm animals wander through the open gate to gaze into the box. Finally, a baby's head appears just as Mother anxiously shoos the animals away and closes the gate. Seeing how sad the baby and animals are, Mother relents and opens the gate, allowing the gentle animals to play with baby. [3]

ANIMALS; BOXES

Rev: CBK

145 *A Boy, a Dog and a Frog.* Mercer Mayer. Dial, 1967. Unp. $8.89. (0-8037-0767-3). **Category:** Wordless **Age:** P–K

Good things come in small packages, and Mayer has created a perfect wordless picture book sized just right for small hands to enjoy. A small boy dressed in over-sized boots and well-equipped with a fishing net and bucket sets off for adventure with his dog. Their slapstick efforts to catch a frog will provoke much mirth. Mayer deftly creates a whole world of emotions and relationships with his soft pen and ink drawings. [1]

DOGS; FROGS; WORDLESS

Rev: ESLC; NYT

146 *A Boy, a Dog, and a Frog.* Mercer Mayer. Phoenix BFA Films & Videos, 1980. Videocassette. 9 min. $155.00. **Category:** Wordless **Age:** P–K

While staying true to Mayer's book (Dial, 1967), this video brings to life the "personalities" of the boy, the dog, and the frog throughout a most playful escapade. Outstanding photography! [1]

DOGS; FROGS; WORDLESS

Rev: BKL 5/1/89

147 *The Boy and the Snow Goose.* The National Film Board of Canada, 1984. Dist. by Bullfrog Films. Videocassette. 11 min. $95.00.

Category: Story **Age:** P–K

A boy cares for an injured snow goose, and a friendship develops. Respecting the way of nature, however, the goose joins the autumn migration, leaving the boy lonely and dreaming of his friend. The snow goose returns briefly in the spring, but while their reunion is loving, they each have found friends among their own kind. The wordless music and softly drawn animation convey the story without undue sentimentality. [1]

GEESE; VALUES

Awards: Special Jury Award, Canadian International Animation Festival

148 *The Boy Who Ate the Moon.* Christopher King. Illus. by John Wallner. Philomel, 1988. Unp. $14.95. (0-399-21459-3). **Category:** Story **Age:** K

In a magical, mystical setting, a young boy fails to heed the warnings of his father and climbs to a treetop to dislodge the moon. Unsuccessful, the boy is blown by the Great West Wind over cities, plains, seas, deserts, and forests. Fortunately, he is blown home just as the sun comes up. Wallner's ethereal illustrations of soft pastels lend a whimsical, airy tone to this flight of fantasy.

IMAGINATION; MOON [2]

Rev: BKL 11/15/88

149 *The Boy Who Loved Frogs: Animal Tales.* Performed by Jay O'Callahan. High Windy Audio, 1987. Audiocassette. 49 min. $9.98.

Category: Story **Age:** K

A long story and three short pieces perfect for family entertainment. "Herman and Marguerite" is a fanciful moral tale about a worm and a caterpillar whose growing friendship encourages each to change and become the best each can be. A compassionate young boy, African animals, and frogs appear in the shorter yarns, whose lively sound effects and modulated cadence will attract kindergartners. [3]

ANIMALS; FABLES

Awards: Parents' Choice Award

150 *Brave Irene.* William Steig. Farrar, Straus & Giroux, 1986. Unp. $13.95. (0-374-30947-7). **Category:** Story **Age:** K

Irene braves a fearful snowstorm to deliver a ball gown for her mother who is poor and ill. The illustrations will make the viewer sympathize with Irene's plight. A perfect story for sharing during the winter months. [1]

ADVENTURE; BRAVERY; GIRLS

Rev: BBC

151 *Brave Irene.* William Steig. Narrated by Lindsey Crouse. Paul Gagne for DMI Productions, 1989. Dist. by Weston Woods Studios. Videocassette. 12 min. $150.00.   **Category:** Story   **Age:** K

Irene must travel through a storm to deliver a gown to the duchess. The wind takes the dress from her, but Irene is determined to finish the trip so she can explain what has happened to the duchess. Amazingly, she finds the gown, the duchess is thrilled, Irene attends the ball, and her mother is proud of her accomplishment. This animated version of Steig's book (Farrar, 1986) does justice to the gamut of emotions Irene experiences.   [1]
ADVENTURE; BRAVERY; GIRLS
Rev: BKL 3/15/90

152 *Bread and Honey.* Frank Asch. Parents Magazine Press, 1981. Unp. $5.95. (0-8193-1078-6).   **Category:** Story   **Age:** P–K

At school, Bear paints a picture of his mother, but on the way home, owl, alligator, rabbit, elephant, lion, and giraffe suggest changes, all of which reflect a characteristic peculiar to each animal. Bear is somewhat doubtful about the finished product, but presents it to Mother, nevertheless. Simple yet colorful illustrations present physical characteristics of the animals in a predictable story.   [3]
BEARS; PAINTING
Rev: ESLC

153 *Bread and Jam for Frances.* Russell Hoban. Illus. by Lillian Hoban. Harper & Row, 1964. 31 pp. $12.95. (0-06-022360-X).
     Category: Story   **Age:** P–K

Frances refuses all but her favorite food—bread and jam. When her family obliges her by serving her only bread and jam, she learns that there can be too much of a good thing. Funny songs that Frances makes up about her food and herself punctuate the text with childlike intensity.   [1]
BADGERS; FOOD
Rev: CBY-87

154 *The Bremen Town Musicians.* Jacob Grimm and Wilhelm K. Grimm. Translated by Anthea Bell. Illus. by Josef Palecek. Picture Book Studio, 1988. Unp. $13.95. (0-88708-071-5).
     Category: Folklore/Folktales/Fairy tales   **Age:** P–K

In a retelling of a Grimm brothers' favorite, an old donkey runs away to join the Bremen Town Band before his master does away with him. Along his way, a menagerie experiencing a similar fate joins him, and together they encounter a band of robbers, which they successfully scare. The full-page primitive illustrations are colorful and effectively complement the story. [2]

ANIMALS; FOLK AND FAIRY TALES

Rev: BKL 11/1/88; ESLC; SLJ 3/89

155 *Brown Bear, Brown Bear, What Do You See?* Bill Martin, Jr. Illus. by Eric Carle. Henry Holt & Co., 1983. Unp. $13.95. (0-8050-0201-4).

Category: Poetry/Nursery rhymes/Songs   **Age:** T–P–K

Large, colorful yet simple illustrations and a rhymed text combine to make this an easy introduction to teaching the concept of color. Children will want to hear this story over and over again, and will quickly begin to participate in responding to the question repeatedly asked. A new edition marking the 25th anniversary of this book includes all new artwork by Carle (Henry Holt, 1992).

ANIMALS; BEARS; COLOR; CUMULATIVE TALES; POETRY [1]

Rev: CBK; ESLC

156 *A Brown Cow.* Bijou Le Tord. Little, Brown & Co., 1989. Unp. $12.95. (0-316-52166-3).   **Category:** Story   **Age:** P–K

In very simple text, a child describes a day in the life of her brown cow. The cow spends her day twitching her ears in the wind, swatting flies with her tail, and eating grass "round and round in her mouth." At the end, the child concludes, "And I love her." [3]

Cows

Rev: BKL 5/15/89

157 *Buffy's Orange Leash.* Stephen Golder and Lise Memling. Illus. by Marcy Ramsey. Kendall Green Publications/Gallaudet University Press, 1988. Unp. $8.95. (0-930323-42-4).   **Category:** Informational   **Age:** P–K

Buffy is friendly, Buffy is smart, and Buffy likes to listen. Buffy is a Hearing Dog who acts as the ears for Mr. and Mrs. Johnson, allowing them to answer the phone, know when their baby cries, respond to a fire alarm, and know when someone is at the door. This story realistically depicts the day-to-day problems that the deaf must handle, and shows how Hearing Dogs are trained to help. [3]

DEAFNESS; DOGS

Rev: BKL 2/15/89

158 *Builder of the Moon.* Tim Wynne-Jones. Illus. by Ian Wallace. Margaret K. McElderry Books, 1988. Unp. $14.95. (0-689-50472-1).

Category: Story **Age:** P–K

Finding a moonbeam message on his floor, "Help! I'm falling apart. The Moon," David gathers his blocks and other needed items and sets off to save the moon. He has all the right sizes, shapes, and colors to build valleys, hills, and mountains. The tiny sliver of moon is whole once more, and David returns home to admire his handiwork. The full color pastel-pencil pictures are perfect for this fantasy. [2]

ADVENTURE; BLOCKS; MOON

Rev: BKL 5/15/89

159 *Bunny Party.* Lena Anderson. Farrar, Straus & Giroux, 1987. Unp. $3.95. (91-29-59134-1). **Category:** Wordless **Age:** T

A toddler rests his head on a table when suddenly a big rabbit brings all the items, one at a time, to make the table ready for a party. First comes the tablecloth, then plates, glasses, flowers, and on it goes. No words are used, but each item added to the table has its own page to highlight the ongoing action. This structure is a clever and inviting way to introduce table manners. [1]

MEALTIME; RABBITS; WORDLESS

Rev: HB 7/89; SLJ 6/89

160 *Bunny Rattle.* Illus. by Cheryl A. Harte. Random House, 1989. Unp. $4.95. (0-394-89956-3).

Category: Participation and manipulative **Age:** I–T

Bunny Rattle romps through tulips, chomps carrots, plays with playmates, and runs to mother, inviting the baby to shake the book to hear all the noise he makes. But when Bunny Rattle sleeps in his basket, baby is cautioned, "Shhh!" Softly padded cloth pages are safe, washable, and durable. The rattle sewn into the final page encourages the child's participation. [2]

RABBITS; SOUNDS

161 *Busy Busy Toddlers.* Photos by Phoebe Dunn. Random House, 1987. Unp. $1.95. (0-394-88604-6). **Category:** Informational **Age:** T

A board book for toddlers who love looking at photographs of other toddlers. Here are 13 different children shown during typical moments of their lives—running, splashing, coloring, eating, and playing. Sure to be a hit and a favorite. [2]

BOARD BOOKS; TODDLERS

Rev: CBY-88

162 *The Cabbages Are Chasing the Rabbits.* Arnold Adoff. Illus. by Janet Stevens. Harcourt Brace Jovanovich, 1985. Unp. $15.95. (0-15-213875-7).

Category: Poetry/Nursery rhymes/Songs **Age:** P–K

A backward nonsense poem about things as they never could be: cabbages chasing rabbits, rabbits chasing dogs, dogs chasing hunters, full of endless repetition to help younger children identify words with pictures and ideas. Realistic and colorful illustrations fill the pages without interfering with the text.
POETRY [2]

Rev: BKL 1/1/88 **Awards:** NCTE Award for Poetry for Children

163 *A Cache of Jewels and Other Collective Nouns.* Ruth Heller. Putnam, 1987. Unp. $10.95. (0-448-19211-X).

Category: Concept/Counting/Alphabet **Age:** P–K

Flowing, rhymed text and spectacular artwork with unusual perspectives make learning collective nouns a delightful experience. Heller's final poem gives further information about collective nouns and other parts of speech and promises books to come on each. [1]
CONCEPTS; WORDS

Rev: CBY-88; SLJ 2/88

164 *A Cake for Barney.* Joyce Dunbar. Illus. by Emilie Boon. Orchard Books, 1988. Unp. $12.95. (0-531-08335-7). **Category:** Story **Age:** P–K

A bear named Barney has a cupcake with five cherries on top and decides to take a leisurely stroll while enjoying his treat. While on his stroll, he encounters a wasp, mouse, cow, squirrel, and crow. Each promises Barney a peaceful walk for the price of a single cherry. With only cake left, Barney is met by big bully Buster Bear, who demands the cake. Barney becomes assertive and eats the cake himself! [2]
ANIMALS; BEARS; BULLYING

Rev: BKL 2/15/88

165 *Can I Keep Him?* Steven Kellogg. Dial, 1971. 32 pp. $12.89. (0-8037-0989-7). **Category:** Story **Age:** P–K

Arnold, a little boy, is lonesome and needs a pet; however, his practical Mother says "no" to the bear, the tiger, the python, etc. But Arnold knows there are lots of nice animals in the world, and he is determined to find at least one for his very own. The text is sparse, but with Kellogg's inimitable cartoon-style illustrations in pen and ink, the story unfolds with his usual sense of fun and tongue-in-cheek humor. [1]
PETS

Rev: NYT

166 *Can You Imagine...? A Counting Book.* Beau Gardner. Putnam, 1987. Unp. $10.95. (0-396-09001-X).

Category: Concept/Counting/Alphabet   **Age:** T–P

For those learning to count from one to 12, Gardner's witty and silly animals such as "1 whale wearing a veil" to "12 swans twirling batons" will delight young readers. The book concludes with a two-page review displaying the numerals and another of the animals lined up across the page in silhouette for extended practice.   [3]

ANIMALS; COUNTING

Rev: CBY-88

167 *Capacity.* Henry Pluckrose. Photos by Chris Fairclough. Franklin Watts, 1988. Unp. $9.90. (0-531-10547-4).

Category: Concept/Counting/Alphabet   **Age:** P–K

Author and photographer combine provocative questions with colorful everyday objects to develop children's concept of mathematics in general and capacity in particular. The artful arrangement of a variety of containers and the thoughtful text will send children out to collect their own measuring items.

MEASUREMENT   [1]

Rev: BKL 11/1/88

168 *Caps for Sale: A Tale of a Peddler, Some Monkeys and Their Monkey Business.* Esphyr Slobodkina. Harper & Row, 1947. Unp. $10.89. (0-06-025778-4).   **Category:** Story   **Age:** P–K

This classic tale is filled with wonderful repetition and illustrated with an Old World flavor. A poor peddler takes a nap after a long walk. But, careful of his merchandise, first he checks "his own checked cap, then the gray caps, then the brown caps, then the blue caps, then the red caps on the very top." He awakens to find a tree full of monkeys, all wearing his caps.   [1]

HATS; MONKEYS

Rev: CBK; ESLC; NYT

169 *Caps, Hats, Socks, and Mittens: A Book about the Four Seasons.* Louise Borden. Illus. by Lillian Hoban. Scholastic, 1989. Unp. $11.95. (0-590-41257-4).   **Category:** Concept/Counting/Alphabet   **Age:** P–K

In clear and sometimes repetitive prose, the author pictures the distinctions of each season: "Winter is hot mugs and hot cups"; "Spring is grass, grass, grass";

"Summer is a jar full of bugs." Though the word pictures are simple, in combination with Hoban's illustrations, they paint an almost poetic celebration of seasonal joy. [2]
CONCEPTS; SEASONS
Rev: BKL 2/15/89

170   A Caribou Alphabet. Mary Beth Owens. Dog Ear Press, 1988. Unp. $13.95. (0-937966-25-8).

Category: Concept/Counting/Alphabet   **Age:** P–K

This ABC book is most unusual in that the progression through the alphabet relates the life of the caribou: E—Escaping, G—Grazing, M—Migrating, etc. The author has effectively used rhymed couplets for the narrative with a matching scene of the animals. Each lowercase and uppercase letter is obvious on the page and often is surrounded by seasonal flowers, which adds both color and beauty. [2]
ALPHABET; REINDEER
Rev: BKL 9/1/88

171   Carl Goes Shopping. Alexandra Day. Farrar, Straus & Giroux, 1989. Unp. $9.95. (0-374-31110-2).   **Category:** Story   **Age:** P–K

A mostly wordless book depicting the adventures of Carl, a rottweiler, and a baby in a department store. Mom goes upstairs to shop and leaves Carl in charge of the baby. What follows in these detailed, impressionistic illustrations is a series of humorous episodes as Carl and the baby explore the store. Both characters' expressions capture their personalities and make us believe the situations. [1]
BABIES; DOGS; SHOPPING
Rev: BKL 1/1/90

172   Carousel. Donald Crews. Greenwillow Books, 1982. 32 pp. $12.88. (0-688-00909-3).   **Category:** Story   **Age:** P–K

The excitement of a ride on a carousel from start to finish is described with simple text and beautiful illustrations. As the carousel begins to move round and round, faster and faster, the viewer feels the motion from Crews' use of the airbrush to simulate the faster movement. Explanation of the carousel as an object located in amusement parks will have to be made for some unfamiliar viewers. [2]
MERRY-GO-ROUNDS
Rev: ESLC

173 *The Carrot Seed.* Ruth Krauss. Illus. by Crockett Johnson. Harper & Row, 1945. Unp. $10.89. (0-06-023351-6). **Category:** Story **Age:** T–P–K

This classic story of a young boy who plants a carrot seed is timeless in its simplicity. The boy tends his garden carefully, pulling weeds, watering, and watching, but his family is sure that nothing will come up. The boy is vindicated when he harvests a giant carrot, which fills a wheelbarrow. Also available in other formats from the National Library for the Blind and Physically Handicapped. [1]

CONFIDENCE; GARDENING

Rev: CBK; CBY-90; ESLC

174 *Cat in the Hat.* Dr. Seuss. Random House, 1957. 72 pp. $6.95. (0-394-80001-X). **Category:** Story **Age:** P–K

After mother leaves for the day, Sally and her brother find themselves confined indoors due to the rain. The children soon discover that their day has been transformed from quiet uneventfulness to utter chaos when a strange, pushy cat and his peculiar friends come for a visit. One of the many Dr. Seuss books children find so appealing due to the silly rhyming text and simple suspense. The cartoonlike characters enhance the story. Also available in other formats from the National Library for the Blind and Physically Handicapped.

CATS; PLAY [1]

Rev: BBC; ESLC; NYT

175 *Catch Me & Kiss Me & Say It Again.* Clyde Watson. Illus. by Wendy Watson. Reprint. Putnam, 1983. 64 pp. $10.95. (0-399-20948-4). **Category:** Poetry/Nursery rhymes/Songs **Age:** T–P

A lively collection of short rhymes, which are often old nursery rhymes made into nonsense words just for the joy of the rhyme on the tongue. Each rhyme has a corresponding illustration showing chubby children and a cat playing, laughing, or dancing. Although the drawings are somewhat subdued in color, they accurately reflect the lightheartedness of the rhymes. [2]

NURSERY RHYMES

Rev: BKL 1/1/88; CBK; NYT

176 *Catching: A Book for Blind and Sighted Children.* Virginia A. Jensen. Putnam, 1983. 23 pp. Paper $12.95. (0-399-20997-2). **Category:** Concept/Counting/Alphabet **Age:** P–K

The raised, textured pictures make this story fun even for children who can't see. Little Rough is tired of being "It" when playing tag with Little Shaggy. To fool Little Shaggy, Little Rough changes shape, turning almost square and

ending up fooling everyone. Using simple raised lines and dots, this tale is a textural delight. [3]
BLINDNESS; SHAPE; SIZE
Rev: ESLC

177 *Celebrations.* Myra Cohn Livingston. Illus. by Leonard Everett Fisher. Holiday House, 1985. 32 pp. $14.95. (0-8234-0550-8).
Category: Poetry/Nursery rhymes/Songs **Age:** P–K

Brief poems for 16 holidays, including one's own birthday. Strongly colored, bold acrylic paintings summarize the days' symbols from a child's point of view. [1]
HOLIDAYS; POETRY
Rev: BKL 1/1/88

178 *A Chair for My Mother.* Vera B. Williams. Greenwillow Books, 1982. Unp. $12.88. (0-688-00915-8). **Category:** Story **Age:** P–K

Wonderfully warm story of a single-parent extended family, using equally warm and colorful watercolor illustrations. Communally saving their spare coins in a large jar, grandma, mother, and daughter share the excitement of purchasing and subsequently enjoying their beloved chair after a fire has destroyed their home and all its furnishings. The lengthy text makes this more suitable for older preschoolers. [1]
FAMILY LIFE; HOUSES; MONEY
Rev: BBC; CBK; ESLC; NYT **Awards:** Caldecott Honor Book

179 *Changes, Changes.* Pat Hutchins. Macmillan, 1987. Unp. Paper $4.95. (0-689-71137-9). **Category:** Wordless **Age:** P–K

The "changes" that take place in this story of a little wooden man and woman and their building blocks are easy to "read" in this wordless book. The bright color illustrations show the couple constructing one object after another, beginning with a house that catches on fire and progressing to other objects: a fire truck, a boat, a locomotive, etc. This book might inspire children to improvise with their own toys and blocks. [1]
DOLLS; TOYS; WORDLESS
Rev: ESLC; NYT **Awards:** ALA Notable Book; NYT Best Illustrated Book

180 *Charlie Anderson.* Barbara Abercrombie. Illus. by Mark Graham. Macmillan, 1990. Unp. $12.95. (0-689-50486-1). **Category:** Story **Age:** P–K

"One cold night a cat walked out of the woods, up the steps, across the deck" and into the lives and hearts of Sarah, Elizabeth, and their mother. Roaming outside one day, Charlie does not return home. While searching for him, the girls discover that Charlie has two homes and two families that love him—just as Elizabeth and Sarah do, now that their parents are divorced. Soft realistic pictures complement the story line. [2]

CATS; DIVORCE

181 *The Checkup.* Helen Oxenbury. Dial, 1983. 24 pp. $3.95. (0-8037-0010-5). **Category:** Story **Age:** T–P

A wee lad's account of his reluctant visit to the doctor told through simple illustrations and brief text. The story begins with the slightly irritated adults in the waiting room, followed by the doctor, who tries to coax the little boy into his examination. Finally, the doctor pronounces the boy healthy enough to head home until next year. [3]

DOCTORS

Rev: CBK

182 *Chester the Chick.* Jane Burton. Random House, 1988. Unp. Paper $1.95. (0-394-89640-8). **Category:** Informational **Age:** K

From egg to rooster, the first year in the life of a chicken is captured in colorful photographs and an informative narrative. [2]

CHICKENS

Rev: CBY-89

183 *The Chick and the Duckling.* Mirra Ginsburg. Translated by V. Suteyev. Illus. by Jose Aruego and Ariane Dewey. Macmillan, 1972. Unp. $14.95. (0-02-735940-9). **Category:** Story **Age:** T–P

When a newly hatched duckling sets off to explore the world, an exuberant chick, who is quick to copy its every action, follows close behind. Together they take a walk, dig a hole, find a worm, and catch a butterfly. After a close call in the pond, however, the chick parts company with the duck. Clear, colorful illustrations with bold outlines appear pleasingly on a large expanse of white space. [1]

CHICKENS; DUCKS; SWIMMING

Rev: ESLC

184 *Chicka Chicka Boom Boom.* Bill Martin, Jr., and John Archambault. Illus. by Lois Ehlert. Simon & Schuster, 1989. Unp. $13.95. (0-671-67949-X).

Category: Concept/Counting/Alphabet **Age:** P–K

The toe-tapping, rhythmic beat of this alphabet book invites the reader to join the letters as they race to the top of the coconut tree. Bright illustrations with colorful borders add to the upbeat mood. This is a must to read aloud and watch the children sway with the rhythm of the words. [1]

ALPHABET

Rev: BKL 10/15/89; CBY-90

185 *Chickadee.* Young Naturalist Foundation, 1979– . $14.95/yr.

Category: Periodical **Age:** P

A nature-oriented magazine and much more. Stories, puzzles, games, experiments, sequencing exercises, and letters as well as pictures from subscribers along with colorful pages make this a favorite for animal lovers and beginning readers. Ten issues per year. [2]

GAMES; NATURE; PUZZLES

186 *A Child Is Born: The Christmas Story.* Elizabeth Winthrop. Illus. by Charles Mikolaycak. Holiday House, 1983. Unp. $14.95. (0-8234-0472-2).

Category: Story **Age:** P–K

Lavishly illustrated, this is a complete retelling of the birth of Christ as written in the King James version of the Bible. Each picture frames the verses, showing an expectant Mary and astonished shepherds. Both children and adults will study and ponder the beautiful story and illustrations. [2]

BIBLE STORIES; CHRISTMAS; JESUS CHRIST

Rev: NYT

187 *Children's All-Star Rhythm Hits.* Jack Capon and Rosemary Hallum. Educational Activities, 1989. Record. 30 min. $10.95.

Category: Poetry/Nursery rhymes/Songs **Age:** P–K

Capon and Hallum have combined many old favorites—"Paw Paw Patch," "Bingo," "Pop Goes the Weasel," "Virginia Reel"—with contemporary activities. The accompanying booklet gives detailed instructions and diagrams for each song. Activities range from physical fitness exercises and games to simple square dances. [2]

DANCING; EXERCISE; SONGS

Rev: BKL 12/15/89

188 *A Children's Zoo.* Tana Hoban. Greenwillow Books, 1985. 24 pp. $12.95. (0-688-05202-9).   **Category:** Informational   **Age:** T–P–K

Ten zoo animals are presented in full-color photographs. Each photo has a facing page with three words that describe the animal as well as the animal's name. These descriptive words are simple and lend themselves to an animal guessing game. A helpful chart, included at the end of the book, can be used before or after a visit to the zoo.   [2]
ANIMALS; ZOOS
Rev: CBK

189 *A Child's First Book of Nursery Tales.* Selma G. Lanes. Illus. by Cyndy Szekeres. Western, 1983. 44 pp. $6.95. (0-307-65577-6).
Category: Folklore/Folktales/Fairy tales   **Age:** T–P

Eight familiar tales featuring nonthreatening retellings of such classics as "The Little Red Hen," "The Three Little Pigs," "Goldilocks and the Three Bears," and "Chicken Little." Each story is from two to five pages and is liberally illustrated with Szekeres's traditionally charming and expressive anthropomorphic creatures. An introductory anthology for the youngest listener.
ANIMALS; FOLK AND FAIRY TALES; NURSERY RHYMES   [3]
Rev: CBK

190 *A Child's Garden of Verses.* Robert Louis Stevenson. Chronicle Books, 1989. 121 pp. $15.95. (0-87701-608-9).
Category: Poetry/Nursery rhymes/Songs   **Age:** P–K

A stunning edition of one of the best-loved collections of poetry in the world, lavishly illustrated by the most distinguished children's book artists of the late 19th and early 20th centuries, including Jesse Wilcox Smith, H. Wilebee le Mair, and Bessie Collins Pease. The illustrations, brimming with color and lush detail, brilliantly capture the universal splendor of a child's imaginative world. Also available in other formats from the National Library for the Blind and Physically Handicapped.   [1]
IMAGINATION; POETRY
Rev: BKL 11/1/89   **Awards:** Redbook's 1989 Top Ten Picture Books of the Year

191 *A Child's Gift of Lullabyes.* J. Aaron Brown and David R. Lehman. Narrated by Tanya Goodman. A Child's Gift of Lullabyes, 1987. Dist. by J. Aaron Brown & Associates. Audiocassette. 60 min. $12.95.
Category: Poetry/Nursery rhymes/Songs   **Age:** I–T–P–K

A collection of nine contemporary, original lullabies, three of which are "Rock-a-Bye," "Lullaby and Goodnight," and "May All Your Dreams Come

True." Side one features vocalist Tanya Goodman with a fully orchestrated background. Side two has only the instrumental background and can be used for listening or singing along. Lyrics are included. [1]

LULLABIES; SONGS

Rev: SLJ 4/89

Awards: Grammy Award Nominee "Best Recording for Children"

---

192 *Choo Choo: The Story of a Little Engine Who Ran Away.* Virginia Lee Burton. Houghton Mifflin, 1937. Unp. $14.95. (0-395-17684-0).

Category: Story   **Age:** P–K

A predictable story full of repetitive sounds that will delight any young listener. The book's large size makes it easy to share with several children at the same time as they are sure to enjoy following all the escapades of this naughty little train, who runs away and learns the hard way that home is best. A good companion story for this would be *The Little Engine That Could.* [2]

TRAINS

Rev: ESLC

---

193 *The Christmas Gift.* Emily A. McCully. Harper & Row, 1988. 32 pp. $12.89. (0-06-024212-4). **Category:** Wordless   **Age:** P–K

The enchanting story of a mouse family's Christmas. Detailed drawings bring to life feelings of joy: favorite songs, anticipation of Christmas morning, gifts, and togetherness. When one little mouse's new airplane breaks, her grandfather takes her to the attic to look for one of his own treasured childhood toys. In a heartwarming gesture of love, Grandfather gives his train to her as she is leaving. [2]

CHRISTMAS; MICE; WORDLESS

Rev: BKL 9/1/88; ESLC

---

194 *The Christmas Pageant.* Jacqueline Rogers. Grosset & Dunlap, 1989. Unp. $12.95. (0-448-40151-7). **Category:** Story   **Age:** P–K

A loosely styled version of the Christmas story told through the preparation for and presentation of a local community's children's pageant. The story begins early in the day as the children gather for dress rehearsal and proceeds through the end of the evening performance. [1]

CHRISTMAS; PLAYS

Rev: BKL 10/15/89; SLJ 10/89

195 ***Christmas Poems.*** Selected by Myra Cohn Livingston. Illus. by Trina Schart Hyman. Holiday House, 1984. 32 pp. $13.95. (0-8234-0508-7).
Category: Poetry/Nursery rhymes/Songs **Age:** K

A collection of poems from a number of outstanding children's poets. The 18 selections span the holiday traditions and their meanings, from the birth of Christ to Santa Claus and his reindeer. Bordered illustrations in shades of red, green, black, and white bring each poem to life. A visual and auditory delight. CHRISTMAS; POETRY [3]
Rev: BKL 1/1/88

196 ***A Christmas Promise.*** Lark Carrier. Picture Book Studio, 1986. Unp. $15.95. (0-88708-032-4). **Category:** Story **Age:** P–K

On the day Amy is to take her Christmas tree indoors, she remembers the birds and animals that have lived in it all year long. When she decides not to take the fir, she is rewarded with a spectacular natural tree decorated by her woodland friends themselves. Pastels and pencil drawings on handmade paper give this story a gentle, dreamlike tone. [3]
ANIMALS; CHRISTMAS; TREES
Rev: ESLC

197 ***Circle Around.*** Tickle Tune Typhoon, 1983. Audiocassette. 37 min. $8.98.
Category: Poetry/Nursery rhymes/Songs **Age:** T–P–K

Varied rhythms and instrumentation along with a lively performance by this Seattle-based troupe make these 12 environmental and health-conscious selections a treat. Tunes are a mix of original and familiar, but each makes the listener want to get up and move. Some selections invite participation. [1]
ECOLOGY; HEALTH; SONGS
Rev: SLJ 4/85 **Awards:** ALSC Notable Recording & Parents' Choice Award

198 ***Circus.*** Lois Ehlert. HarperCollins, 1992. Unp. $15.00. (0-06-020252-1).
Category: Story **Age:** P–K

In a grand work of art, the author/illustrator has created the Greatest Show on Earth with boldly colored collage illustrations. Acts include Samu, the fiercest tiger in the world, jumping through a hoop, marching snakes, leaping lizards, and flying zucchinis! [1]
ANIMALS; CIRCUS

199 *Circus Baby.* Maud Petersham and Miska Petersham. Macmillan, 1950. Unp. $13.95. (0-02-771670-8). **Category:** Story **Age:** P–K

Mother Elephant wants her baby to eat like the clown family's baby—in a chair with a spoon. She soon learns her baby needs to eat the way elephants eat, because, after all, he is an elephant. Young children will giggle at Baby Elephant's efforts to eat with a spoon and will appreciate the inevitable outcome. Also available in other formats from the National Library for the Blind and Physically Handicapped. [2]

BABIES; CIRCUS; ELEPHANTS

Rev: ESLC

200 *Circus Circus.* Lely Yashar. Media Inc, 1986. Videocassette. 6 min. $125.00. **Category:** Informational **Age:** K

The episode begins with a little girl drawing on a computer with a stylus and pad to create a circus and then quickly moves to show her participation in circus acts and her enjoyment of the animals. Use of animation and computer-generated music will captivate the imagination of the viewer. An explanation of the steps employed to make the production follows the first viewing. [3]

ART; CIRCUS; IMAGINATION

Rev: BKL 8/89

201 *City Seen from A to Z.* Rachel Isadora. Greenwillow Books, 1983. Unp. $11.88. (0-688-01803-3).

Category: Concept/Counting/Alphabet **Age:** P–K

Scenes of city life are depicted with 26 wonderful black-and-white drawings. Each picture is accompanied by a letter and an appropriate noun. Drawings show a multiethnic setting. From sidewalks to the subway, from the park to the beach, adults and children work and play, and the city is brought to life.

ALPHABET; CITIES AND TOWNS [1]

Rev: CBK; ESLC

202 *Clap Your Hands.* Lorinda Bryan Cauley. Putnam, 1992. Unp. $14.95. (0-399-22118-2). **Category:** Participation and manipulative **Age:** P–K

An ideal listening exercise perfect for sharing aloud. Rhymes sing out instructions (as in square dancing) that will have participants roaring, wiggling, spinning, counting, and more. The outstanding illustrations add to the fun and humor for all. [1]

PARTICIPATION; PLAY

203 ***Classic Children's Tales.*** Performed by Jackie Torrence. Rounder Records, 1989. Dist. by Roundup Records. Audiocassette. 44 min. $9.00.
Category: Folklore/Folktales/Fairy tales **Age:** P–K

Jackie Torrence uses her expressive and spirited voice to share several beloved tales, including "The Gingerbread Man," "Little Red Riding Hood," and "The Three Billy Goats Gruff." Although the tales stand well without background accompaniment or sound effects, children accustomed to such may need encouragement to create an image by closing their eyes. An excellent introduction to pure storytelling for young children. [1]
FOLK AND FAIRY TALES

204 ***Classroom Holidays.*** Miriam Cohen. Illus. by Lillian Hoban. Spoken Arts, 1988. Filmstrip. 7 min. $139.95. **Category:** Story **Age:** K

Four of the popular Cohen/Hoban books—*Liar, Liar, Pants on Fire; Don't Eat Too Much Turkey!; Be My Valentine;* and *Starting First Grade*—are included in this set of four filmstrips with audiocassettes. A teachers' guide suggests ways to use each filmstrip. Each kit deals with understanding feelings and getting along with peers as the child handles competition and selfishness. Three of the stories fit into the holidays; the fourth is about organizing a class play.
FRIENDSHIP; HOLIDAYS; SCHOOL [2]

205 ***Clementine's Winter Wardrobe.*** Kate Spohn. Orchard Books, 1989. Unp. $13.95. (0-531-08441-8). **Category:** Story **Age:** P–K

Clementine chooses her winter wardrobe from a dazzling array of warm clothing. Each piece of apparel is shown on a full-page spread with a choice of many colors and styles. From long johns to mittens, children will enjoy deciding what Clementine will select to wear. [1]
CATS; CLOTHING
Rev: BKL 9/15/89

206 ***Clifford the Big Red Dog.*** Norman Bridwell. Scholastic, 1985. Unp. $8.95. (0-590-40743-0). **Category:** Story **Age:** P–K

The escapades of a giant red dog are humorously related by his owner, Emily Elizabeth. Very easy to read and accompanied by colorful illustrations. This book will find a welcome home with any young reader, even those who do not have a dog in the house. Also available in big-book format for sharing with large groups. [1]
DOGS; HUMOR
Rev: CBK; ESLC

207 *Clive Eats Alligators.* Alison Lester. Houghton Mifflin, 1986. Unp. $12.95. (0-395-40775-3). **Category:** Story **Age:** P–K

Seven children, each with individual likes and preferences, are shown in a variety of activities, from eating to playing to shopping to bedtime. Humorous illustrations and text continue to delight readers as they guess which character is missing this time and what each is up to.   [3]
SELF-CONCEPT

Rev: BBC

208 *Clothes.* Ann Morris. Illus. by Maureen Roffey. Ideals Publishing Corporation, 1988. Unp. $2.95. (0-8249-8290-8).

Category: Informational **Age:** T

One article of clothing is clearly drawn on each side of the thick cardboard pages of this tiny chunky board book. Each garment is labeled with the word printed in bold lowercase letters. Clothes pictured include sleepwear and outside wear for summer and winter.   [2]
BOARD BOOKS; CLOTHING

209 *Cloudy with a Chance of Meatballs.* Judith Barrett. Illus. by Ron Barrett. Atheneum, 1978. Unp. $13.95. (0-689-30647-4).

Category: Story **Age:** K

The weather takes a culinary turn for the worse in the town of Chewandswallow, where the normal rain of food becomes an onslaught of monstrous morsels. Clever illustrations in black ink with watercolor add to the tongue-in-cheek humor of the book.   [1]
CLOUDS; FOOD; HUMOR

Rev: CBK

210 *The Clown of God.* Tomie dePaola. Harcourt Brace Jovanovich, 1978. Unp. $13.95. (0-15-219175-5). **Category:** Story **Age:** K

An orphan named Giovanni makes his living by juggling in the streets, becomes a famous juggler, and spends his life traveling throughout Italy. With age, Giovanni loses his ability to juggle and becomes a beggar. On Christmas Eve, he takes shelter in a cathedral, where he makes a statue of the Christ child smile at his juggling, and then he dies. Watercolor illustrations complement the text perfectly.   [2]
CHRISTMAS; FOLK AND FAIRY TALES; JUGGLERS

Rev: BBC

211 ***The Cobweb Curtain: A Christmas Story.*** Jenny Koralek. Illus. by Pauline Baynes. Henry Holt & Co., 1989. Unp. $13.95. (0-8050-1051-3).
Category: Folklore/Folktales/Fairy tales   **Age:** P–K

A retelling of the birth of Christ in a Bethlehem stable. Based on a legend by William Barclay, the simply told story centers on an explanation of the origin of tinsel now used on Christmas trees. The colorful yet muted pictures help create the effect of night for many of the scenes. Young children will enjoy seeing the connection between the spider's silky web and the beauty of the silver tinsel. [3]
CHRISTMAS; FOLK AND FAIRY TALES; SPIDERS
Rev: BKL 10/1/89; SLJ 10/89

212 ***Color Dance.*** Ann Jonas. Greenwillow Books, 1989. 32 pp. $13.88. (0-688-05991-0).   **Category:** Concept/Counting/Alphabet   **Age:** P–K

Flowing red, yellow, and blue scarves carried by young dancers overlap and carry the child beyond mere color identification into "What happens when we combine colors?" Jonas even moves beyond secondary colors into tertiaries such as magenta, chartreuse, and vermillion. The book concludes with a color wheel and further explanations of color concepts. [1]
COLOR; DANCING
Rev: BKL 8/89

213 ***Color Farm.*** Lois Ehlert. Lippincott, 1990. Unp. $12.95. (0-397-32440-5).
Category: Concept/Counting/Alphabet   **Age:** P–K

An elegantly designed book that focuses on the concepts of shape and color in its depiction of abstractly presented animals. Basic shapes, such as square, rectangle, and circle, graduate to less familiar ones, such as octagon and pentagon, through a unique use of page overlays. Bold, primary colors catch the eye, and the total result keeps the reader engrossed. [1]
COLOR; FARMS; SHAPE

214 ***Color Me a Rainbow: Color Concepts for Early Childhood.*** Performed by Jerry Caspell. Melody House, 1973. Record. 17 min. $9.95.
Category: Concept/Counting/Alphabet   **Age:** P–K

A variety of songs, poetry and drama, and music and motion are used to teach basic colors and their blends. In addition to the overall focus on colors, activities include the concepts of direction, shapes, and parts of the body. Listeners can also delve into emotions: "What color do you feel when you feel happy?

scared? cold?" The familiar tale of the three little pigs is offered for dramatic interpretation involving colors. [1]
COLOR; SHAPE; SONGS

215 *Color Zoo.* Lois Ehlert. Harper & Row, 1989. Unp. $12.89. (0-397-32260-7). **Category:** Concept/Counting/Alphabet **Age:** T–P–K

This innovative concept book uses brilliant color and stacked geometric cut-out pages to create animal figures. As pages are turned, a tiger becomes a deer, a mouse, and then a fox. Three sets of such transformations are included. Shapes are named on the reverse side of the turned page. Final pages identify shapes, colors, and animals. Children will return to this imaginative book again and again. [1]
COLOR; SHAPE
Rev: BKL 5/15/89 **Awards:** Caldecott Honor Book

216 *Colors.* Gwenda Turner. Viking Kestrel, 1989. Unp. $9.95. (0-670-82552-2). **Category:** Concept/Counting/Alphabet **Age:** T–P

Ten vivid colors are shown first with face paintings (red hearts on a girl's cheeks, for example) and then with children and/or animals engaged in activities using those colors (boy and girl savoring red apples). Watercolor illustrations convey almost photographic realism, capturing the colorful essence of childhood. [1]
COLOR; PAINTING

217 *Come Out, Jessie!* Harriet Ziefert. Illus. by Mavis Smith. Random House, 1988. Unp. $5.95. (0-394-89679-3).
Category: Participation and manipulative **Age:** P–K

Die-cut pages allow the reader to see through to the next page. Jessie's friend John asks Jessie to come out to play hopscotch. Jessie tells him to count to 50 while she gets chalk, cookies, and ice cream bars and feeds the cat. The unique illustrations allow the viewer to see inside the cat's house, a drawer, the freezer, a cookie jar, and Jessie's backpack. A subtle lesson on sharing is also provided. [2]
FRIENDSHIP; GAMES; SHARING
Rev: CBY-89

218 *Come Play with Us.* Anne S. O'Brien. Henry Holt & Co., 1985. 14 pp. Paper $3.95. (0-03-005008-1). **Category:** Story **Age:** P

A self-concept book designed for children going to day care for the first time. Rachel's first-day feelings—anxiety over being left, the enjoyment of play with other children, and, finally, the joy of her father's return—are shared. Images of children are beautifully captured on wide, two-page layouts in a board book format. The text is comforting and direct. Ideal for parents to share with their preschooler. [3]
BOARD BOOKS; DAY CARE CENTERS; PLAY; SELF-CONCEPT
Rev: CBK

219   ***Come with Me.*** Ashley Wolff. Dutton, 1990. Unp. $12.95. (0-525-44555-2).   **Category:** Story   **Age:** P–K
A little boy tells his dog some puppy stories about the wonderful things they will do when she is old enough to leave her mother and come live with him. Beautiful full-color double-page spreads in springtime watercolors are a departure from Wolff's usual woodcuts. The lyrical text and large illustrations make this book excellent for group read-aloud in addition to one-on-one sharing. [2]
DOGS

220   ***Cookie's Week.*** Cindy Ward. Illus. by Tomie dePaola. Putnam, 1988. Unp. $10.95. (0-399-21498-4).   **Category:** Story   **Age:** T–P
Each day of the week, Cookie, a mischievous family cat, manages to find a new and destructive activity, from falling into the toilet and knocking over plants, to climbing the curtains. Cookie's outrageous antics are enlivened by illustrations featuring flowing lines and splashes of vivid colors. The playful illustrations, physical humor, and bold, simple text make this an ideal choice for the toddler and preschool cat-loving crowd. [2]
CATS; DAYS OF THE WEEK; MONTHS OF THE YEAR
Rev: BKL 5/15/88

221   ***Corduroy.*** Don Freeman. Viking Penguin, 1968. 32 pp. $10.95. (0-670-24133-4).   **Category:** Story   **Age:** P–K
While he is in a department store, a teddy bear named Corduroy searches for the missing button from his overalls. Several adventures befall him until a caring little girl buys him, takes him home, and sews on his missing button. Told with warmth and gentle humor, this is a favorite with young listeners. [1]
AFRO-AMERICANS; TEDDY BEARS; TOYS
Rev: BBC; CBK; ESLC; NYT

222 *Corduroy.* Don Freeman. Joe Mantegna and Gary Templeton, 1984. Dist. by Weston Woods Studios. Videocassette. 16 min. $50.00.

Category: Story **Age:** P–K

A stuffed toy bear comes alive at night in a department store to search for his lost button. He hopes that someone will then buy him. A little girl comes the next day and purchases him, promising to sew on a new button. This live action production of the book by Don Freeman (Viking, 1968) portrays a heartwarming story of devotion and friendship. [1]
AFRO-AMERICANS; TEDDY BEARS; TOYS

223 *Count-a-Saurus.* Nancy Blumenthal. Illus. by Robert Jay Kaufman. Four Winds, 1989. 24 pp. $12.95. (0-02-749391-1).

Category: Concept/Counting/Alphabet **Age:** P–K

Dinophiles will relish this counting book in rhyme with its whimsical reptiles dashing across the pages. Each plate includes a pronunciation guide for the featured dinosaur's name. A clever "append-a-saurus" closes the book and reveals interesting facts on which the illustrations are based. [1]
COUNTING; DINOSAURS
Rev: BKL 3/1/89

224 *Counting.* Henry Pluckrose. Photos by Chris Fairclough. Franklin Watts, 1988. Unp. $9.90. (0-531-10524-5).

Category: Concept/Counting/Alphabet **Age:** P–K

Clear photographs give readers many opportunities to count familiar objects such as shoes, toys, and chairs. Numerals are introduced, as are the concepts of less than and more than. Counters are arranged in regular patterns, and readers are encouraged to create their own arrangements. Lots of opportunity for adult-child interaction while using this advanced book to explore counting skills and concepts. [1]
COUNTING
Rev: BKL 5/1/88

225 *Country Bear's Good Neighbor.* Larry D. Brimner. Illus. by Ruth T. Councell. Orchard Books, 1988. Unp. $12.95. (0-531-08308-X).

Category: Story **Age:** P–K

The little girl in overalls does not understand why her neighbor, Country Bear, is borrowing so many things from her. When the bear brings her a "Good neighbor cake," she learns about the joys of sharing. The recipe for the cake is included. [2]
FRIENDSHIP; SHARING
Rev: BKL 3/1/88; SLJ 5/89

226 *A Country Far Away.* Nigel Gray. Illus. by Philippe Dupasquier. Orchard Books, 1988. Unp. $12.95. (0-531-08392-6).

Category: Story Age: P–K

A pictorial study of the everyday lives of two boys—one African and one American. The illustrations divide the page and detail their differences and similarities as each boy goes to school, goes shopping, and plays outside. A unique introduction to cultural diversity for young children. [2]
AFRICA; BOYS
Rev: BKL 11/15/89

227 *Crash! Bang! Boom! A Book of Sounds.* Peter Spier. Doubleday, 1990. Unp. $5.95. (0-385-26569-7).

Category: Concept/Counting/Alphabet Age: P–K

A veritable feast of sounds from every part of a child's life, the book conveys the importance of sounds in daily doings. Bright, colorful drawings attached to hundreds of sound words from the bathroom, the kitchen, the farm, the school, the playground, the sports field, and the like make the book come to life. [1]
HEARING; CONCEPTS; SOUNDS
Rev: CBK; ESLC; NYT

228 *Crazy Clothes.* Niki Yektai. Illus. by Suçie Stevenson. Bradbury, 1988. Unp. $12.95. (0-02-793692-9). Category: Story Age: P–K

When Patrick tries to show his mother how well he can dress himself, his clothes become stubborn and insist on going on the wrong parts of his body. His charade is ended by his mother, who counts to 100 while Patrick dresses properly. Stevenson's cartoon drawings effectively show Patrick's antics. [3]
CLOTHING
Rev: BKL 5/15/88

229 *Crocodile Beat.* Gail Jorgensen. Illus. by Patricia Mullins. Bradbury, 1989. Unp. $13.95. (0-02-748010-0). **Category:** Story **Age:** P

An Australian story about a lion who saves his jungle friends from the jaws of the crocodile. Uniquely illustrated with tissue collage, rubber stamps, and crayon in double-page spreads with vibrant colors. Rhyming text and numerous animal sounds make this an excellent choice for reading aloud. [2]
CROCODILES; JUNGLE; RHYMES
Rev: BKL 11/1/89

230 *Curious George.* H. A. Rey. Reprint. Houghton Mifflin, 1973. 56 pp. $12.95. (0-395-15993-8). **Category:** Story **Age:** P–K

Because of his curiosity, a small monkey in Africa is captured by a man wearing a big yellow hat. His curiosity continues to get the little monkey into trouble several times before the man finally gets George to the zoo. Full-page color illustrations have a timelessness about them, which will continue to appeal to young children for years to come. [1]
HUMOR; MONKEYS
Rev: CBK; ESLC

231 *Curious George Goes to School.* H. A. Rey and Margaret Rey. Edited by Margaret Rey and Allan J. Shalleck. Houghton Mifflin, 1989. 30 pp. $9.95. (0-395-51944-6). **Category:** Story **Age:** P–K

Curious George, a little monkey, and his friend, the man in the yellow hat, visit a school. As always, George is curious and finds his way into the Art Room. George paints a picture and decides to turn the fan on, which scatters all the paintings everywhere. While picking them up, he finds a missing piece of artwork and becomes the hero of the day. [2]
HUMOR; MONKEYS; SCHOOL
Rev: ESLC

232 *Daddy Has a Pair of Striped Shorts.* Mimi Otey. Farrar, Straus & Giroux, 1990. Unp. $13.95. (0-374-31675-9). **Category:** Story **Age:** P–K

A funny, warm, and touching story. A father's clothes are loud and they clash. For all the embarassment this may cause his children, he is loving and loved. Positive and nurturing depiction of a father's participation in the life of his children, family, and community. [1]
FAMILY LIFE; FATHERS

233 **Daddy, Play with Me!** Shigeo Watanabe. Illus. by Yasuo Ohtomo. Philomel, 1985. Unp. $8.95. (0-399-21211-6). **Category:** Story **Age:** T–P

Wonderful illustrations depicting a father and child enjoying each other. Play activities include dancing on Dad's feet, playing horse, and piggyback. Part of I Can Do It All by Myself series. [2]

BEARS; FATHERS; PLAY

Rev: ESLC

234 **Dance-a-Story Sing-a-Song.** Marcia Berman and Anne Barlin. B B Records, 1980. Record. 32 min. $9.95.

Category: Poetry/Nursery rhymes/Songs **Age:** T–P–K

A fun way for children to explore movement and different countries through their songs. On side one, the child learns the difference between tension and relaxation by imitating the movements of a wooden doll. Side two has nine multicultural (American, Japanese, Dutch, Jewish, etc.) songs and stories, which give insights into different cultures. Lyrics and suggestions for using the songs are included. [2]

DANCING; SONGS

235 **Dance, Tanya.** Patricia Lee Gauch. Illus. by Satomi Ichikawa. Philomel, 1989. Unp. $13.95. (0-399-21521-2). **Category:** Story **Age:** P–K

While her older sister practices her ballet positions, Tanya does too, although she has been told she is too young for lessons. But when she does her own performance after her sister's recital, she is presented with her own leotards and slippers in order to begin ballet school. Soft-hued watercolor illustrations capture the movement of the ballet as well as the joy of this young dancer. [2]

BALLET; DANCING

Rev: BKL 9/1/89; CBY-90

236 **The Dancing Granny.** Ashley Bryan. Macmillan, 1987. Unp. Paper $6.95. (0-689-71149-2). **Category:** Folklore/Folktales/Fairy tales **Age:** P–K

Granny Anika cooks and works in her garden as she sings, but what she really likes to do is dance. Spider Ananse does not like to work, but he really likes the good vegetables in Granny's garden. He sings to Granny until her feet get happy and she dances off. Spider helps himself to her fine produce. Granny finally finds a way to keep Spider out of her garden. The rhyme and repetition of this tale establish a dancing mood. [2]

AFRICA; DANCING; FOLK AND FAIRY TALES

Rev: NYT

237   *Danny and the Dinosaur.* Syd Hoff. Harper & Row, 1958. 64 pp. $10.89.
(0-06-022466-5).   **Category:** Story   **Age:** P–K

Danny and a museum dinosaur spend a wonderful day playing together in this
beginning reader. The cartoon drawings in the near-classic fantasy and the
story's improbable silliness will delight another generation of 4s and 5s.   [1]
DINOSAURS; FRIENDSHIP
Rev: CBK; NYT

238   *Dawn.* Molly G. Bang. Morrow Jr. Books, 1983. 32 pp. $12.88. (0-688-
02404-1).   **Category:** Folklore/Folktales/Fairy tales   **Age:** K

An adaptation of the Japanese folktale. A shipbuilder rescues and nurses back
to health an injured Canada goose. Sometime later, a woman appears, who offers to weave sails. The two marry and have a little girl. The husband
promises never to watch his wife while she is weaving, but one day he gets
impatient and opens the door, only to discover a goose plucking feathers from
her breast and weaving sails. A stirring tale of love.   [1]
FAMILY LIFE; FOLK AND FAIRY TALES
Rev: NYT

239   *The Day Jimmy's Boa Ate the Wash.* Trinka H. Noble. Illus. by Steven Kellogg. Dial, 1980. Unp. $13.89. (0-8037-1724-5).

                                       Category: Story   **Age:** P–K

It's a toss-up which is funnier: Noble's story or Kellogg's illustrations of a hilarious class trip to a farm. A young girl answers her mother's questions about
the trip in a deadpan manner: "Oh boring until the cow started crying," which
leads to the recounting of a series of misadventures all triggered by Jimmy's
boa constrictor. Kellogg's colorful drawings capture all the wild adventures of
this class outing.   [1]
ANIMALS; FARMS; SNAKES
Rev: BBC; NYT

240   *Daytime.* Diane Wilmer. Illus. by Nicola Smee. Macmillan, 1987. 10 pp.
Paper $3.95. (0-689-71240-5).   **Category:** Story   **Age:** I–T

A young boy wanders through his house looking for the members of his family. "Where's Dad? Here he is." Each person is involved in various party preparation activities. Dad is blowing up balloons; Mom is making cupcakes; the
dog and cat are playing with confetti. A final page finds the entire family together at the table celebrating the boy's birthday. This sturdy board book has
bright, colorful, realistic illustrations.   [3]
BIRTHDAYS; BOARD BOOKS; DAY; FAMILY LIFE
Rev: BKL 1/15/89

241 **_The Deep Blue Sea._** Bijou Le Tord. Orchard Books, 1990. 32 pp. $13.95.
(0-531-08453-1). **Category:** Story **Age:** T–P–K

In simple, gentle words, children discover that God created the world, plants, and animals to live in harmony. People and families are pictured and joined in the whole comfortable life on earth as well as in space. Soft, watercolor paintings reveal a world with purpose and hope. This is a satisfying and thankful book. [2]

CREATION; GOD

Rev: BKL 3/15/90

242 **_Deep In the Forest._** Brinton Turkle. Dutton, 1976. Unp. $12.95. (0-525-28617-9). **Category:** Folklore/Folktales/Fairy tales **Age:** P–K

The reverse of Goldilocks and her bears, this story shows what might happen to Baby Bear if he invades Goldie's home. He eats the porridge, breaks her bowl, wrecks the chairs, and bounces on Mama's and Papa's beds. The humans come home, and the bear is just a bit faster than the family in making his exit. The heavily shaded pencil drawings show a neat woodland home, a blond family, and an adorable cub. [1]

BEARS; FOLK AND FAIRY TALES

Rev: CBK; ESLC

243 **_Deep In the Jungle._** Joe Scruggs. Educational Graphics Press, 1987. Audiocassette. 40 min. $9.95.
Category: Poetry/Nursery rhymes/Songs **Age:** P–K

A humorous assortment of original tunes and new versions of old favorites, such as "Eensy Weensy Spider," "Aunt Lucy," and "Old MacDonald," are presented in a soothing country folk style. Children and parents will be tickled by musical discussions of familiar topics: naps, refrigerator art, and unique birthday presents for Mom. [2]

MUSIC; NURSERY RHYMES; SONGS

Awards: Parents' Choice Award

244 **_Diaper Gym: Fun Activities for Babies on the Move._** Kimbo Educational, 1985. Audiocassette. 30 min. $10.95.
Category: Poetry/Nursery rhymes/Songs **Age:** I–T

Exercises set to traditional and "show" tunes about babies. The purpose is to stimulate interaction and fun between adult and child as much as to provide healthful exercises. A new set of rhymes for those who have forgotten their Mother Goose. Includes exercise instructions for parents. [1]

EXERCISE; GYMNASTICS; SONGS

Awards: Parents' Choice Honors

245 *Digging Up Dinosaurs.* Aliki. Harper & Row, 1981. 40 pp. $12.89. (0-690-04099-7). **Category:** Informational **Age:** P–K

Lighthearted but informational look at how dinosaur bones get into museums and where they come from. A clear, easy-to-read text explains the process of excavating bones, what scientists learn from them, and how the bones are put back together. Accompanied by clear, cartoonlike illustrations. [2]

DINOSAURS; MUSEUMS

Rev: NYT

246 *Dilly Dilly Piccalilli: Poems for the Very Young.* Myra Cohn Livingston. Illus. by Eileen Christelow. Margaret K. McElderry Books, 1989. 68 pp. $12.95. (0-689-50466-7).

Category: Poetry/Nursery rhymes/Songs **Age:** I–T–P–K

Works by Edward Lear, Christina Rossetti, Robert Louis Stevenson, and Walter de la Mare are featured in this anthology, as are works by contemporary poets. Whether the poems celebrate nature, capture playful moments, or feature humor and nonsense, young listeners will appreciate the rhyme and the rhythm of the short poems offered in this small, sparsely illustrated book.

POETRY [2]

Rev: BKL 6/1/89

247 *Dinah's Mad, Bad Wishes.* Barbara M. Joosse. Illus. by Emily Arnold McCully. Harper & Row, 1989. 32 pp. $12.89. (0-06-023099-1).

Category: Story **Age:** P–K

Mother and daughter are very angry with one another, but both whiz, bump, and wish their disturbing feelings away until they reconcile and "only the loving was left." A simple, reassuring story about a frequent, strong family emotion. The cartoonlike drawings add to the humor and spirit of forgiveness.

ANGER; MOTHERS AND DAUGHTERS [3]

Rev: BKL 5/1/89; ESLC

248 *The Dingles.* National Film Board of Canada, 1989. Dist. by Bullfrog Films. Videocassette. 8 min. $145.00. **Category:** Story **Age:** P–K

Grandmotherly Doris Dingle and her three cats—Donna, DeeDee, and Dale
—live happy, carefree lives. Their tranquility is interrupted one day, however,
when a fierce, unexpected windstorm nearly blows them away. Resourceful
Doris cleverly saves them all. In the aftermath, the four friends settle comfort-
ably for the night in Doris's ample bed, with adversity surmounted and security restored.   [2]
CATS; HUMOR; STORMS

249   *Dinosaurs, Dinosaurs.* Byron Barton. Harper & Row, 1989. Unp. $13.89.
        (0-690-04768-1).   **Category:** Informational **Age:** P–K

Vibrant childlike illustrations and simple, bold text describe the basic characteristics of these popular prehistoric creatures. Endpapers portray the dinosaurs shown within the book, including scientific names and pronunciations.
Dinosaur fans not yet able to comprehend more detailed information will be
delighted with this enticing book.   [1]
DINOSAURS
Rev: BKL 3/15/89; CBY-90

250   *Dinosaurs' Halloween.* Liza Donnelly. Scholastic, 1987. Unp. $12.95. (0-
        590-41025-3).   **Category:** Story **Age:** P–K

Dressed as dinosaurs, a boy and his dog make a new friend as they are trick-or-
treating. The friend, a most unusual character, helps them out when they are
confronted by bullies who are determined to take all their treats. The colorful
and humorous illustrations make this a delightful story for adults to share with
young children.   [3]
BULLYING; DINOSAURS; HALLOWEEN
Rev: ESLC

251   *Dinosaurs Never Say Please and Other Stories.* Performed by Bill Harley.
        Round River Productions, 1987. Audiocassette. 40 min. $9.98.
                                                           Category: Story **Age:** K

Four stories with appropriate voice changes for each character are told in a
pleasant manner by Harley. "Dinosaurs Never Say Please" describes a boy
who learns the importance of saying "please." The fate of those who fail to
listen is related in "I'm Busy." "Bojabi" is an African cumulative tale which
includes an original song. "Master of All Masters" is taken from the book of
Joseph Jacobs and is slightly changed and expanded.   [2]
CLEVERNESS; DINOSAURS
Rev: BKL 1/15/90

252 *Do Not Disturb.* Nancy Tafuri. Greenwillow Books, 1987. 24 pp. $11.88.
(0-688-06542-2). **Category:** Story **Age:** P–K

A family goes camping near a lake on the first day of summer. They are unaware that they are disturbing the wildlife as they make camp, swim in the lake, play soccer, and cook dinner. Only after the family retires to their tent do the animals return to their formerly disturbed habitat to sing their nighttime songs. [3]
ANIMALS; CAMPING
Rev: CBY-88; ESLC

253 *Do You Want to Be My Friend?* Eric Carle. Harper & Row, 1971. Unp.
$13.89. (0-690-24277-8). **Category:** Wordless **Age:** T–P–K

Almost wordless, the tale begins with a small gray mouse and the title question that he asks of various animals. The first page shows a brown tail on the right. On the next page, it is revealed as belonging to a horse, while yet another tail is shown. This keeps eyes moving from left to right and encourages habits necessary to beginning readers. Carle's watercolor cutouts of animals are simple and vibrant. [2]
ANIMALS; FRIENDSHIP; WORDLESS
Rev: CBY-88; ESLC

254 *Doctor De Soto.* William Steig. Farrar, Straus & Giroux, 1982. Unp.
$13.95. (0-374-31803-4). **Category:** Story **Age:** P–K

Doctor De Soto, a competent and painless dentist, and his able assistant, Mrs. De Soto, cope with the toothaches of animals large and small. Since he is a mouse, Doctor De Soto normally refuses to treat animals who crave the taste of mice, but he makes an exception for the fox who shows up begging for relief. How the mice outwit the ungrateful fox, who has decided to eat them anyway, makes for delightfully funny reading. [2]
DENTISTS; FOXES; MICE
Rev: BBC; NYT

255 *Doggies.* Sandra Boynton. Simon & Schuster, 1984. Unp. Paper $3.95.
(0-671-49318-3). **Category:** Participation and manipulative **Age:** I–T

Boynton has managed to bring great humor to a simple board book. Each different type of "doggie" has both a unique bark and a ridiculous expression on its face. This is one that adults can enjoy along with the child.   [1]
BOARD BOOKS; DOGS; HUMOR; PARTICIPATION
Rev: CBK

256   ***Donald Says Thumbs Down.*** Nancy E. Cooney. Illus. by Maxie Chambliss. Putnam, 1987. Unp. $11.95. (0-399-21373-2).

Category: Story   **Age:** P–K

Preschooler Donald is a big boy in many ways. But, try as he might, he cannot break the thumbsucking habit he developed as a baby. After trying a variety of solutions that do not seem to work, he finally talks to his mother about his dilemma, and she helps him to direct his attention to other activities. Although simple line drawings are used, the characters' faces are expressive and reflective of the story's tone.   [2]
FINGER-SUCKING; GROWING UP
Rev: ESLC

257   ***Don't Touch My Room.*** Patricia Lakin. Illus. by Patience Brewster. Little, Brown & Co., 1988. 32 pp. $12.95. (0-316-51230-3).

Category: Story   **Age:** P–K

Aaron does not want his room or his life to change and does not want a little brother. As he fears, the changes do come, and adjustments have to be made. In spite of it all, Aaron grows from not wanting to share his room or toys, to sharing even his secret room with Benji, whom he learns to love. Colorful, detailed illustrations enhance the perspective.   [1]
BABIES; SIBLING RIVALRY
Rev: ESLC; NYT

258   ***The Doorbell Rang.*** Pat Hutchins. Greenwillow Books, 1986. Unp. $12.88. (0-688-05252-5).   **Category:** Story   **Age:** P–K

What could be better than a plate of cookies? Two friends to share them with! However, the children's willingness to share wanes with each ring of the doorbell, as more and more friends come to share the cookies. When there is left only one cookie apiece, the doorbell rings again. But never fear, it is Grandmother with another plate full of cookies. A fun, predictable book with glorious illustrations.   [1]
COOKING; GRANDMOTHERS; SHARING
Rev: BBC; CBY-87; ESLC

259 *Dots, Spots, Speckles, and Stripes.* Tana Hoban. Greenwillow Books, 1987. Unp. $11.88. (0-688-06863-4).

Category: Concept/Counting/Alphabet   **Age:** P–K

A wordless book of full-color photographs used to teach the differences between dots, spots, speckles, and stripes. Illustrations are clear and crisp, showing a variety of scenes from both the city and the country.   [2]

CONCEPTS; WORDLESS

Rev: CBY-88

260 *The Dream Child.* David McPhail. Narrated by Myvanwy Jenn. Random House/Educational Enrichment Materials, 1985. Dist. by American School Publishers. Filmstrip. 5 min. $26.00.

Category: Story   **Age:** P–K

Dream Child and Tame Bear explore nighttime fantasies in their winged boat. McPail's rich watercolors, Guth's original score and Jenn's artful narration produce a truly exceptional dreamworld fantasy (Dutton, 1985). Accompanied with audiocassette.   [1]

DREAMS; IMAGINATION

Rev: SLJ 4/87   **Awards:** ALSC Notable Filmstrip

261 *Dream Dancin'.* Linda Saxton Brown. Linda Saxton Brown, 1988. Dist. by Tahoe Crafts Printing. Audiocassette. 35 min. $9.95.

Category: Poetry/Nursery rhymes/Songs   **Age:** I–T

Beautifully sung and well paced, this collection of lullabies by Brown provides a trip through memory. Some, like "Rock-a-bye" and "Hush Little Baby," are traditional songs from America's past, but others, like "Jesse's Song," are new and equally delightful. The folksinging style suits the music. All the words are provided for singing along.   [1]

BABIES; LULLABIES; SONGS

Rev: BKL 11/1/89

262 *Dreams.* Peter Spier. Doubleday, 1986. Unp. $11.95. (0-385-19337-8).

Category: Wordless   **Age:** P–K

As a young boy and girl relax in a field of flowers, they look up at the changing clouds in the sky. The clouds take on various shapes, and the imaginations of the children turn them into scenes of beauty and adventure. A single line of

text concludes the book: "And the next time you gaze at the sky: dream dreams!" [1]
CLOUDS; DREAMS; IMAGINATION
Rev: ESLC

263 *Dry or Wet?* Bruce McMillan. Lothrop, Lee & Shepard, 1988. 32 pp. $12.88. (0-688-07101-5). **Category:** Wordless **Age:** P

Bold, eye-catching color photographs depict happy children involved in dry and wet situations and activities. The viewer is invited to decide which is dry and which is wet, as joyful children swim and play with water in this wordless concept book. [1]
CONCEPTS; WORDLESS
Rev: BKL 3/1/88

264 *D.W. Flips!* Marc Brown. Little, Brown & Co., 1987. Unp. $10.95. (0-316-11239-9). **Category:** Story **Age:** P–K

D.W. resents being put into the beginning gymnastics class, because she is sure she can already do flips, but to her dismay she cannot even do a forward roll. Humorous pastel illustrations show her practicing at home while shaking the plaster off the ceiling as well as at the supermarket bumping into a fruit display. Her persistence pays off, and at her next class, D.W. flips. Young children will rejoice in her success. [3]
ANTEATERS; GYMNASTICS
Rev: CBY-88; ESLC

265 *Dylan's Day Out.* Peter Catalanotto. Orchard Books, 1989. Unp. $14.99. (0-531-08429-9). **Category:** Story **Age:** K

Dylan escapes the boredom of being left at home when his owner accidentally leaves the door open. Before the day is done, the dalmatian's adventures include exploring trash cans and getting into a soccer game between penguins and skunks. Although Catalanotto uses color, the black and white emphasis is striking. Kindergartners will enjoy the story; adults will laugh at the subtle humor in many of the illustrations. [1]
DOGS
Rev: BKL 10/1/89

266 *Each Peach, Pear, Plum: An I-Spy Story.* Janet Ahlberg and Allan Ahlberg. Viking Kestrel, 1978. Unp. $11.95. (0-670-28705-9). **Category:** Participation and manipulative **Age:** T–P

An "I spy" book with two sets of well-known nursery rhyme characters illustrated on each page. One set is prominently displayed, while the other requires some careful scrutiny of the illustration. An accompanying rhyme identifies both so that children will know what to look for. Continuity is achieved as each hidden character becomes the featured character on the following page. Lots of fun for all. [1]

GAMES; PARTICIPATION

Rev: BBC; CBK; ESLC; NYT

267 *Early Morning in the Barn.* Nancy Tafuri. Greenwillow Books, 1983. Unp. $14.88. (0-688-02329-0). **Category:** Wordless **Age:** T–P

A crowing rooster announces a new day and awakens the other barnyard animals. Full-page pictures are bright and cheerful and hold surprises for the watchful eye. [2]

ANIMALS; WORDLESS

Rev: ESLC

268 *Earth Mother Lullabies from Around the World, Vol. 2.* Pamela Ballingham and Tim Ballingham. Earth Mother Productions, 1987. Audiocassette. 49 min. $9.98.

Category: Poetry/Nursery rhymes/Songs **Age:** T–P–K

A collection of lullabies as culturally diverse as ancient Syrian, Yiddish, and African-American. Pleasing vocals are accompanied by flute, keyboard, guitar, and harp in soothing selections. [2]

LULLABIES; SONGS

Rev: SLJ 4/88 **Awards:** ALSC Notable Recording

269 *Easter.* Gail Gibbons. Holiday House, 1989. Unp. $13.95. (0-8234-0737-3). **Category:** Informational **Age:** P–K

This is a much needed information book on the Easter holiday. It tells why Easter is celebrated and does not skirt the direct relationship between the death and resurrection of Jesus Christ. Gibbons also includes the traditions of Easter—the Easter bunny, colored eggs, and the Easter lily. An appendix of Easter holy days is included. Illustrations are presented in a picture frame format in which objects move outside their frames. [1]

EASTER

Rev: BKL 4/1/89

270 *Easter Parade.* Mary Chalmers. Harper & Row, 1988. Unp. $11.89. (0-06-021233-0). **Category:** Story **Age:** T–P).

Rabbits, chickens, and ducks meet at Easter Farm each spring to load up for the Easter Parade. They make an Easter basket for each animal but find there is one left after delivering them. Bluebird finally tells them they forgot Ladybug. After completing this last delivery, they then go back to their homes until the next spring. The winsome pictures filled with activity make the book attractive to a young audience. [2]
ANIMALS; EASTER
Rev: BKL 1/15/88

271 *Eat up, Gemma.* Sarah Hayes. Illus. by Jan Ormerod. Lothrop, Lee & Shepard, 1988. 32 pp. $13.00. (0-688-08149-5).
Category: Story **Age:** T–P

No matter how hard the family tries, Gemma cannot be persuaded to eat; all she wants to do is play with her food. Her brother watches from a distance and then devises a plan that works. The story is an accurate depiction of infancy, and one of the many challenges every parent must endure. Ormerod's illustrations show the warmth this black family has for its youngest member. [1]
AFRO-AMERICANS; BABIES; FAMILY LIFE
Rev: BKL 9/1/88; CBY-90; ESLC

272 *Eating the Alphabet: Fruits and Vegetables from A to Z.* Lois Ehlert. Harcourt Brace Jovanovich, 1989. Unp. $13.95. (0-15-224435-2).
Category: Concept/Counting/Alphabet **Age:** T–P–K

A cornucopia of colorful fruits and vegetables is splashed across the pages of this delectable book. Both children and parents will be introduced to the alphabet and a variety of foods. Oh, what fun to really eat through this alphabet. Not just the trusty old A for apple, but apricots, artichokes, and avocados. A glossary provides additional information, including pronunciation and origin of each food shown. [1]
ALPHABET; FRUIT; VEGETABLES
Rev: BKL 3/15/89

273 *The Egg Tree.* Katherine Milhous. Reprint. Scribner's, 1971. 32 pp. $12.95. (0-684-12716-4). **Category:** Story **Age:** P–K

With colored eggs found on their Easter egg hunt and cherished eggs decorated long ago, a Pennsylvania Dutch family creates an egg tree to be viewed by many visitors. Directions for making a similar tree appear on the dust

jacket. Colorful, though muted illustrations and an effusive text, reminiscent of an era long past, will still appeal to young children. [3]
EASTER; FAMILY LIFE
Rev: NYT   **Awards:** Caldecott Medal

274   ***Elbert's Bad Word.*** Audrey Wood. Illus. by Audrey Wood and Don Wood. Harcourt Brace Jovanovich, 1988. Unp. $13.95. (0-15-225320-3).

Category: Story   **Age:** P–K

While playing croquet, young Elbert catches a bad word, all hairy and ugly as it flies through the air, and he puts it in his pocket. Without Elbert's knowledge, it leaves his pocket and flies into his mouth. When a mallet drops on his foot, the bad word loudly springs out. After Elbert's mother washes his mouth, Elbert visits the resident gardener/ wizard who feeds Elbert a cake made from alternative, acceptable words. [3]
MAGIC; SWEARING
Rev: BKL 10/1/88

275   ***The Elephant and the Bad Baby.*** Elfrida Vipont. Illus. by Raymond Briggs. Reprint. Coward McCann, 1986. Unp. $12.95. (0-698-30752-6).

Category: Story   **Age:** P–K

The Bad Baby always says yes to the Elephant's offer of treats as they rampage past the ice cream stand, butcher shop, bakery, snack shop, grocery store, candy store, and fruit stand. But their exploits come to a screeching halt when the Elephant realizes that the Bad Baby "never once said please," until the unexpected, happy ending. The antics of the beguiling pair are charmingly illustrated in full-page color paintings. [2]
BABIES; CUMULATIVE TALES; ELEPHANTS; STEALING
Rev: ESLC; NYT

276   ***Elfabet: An ABC of Elves.*** Jane Yolen. Illus. by Lauren Mills. Little, Brown & Co., 1990. Unp. $14.95. (0-316-96900-1).

Category: Concept/Counting/Alphabet   **Age:** P–K

Winsome elves cavort through the alphabet. Each page is bordered with beautifully detailed flowers and filled with appropriate objects and animals involved with the elves' antics. A key to all objects is provided at the book's end.
ALPHABET [2]

277 **Elizabeth Hen.** Siobhan Dodds. Little, Brown & Co., 1988. Unp. $9.95. (0-316-18818-2). **Category:** Concept/Counting/Alphabet **Age:** T–P

As Elizabeth Hen parades proudly through the farmyard telling her friends about the egg she laid, young children will enjoy counting the ever-increasing offspring of the animals Elizabeth meets: from the cow with her two calves and the sheep with her three lambs to the rabbit with her 10 babies. She returns to her nest just in time to discover that her own egg is hatching.   [2]
ANIMALS; CHICKENS; COUNTING; FARMS
Rev: BKL 3/15/88

278 **Ellie's Doorstep.** Alison Catley. Barron's Educational Series, 1989. Unp. $10.95. (0-8120-5966-2). **Category:** Story **Age:** P–K

Ellie, aged 3½, sits on her doorstep every day and pretends to be a wizard, a teacher, and a grownup while she plays with her friends, both real and imagined. Each night Daddy carries Ellie up to bed to hear her adventures and read a favorite story. Rhymed text and colored pencil illustrations show a happy girl playing with her stuffed animals and creating magic through her imagination.   [3]
IMAGINATION; TOYS
Rev: BKL 4/15/89

279 **Elmer and the Chickens vs. the Big League.** Brian McConnachie. Illus. by Harvey Stevenson. Crown, 1992. Unp. $14.00. (0-517-57617-1). **Category:** Story **Age:** P–K

Elmer's brother promised to take him to a game, but not today. Left alone, Elmer's imagination transforms the barnyard into a baseball stadium. Recruiting the chickens as teammates, Elmer pitches his first major league game. That is until Mom calls him in for dinner.   [2]
BASEBALL; BROTHERS; CHICKENS; IMAGINATION

280 **The Emergency Room.** Anne Rockwell. Illus. by Harlow Rockwell. Macmillan, 1985. 24 pp. $13.95. (0-02-777300-0). **Category:** Informational **Age:** T–P–K

Straightforward and elementary introduction to the emergency room. Crisp, clean watercolor illustrations depict such items as wheelchairs, stretchers, oxygen tanks, and X-ray and blood pressure machines. Good for preemergency and postemergency room visit sharing time.   [3]
HOSPITALS
Rev: NYT

281 *Emma's Pet.* David McPhail. Narrated by Larry Robinson. Live Oak Media, 1986. Filmstrip with audiocassette. 4 min. $24.95.

Category: Story   **Age:** P–K

After searching everywhere, Emma finds just the right pet at home. She tries a frog, turtle, bird, and fish only to find they were not so good for hugs. When she returns home after her adventures, her father has hugs for her. The blending of delightful sounds, soft colors, and warm hugs makes this a visual adventure for the very young (Dutton, 1987). [2]

ANIMALS; FAMILY LIFE; PETS

Rev: SLJ 4/88   **Awards:** ALSC Notable Recording

282 *The Emperor and the Kite.* Jane Yolen. Illus. by Ed Young. Philomel, 1988. Unp. $14.95. (0-399-21499-2).

Category: Folklore/Folktales/Fairy tales   **Age:** P–K

When the emperor is kidnapped by evil men, his littlest daughter uses her kite to send food up to him in his prison tower and eventually devises a plan to rescue him with her kite. In this tale of loyalty, love, and courage, the rescued emperor finally learns never to neglect anyone, great or small. The vibrance of Young's watercolors invigorates the story from cover to cover. [1]

CHINA; FOLK AND FAIRY TALES; KITES; ROYALTY

Rev: BKL 6/1/88   **Awards:** Caldecott Honor Book

283 *The Emperor & the Nightingale.* Hans Christian Andersen. Narrated by Glenn Close. Sony Video, 1987. Dist. by Teacher's Discovery. Videocassette. 40 min. $14.95.

Category: Folklore/Folktales/Fairy tales   **Age:** P–K

Illustrations and music are colorful, oriental, exotic—almost three-dimensional. The nightingale, discovered by the emperor's court, is soon replaced by a jewel-encrusted artificial copy of the "little grey, ordinary" bird, so she flies away. Upon hearing of the emperor's illness, she returns to sing him back to hope and life with her "freely given enchantment." [1]

BIRDS; CHINA; FOLK AND FAIRY TALES

Rev: BKL 2/1/88

284 *The Empty Pot.* Demi. Henry Holt & Co., 1990. 32 pp. $15.95. (0-8050-1217-6).   **Category:** Folklore/Folktales/Fairy tales   **Age:** P–K

Chinese tale of being honest, doing one's best, and taking pride in these virtues. The emperor has decided his successor will be whoever grows the most beautiful flower from seeds he has cooked. Ping carefully and diligently tends his seed, but to no avail. Of all the children only Ping appears with an empty

pot. The emperor rewards his courage and honesty. Detailed pen and water-color illustrations are framed and centered.   [2]
CHINA; FOLK AND FAIRY TALES; HONESTY

285   **Eric Needs Stitches.** Barbara P. Marino. Photos by Richard Rudinski. Harper & Row, 1979. 32 pp. $12.70. (0-397-32374-3).

Category: Informational   **Age:** P–K

Factual information about visiting a hospital emergency room is given in this story about a young boy who falls off his bike and needs stitches. Black-and-white photographs on each page illustrate the book, which was written by an emergency room nurse.   [1]
HOSPITALS; MEDICINE
Rev: ESLC

286   **Ernest and Celestine.** Gabrielle Vincent. Morrow Jr. Books, 1986. Unp. $3.95. (0-688-06525-2).   **Category:** Story   **Age:** P–K

The first in a series of stories about Ernest, the bear, and Celestine, the mouse. In this tale, Celestine loses Gideon, her stuffed bird doll. Ernest tries to comfort her, but Celestine wants only Gideon, no other doll. Ernest creatively solves the problem for a charming ending. Young children will identify with Celestine's sadness at the loss of a beloved toy.   [2]
ANIMALS; FRIENDSHIP; TOYS
Rev: NYT

287   **Even If I Did Something Awful?** Barbara S. Hazen. Illus. by Nancy Kincade. Atheneum, 1981. 32 pp. $11.95. (0-689-30843-4).

Category: Story   **Age:** P–K

A reassuring tale about the endurance of love. Fearing the worst when an accident breaks her mom's favorite vase, the child first discusses with the mother other tragedies, such as crayon on the carpet or pinching the baby, before the truth is told. Using color-washed drawings to portray a young girl's fantasies within the setting of a cozy home, this comforting story reminds one that love transcends such minor tragedies.   [1]
LOVE; MOTHERS; QUESTIONING
Rev: CBK; SLJ 11/81

288   **Even Trolls Have Moms.** Performed by Joe Scruggs. Educational Graphics Press, 1988. Audiocassette. 30 min. $9.95.

Category: Poetry/Nursery rhymes/Songs   **Age:** K

The driving beat of these original ballads of contemporary urban life will attract kids long before they understand the humor. In "Nuke It," Scruggs' hymn to the microwave dinner, the kids sing "We like fast food to go/And making leftovers glow/When we've nuked them . . . in the microwave." Messy rooms, first day at kindergarten blues, and dirty clothes are subjects that will amuse a growing child well into the elementary years. [3]
SONGS
Rev: BKL 9/15/89 & 1/15/90

289 *Everett Anderson's Goodbye.* Lucille Clifton. Illus. by Ann Grifalconi. Henry Holt & Co., 1983. 32 pp. $10.95. (0-8050-0235-9).

Category: Story **Age:** P–K

An affirming book about a child's grief following his father's death. Excellent for the accurately presented stages of grief without forcing the rhyme of the poetic form. The reader easily identifies with young Everett's feelings and the loving relationship in this familiar minority family. [1]
DEATH; FAMILY LIFE
Rev: BKL 1/1/88

290 *Everything Grows.* Raffi. A & M Records, 1987. Audiocassette. 37 min. $8.98. **Category:** Poetry/Nursery rhymes/Songs **Age:** T–P

Providing entertainment for the entire family, Raffi delights the youngest to the oldest listener with a collection of old, familiar songs from around the world and new ones from France, Japan, and Poland. [2]
SONGS
Rev: SLJ 4/88 **Awards:** ALSC Notable Recording

291 *The Fabulous Five: Our Senses.* Produced by Peter Cochran and Kathleen Cochran. Rainbow Educational Video, 1989. Videocassette. 20 min. $89.00. **Category:** Informational **Age:** K

A pleasant narrator exposes the viewer to an escapade of sensory experiences. Suggested activities are provided for each of the five senses. Exquisite photography makes the video outstanding and memorable. The package also includes a guide. [1]
SENSORY
Rev: BKL 8/89

292 *Family.* Helen Oxenbury. Simon & Schuster, 1981. Unp. $3.50. (0-671-
42110-7).   **Category:** Concept/Counting/Alphabet **Age:** T

Depicts family members and how they might appear to young children. Non-
primary colors give soft, warm feelings to this Oxenbury board book. The text
is limited to one word that names the family member in a large-type print.
Ideal for parents to share with toddlers.   [2]
BABIES; BOARD BOOKS; CONCEPTS; FAMILY LIFE
Rev: BKL 5/1/81; SLJ 10/81

293 *The Family Read-Aloud Christmas Treasury.* Compiled by Alice Low. Illus.
by Marc Brown. Little, Brown & Co., 1989. 136 pp. $17.95. (0-316-
53371-8).   **Category:** Story   **Age:** P–K

A wonderfully nostalgic anthology of stories, songs, and poems relating to the
Christmas season. Included are Beverly Cleary, the Brothers Grimm, David
McCord, Roger Duvoisin, and Edgar Allan Poe along with many familiar
others. Selections are enlivened by the delightful and inimitable watercolor il-
lustrations of Marc Brown. Multiple uses await those who choose this title.
CHRISTMAS; MUSIC; POETRY   [2]
Rev: BKL 11/1/89

294 *Family Vacation.* Performed by Rosenshontz. RS Records, 1988. Audiocassette. 40 min. $9.98.
                            Category: Poetry/Nursery rhymes/Songs **Age:** P–K

The duo of Gary Rosen and Bill Shontz (Rosenshontz) rocks 'n' rolls its way
through lyrics about everyday life. Most noteworthy are "Family Vacation,"
"Peanut Butter Blues," and "Pizza." The lively rhythm and catchy lyrics will
draw listeners of all ages into the songs.   [2]
SONGS
Rev: BKL 6/15/89

295 *Farm Noises.* Jane Miller. Simon & Schuster, 1989. Unp. Paper $8.95. (0-
671-67450-1).   **Category:** Informational   **Age:** T–P

Big, bright, clear photographs of farm animals and objects are used to show
the farm environment. The simple text describes the sounds they make.
There is opportunity for interaction as young children are encouraged to
mimic the sounds.   [1]
FARMS; SOUNDS
Rev: CBY-90

296 *The Farmer.* Rosalinda Kightley. Macmillan, 1988. Unp. $11.95. (0-02-750290-2). **Category:** Informational **Age:** T–P–K

The large, colorful pictures of this simple rhyming book make it easy to use for story hour presentation about farm life. A double-page spread is devoted to each farm chore, ranging from driving sheep out to pasture to oiling a tractor. Illustrations are gentle and inviting in their simple style. [2]
COUNTRY LIFE; FARMERS; FARMS
Rev: BKL 4/1/88

297 *The Farmer in the Dell.* Illus. by Kathy Parkinson. Albert Whitman & Co., 1988. Unp. $12.95. (0-8075-2271-6). **Category:** Poetry/Nursery rhymes/Songs **Age:** P–K

An illustrated version of the nursery rhyme, rendered in subdued shades with beige, brown, and blue. The parent sharing the book with a young child is bound to feel a real sense of nostaglia when experiencing these drawings.
FARMERS; NURSERY RHYMES; SONGS [3]
Rev: BKL 5/1/88

298 *Farming.* Gail Gibbons. Holiday House, 1988. Unp. $13.95. (0-8234-0682-2). **Category:** Informational **Age:** K

A basic introduction to farms. This composite farm includes a dairy, hay fields, cornfields, an apple orchard, beehives, a vegetable garden, a maple sugar house, chickens, and other farm animals. The external and internal farm activities are placed in seasonal settings. Gibbons' clean-cut watercolors convey the information succinctly. [2]
FARMS; SEASONS
Rev: BKL 6/1/88

299 *Fast-Slow, High-Low: A Book of Opposites.* Peter Spier. Doubleday, 1988. Unp. Paper $5.95. (0-385-24093-7). **Category:** Wordless **Age:** P

This wordless book of opposites includes size, texture, and temperature. Each page is "titled" with the concept to be explored. Spier's small, colorful drawings of ordinary things and events serve to demonstrate each opposite. Objects and happenings chosen will be familiar to small children, and the artist's clear depiction leaves little doubt as to what should be gleaned from each of the many examples on a single page. [1]
CONCEPTS; OPPOSITES; WORDLESS
Rev: CBK; ESLC

300 ***Father Fox's Pennyrhymes.*** Clyde Watson. Illus. by Wendy Watson. Harper & Row, 1971. 56 pp. 13.89. (0-690-29214-7).
Category: Poetry/Nursery rhymes/Songs **Age:** I–T–P–K

Father Fox is close kin to Mother Goose and Brer Rabbit. These thoroughly American rhymes are resonant of other children's rhymes but at the same time new and silly. The accompanying illustrations show familiar animals in cartoonlike panels rollicking in tune to their verses. Also available in other formats from the National Library for the Blind and Physically Handicapped.
LIMERICKS; NURSERY RHYMES   [2]
Rev: CBY-88; NYT

301 ***Feel the Wind.*** Arthur Dorros. Thomas Y. Crowell, 1989. 32 pp. $12.89. (0-690-04741-X). **Category:** Informational **Age:** P–K

Succinctly explains what causes the wind, thus determining our weather, creating power, and altering our landscape. Watercolor drawings are complementary throughout, giving meaning to and creating an interest in the informative text. Instructions for making a weather vane are incorporated within the body of the text.   [2]
WIND
Rev: BKL 4/1/89

302 ***Feelings.*** Aliki. Greenwillow Books, 1984. 32 pp. $11.88. (0-688-03832-8). **Category:** Concept/Counting/Alphabet **Age:** P–K

Using cartoons, two-page spreads, and wordless panels with minimal illustrations and simple captions, Aliki presents a full range of youthful emotions: anger, joy, depression, jealousy, quiet satisfaction, etc. Ranging from the most peaceful to the most disruptive, the book faces head-on the indescribable as well as the ambivalent, giving illustration if not words to the changeability of the human mind.   [2]
CONCEPTS; EMOTIONS
Rev: NYT

303 ***Feet!*** Peter Parnall. Macmillan, 1988. 32 pp. $13.95. (0-02-770110-7).
Category: Concept/Counting/Alphabet **Age:** P–K

A variety of animals' feet parade across the jacket and pages of this book. Small drawings of the animals are hidden within the pages for the viewer to find. Feet are identified as FAST, HAIRY, THIN, etc. Delicate pen and ink drawings contrast with the bright colors to create sophisticated illustrations in this concept book.   [2]
CONCEPTS; FEET
Rev: BKL 10/1/88

304   *Finger Magic Books: Bear Magic; Bunny Magic; Turtle Magic; Spider Magic.* Illus. by Mitchell Rose. Revised. Schneider Educational Products, 1991. Unp. $5.95. (1-877779-19-9).

Category: Poetry/Nursery rhymes/Songs   Age: I–T–P

This set of board books presents four individual finger plays with a "tuck-and-go" felt finger puppet of the title character. "Bunny Magic" and "Bear Magic" are original compositions. "Spider Magic" is known as "Itsy, Bitsy Spider;" "Turtle Magic" is the familiar poem by Vachel Lindsay. Illustrations feature bright graphics, bold outlines in black, and instructions for hand movements. Spanish-English version available.   [3]
BOARD BOOKS; POETRY

305   *Finger Plays for Nursery & Kindergarten.* Emilie Poulsson. Music by Cornelia C. Roeske. Illus. by L. J. Bridgman. Dover Publications, 1971. 80 pp. Paper $2.25. (0-486-22588-7).

Category: Poetry/Nursery rhymes/Songs   Age: P–K

Eighteen finger plays are featured with their accompanying poems and lyrics. The pen and ink illustrations are old-fashioned in style but complement the tried-and-true verses and songs. The finger plays are simple and achievable, with easy-to-follow directions.   [2]
FINGER PLAY; GAMES; SONGS
Rev: CBK

306   *Finger Rhymes.* Marc Brown. Dutton, 1980. 32 pp. $11.95. (0-525-29732-4).   Category: Poetry/Nursery rhymes/Songs   Age: I–T–P–K

All the rhymes included involve fingers to act them out, ranging from the familiar "Eentsy Weentsy Spider" to the more obscure. Small graphics at the start of each line show the hand action effectively and unobtrusively, while the black-and-white pencil and pen illustrations suggest the scene.   [1]
FINGER PLAY; NURSERY RHYMES
Rev: CBK; NYT

307   *Fire Engine Shapes.* Bruce McMillan. Lothrop, Lee & Shepard, 1988. 32 pp. $12.88. (0-688-07843-5).

Category: Concept/Counting/Alphabet   Age: T–P

Using the ever-popular fire engine, McMillan introduces seven shapes. Full-color close-up photos depict the circles in wheels, rectangles in lights, squares

in the ladder, etc. A little girl dressed in yellow overalls is shown in part or wholly in all the photos. A handy chart at the back shows the shapes, gives their definitions, and lists the pages on which they are found. [1]
CONCEPTS; FIRE ENGINES; SHAPE
Rev: BKL 9/1/88

308 **Fire Fighters A to Z.** Jean Johnson. Photos by Jean Johnson. Walker & Co, 1985. 39 pp. $12.95. (0-8027-6589-0).
Category: Concept/Counting/Alphabet   **Age:** P–K
From A for alarm to Z for zone, each letter of the alphabet represents a different aspect of firefighting. Brief text and black and white photographs depict men and women with their clothing and equipment in the station and at the scene of a fire. Includes an appendix about the importance of these community helpers. [2]
ALPHABET; FIREFIGHTERS
Rev: BBC; ESLC

309 **First Comes Spring.** Anne Rockwell. Thomas Y. Crowell, 1985. Unp. $11.89. (0-690-04455-0).   **Category:** Story   **Age:** P
A little bear follows the seasons' activities, dressed appropriately for the winter. Simple, brightly colored double-page spreads feature busy bears working and playing. Young viewers will have fun guessing the seasonal activities, then turning the page for the explanations. [2]
BEARS; SPRING
Rev: CBK; ESLC

310 **First Flight.** David McPhail. Joy Street Books/Little, Brown & Co., 1987. 32 pp. $13.95. (0-316-56323-4).   **Category:** Story   **Age:** P–K
McPhail's lively illustrations add to a little boy's tale of his first airplane flight. Accompanied by a nervous teddy bear, the young hero imparts the dos and don'ts of air travel with infectious humor and a sense of adventure. Ideal for the parent to take along to share during a child's first flight, no matter how old the child. [2]
FLIGHT; TEDDY BEARS
Rev: CBY-88; NYT

311 **First Snow.** Emily Arnold McCully. Harper & Row, 1985. 32 pp. $12.89. (0-06-024129-2).   **Category:** Wordless   **Age:** P–K

The large mouse family piles into the family truck for a trip to the hills for some frolicking, fresh-air fun at the sign of the season's first snowfall. Splashes of color (scarves, caps, and mittens) against the background of snow-covered hills deftly and expertly define the joyful action in this wordless picture book.
MICE; SNOW; WORDLESS   [2]
Rev: BBC; ESLC

312   *The First Snowfall.* Anne Rockwell and Harlow Rockwell. Macmillan, 1987. Unp. $12.95. (0-02-777770-7).   **Category:** Story   **Age:** T–P

Large, colorful illustrations with well-defined outlines brighten up a child's adventure through a snow-filled day. She bundles up and romps through her yard, using a snow shovel, making a snowman, going sledding, and topping off her fun with a mug of hot cocoa.   [3]
SNOW; WINTER
Rev: CBY-88; ESLC

313   *First Things First: A Baby's Companion.* Charlotte Voake. Little, Brown & Co., 1988. 45 pp. $12.95. (0-316-90510-0).
                                  Category: Concept/Counting/Alphabet   **Age:** I–T–P

This imaginative potpourri of information features the ABCs, days of the week, numbers, animals, colors, shapes, fruits, insects, and flowers along with some nonsense verses and several classic childhood favorites. Humorous sketches and illustrations appear throughout. Because of the layout and the variety of information presented, both young children and adults will enjoy reading the material again and again.   [1]
ALPHABET; ANIMALS; COUNTING
Rev: BKL 11/15/88

314   *Fish Eyes: A Book You Can Count On.* Lois Ehlert. Harcourt Brace Jovanovich, 1990. Unp. $13.95. (0-15-228050-2).
                                  Category: Concept/Counting/Alphabet   **Age:** T–P–K

Rhymed text and psychedelic colored fish with cut-out eyes that change colors make counting a delight. The child is invited to don scales, fins, and tail, dive beneath the sea, and explore basic addition and counting concepts with the friendly narrator fish.   [1]
COUNTING; FISH; POETRY
Awards: Parents' Choice Honors Award

315 *Fish for Supper.* M. B. Goffstein. Dial, 1976. Unp. $8.89. (0-8037-2572-8).
Category: Story **Age:** P–K

This circular story tells of Grandmother, who gets up at five in the morning, has her breakfast, and then rows her little boat onto the water, where she fishes all day. She rows home, cooks her catch for supper, and does the dishes fast, fast, fast, so that she can get to bed and get up at five the next morning to go fishing once again. An excellent title for discussion with mature listeners on the problems of too much routine. [2]
FISHING; GRANDMOTHERS; OLD AGE
Rev: ESLC

316 *Fish Is Fish.* Leo Lionni. Pantheon Books, 1970. Unp. $12.99. (0-394-90440-0).
Category: Story **Age:** P–K

A minnow and a tadpole become friends; then the tadpole, who has become a frog, goes out into the world. One day, he returns and tells the fish all of the wonderful things he has seen. Outstanding illustrations show the outlandish things that the fish thinks the frog is describing. Children will definitely enjoy the humorous drawings by Lionni. [3]
FISH; FROGS; GROWING UP
Rev: CBY-88; ESLC

317 *Five Little Monkeys Jumping on the Bed.* Retold and illustrated by Eileen Christelow. Ticknor & Fields, 1989. Unp. $13.95. (0-89919-769-8).
Category: Concept/Counting/Alphabet **Age:** T–P–K

Five little monkeys obediently perform their bedtime tasks but cannot resist jumping on the bed. One by one, each monkey falls, bumping his or her head. Eventually all five have bumps on their head and go to sleep. At last, the mama monkey can go to bed—and jump on it! This simple counting book with soft, warm, amusing illustrations will delight young children. [1]
COUNTING; MONKEYS
Rev: BKL 6/1/89

318 *Five Minutes' Peace.* Jill Murphy. Putnam, 1986. Unp. $10.95. (0-399-21354-6).
Category: Story **Age:** P–K

In search of a brief interlude of peace and quiet (too much to ask when one has three children?), Mrs. Large steals off with teapot and newspaper to soak in the tub. But not for long! One by one, her children find her until everyone is in the tub. Once again, Mrs. Large slips away—for how long? Entertaining illustrations capture and delight readers and listeners alike. [3]
BATHS; ELEPHANTS
Rev: ESLC; NYT

319 *Flying.* Donald Crews. Greenwillow Books, 1986. 32 pp. $11.88. (0-688-04319-4). **Category:** Story **Age:** P–K

Flying over rivers, cities, and mountains and across the country, this armchair book is full of movement and color. The venture of a twin-propeller aircraft is revealed by simple graphic forms, making the book a fine introduction for novice travelers and lots of fun for young airplane lovers as well. [2]

AIRPLANES; FLIGHT

Rev: BBC

320 *Foolish Rabbit's Big Mistake.* Rafe Martin. Illus. by Ed Young. Putnam, 1985. Unp. $14.95. (0-399-21178-0).

Category: Folklore/Folktales/Fairy tales **Age:** P–K

An ancient Indian tale much like Chicken Little. A rabbit, scared by the sound of an apple falling from a tree, thinks the Earth is breaking up. As he runs away, he tells other animals, who join in his fear and flight. The brave lion stops the stampede and forces the rabbit to identify and confront his fear. Intensely powerful paintings bring the story to life for all. A splendid version of a popular tale. [2]

ANIMALS; FEAR; FOLK AND FAIRY TALES

Rev: NYT

321 *Four Tales by Beatrix Potter.* Beatrix Potter. United Learning, 1986. Filmstrip. 29 min. $135.00. **Category:** Story **Age:** T–P

Four familiar tales by Potter are displayed in a visual format appropriate for sharing with a large group: "Peter Rabbit," "Benjamin Bunny," "Flopsy Bunnies," and "Tom Kitten." Musical accompaniment in selected places helps to support the text. Although the illustrations are not the originals, they are close enough if children also want to see the books. Audiocassettes and teacher's guide with summary, questions, and script are provided. [1]

CATS; RABBITS

322 *Fox's Dream.* Keizaburo Tejima. Philomel, 1987. Unp. $14.95. (0-399-21455-0). **Category:** Story **Age:** P–K

A fox, wandering through the woods on a snowy winter day, is so lonely that he imagines other animals in the icy branches of the trees. Finally, he comes upon a vixen and is lonely no more. Exquisite woodcuts are accentuated by colors to make the reader feel the cold winter as well as the warmth of the fox's memories. [1]

DREAMS; FOXES

Rev: ESLC; NYT **Awards:** New York Times Best Illustrated Children's Book

323 *Fox's Dream.* Keizaburo Tejima. Random House/Educational Enrichment Materials, 1989. Dist. by American School Publishers. Filmstrip. 6 min. $30.00.   **Category:** Story **Age:** P–K

Caught in winter's frozen magic, a fox imagines frozen figures in the forest. He dreams of spring and of finding a mate. Delicate music on the accompanying audiocassette combines with Tejima's exquisite woodcuts to create a woodland wonder. Suggested spin-off activities include exploring Haiku poetry, researching fox habits, and locating major forests (Philomel, 1987).   [2]
DREAMS; FOXES
Rev: BKL 1/15/90

324 *Fran Anvi Sings Artichokes and Brussel Sprouts.* Performed by Fran Anvi and others. Lemonstone Records, 1988. Dist. by Alcazar Records. Audiocassette. 42 min. $9.98.
                                   Category: Poetry/Nursery rhymes/Songs **Age:** T–P–K

Foot stomping, toe tapping, hand clapping, and singing are the order of the day when young children hear these story, movement, and sing-along songs. Lyrics included.   [3]
SONGS
Rev: BKL 4/15/89 & 1/15/90

325 *Frank and Ernest.* Alexandra Day. Scholastic, 1988. Unp. $12.95. (0-590-41557-3).   **Category:** Story **Age:** K

When Frank and Ernest volunteer to manage a diner, they study up on the special language of food ordering. If you want Jell-O at Sally's Diner, you'll hear, "I need a nervous pudding." Additional food phrases can be found inside the front and back covers and on the endpapers. Children five and older will get as much of a kick out of the bear-and-elephant duo who dish up the orders as they will from the novel language.   [2]
ANIMALS; BEARS; ELEPHANTS
Rev: BKL 12/15/88

326 *Frederick.* Leo Lionni. Pantheon Books, 1967. 28 pp. $12.99. (0-394-91040-0).   **Category:** Story **Age:** T–P–K

While all the other field mice gather food for the winter, Frederick stores memories of the sun's warmth and of nature's colors, as well as many words to use during the long days ahead. His stored treasures become the miracle that brings the little creatures through the dark, dreary days ahead. A comforting look at the change of seasons and life. [1]

ANIMALS; MICE; SEASONS

Rev: CBY-88; ESLC; NYT

327 *Frederick and Ten Other Stories of Mice, Snails, Fish and Other Beings.* Leo Lionni. Narrated by Carol Channing. Harper Audio, 1976. Audiocassette. 52 min. $8.98. **Category:** Story **Age:** T–P–K

Lionni's wonderful story of Frederick, the shy mouse-pet, plus 10 more animal fables that focus on the celebration of our earth, the creative arts, and the use of language to work together to solve our difficulties. Channing's considerable comedic gifts and mercurial voice infuse Lionni's wise characters with joyous life. [2]

ANIMALS; FABLES; HOUSES

Rev: ESLC

328 *Frederick's Fables: A Leo Lionni Treasury of Favorite Stories.* Leo Lionni. Pantheon Books, 1985. 144 pp. $50.00. (0-394-87812-4). **Category:** Story **Age:** P–K

Lionni is a master both of the simple, poignant story told by using animal characters and of expressing the deepest meanings inherent in these stories through wonderfully imaginative and richly colored pictures. Bettelheim has written the thought-provoking introduction to enhance the anthology of 13 Lionni stories, which include "Frederick"; "Fish Is Fish"; "Geraldine, the Music Mouse"; and "Swimmy." [1]

ANIMALS; FABLES

Rev: ESLC

329 *Freight Train.* Donald Crews. Greenwillow Books, 1978. 32 pp. $11.88. (0-688-84165-1). **Category:** Story **Age:** T–P–K

As the black engine pulls its purple, blue, green, yellow, and orange cars (and red caboose, of course) through tunnels, by cities, and across trestles in daylight and at night, it gathers speed. The viewer is quickly caught up in the

action of the illustrations as they move across the pages faster and faster and faster until the train is . . . gone. [1]
TRAINS
Rev: BBC; CBK; ESLC; NYT **Awards:** Caldecott Honor Book

330 *Friend Dog.* Robert Wahl. Illus. by Joe Ewers. Little, Brown & Co., 1988. Unp. $12.95. (0-316-91710-9). **Category:** Story **Age:** T–P

Exceptionally well-written rhyming story about a toddler's meeting his new puppy. The world is shown from the toddler's short-legged point of view, with the feet and legs of the mother showing. The illustrations are humorous, as they depict the child and the dog imitating each other. [1]
BABIES; DOGS; FRIENDSHIP
Rev: BKL 10/15/88

331 *The Friendly Beasts: An Old English Christmas Carol.* Tomie dePaola. Putnam, 1981. Unp. $14.95. (0-399-20739-2).
Category: Poetry/Nursery rhymes/Songs **Age:** T–P–K

Muted colors and a strong sense of form create soft but solid, dignified illustrations of this classic English Christmas song. Double-page artwork alternates with pictures on the one page and text on the other. Illustrations are strong against a cream-colored background with a three-color/line border framing each page. Music and entire song text are provided. [3]
CHRISTMAS; MUSIC; SONGS
Rev: BKL 1/1/88

332 *Friends.* Rachel Isadora. Greenwillow Books, 1990. Unp. $12.95. (0-688-08264-5). **Category:** Concept/Counting/Alphabet **Age:** T–P

Life is more fun when it's shared. Isadora successfully captures the serendipity of first friendship. Bright watercolor, double-page spreads display children visiting, building, drawing, reading, and so forth. [2]
CONCEPTS; FRIENDSHIP
Rev: BKL 2/15/90

333 *The Frog Alphabet Book: . . . And Other Awesome Amphibians.* Jerry Pallotta. Illus. by Ralph Masiello. Charlesbridge, 1990. Unp. $11.95. (0-88106-463-7). **Category:** Informational **Age:** P–K

Frogs, toads, salamanders, newts, and caecilians are all briefly discussed in simple, entertaining language, accompanied by full-page illustrations in glowing colors and realistic detail. Large uppercase and lowercase letters are found

on each page with various amphibians from the Amazon horned frog to the zig-zag salamander. A good introduction for young children to some of nature's unusual creatures. [2]
ALPHABET; FROGS
Rev: BKL 9/1/90

334   Frog and Toad. Arnold Lobel. Listening Library, 1987. Audiocassette. 90 min. $15.95.   **Category:** Story   **Age:** P–K

Children are sure to enjoy hearing the author read these popular Frog and Toad books. The complete text of "Frog and Toad Are Friends," "Frog and Toad All Year," "Frog and Toad Together," and "Days with Frog and Toad" are read on two audiocassettes by Arnold Lobel at a pace that youngsters will find easy to listen to or follow along with the books. [2]
FRIENDSHIP; FROGS

335   Frog and Toad Are Friends. Arnold Lobel. Harper & Row, 1970. 64 pp. $10.89. (0-06-023957-3).   **Category:** Story   **Age:** P–K

Who helped Toad find his lost button? His best friend, Frog. Who made tea for Frog when he was sick? His best friend, Toad. In five chapters, which can be read continuously or as separate stories, these two best friends share excitement, gaiety, and tender affection. This is what friendship is all about. Also available in other formats from the National Library for the Blind and Physically Handicapped. [1]
FRIENDSHIP; FROGS
Rev: CBK   Awards: Caldecott Honor Book

336   Frog and Toad Are Friends. Arnold Lobel. Churchill Films, 1985. Videocassette. 18 min. $295.00.   **Category:** Story   **Age:** P–K

Frog and Toad, in three-dimensional animation, provide viewers with five episodes of the trials and humor of friendship. Those familiar with the Caldecott Honor Book (Harper, 1970) will be pleased with the use of music and vocalization that meld this into a unified, high-quality production. [1]
FRIENDSHIP; FROGS
Rev: SLJ 4/87   Awards: ALSC Notable Film/Video

337 *Frog and Toad Together.* Arnold Lobel. Churchill Films, 1987. Videocassette. 18 min. $295.00.   **Category:** Story **Age:** K

Presented in claymation, the characters are given a marvelous interpretation in the following favorite stories: "The Garden," "Cookies," "Dragons and Giants," and "The Dream." Gentle in spirit, there is still enough activity to entice the young child (Harper, 1972).   [1]
FRIENDSHIP; FROGS; TOADS
Rev: SLJ 4/89   **Awards:** ALSC Notable Film/Video; Parents' Choice Award

338 *Frog In Love.* Max Velthuis. Translated by Anthea Bell. Farrar, Straus & Giroux, 1989. Unp. $11.95. (0-374-32465-4).
                                                         Category: Story **Age:** P–K

Too shy to express his love for duck, frog tries to please her with gifts and extraordinary accomplishments. When he jumps too high and hurts himself, duck rushes to his side and it's love forever. The tempera illustrations capture the feelings and intensity of the story. The message of antiracism is clear: a frog and a duck, green and white—love knows no boundaries.   [2]
FROGS
Rev: BKL 12/15/89

339 *Frog on His Own.* Mercer Mayer. Phoenix BFA Films & Videos, 1989. Videocassette. 14 min. $260.00.   **Category:** Wordless **Age:** P–K

Just return the frog home; what could be easier, right? Wrong! This trip through a city park is as hilarious as it is imaginative. Get ready to laugh (Dial, 1973).   [1]
DOGS; FROGS; WORDLESS
Rev: BKL 1/15/90

340 *A Frog Prince.* Alix Berenzy. Henry Holt & Co., 1989. 32 pp. $13.95. (0-8050-0426-2).   **Category:** Folklore/Folktales/Fairy tales **Age:** K

Beginning like Grimm's fairy tale of the frog who loved a princess but was rejected by her, this story leads to new adventures and a surprise ending, told from the frog's point of view. The rich, dark colors set the mood and add to the sense of adventure and fantasy. A good choice to read aloud.   [2]
FOLK AND FAIRY TALES
Rev: BKL 12/15/89

341   *Froggie Went A-Courting.* Retold and illustrated by Chris Conover. Farrar,
       Straus & Giroux, 1986. Unp. $12.95. (0-374-32466-2).
                              Category: Poetry/Nursery rhymes/Songs   **Age:** P–K

A delightful retelling of a favorite, whimsical children's ballad in which a frog
marries a mouse, this version will capture the attention of young and old alike.
Conover's illustrations are exquisite, with intense color and attention to detail
that create a visual feast, including several double-page spreads. Music and
lyrics are provided at the back of the book to make this a sing-along favorite.
FROGS; SONGS; WEDDINGS   [3]
Rev: CBY-88; ESLC

342   *Funnybones.* Janet Ahlberg and Allan Ahlberg. Greenwillow Books, 1980.
       Unp. $11.88. (0-688-84238-0).   **Category:** Story   **Age:** K

When two skeletons—a big one and a little one—decide to take the dog skeleton for a walk and frighten somebody one night, they take time to play both in
the park and with the skeleton animals at the zoo but cannot find anyone to
frighten. So they take turns frightening each other all the way home. Children
will be most amused when the dog skeleton has an accident, ends up a pile of
bones, and is put back together incorrectly.   [3]
HUMOR
Rev: BBC

343   *Games for the Road: First Aid for Traveling Families.* Valentine Produc-
       tions, 1988. Audiocassette. 40 min. $8.50.
                                      Category: Informational   **Age:** P–K

A long car trip has the family frazzled until a gravelly voiced Fairy Game
Mother gives directions for games the whole family can play. Many of these
rely on reading, spelling, or math skills. Verbal sparring between Dad and the
fairy will appeal to grown-ups. "Games for Rainy Days," another cassette similar in format, features the same children and fairy, with Mother drawn in for
assistance. Upbeat music fills in the spaces.   [2]
GAMES
Rev: BKL 6/15/88

344   *George and Martha.* James Marshall. Houghton Mifflin, 1972. 48 pp.
       $12.95. (0-395-16619-5).   **Category:** Story   **Age:** P–K

The first book in a series that centers on two hilarious hippos. This title comprises five short stories, with one about the two friends: Martha, who loves to
make split pea soup, and George, who does not like to eat it. George and

Martha learn that a real friendship means being honest with each other, because that's what friends are for. [1]

FRIENDSHIP; HIPPOPOTAMUSES

Rev: BBC; CBK; ESLC; NYT

345 *Geraldine's Big Snow.* Holly Keller. Greenwillow Books, 1988. 24 pp. $11.95. (0-688-07514-2). **Category:** Story **Age:** T–P–K

All day long Geraldine the pig is waiting. She readies her boots and sled. She watches the grown-ups making preparations for the big snowstorm that is coming. But nothing happens. She waits and waits, disappointed when night falls and the ground is still dry. But while she sleeps, the clouds work their magic, and little Geraldine awakens to a glorious snow-covered world. [3]

GIRLS; SNOW; WINTER

Rev: BKL 8/88; CBY-89; ESLC

346 *Geraldine's Blanket.* Holly Keller. Greenwillow Books, 1984. Unp. $11.88. (0-688-02540-4). **Category:** Story **Age:** T–P–K

Geraldine the pig receives a security blanket from her aunt as a birthday present. As she grows older, the blanket gets tattered from continued use, but Geraldine cleverly satisfies the critics with her own resolution. She makes the blanket into a dress for her favorite doll, who always travels with her. A creative response, illustrated with pink cartoons, underscores the joke on others with lightness and brevity. [2]

BLANKET; PIGS

Rev: CBK; NYT; PP

347 *The Giant Jam Sandwich.* John V. Lord. Verses by Janet Burroway. Houghton Mifflin, 1972. 32 pp. Paper $3.95. (0-395-44237-0). **Category:** Story **Age:** P–K

This is a rhyming story that tells how a town defeats the invasion of four million wasps by trapping them in a giant jam sandwich. The story suggests the advantages of cooperation. Pictures are bright and colorful, although they might not show well for a large group. [2]

ADVENTURE; FOOD

Rev: ESLC

348 *The Giant's Toe.* Brock Cole. Farrar, Straus & Giroux, 1986. Unp. $13.95. (0-374-32559-6). **Category:** Folklore/Folktales/Fairy tales **Age:** K

In this whimsical spin-off of "Jack and the Beanstalk," the giant accidentally cuts off his toe, which turns into a young boy. The giant, irritated by the toe/boy's attitude, decides to get rid of him but is outwitted at each juncture. When the toe/boy gets rid of the pesky Jack, the giant decides to keep him. Humorous watercolor illustrations complement the text. [3]

FOLK AND FAIRY TALES; GIANTS; HUMOR

Rev: BBC; ESLC

349 *Gila Monsters Meet You at the Airport.* Marjorie W. Sharmat. Illus. by Byron Barton. Aladdin, 1990. Unp. Paper 3.95. (0-689-71383-5). Dist. by Macmillan. **Category:** Story **Age:** P-K

One boy is moving west from New York; the other to New York from the West. Each has fears based on stereotypes of life in the different regions. Life in the "West" means chasing buffaloes, cowboy clothes, cowboy food, and too hot to live, doesn't it? In New York, it's winter all year round, everyone's a gangster, and there are alligators in the sewers, right? [3]

FEAR; MOVING; STEREOTYPES

Rev: CBK; NYT

350 *Give a Dog a Bone.* Brian Wildsmith. Pantheon Books, 1985. Unp. $10.95. (0-394-87709-8). **Category:** Story **Age:** P-K

Wildsmith uses a split-page format to provide for the surprises that accompany the poor dog, Stray, who proceeds to lose one bone after another. Stray loses his bones to a steamroller, a street cleaner, a dirt mover, and a lion. His pursuit of a bone and a home are rewarded in the end. [2]

DOGS

Rev: ESLC

351 *Give Us This Day: The Lord's Prayer.* Illus. by Tasha Tudor. Philomel, 1987. Unp. $8.95. (0-399-21442-9). **Category:** Concept/Counting/Alphabet **Age:** P-K

Tudor has illustrated this well-known prayer in delicate watercolors framed by wreaths of flowers in a manner that expresses faith and tranquility. The peaceful village scenes drawn from rural New England memories perfectly convey the feeling of the prayer. The illustrations are sure to help a young child understand the meaning of these oft-repeated words. [3]

CONCEPTS; PRAYERS

Rev: BKL 2/1/88

352 ***The Glorious ABC.*** Selected by Cooper Edens. Atheneum, 1990. 32 pp. $14.95. (0-689-31605-4).

Category: Concept/Counting/Alphabet   **Age:** P–K

Magnificent compilation of illustrations by well-known children's book illustrators from the late 19th and early 20th centuries. Each illustration depicts one letter and one word with a unique individuality all its own. The alphabet may never seem as varied nor as splendid again.   [2]
ALPHABET

353 ***The Glorious Mother Goose.*** Selected by Cooper Edens. Atheneum, 1988. 96 pp. $15.95. (0-689-31434-5).

Category: Poetry/Nursery rhymes/Songs   **Age:** T–P

Forty-two of the most familiar rhymes compose this collection, with each illustrated by past interpreters. Represented are well-known artists such as Brooke, Greenaway, Rackham, Richardson, and Crane. Taken together, the illustrations evoke a rich heritage from the Mother Goose tradition.   [2]
MOTHER GOOSE; NURSERY RHYMES
Rev: BKL 11/15/88

354 ***Go to Sleep, Nicholas Joe.*** Marjorie Weinman Sharmat. Illus. by John Himmelman. Harper & Row, 1988. 32 pp. $11.89. (0-06-025504-8).

Category: Story   **Age:** P–K

Who hasn't wanted to trade places with the person who is giving the order to go to bed? After refusing to go to sleep because he can hear other kids playing and ice cream trucks jingling, Nicholas Joe begins to travel around, putting everyone else to sleep. The people he meets ask him for favorite toys, drinks of water, etc., before they can go to sleep. The colorful drawings with expressive faces enhance the story.   [2]
BEDTIME; BOYS
Rev: BKL 2/15/88

355 ***Goat's Trail.*** Brian Wildsmith. Alfred A. Knopf, 1986. Unp. $10.95. (0-394-88276-8).   **Category:** Story   **Age:** T–P–K

A lonely goat living high in the mountains decides to explore the town below. On his way into town, he invites a sheep, a cow, and a pig to follow him. Once in town, they cause such commotion that finally no one will follow the goat, and everyone goes home. The watercolors are bright and cheerful, and die-cut windows allow children to see what is happening in either direction.   [2]
ANIMALS; GOATS; TOY AND MOVABLE BOOKS
Rev: CBY-87; ESLC

356   *Gobble, Growl, Grunt: A Book of Animal Sounds.* Peter Spier. Doubleday, 1988. Unp. $6.95. (0-385-24094-5).

Category: Concept/Counting/Alphabet   **Age:** I–T

Every child will want to gobble, growl, and grunt with Spier's raucous, but realistically depicted animals. The beauty of this book of animals and their noises is the pacing. For openers, there's the barnyard, the pond and the forest, a whole page with elephants and monkeys, then to the Arctic, and back to the forest again. This book cannot be read quietly; it sings, shouts, and dances. And it will be asked for again and again.   [2]

ANIMALS; CONCEPTS; SOUNDS

Rev: CBK; ESLC

357   *Going to Day Care.* Fred Rogers. Photos by Jim Judkis. Putnam/Family Communications, 1985. Unp. $12.95. (0-399-21235-3).

Category: Informational   **Age:** T–P

Separation anxiety is alleviated via actual photos depicting exactly what a child can expect at day care. Text contains questions that allow the child to verbalize fears. Once again, Mr. Rogers provides help for both adult and child with another of his First Experiences books.   [1]

DAY CARE CENTERS

Rev: CBK

358   *Going to My Nursery School.* Susan Kuklin. Bradbury, 1990. Unp. $12.95. (0-02-751237-1).   **Category:** Informational   **Age:** P

For any youngster who is getting ready for day care or nursery school, this is the ideal book to be shared with a parent. Loaded with helpful information on what to expect, the text and pictures display activities and places such as hanging up outdoor clothes, workstations for play, fun at the water table, painting, building blocks, and more. Colorful photographs make the book visually appealing and realistic.   [2]

DAY CARE CENTERS

359   *The Golden Egg Book.* Margaret Wise Brown. Illus. by Leonard Weisgard. Reprint. Western, 1976. Unp. $9.15. (0-307-60462-4).

Category: Story   **Age:** T–P

Color illustrations fairly bursting with spring flowers surround each egg-shaped oval in this story of beginning life and friendship that was first published in 1947. Unsuccessful in his attempts to find out what might be inside an egg that he has found, Bunny falls asleep curled up next to it. As Bunny

sleeps, Duck hatches. What joy to find a friend and realize that neither would have to be alone again. [2]
DUCKS; EGGS; RABBITS
Rev: CBK

360   *Goldilocks and the Three Bears.* Retold by Jan Brett. Putnam, 1987. Unp. $13.95. (0-396-08925-9).
Category: Folklore/Folktales/Fairy tales   **Age:** T–P–K

Adapted from Lang's version, a beautiful, blonde Goldilocks makes her way through the three bears' house, while they stroll through the woods waiting for their porridge to cool. She helps herself to porridge, breaks the chair of Baby Bear, and falls asleep in his bed. When the bears return, they discover the damage and the girl. When awakened, Goldilocks runs from the house and is never seen again. Lush illustrations by Brett. [1]
BEARS; FOLK AND FAIRY TALES
Rev: CBY-88; ESLC; PP

361   *The Good-Bye Book.* Judith Viorst. Illus. by Kay Chorao. Atheneum, 1988. 32 pp. $12.95. (0-689-31308-X).   **Category:** Story   **Age:** T–P

The pangs of separation are at the core of a small boy's familiar attempts to change his parents' plans for an evening at a French restaurant. He suggests, he pleads, he bargains—but to no avail. The sitter arrives, and the little fellow's frustration prompts a threat that he will not say good-bye—NEVER! A wordless ending shows a smiling baby-sitter patiently waiting with a lapful of storybooks. [1]
BABY-SITTING; FAMILY LIFE; SEPARATION
Rev: BKL 2/15/88; CBY-89; ESLC

362   *Good-bye, Sammy.* Liza Ketchum Murrow. Illus. by Gail Owens. Holiday House, 1989. Unp. $13.95. (0-8234-0726-8).
Category: Story   **Age:** P–K

A boy tells of adventures while visiting his grandparents and playing with Sammy, his old stuffed rabbit. On returning home, he realizes he left Sammy on the plane and must accept that Sammy cannot be found. Although the boy's mother convinces him that another rabbit can be purchased, he continues to miss the "old soft smell" of his faithful partner. Comforting for those experiencing the trauma of such a loss. [2]
RABBITS; SADNESS; TOYS
Rev: CBY-90; BKL 4/15/89; SLJ 7/89

363   Good Dog, Carl. Alexandra Day. Green Tiger Press, 1985. Unp. $11.95. (0-88138-062-8).   **Category:** Story   **Age:** T–P

Mother asks Carl, a rottweiler, to look after her baby during her absence. The dog decides to do more than just watch: he entertains. Beginning with an escape from the crib and a ride through the house, down the laundry chute, to a swim in the aquarium, a brief snack, and a bath to get clean before Mom returns, this is a book to be enjoyed by children and adults alike. The tempera illustrations capture the essence of the story.   [1]
BABIES; BABY-SITTING; DOGS

364   Good Morning, Chick. Mirra Ginsburg. Illus. by Byron Barton. Greenwillow Books, 1980. 32 pp. $12.88. (0-688-84284-4).

Category: Story   **Age:** T–P

Little Chick hatches, has several adventures, and returns safely to Spotted Hen. Repetition of the phrase "like this" will satisfy and involve even the youngest reader.   [2]
CHICKENS; SOUNDS
Rev: BBC; CBK; NYT

365   Good Morning, Good Night. Music for Little People, 1988. Audiocassette. 53 min. $9.95.   **Category:** Poetry/Nursery rhymes/Songs   **Age:** P–K

Many of the selections in this unique compilation use well-known poems by poets such as Stevenson and Wordsworth set to original music. Using a variety of instruments and voices, the selections feature women, men, and even children singing lead vocals. "Good Morning" is lively and upbeat; the flip side, "Good Night," is designed for bedtimes. A fine choice for morning time, nighttime, and even in-between times.   [1]
MORNING; NIGHT; POETRY
Awards: Parents' Choice Award

366   Goodnight, Goodnight. Eve Rice. Greenwillow Books, 1980. Unp. $11.88. (0-688-84254-2).   **Category:** Story   **Age:** T–P

Town life is pictured in a succession of convincing evening vignettes of crisp black and white crayon finely highlighted in yellow. Night descends reassuringly everywhere for everyone—even for an appealing little kitten, who would clearly rather play than sleep. One story with which all children can identify.
CATS; NIGHT   [3]
Rev: BBC; CBK; ESLC

367   ***Goodnight Moon.*** Margaret Wise Brown. Illus. by Clement Hurd. Harper & Row, 1947. 30 pp. $11.89. (0-06-020706-X).

Category: Story   **Age:** I–T–P

A young rabbit says goodnight to familiar objects in his bedroom, as gradually darkening illustrations give way to growing cozy nighttime. Simple repetition as well as simple illustrations combine with the rhyming text to create a soothing bedtime ritual book. This classic must be in every young child's library. Also available in other formats from the National Library for the Blind and Physically Handicapped. [1]

BEDTIME; NIGHT; RABBITS

Rev: BBC; CBK; ESLC; NYT

368   ***Good-Night, Owl.*** Pat Hutchins. Macmillan, 1972. 32 pp. $12.95. (0-02-745900-4).

Category: Story   **Age:** T–P–K

Poor Owl tried to sleep, but the bees, the squirrels, and a variety of feathered fellows made such a racket that he could not get a moment's rest. Then "darkness fell and the moon came up. And there wasn't a sound." And Owl had his revenge. A rhythmic and repetitive text filled with onomatopoeic woodland sounds invites listener participation. The plot is mirrored by the bold, graphic illustrations. [1]

OWLS; SLEEP; TREES

Rev: ESLC

369   ***Gorilla.*** Anthony Browne. Alfred A. Knopf, 1983. Unp. $8.95. (0-394-87525-7).

Category: Story   **Age:** P–K

Browne has created an emotionally satisfying fantasy about a lonely and neglected little girl who loves gorillas. Hannah finds a birthday surprise on her bed in the middle of the night: a gorilla, but it is only a toy one. Magically, the toy becomes real and takes her to the zoo to see other primates. The remarkably realistic illustrations skillfully use rich color, texture, and subtle humor to heighten the story. [2]

ANIMALS; GORILLAS; IMAGINATION

Rev: BBC   **Awards:** Kate Greenaway Award

370   ***Grandaddy's Place.*** Helen V. Griffith. Illus. by James Stevenson. Greenwillow Books, 1987. 40 pp. $12.88. (0-688-06254-7).

Category: Story   **Age:** K

"When they got to Granddaddy's place, Janetta didn't like it at all." But after a few days of adjustment and some front-porch storytelling, she comes to love her grandfather, his mule, and the "mean looking cat." Expressive pen and watercolor illustrations convey the warmth and humor of this gentle, understated story. [3]

COUNTRY LIFE; GRANDFATHERS

Rev: CBY-88

371 *Grandma's Patchwork Quilt: A Children's Sampler.* American Melody, 1987. Audiocassette. 30 min. $9.98.

Category: Poetry/Nursery rhymes/Songs **Age:** P–K

Performers Cathy Fink, Jonathan Edwards, John McCutcheon, Larry Penn, and Phil and Naomi Rosenthal present a cheerful, toe-tapping album. A mixture of traditional songs and original numbers, the style is bluegrass, with guitar, mandolin, bass, and fiddle. Songs include "Buffalo Gals," "The Three Blind Mice," "The Pumpkin Man," "A Duck Named Earl," and "You Can't Make a Turtle Come Out." Pleasing voices provide for cozy listening. [2]

SONGS

Rev: BKL 2/15/88 **Awards:** Parents' Choice Award

372 *Grandpa.* Barbara Borack. Illus. by Ben Shecter. Harper & Row, 1967. 32 pp. $13.89. (0-06-020628-4). **Category:** Story **Age:** P–K

Grandpa and Marilyn are best friends. They play hide-and-seek, slurp soup together, and share secrets and silences. Grandma says they "make a pair." And what a pair! Ben Shecter's illustrations enhance the text, revealing the humor, warmth, and affection that a young girl shares with her grandfather. [1]

GRANDFATHERS

Rev: ESLC; CBK

373 *Green Eggs & Ham.* Dr. Seuss. Beginner Books, 1960. 72 pp. $6.95. (0-394-80016-8). **Category:** Story **Age:** T–P–K

Sam-I-am wants his friend to try some of his green eggs and ham. When his friend refuses, Sam goes to great lengths to make him change his mind. Finally, Sam's persistence pays off when his friend decides to try just one bite, and discovers that it is indeed delicious! A story to appeal to all who may have refused foods before trying them. The rhyme as well as the format make this appealing to toddlers and many others. [2]

FOOD

Rev: NYT

374 *Growing: From First Cry to First Step.* Fiona Pragoff. Doubleday, 1987. Unp. Paper $6.95. (0-385-24174-7).

Category: Concept/Counting/Alphabet **Age:** I–T–P

Outstanding full-color photographs illustrate a small child's growth from a first cry to some first steps. An excellent variety of children from various cultures are pictured. A single-word caption in lowercase letters accompanies each picture. Several double-page spreads provide variety in the format. This spiral-bound book is printed on heavy, wipe-clean cardstock that encases the binding. [1]

BABIES; CONCEPTS; GROWING UP

Rev: BKL 1/15/88

375 *Growing Colors.* Bruce McMillan. Lothrop, Lee & Shepard, 1988. 40 pp. $12.88. (0-688-07845-1).

Category: Concept/Counting/Alphabet **Age:** T–P–K

Using the colors in nature, this photographer captures the essence of yellow squash, tan melons, and purple beans, to name only a few of the vegetables and fruits that grow in, on, or above the ground. The pictures are so crisp and clear that the viewer is moved to pick and taste the objects on the pages of the book. McMillan includes a glossary and an author's note in an appendix. [1]

COLOR; FRUIT; VEGETABLES

Rev: BKL 9/1/88

376 *Guess Where You're Going, Guess What You'll Do.* A. F. Bauman. Illus. by True Kelley. Houghton Mifflin, 1989. 32 pp. $13.95. (0-395-50211-X).

Category: Story **Age:** P–K

Verbal and visual clues invite the child to guess or predict where one would go and what would be done given a certain set of circumstances and preparations. Each clue page is followed by a double-page spread of the activities and location that the child has no doubt already guessed. Colorful cartoon-style drawings offer much detail and multiple activities for the child to pore over.

PUZZLES [3]

Rev: BKL 11/1/89

377 *Hairy Man.* Performed by David Holt. High Windy Audio, 1981. Audiocassette. 44 min. $9.95. **Category:** Story **Age:** K

These six traditional and contemporary tales are filled with the humor, magic, and drama characteristic of the best down-home southern storytelling. The lively stories joined with snappy lyrics, banjo music, and sound effects offer an irresistible listening treat. [3]

SONGS

Awards: Parents' Choice Award

378 *Half a Moon and One Whole Star.* Crescent Dragonwagon. Illus. by Jerry Pinkney. Macmillan, 1986. 32 pp. $13.95. (0-02-733120-2).

Category: Poetry/Nursery rhymes/Songs **Age:** P–K

Beautiful watercolor illustrations create perfect visualization of and interaction with the theme of this lovely poem about nighttime. The poem describes Susan, a young girl, and the nighttime happenings that accompany her "almost sleeping." Crickets chirp, the next day's bread is baked, and even a blues saxophone is included. Beautifully written lines make this just right to read aloud. [1]

NIGHT; POETRY; SLEEP

Rev: CBY-87; ESLC

379 *A Halloween Mask for Monster.* Virginia Mueller. Illus. by Lynn Munsinger. Albert Whitman & Co., 1986. Unp. $10.95. (0-8075-3134-0).

Category: Story **Age:** T

Vivid illustrations complement the simple, appealing, repetitive text in which a young monster tries to find the perfect mask for Halloween. Toddlers will delight in the types of masks that are too scary for the monster. [2]

HALLOWEEN; MONSTERS

Rev: ESLC

380 *Hand Rhymes.* Collected and illustrated by Marc Brown. Dutton, 1985. 32 pp. $12.95. (0-525-44201-4).

Category: Poetry/Nursery rhymes/Songs **Age:** T–P–K

Collected rhymes offer the youngest audiences a lilting introduction to poetry through participatory action. Short selections with small, explanatory pictures next to each sentence show the motions to use in emphasizing the words' actions. A combination of evocative, pastel illustrations and simple text makes this title ideal to share with young children. Also available from Random House in sound filmstrip. [1]

FINGER PLAY; NURSERY RHYMES

Rev: ESLC

381   *Hand Rhymes.* Marc Brown. Random House/Miller-Brody, 1986. Dist. by American School Publishers. Filmstrip. 21 min. $25.00.

Category: Poetry/Nursery rhymes/Songs   **Age:** T–P–K

Who can resist an invitation to "sing along with your hands"? Upbeat music on the accompanying audiocassette combines with Brown's hand rhymes to produce a great sharing time for kids and grown-ups. Seasonal as well as general activities make this a year-round winner (Dutton, 1985).   [2]

FINGER PLAY; NURSERY RHYMES

Rev: SLJ 4/88   **Awards:** ALSC Notable Filmstrip

382   *Hands.* Ruth Thomson. Photos by Mike Galletly. Franklin Watts, 1988. 32 pp. $10.40. (0-531-10617-9).   **Category:** Informational   **Age:** P–K

Readers take a close look at their hands. Splendid, colorful photographs amplify the simple text, encouraging discussion and investigation. From "bones" to "X-ray," information is well indexed on the concluding page. Other titles in this series explore eyes, faces, feet, hair, and teeth.   [1]

HANDS

Rev: BKL 2/1/89

383   *Hanimals.* Mario Mariolti. Photos by Roberto Marchiori. Green Tiger Press, 1982. Unp. Paper $7.95. (0-914676-90-3).

Category: Wordless   **Age:** P–K

This unusual wordless book shows what can happen when a creative artist combines water-based paint and glued-on eyes with the human hand. Roosters, zebras, elephants, and octopuses are just a few of the brilliantly colored "hanimals" photographed against starkly contrasting, solid backgrounds.   [3]

ANIMALS; HANDS; PAINTING; WORDLESS

Rev: SLJ 4/83

384   *Hansel and Gretel.* Jacob and Wilhelm Grimm. Retold by Rika Lesser. Illus. by Paul O. Zelinsky. Putnam, 1985. Unp. $14.95. (0-399-21733-9).

Category: Folklore/Folktales/Fairy tales   **Age:** K

Faced with starvation, parents leave their two children lost in the woods. Taken in by an evil witch who wishes to eat them, Gretel pushes the witch into an oven, the children escape with her wealth, and they return home. Zelinsky's vivid oil paints are a perfect match for the Grimm tale. Although this classic tale deals with the topic of child abuse, it has modern implications and is excellent for discussion.   [1]

CHILD ABUSE; FOLK AND FAIRY TALES; STARVATION; WITCHES

Rev: NYT   **Awards:** Caldecott Honor Book

385 *Hansel and Gretel.* Jacob and Wilhelm Grimm. Retold by Rika Lesser. Illus. by Paul O. Zelinsky. Random House/Miller-Brody, 1986. Dist. by American School Publishers. Filmstrip. 15 min. $26.00.

Category: Folklore/Folktales/Fairy tales **Age:** K

Zelinsky's richly colored and textured illustrations and Rita Lesser's adaptation convey all the mystery, horror, and magic of the Grimm classic. Spin-off activities in literature, art, music, and drama are included (Putnam, 1985).

CHILD ABUSE; FOLK AND FAIRY TALES; STARVATION; WITCHES [1]

Rev: SLJ 4/87 **Awards:** ALSC Notable Filmstrip

386 *Hanukkah.* Miriam Chaikin. Illus. by Ellen Weiss. Holiday House, 1990. Unp. $14.95. (0-8234-0816-7). **Category:** Informational **Age:** P–K

Antiochus's oppression of the Jews, their flight to the hills, the Maccabean victory, the triumphant return to Jerusalem, and the miraculous vial of oil reveal the history of Hanukkah, the Jewish Festival of Lights. Modern observance of this holiday is also explained. [2]

HANUKKAH

387 *Happy Baby.* Chris Sage. Illus. by Angie Sage. Dial, 1990. Unp. $5.95. (0-8037-0883-1). **Category:** Concept/Counting/Alphabet **Age:** I–T

Baby gleefully plays with his toes, blocks, teddy, keys, and other toys and concludes, "I'm a happy baby . . . but I'm not that happy!" The final page reveals the fickle moods of infancy with a very unhappy, howling baby. This sturdy, laminated board book with rounded corners and big, bright illustrations is sure to be a hit with "happy" babies and their parents. [2]

BABIES; BOARD BOOKS; CONCEPTS; PLAY

388 *Happy Birthday.* Sharon, Lois, and Bram. A & M Records, n.d. Audiocassette. 43 min. $8.98.

Category: Poetry/Nursery rhymes/Songs **Age:** P–K

Noisy fun for all! The three performers encourage listeners to participate and enjoy songs that celebrate one of the happiest times of a child's year: the birthday. The mix of country, waltz, calypso, and swing rhythms makes the tape memorable. Ideal for sharing before, during, and after the party. [2]

BIRTHDAYS; SONGS

Rev: BKL 6/15/89; SLJ 4/89 **Awards:** ALSC Notable Recording

389   *Happy Birthday, Moon.* Frank Asch. Simon & Schuster, 1985. Unp. $12.95. (0-671-66454-9).   **Category:** Story   **Age:** T–P

Flat, childlike illustrations in soft, muted colors combine with the presentation of natural phenomena—echoes, the moon's movement, the wind—and form this gentle story of Bear's starry, moonlit (but never dark) adventure.   [1]
BEARS; BIRTHDAYS; MOON
Rev: CBK

390   *Happy Birthday, Moon.* Frank Asch. Narrated by Melissa Leebaert. Weston Woods Studios, 1985. Videocassette. 7 min. $60.00.

   Category: Story   **Age:** T–P

Bear climbs to the top of a mountain to ask the moon what it wants for its birthday, and "Thinking echos" are the moon's answers. Bear quickly develops a touching friendship with the moon. From the book by Frank Asch (Simon & Schuster).   [1]
BEARS; BIRTHDAYS; MOON
Rev: SLJ 4/87   **Awards:** ALSC Notable Film/Video

391   *Happy Birthday, Sam.* Pat Hutchins. Greenwillow Books, 1978. 32 pp. $11.88. (0-688-84160-0).   **Category:** Story   **Age:** T–P

It is Sam's birthday, but he is still too short to turn on the light switch, reach his clothes in the closet, reach the water spigot, or even sail his new boat in the sink. However, when the postman delivers Grandpa's present—a new chair for Sam—he can finally reach and do it all. And when Grandpa arrives for the birthday party, Sam opens the front door all by himself with the use of his new chair.   [2]
BIRTHDAYS; SELF-CONCEPT; SIZE
Rev: BBC; CBK; ESLC

392   *The Happy Day.* Ruth Krauss. Illus. by Marc Simont. Harper & Row, 1949. Unp. $11.89. (0-06-023396-6).   **Category:** Story   **Age:** P–K

Large-size black and white charcoal drawings show different animals asleep in their winter homes as gentle snowflakes dot the countryside. Suddenly, the various animals—bears, field mice, and squirrels—awake, sniffing something in the air. Krauss's tale builds enormous suspense with a simple text accessible to the beginning reader. Simon's illustrations set just the right mood of anticipation and action.   [3]
ANIMALS; SPRING
Rev: CBY-90; ESLC   **Awards:** Caldecott Honor Book

393 *Happy Day; and, Where Does the Butterfly Go When It Rains?* Ruth Krauss and May Garelick. Illus. by Marc Leonard. Narrated by John Cunningham. Weston Woods Studios, 1962. Filmstrip. 5 min. $30.00.

Category: Story **Age:** P–K

In "The Happy Day," bears and other animals gather together to enjoy the first signs of spring. In "Where Does a Butterfly Go When it Rains?" the narrator explains where various animals go during rainstorms. The text of each story is given on each frame. Audiocassette and script are included. [3]
ANIMALS; RAIN; SPRING

394 *Happy Passover, Rosie.* Jane B. Zalben. Henry Holt & Co., 1990. Unp. $13.95. (0-8050-1221-4). **Category:** Story **Age:** P–K

The Bear family celebrates the Passover seder through the eyes of Rosie, the youngest member of the family. She is given the most important role, that of answering the Four Questions at the seder. The preparation, the arrival of guests, and details of the celebration are included within the story. Additional information on "The Four Questions" and "The Seder Plate" is included in an appendix. [2]
BEARS; PASSOVER
Rev: BKL 3/15/90

395 *Harold and the Purple Crayon.* Crockett Johnson. Harper & Row, 1955. Unp. $10.89. (0-06-022936-5). **Category:** Story **Age:** T–P–K

Harold creates his own adventure-filled, child-sized world, using only a crayon. Looking innocent and wide-eyed in his sleepers, he is a fast thinker when things get tough. When he tires of climbing mountains and escaping monsters, he wishes to go home. Harold remembers he can always see the moon from his window. He "makes" the bed, "draws up" his covers, and the purple crayon drops to the floor as Harold drops off to sleep. [2]
ART; IMAGINATION
Rev: ESLC; NYT

396 *Harry, the Dirty Dog.* Gene Zion. Illus. by Margaret Bloy Graham. Harper & Row, 1956. 32 pp. $12.89. (0-06-026866-2).

Category: Story **Age:** P–K

Harry is a white dog with black spots who hates baths. One day he hides the scrub brush and runs away in order to end them. He plays all day in the dirtiest places and, when he gets hungry, returns home only to find that his family

does not know him because now he is a black dog with white spots. Many children will identify with Harry's bathing dilemma. Also available in other formats from the National Library for the Blind and Physically Handicapped.
BATHS; DOGS [2]
Rev: BBC; CBK; ESLC

397 *Harry, the Dirty Dog.* Gene Zion. Directed and produced by Pete Matu-lavich. Barr Films, 1987. Videocassette. 18 min. $295.00.
Category: Story **Age:** P–K

To avoid a bath, Harry, the lovable dog, runs away from home, thus beginning an entertaining adventure involving a ride in a garbage truck, rounding up cattle on a farm, jumping hurdles at a riding stable, a paint fight, and the dog catcher. Finally, tired and hungry, he returns home where he is not immediately recognized by his family (Harper, 1956). [2]
BATHS; DOGS
Rev: BKL 4/15/88

398 *Has Anyone Here Seen William?* Bob Graham. Little, Brown & Co., 1989. Unp. $11.95. (0-316-32313-6). **Category:** Story **Age:** P–K

When William takes his first step, he immediately follows it with another . . . and another. He's just like his Teddy Bear—wind him up and off he goes. Children will delight in William's adventures as his newly acquired ability to walk carries him from one humorous situation to another. Graham's colorful cartoon illustrations add to the fun. [3]
FAMILY LIFE
Rev: BKL 6/1/89

399 *Have You Seen My Cat?* Eric Carle. Reprint. Picture Book Studio, 1987. Unp. $14.95. (0-88708-054-5). **Category:** Story **Age:** T–P

Asking a series of strangers if they have seen his cat, a young boy repeatedly rejects a lion, jaguar, cheetah, bobcat, panther, tiger, puma, and Persian by saying, "That's not MY cat." After a worldwide search, a couple in a typical U.S. city park help the boy to find his cat and her new kittens. Illustrations are in Carle's familiar, bright collage style. [2]
CATS
Rev: ESLC

400 *Have You Seen My Duckling?* Nancy Tafuri. Greenwillow Books, 1984. Unp. $13.88. (0-688-02798-9). **Category:** Story **Age:** T–P–K

Mother duck loses her free-spirited eighth offspring to a butterfly chase across the top of the pages. She and the seven other ducklings search the marshlands and their neighbors, while the "lost" duckling remains cleverly camouflaged. Finally found, it rejoins the end of the queue. Vivid two-page spreads with close-ups of pond flora and fauna give a realistic, careful glimpse from a duck's-eye view. [1]

DUCKS; FAMILY LIFE

Rev: BBC; ESLC; NYT   **Awards:** Caldecott Honor Book

401 *Have You Seen My Finger?* Gene Baer. Random House, 1992. Unp. $5.99. (0-679-81382-9).

Category: Participation and manipulation   **Age:** T–P

This board book requires help in telling its story. On each page a finger needs to be poked through a hole to complete the illustration. The finger becomes a chicken's beak, a witch's nose, a boy's tongue, a tortoise's ear, and an elephant's trunk. This one's sure to elicit a "That was fun; let's do it again!"

BOARD BOOKS; PARTICIPATION [2]

402 *Heckedy Peg.* Audrey Wood. Illus. by Don Wood. Narrated by Pauline Brailsford. Random House/Educational Enrichment Materials, n.d. Dist. by American School Publishers. Filmstrip. 10 min. $30.00.

Category: Folklore/Folktales/Fairy tales   **Age:** K

Ignoring their mother's warnings, seven children admit Heckedy Peg into their home and are immediately turned into dishes for the witch's dinner. The Woods' spectacular picture book is skillfully enhanced with English folk music and Brailsford's superb narration (Harcourt, 1987). Accompanied with audiocassette. [1]

FOLK AND FAIRY TALES; WITCHES

Rev: BKL 1/15/90

403 *Hector Protector and As I Went over the Water: Two Nursery Rhymes.* Maurice Sendak. Harper & Row, 1990. Unp. Paper $5.95. (0-06-443237-8).   **Category:** Poetry/Nursery rhymes/Songs   **Age:** P

Delightful, humorous color illustrations highlight two short Mother Goose rhymes, bringing to life the mischief and daring of two young world adventurers. Not even a lion, a snake, or a sea monster can stop these two from accomplishing their feats. [2]

MOTHER GOOSE; NURSERY RHYMES

Rev: NYT

404 ***The Helen Oxenbury Nursery Story Book.*** Retold and illustrated by Helen Oxenbury. Alfred A. Knopf, 1985. 72 pp. $12.99. (0-394-87519-2).

Category: Folklore/Folktales/Fairy tales **Age:** P–K

Oxenbury retells 10 delightful nursery tales, including "Goldilocks," "The Three Little Pigs," and "Henny Penny." Each story is about seven pages long with several bright, full-page, and double-spread illustrations. [2]
FOLK AND FAIRY TALES
Rev: CBK; NYT

405 ***Hello Everybody! Playsongs and Rhymes from a Toddler's World.*** Rachel Buchman. A Gentle Wind, 1986. Audiocassette. 40 min. $7.95.

Category: Poetry/Nursery rhymes/Songs **Age:** T–P

Buchman accompanies herself on guitar as she performs 18 traditional and original songs that will appeal to older children as well as to toddlers, for whom the music is intended. With plenty of repetition, catchy tunes, silliness, and simple lyrics, the songs will keep children singing and laughing for hours. Finger plays and songs appropriate for dramatic play will increase its popularity among caregivers. [2]
CLOTHING; IMAGINATION; SONGS
Rev: BKL 3/15/87; SLJ 9/87
Awards: Booklist's Notable Recordings and Parents' Choice

406 ***Hello Rachel! Hello Children! Songs and Singing Games from the U.S. and Around the World.*** Performed by Rachel Buchman. Rounder Records, 1988. Dist. by Roundup Records. Audiocassette. 38 min. $9.00.

Category: Poetry/Nursery rhymes/Songs **Age:** K

This unique collection of multiethnic folk songs provides musical fun for all children. In this variety of sing-alongs and games, Buchman is expressing the common denominators among children of all cultures: love, humor, music, and the fun of being a child. Singing along in another language, children are able to transcend cultural barriers and see the similarities in their lives. [1]
MUSIC; SONGS

407 ***The Helpful Shoelace.*** Illus. by Pam Adams. Child's Play, 1987. Unp. $7.95. (0-85953-297-6).

Category: Participation and manipulative **Age:** P–K

A spiral-bound participation book about a king's used shoelace that finds its usefulness in helping others. A reader and participant are needed as the shoestring is manipulated in and out of the holes in the pages. The shoestring is threaded through individual pages to simulate a mended archer's bow, a repaired hair ribbon, and a harp string. The book encourages fine motor control and practice of a difficult skill.   [2]
PARTICIPATION; SHOES

408   *Henny Penny.* H. Werner Zimmerman. Scholastic, 1989. 28 pp. $8.95. (0-590-42390-8).   **Category:** Folklore/Folktales/Fairy tales   **Age:** T–P–K

This favorite old tale of the hen and her silly feathered friends is delightfully illustrated with bright watercolors. The tale is true to tradition, but children must follow the pictures to find out the surprise ending. Repetition and humor make this perfect for reading aloud and for beginning readers.   [1]
CHICKENS; FOLK AND FAIRY TALES; FOXES
Rev: BKL 12/15/89

409   *Henry's Awful Mistake.* Robert Quackenbush. Parents Magazine Press, 1980. Unp. $5.95. (0-8193-1040-9).   **Category:** Story   **Age:** P–K

Henry the duck uses wise precautions when trying to rid his house of an ant as he prepares for a guest. However, he forgets to use restraint at times. This humorous story with colorful illustrations will entertain young audiences and offer the opportunity for listeners to predict outcomes. Children will enjoy the bright, colorful illustrations and be able to locate the ant on almost every page.
ANTS; DUCKS; HUMOR   [3]
Rev: SLJ 5/81

410   *Here Are My Hands.* Bill Martin, Jr. and John Archambault. Illus. by Ted Rand. Henry Holt & Co., 1987. 32 pp. $14.95. (0-8050-0328-2).
Category: Concept/Counting/Alphabet   **Age:** T–P–K

Children are encouraged to respond spontaneously to a rhyming text that deals with the parts of the human body. Full-color, up-close, two-page spreads feature children from a variety of cultural backgrounds.   [1]
CONCEPTS; HANDS
Rev: ESLC

411   *Here Comes the Cat!* Frank Asch. Illus. by Vladimir Vagin. Scholastic, 1989. Unp. $11.95. (0-590-41859-9).   **Category:** Story   **Age:** T–P–K

A mouse travels the countryside, shouting warnings of "Here comes the cat!" in both English and Russian to groups of mice on each page. When the cat finally arrives pulling a cartload of cheese, the mice feed him milk and comb his fur. Action-filled pictures showing an unusual friendship will keep children turning pages to find out what the cat is going to do. [1]

CATS; FRIENDSHIP; MICE

412   *Here I Am, an Only Child.* Marlene F. Shyer. Illus. by Donald Carrick. Scribner's, 1985. 32 pp. $12.95. (0-684-18296-3).

Category: Story   **Age:** P–K

The pros and cons of life as an only child are described by a young boy. He would like to have a sibling to share fun times and responsibilities and to blame when things go wrong. Carrick's full-color, double-page illustrations convey a warm and encouraging message to those who share this book. Yes, there are problems, but life as an only child can definitely turn out "a winner."

FAMILY LIFE [2]

Rev: NYT

413   *Here We Go, Parts 1 and 2.* Narrated by Lynn Redgrave. Produced by J. Stein Kaplan. Never a Dull Moment Productions, 1986. Videocassette. 33 min. $29.95.   **Category:** Informational   **Age:** P–K

Young children love vehicles, so they will be happy to climb aboard the variety of British and American conveyances featured in these entertaining trips. Lynn Redgrave introduces and briefly describes the vehicles, but multiethnic children do most of the narration, accompanied by music appropriate to the water, land, and air excursions. Fun armchair travel. [2]

TRAVEL

Rev: BKL 7/89   **Awards:** Parents' Choice Gold Seal Video Award

414   *Herman the Helper.* Robert Kraus. Illus. by Jose Aruego and Ariane Dewey. Simon & Schuster, 1987. Unp. Paper $10.95. (0-671-66270-8).

Category: Story   **Age:** T–P–K

Herman, the well-mannered little boy octopus, helps everyone: friends, parents, enemies, the young, and the old—even himself. Colorful illustrations capture the expressions of all the animals, and Herman's small size makes him identifiable for young children. [2]

HELPFULNESS; OCTOPUSES; SEA AND SEASHORE

Rev: ESLC

415 *Highlights for Children.* Highlights for Children, 1946– . $19.95/yr.

Category: Periodical **Age:** K

Although most of the content is more appropriate for the older youngster, a number of pages are obviously suitable "for wee folks." Picture identification, read-aloud stories, riddles, hidden pictures, matching puzzles, things to make, and pictures drawn by subscribers are found in most issues. A guide for usage by parents and teachers is appended to the table of contents. Eleven issues per year. [1]

CONCEPTS; PUZZLES; READING

Rev: ESLC

416 *Hilary Knight's the Twelve Days of Christmas.* Hilary Knight. Macmillan, 1987. 34 pp. Paper $4.95. (0-689-71150-6).

Category: Poetry/Nursery rhymes/Songs **Age:** P–K

The familiar words of the Christmas song form the backdrop for the story of Benjamin Bear's selecting gifts for his beloved Bedelia. Children will be captivated by the detail in Knight's watercolors as she depicts the bears and their animal friends decorating their farm and woodland homes for Christmas. [3]

CHRISTMAS; HUMOR; SONGS

Rev: BKL 1/1/88

417 *The Hill Farm.* Mark Baker. Pyramid Film & Video, 1989. Videocassette. 18 min. $325.00.

Category: Story **Age:** P–K

The demanding and cyclical routine of daily life on a farm is juxtaposed with poignant intrusions by groups of campers and hunters. The outstanding music and animation combine to captivate viewers from start to finish. [3]

ANIMALS; FARMS

Awards: Academy Award Nomination, 1989

418 *A Hole Is to Dig: A First Book of Definitions.* Ruth Krauss. Illus. by Maurice Sendak. Harper & Row, 1952. Unp. $3.95. (0-06-443205-X).

Category: Concept/Counting/Alphabet **Age:** P–K

"Toes are to wiggle," "dishes are to do," and "rugs are so you don't get splinters in you" in this book of definitions. Sendak's black-and-white line drawings enhance the text with active, happy children. [2]

CONCEPTS; DICTIONARIES; HUMOR

Rev: ESLC; NYT

419   *Holes and Peeks.* Ann Jonas. Greenwillow Books, 1984. Unp. $11.88. (0-688-02538-2).   **Category:** Story **Age:** T–P

An experience with not only how scary certain holes such as toilets and drains can be but also how finding things to look through can be fun. Illustrations are colorful and at the child's eye level.   [2]
FEAR; SIZE
Rev: ESLC; NYT

420   *Holiday Fairy Tales.* Read by Frances Sternhagen and others. Spoken Arts, 1982. Filmstrip. 38 min. $139.95.
                     Category: Folklore/Folktales/Fairy tales **Age:** K

Four wonderfully illustrated, narrated folktales put to music that are exceptionally well done. A clever way to integrate fairy tales into holidays. They include "Rapunzel' (Halloween), "The Shoemaker and the Elves" (Christmas), "Twelve Months" (New Year's), and "The Selfish Giant" (Easter). Contains four filmstrips and audiocassettes with guides.   [3]
FOLK AND FAIRY TALES; HOLIDAYS

421   *Homes.* Jan Pienkowski. Simon & Schuster, 1988. Unp. $2.95. (0-671-70478-8).   **Category:** Concept/Counting/Alphabet **Age:** I–T

From caveman to modern man, from horses to snails, we all have distinctive, unique homes. This brightly colored, simply illustrated, 3-inch-square board book with rounded corners is ideal for small hands. Especially meaningful is the last picture of the planet Earth with the question, "Whose home?"   [1]
BOARD BOOKS; CONCEPTS; HOUSES

422   *Hop on Pop.* Dr. Seuss. Random House, 1987. Unp. Paper $6.95. (0-394-89222-4).   **Category:** Poetry/Nursery rhymes/Songs **Age:** T–P–K

Beginning sight words are used in silly Seuss sentences. Amusing creatures cavort across the pages depicting "ALL FALL. Fall off the wall" and "THING SING. That thing can sing." The nonsense rhymes will work well for beginning readers. Accompanying audiocassette package features both a read-along side for beginning readers and a listening side.   [2]
HUMOR; POETRY
Rev: ESLC

423   *Horton Hears a Who.* Dr. Seuss. Random House, 1954. Unp. $11.99. (0-394-90078-2).   **Category:** Story **Age:** P–K

"A person's a person, no matter how small," says Horton the elephant as he sets about to save the Whos, who live on a tiny dust speck. Since he is the only animal who can hear the inhabitants of Who-ville, the other animals think he is crazy and attempt to put him in a cage while they destroy the speck of dust. A delightful fantasy that children will want to have read over and over again. Also available in other formats from the National Library for the Blind and Physically Handicapped. [1]

HUMOR; KINDNESS; POETRY

Rev: ESLC

424   *Hot Hippo.* Mwenye Hadithi. Illus. by Adrienne Kennaway. Narrated by Terry Alexander. Weston Woods Studios, 1987. Filmstrip. 5 min. $30.00.

Category: Folklore/Folktales/Fairy tales   **Age:** P–K

Ngai, the god of Everything and Everywhere, finally gives Hippo permission to live in the rivers and streams. Hippo promises not to eat Ngai's little fishes and must float to the surface now and then and open his mouth to show Ngai that he has not eaten any fish. The tale explains why hippopotamuses behave the way they do. An audiocassette with script is included. [3]

FOLK AND FAIRY TALES; HIPPOPOTAMUSES

Rev: BKL 5/15/88

425   *Hound and Bear.* Dick Gackenbach. Houghton Mifflin, 1976. Unp. $14.95. (0-8164-3170-1).   **Category:** Story   **Age:** P–K

The tricks Hound plays on his friend Bear always seem to backfire. Hound begins to realize that tricks do not help develop friendships and so changes his ways. The final chapter of this three-chapter story presents Hound giving a surprise gift to Bear and promising, "No more tricks." The monochromatic illustrations seem a bit drab at first but actually lend themselves to the kind of warm story associated with Gackenbach. [2]

BEARS; DOGS; FRIENDSHIP

Rev: ESLC

426   *A House for Hermit Crab.* Eric Carle. Picture Book Studio, 1987. Unp. $15.95. (0-88708-056-1).   **Category:** Story   **Age:** P–K

Bright collages of underwater creatures come to life in this charming story of Hermit Crab. Because he keeps outgrowing his shell, he has to look for another throughout the year. Other small creatures join him in and on his shell house. After a year, Crab must move to a new house, but only after another

crab comes along to take up residence. Carle includes information about hermit crabs, a list of new words, and a calendar. [3]
CRABS; SEA AND SEASHORE
Rev: BKL 5/1/88; CBY-89; ESLC;

427   *How a House Is Built.* Gail Gibbons. Holiday House, 1990. Unp. $13.95. (0-8234-0841-8).   **Category:** Informational   **Age:** P–K
From the architect's plans through the various stages of contracting, Gibbons explains in detail the construction of a house and the roles of those involved in the process. Modern houses of various materials are illustrated at the beginning of the book; shelters used in the past are shown at the end. [1]
CAREERS; HOUSES

428   *How Do I Put It On?* Shigeo Watanabe. Illus. by Yasuo Ohtomo. Philomel, 1977. 28 pp. $10.95. (0-399-20761-9).   **Category:** Story   **Age:** T–P
Humorous, colored pencil drawings illustrate the incorrect and correct ways to wear various articles of clothing. Children will laugh at the "mistakes" of this bear as it learns how to dress itself, finally proclaiming, "I got dressed all by myself." First in the I Can Do It All By Myself series. [3]
BEARS; CLOTHING
Rev: CBK; NYT

429   *How My Parents Learned to Eat.* Ina R. Friedman. Illus. by Allen Say. Houghton Mifflin, 1984. Unp. $12.95. (0-395-35379-3).
Category: Story   **Age:** K
"In our house, some days we eat with chopsticks and some days we eat with knives and forks." To explain this first sentence, a young girl tells, with lots of humor, of the courtship of her American sailor father and her Japanese mother. Also interwoven in the story is additional information on the two cultures. Delightful and informative. [2]
JAPAN; MANNERS
Rev: NYT

430   *How the Camel Got His Hump & How the Rhinoceros Got His Skin.* Rudyard Kipling. Illus. by Tim Raglin. Narrated by Jack Nicholson. Sony Video, 1987. Dist. by Teacher's Discovery. Videocassette. 30 min. $14.95.
Category: Folklore/Folktales/Fairy tales   **Age:** P–K

The voice of Nicholson, the illustrations of Raglin, and the a cappella vocals of Bobby McFerrin truly unite to complement each other while they enchant, entertain, and educate the viewer. "I'm not sure I believe it, but ..." says the narrator. The first story is about a Parsi's revenge on a rhino with no manners. The second is about when the world was new and the camel had no hump but plenty of "excruciating idleness." [2]

CAMELS; FOLK AND FAIRY TALES; RHINOCEROSES

Rev: BKL 2/1/88

431 *How the Grinch Stole Christmas.* Dr. Seuss. Random House, 1957. Unp. $7.99. (0-394-90079-0). **Category:** Story **Age:** P–K

When the Grinch tries to steal Christmas from the town of Who-ville by taking away all the presents, Christmas trees, and decorations, he discovers that, "Maybe Christmas doesn't come from a store. Maybe Christmas perhaps means a little bit more!" In the style that is uniquely Dr. Seuss, this is a Christmas classic. Also available in other formats from the National Library for the Blind and Physically Handicapped. [1]

CHRISTMAS; POETRY

Rev: ESLC; NYT

432 *How You Were Born.* Joanna Cole. Morrow Jr. Books, 1984. 48 pp. $12.95. (0-688-01710-X). **Category:** Informational **Age:** P–K

An easy and good-natured book, this account follows human development from egg cell and life to the birth process and baby. Both artwork and photographs are calm and clear. The writing is quiet and factual. Good answers are available here on demand. [2]

SEX INSTRUCTION

Rev: NYT

433 *Howjadoo.* John McCutcheon. Rounder Records, 1987. Dist. by Roundup Records. Audiocassette. 40 min. $9.98.
Category: Poetry/Nursery rhymes/Songs **Age:** P–K

Performed by John McCutcheon and a chorus of youngsters accompanied by instruments, *Howjadoo* is a listening delight. Original songs like "Howjadoo," "Rubber Blubber Whale," and "Babysitter" will have kids toe tapping and singing along, while "Peanut Butter" will have them eating peanut butter so they can scrape it off the top of their mouth. (A coloring book with lyrics to songs can be ordered for $1.) [2]

Music; Songs

Rev: SLJ 4/87 **Awards:** ALSC Notable Recording

434 *Hugs and Kisses.* Kathy Hirsh-Pasek and Mona Goldman Zakheim. Kamotion, 1990. Dist. by Special Things Distributing. Audiocassette. 33 min. $8.98. **Category:** Poetry/Nursery rhymes/Songs **Age:** P–K

Real-life experiences are addressed in this cassette of songs for children. Both children and adults sing songs about subjects such as boo-boos, cleaning up messes, lost mittens, eating a cookie, and being sorry. Simply orchestrated songs with well-defined rhythms and simple refrains present instructional as well as informational observations about activities and feelings in a young child's life. [3]

Songs

435 *Humphrey's Bear.* Jan Wahl. Illus. by William Joyce. Henry Holt & Co., 1987. Unp. $12.95. (0-8050-0332-0). **Category:** Story **Age:** K

Feeling threatened that his father might take his toy bear away from him, Humphrey dreams of going to sea with his bear. When he awakens, he is in his bedroom. His father stands nearby holding bear—once his own bear. He shares with Humphrey that he and bear had gone on the same adventure. Dreamlike illustrations contribute to this warm, reassuring story. Also available in other formats from the National Library for the Blind and Physically Handicapped. [2]

Bedtime; Teddy bears

Rev: CBY-88; NYT

436 *Humpty Dumpty's Magazine.* Children's Better Health Institute, 1952– $11.95/yr. **Category:** Periodical **Age:** P–K

Read-alouds, completion activities, simple rebus stories, hidden-picture games, dot-to-dots, poetry, and attractive color as well as black-and-white drawings are included in this health-oriented magazine. A balance between what the adult must share and what the child completes alone is present in each issue. Eight issues per year. [2]

Games; Health; Reading

Rev: ESLC

437 *Hurray for Captain Janel And Other Liberated Stories for Children.* Read by Tammy Grimes. Harper Audio, 1976. Audiocassette. 57 min. $9.95.

Category: Story   **Age:** K

Ten nonsexist stories, including "Hurray for Captain Jane," "Emily and the Klunky Baby and the Next-Door Dog," and "Ira Sleeps Over." Grimes's voice is perfect for these funny and sensitive stories.   [1]

SELF-CONCEPT

Rev: ESLC

438 *Hush, Little Baby.* Margot Zemach. Reprint. Dutton, 1987. Unp. $11.95. (0-525-44296-0).   **Category:** Poetry/Nursery rhymes/Songs   **Age:** I–T–P

Hilarious color tempera illustrations add zest to this chaotic portrayal of a squalling baby who is promised a strange assortment of items, from a mockingbird to a horse and cart—all just to stop crying. Musical notes for the song are included.   [3]

BABIES; SONGS

Rev: CBK; CBY-88

439 *I Am Not a Crybaby!* Norma Simon. Illus. by Helen Cogancherry. Albert Whitman & Co., 1989. Unp. $12.95. (0-8075-3447-1).

Category: Informational   **Age:** P–K

A variety of child narrators present situations in which they were physically and emotionally hurt: a broken leg, being called fat, parents fighting, a pet dying. Some situations show a child being brave and not crying; others show happy tears. One child mentions, "Everyone feels like crying sometimes." Realistic color illustrations depicting many different children and families further support the comforting message.   [2]

SADNESS

Rev: BKL 4/15/89

440 *I Can't Get My Turtle to Move.* Elizabeth Lee O'Donnell. Illus. by Maxie Chambliss. Morrow Jr. Books, 1989. 32 pp. $11.88. (0-688-07324-7).

Category: Concept/Counting/Alphabet   **Age:** T–P

Charming groups of busy animals and insects demonstrate the concept of counting from one to 10. The one turtle will not budge, and little ones will enjoy repeating on every page, "But I can't get my turtle to move." At the end of the story, the promise of lunch brings the turtle out of his shell.   [2]

CONCEPTS; TURTLES

Rev: CBY-90

441 *I Can't Sleep.* Philippe Dupasquier. Orchard Books, 1990. Unp. $13.95.
(0-531-08474-4). **Category:** Wordless **Age:** P–K

When Dad, then the kids, and finally Mom (and even the cat) can't sleep, it
provides an excuse for a midnight feast and stargazing fest. Just when Mom
and Dad think everyone is tucked back into bed, here come the kids (and the
cat) to pile into their big bed for a late sleep-in the next morning. [1]
NIGHT; SLEEP; WORDLESS

442 *I Forgot.* Sucie Stevenson. Orchard Books, 1988. Unp. $11.95. (0-531-
08344-6). **Category:** Story **Age:** P

Arthur Platypus has terrible trouble remembering everything, from where his
lunchbox is to the names of the oceans. He never seems to know the things he
just learned for school, and all kinds of reminder systems have failed. Just
when it looks hopeless, Arthur remembers his mother's birthday. The story is
involving; the forgotten things realistic. Children will enjoy the way Arthur
remembers the really important things in the end. [3]
BIRTHDAYS; FORGETFULNESS; PLATYPUS
Rev: BKL 2/15/88; SLJ 5/88

443 *I Had a Friend Named Peter: Talking to Children About the Death of a
Friend.* Janice Cohn. Illus. by Gail Owens. Morrow Jr. Books, 1987. Unp.
$13.00. (0-688-06685-2). **Category:** Informational **Age:** P–K

Beginning with a five-page introduction for adults on how to discuss death
with children, the story deals with the death of a nursery school boy named
Peter who was killed by a car. His playmate Betsy is trying to understand and
cope with this loss. May be shared by parents and children to help them deal
with a difficult time. [3]
DEATH
Rev: NYT

444 *I Have a Friend.* Keiko Narahashi. Margaret K. McElderry Books, 1987.
Unp. $12.95. (0-689-50432-2).
Category: Story **Age:** P–K

A little boy tells about his shadow and what they do together. The clear, colorful watercolor illustrations complement the text and help convey the basic scientific concept of shadows to the young child. [2]
BOYS; CONCEPTS; SHADOWS
Rev: CBY-88; ESLC

445 *I Have a Friend.* Keiko Narahashi. Narrated by Colin Carman. Random House/Educational Enrichment Materials, 1989. Dist. by American School Publishers. Filmstrip. 8 min. $30.00.

Category: Story **Age:** P–K

What friend is sometimes short and fat, sometimes tall enough to reach treetops, and almost always there? Narahashi's delightful watercolor illustrations and Arthur Custer's original score explore the very special relationship of a young boy and his shadow. Accompanied by an audiocassette. [2]
BOYS; CONCEPTS; SHADOWS
Rev: BKL 1/15/90

446 *I Hear.* Rachel Isadora. Greenwillow Books, 1985. Unp. $11.88. (0-688-04062-4).

Category: Story **Age:** I–T

In a simple, enlarged text, Isadora presents a combination of word and sound associations for a very young child to share with adults. Watercolor illustrations provide soft visuals with which a youngster can easily identify, as well as a background for language experiences and development for the child just learning to talk. [1]
BABIES; HEARING
Rev: BBC

447 *I Know a Lady.* Charlotte Zolotow. Illus. by James Stevenson. Greenwillow Books, 1984. Unp. $11.88. (0-688-03838-7).

Category: Story **Age:** P–K

A little girl describes the loving relationship between an older lady and the neighborhood children. Through all the seasons, the lady finds ways to share her love. Whether it is by sharing flowers from her garden, treats on Halloween and Christmas, or just smiles, the love between the old and the young jumps off the pages. Illustrations have a small-town, New England feel. A perfect book for sharing. [3]
FRIENDSHIP; LOVE; OLD AGE
Rev: CBK; NYT

448 *I Like Books.* Anthony Browne. Alfred A. Knopf, 1988. Unp. $10.99. (0-394-94186-1).

Category: Concept/Counting/Alphabet **Age:** T–P

Simple, colorful illustrations of an endearing chimpanzee introduce the youngest child to the world of print. A celebration of reading, Browne's work invites children to enjoy and explore funny books, scary books, fairy tales, and an array of other interesting subjects. Certain to inspire beginning readers from toddlerhood through the preschool years, this title whets the appetite for more books. [2]
CHIMPANZEES; CONCEPTS; READING
Rev: BKL 8/89; CBY-90

449 *I Like Dessert.* David S. Polansky. Great American Music, 1987. Audiocassette. 31 min. $10.95.

Category: Poetry/Nursery rhymes/Songs   **Age:** P–K

Children who enjoy music will immediately swing and dance to the songs of Polansky. The theme song, "I Like Dessert," is only one of the sweets served to listeners. Going to school, being different, dealing with bullies and anger, and the end of the day are all subjects covered in this smorgasbord of rhythms and lyrics. Clever lyrics are performed by children as well as adults. Lyrics included.   [1]

SONGS

Rev: BKL 2/15/88

450 *I Like to Be Little.* Charlotte Zolotow. Illus. by Erik Blegvad. Thomas Y. Crowell, 1987. 32 pp. $11.89. (0-690-04674-X).

Category: Story   **Age:** P–K

A little girl enumerates to her mother all the reasons she likes to be little: jumping in the leaf piles in autumn, making a house under the dining room table, eating the first snow as it falls, etc. Soft watercolors extend the warmth of this gentle and loving story.   [3]

GIRLS; GROWTH

Rev: ESLC

451 *I Love You, Mouse.* John Graham. Illus. by Tomie dePaola. Harcourt Brace Jovanovich, 1976. Unp. $12.95. (0-15-238005-1).

Category: Story   **Age:** P–K

A young boy greets a variety of animals, including a mouse, dog, pig, chicken, sheep, bear, frog, duck, goose, rabbit, and owl. As the boy tells each animal how he would care for it, the reader/listener receives information about the creature: its habitat, its food, and one other characteristic. This predictable book would be useful in teaching about animals and/or discussing father-son relationships.   [2]

ANIMALS; IMAGINATION

Rev: ESLC

452 *I Wanna Tickle the Fish.* Sung by Lisa Atkinson. A Gentle Wind, 1987. Audiocassette. 30 min. $7.95.

Category: Poetry/Nursery rhymes/Songs   **Age:** T–P–K

A collection of original songs by Lisa Atkinson presents lighthearted tunes that address the importance of self-esteem and positive values. Through a variety of music, including a waltz and a marching song, this piece proves delightfully entertaining. The title song suggests that adults might learn how to relax if they observed children. [2]

SELF-CONCEPT; SONGS

Rev: BKL 6/15/88 **Awards:** Parents' Choice Award

453 *I Was So Mad!* Norma Simon. Illus. by Dora Leder. Albert Whitman & Co., 1974. Unp. $10.95. (0-8075-3520-6).

Category: Informational **Age:** P–K

Eighteen vignettes provide different scenarios exploring anger, such as anger resulting from frustration while learning new things, having to come in from playing, being teased, being scared, etc. The author stresses that, although some things in life just make you mad, being mad is not being bad. [1]

ANGER; EMOTIONS

Rev: CBK

454 *I Went Walking.* Sue Williams. Illus. by Julie Vivas. Harcourt Brace Jovanovich, 1990. 32 pp. $13.95. (0-15-200471-8).

Category: Concept/Counting/Alphabet **Age:** I–T–P

The simple repetitive phrases "I went walking" and "What did you see?" set the framework for this predictable story. A variety of farm animals are discovered by the disheveled boy. Large, bold, color illustrations are placed on a stark white background. The predictive nature of the question-and-answer format and the action-packed illustrations provide the reader and listener with a fun-for-all experience. [1]

ANIMALS; CONCEPTS; WALKING

Rev: BKL 9/1/90; HB 11/12/90; SLJ 10/90

455 *I Wish Daddy Didn't Drink So Much.* Judith Vigna. Albert Whitman & Co., 1988. Unp. $12.95. (0-8075-3523-0).

Category: Informational **Age:** P–K

A sensitive and caring story of how the disease of alcoholism affects every member of a family. For Christmas, Lisa's father gives her a beautiful sled and a broken promise. Anger, arguments, disappointment, and distrust are touched upon. Stressed are the facts that alcoholism cannot be cured but that no one is alone, that there is support. [3]

ALCOHOLISM; DISEASE; FAMILY LIFE

Rev: BKL 10/1/88; ESLC

456 *If I Had a Pig.* Mick Inkpen. Little, Brown & Co., 1988. Unp. $7.95. (0-316-41887-0).   **Category:** Story   **Age:** T–P

What would this little boy do if he had a pig to call his own? Well, there is no end to the fun they'd have. Painting pictures, hide-and-seek, staying in the tub until they were wrinkly, puddle walking, and bedtime stories are just the beginning of the good times and close friendship he and his porcine pal would share.   [2]

PETS; PIGS

Rev: BKL 1/1/89

457 *If I Ran the Circus.* Dr. Seuss. Random House, 1956. Unp. $9.95. (0-394-80080-X).   **Category:** Story   **Age:** P–K

Narrating in nonsense verse, a young boy named Morris McGurk imagines what could happen if he ran a circus behind Mr. Sneelock's store. The rhyming text has strong ear appeal and will delight children whose language development is just beginning. Typical of the author's writing, this is a challenging read-aloud book.   [2]

CIRCUS; POETRY

Rev: ESLC

458 *If I Were a Penguin . . . .* Heidi Goennel. Little, Brown & Co., 1989. Unp. $14.95. (0-316-31841-8).   **Category:** Story   **Age:** T–P

Simple, large, bright pictures rendered in bold colors highlight a story about a child imagining being a series of animals. The words are few and printed in large type. Via large pages and strong illustrations, this pattern story lends itself to sharing with a group of youngsters. After considering the options of being creatures ranging from penguins to camels, the narrator decides, "Mostly I'm happy just to be me."   [2]

ANIMALS; SELF-CONCEPT

Rev: BKL 4/1/89

459 *If You Give a Mouse a Cookie.* Laura Joffe Numeroff. Illus. by Felicia Bond. Harper & Row, 1985. 32 pp. $11.89. (0-06-024587-5).

Category: Story   **Age:** P–K

One thing leads to another in this highly amusing tale. A young boy is kept busy fulfilling the numerous requests of a visiting mouse. The chain of events comes full circle, to the delight of the reader. Large, colorful illustrations add detail to the antics and enhance the humor of the story, making it a favorite

with children of all ages. Also available in other formats from the National Library for the Blind and Physically Handicapped. Equally enjoyable and appropriate for these ages is the Numeroff and Bond book titled *If You Give a Moose a Muffin* (HarperCollins, 1991). [1]
KINDNESS; MICE
Rev: CBK

460 *I'll Always Love You.* Hans Wilhelm. Crown, 1985. Unp. $11.95. (0-517-57759-3). **Category:** Story **Age:** P–K

A boy and his beloved dog grow up together. When the dog grows old and finally dies, the boy mourns his terrible loss but finds comfort in the fact that he never forgot to tell the dog every night, "I'll always love you." A beautiful story, with humor as well as a serious message about the power of saying the words, "I love you." [1]
DEATH; DOGS; LOVE
Rev: ESLC

461 *I'll Try.* Karen Erickson. Illus. by Maureen Roffey. Viking Penguin, 1987. Unp. $4.95. (0-670-81572-1).
Category: Concept/Counting/Alphabet **Age:** T–P

Learning to clothe oneself can be a very "trying" experience, but with patience and practice it can be mastered. A simple text and delightfully simple illustrations make this an ideal selection for the toddler struggling to endure the process. [3]
CLOTHING; CONCEPTS
Rev: BKL 8/87; CBY-88; SLJ 6/88

462 *I'm a Little Mouse: A Touch & Feel Book.* Noelle Carter and David Carter. Henry Holt & Co., 1990. Unp. $10.95. (0-8050-1420-9).
Category: Participation and manipulative **Age:** T–P

Little Mouse is soft and fuzzy and encounters many friends of different textures before he finds his equally soft, fuzzy mother mouse. Animal choices—shaggy bear, slippery fish, scaly snake, and bumpy turtle—provide a wide visual range as well as delightful tactile experiences. Sure to be a well-loved book.
ANIMALS; PARTICIPATION; TOUCHING [1]

463 *I'm Busy, Too.* Norma Simon. Illus. by Dora Leder. Albert Whitman & Co., 1980. Unp. $10.95. (0-8075-3464-1). **Category:** Story **Age:** P

Three preschool children are shown during a typical day at a center while their parents go off to work. Each comes from a very different but loving family. The day begins with each family's morning routine, continues with their work activities, and concludes with the evening, which is a time for caring and sharing the day's events with other family members before going to bed for the night. [3]

DAY CARE CENTERS; FAMILY LIFE; PLAY

Rev: ESLC

---

464 *I'm Just a Kid.* Performed by Rory. Roar Music, 1988. Dist. by Alcazar Records. Audiocassette. 30 min. $9.98.

Category: Poetry/Nursery rhymes/Songs **Age:** P–K

Ten catchy tunes cover diverse categories such as rainy days, bubble baths, conducting a band, and friends. A particularly fun song, sure to be loved by parents and children, is one called "You're Drivin' Me Crazy!" sung from both the parent's and child's point of view. Several of these tunes will become sing-along favorites, and with the lyrics enclosed for these original tunes, it will be easy for the child to join in. [2]

EMOTIONS; MUSIC; SONGS

Rev: BKL 2/15/89

---

465 *I'm Not Moving, Mama!* Nancy White Carlstrom. Illus. by Thor Wickstrom. Macmillan, 1990. Unp. $13.95. (0-02-717286-4).

Category: Story **Age:** P–K

As Mother packs little mouse's favorite things, he declares he is not moving, remembering his favorite places in and around the old house. Mother explains and cajoles little mouse, but he is not convinced until she tells him that they would not be able to live in the new place without him. A child's fear and regrets about moving are beautifully portrayed, using cartoon-style mouse characters in colorful framed illustrations. [3]

MOTHERS; MOVING

---

466 *I'm Terrific.* Marjorie W. Sharmat. Illus. by Kay Chorao. Holiday House, 1977. Unp. $12.95. (0-8234-0282-7). **Category:** Story **Age:** K

Jason Everett Bear has an ego problem and consequently is losing friends quickly. His mother helps him through a period of figuring out who he is, so

Jason not only ends up liking himself better, but he also makes a new friend in the process. [2]

ANIMALS; BEARS; SELF-CONCEPT

Rev: NYT

---

467 *I'm Wonderful! (Fun Dance Kids Video).* Directed by Jack Hunter. Peg Emerson for WGTE Toledo Public TV, 1988. Dist. by Family Express Video. Videocassette. 30 min. $14.95.

Category: Participation and manipulative **Age:** T–P

Owen Anderson, the host, takes the viewer through facial aerobics, physical storytelling involving the whole body, shadow puppets, and much more. His talent as a mime will captivate, amuse, and entertain. An invitation by the presenter for the child to participate will entice the child to see the program again and again. [1]

ENTERTAINMENT; EXERCISE

Rev: BKL 2/1/89

---

468 *Imagine Yourself to Sleep: A Getting to Sleep Tape for Kids.* Bett L. Sanders and Chuck Cummings. Audio Outings, 1988. Audiocassette. 60 min. $9.98. **Category:** Poetry/Nursery rhymes/Songs **Age:** K

Soft narrator voices and bird songs on side one and a bouncing ball on side two create a soothing, hypnotic effect. The last segments of both sides offer woodland sounds or ocean waves with no verbal interruption. This presentation should calm the child (and the tense adult), inducing relaxation and rest. [2]

SLEEP; SOUNDS

Rev: SLJ 7/89

---

469 *Imogene's Antlers.* David Small. Crown, 1985. Unp. $10.95. (0-517-55564-6). **Category:** Story **Age:** P–K

Imogene wakes up to find antlers growing out of her head. Even though her mother keeps fainting at the sight of them, they do have some usefulness. The next morning, Imogene awakens, minus antlers, but. . . . A fun book, from its beginning to its surprise ending. [1]

ANIMALS; HUMOR

Rev: ESLC **Awards:** Reading Rainbow Book; Parent's Choice Award

---

470 *The Important Book.* Margaret Wise Brown. Illus. by Leonard Weisgard. Harper & Row, 1949. Unp. $11.89. (0-06-020721-3).

Category: Concept/Counting/Alphabet **Age:** P

This 1949 classic lists the qualities of things from spoons to shoes: how they look, feel, and taste—supported by simple illustrations. The book culminates in affirming the importance of the young listener. Children may be stimulated to develop observations of familiar objects in their own world of experiences.
CONCEPTS; SELF-CONCEPT   [1]
Rev: CBK; ESLC

471   In Our House. Anne Rockwell. Thomas Y. Crowell, 1985. Unp. $11.89. (0-690-04488-7).   **Category:** Story   **Age:** P–K

Baby Bear proudly takes the viewer on a tour of his house. Rockwell first presents each room in a large double spread. The next double spread comprises smaller pictures of many activities that take place in each, with short captions. We travel from living room to basement to attic, with a stop in Baby Bear's room. Children will linger in each room, examining many possibilities for activities offered by the items shown.   [2]
BEARS; CONCEPTS; HOUSES
Rev: ESLC; CBK

472   In the Desert (Series: Nature's Footprints). Q. L. Pearce and W. J. Pearce. Illus. by Delana Bettoli. Silver Press/Silver Burdett Press, 1990. Unp. $8.98. (0-671-68825-1).   **Category:** Informational   **Age:** P–K

Pairs of animals depicted in their native habitat are described. Detailed color illustrations, paired with individual footprints, are excellent for sharpening observation skills in this version of hide-and-seek. Ten animals are featured in each book.   [1]
ANIMALS; DESERT; NATURE

473   In the Hospital: A Guide for Parents, Nurses and Others Who Care. Peter Alsop and Bill Harley. Moose School Records, 1989. Audiocassette. 53 min. $8.98.   **Category:** Informational   **Age:** K

Humorous and touching stories and songs for and about children in the hospital. Covers sensitive issues to help adults and children communicate more openly. Produced by two nationally known, award-winning singers/songwriters/storytellers. Accompanying book contains all words and lyrics plus notes and suggestions to parents and other caregivers.   [2]
HOSPITALS
Awards: Parents' Choice Award

474 *In the Middle of the Night.* Kathy Henderson. Illus. by Jennifer Eachus. Macmillan, 1992. Unp. $13.95. (0-02-743545-8).

Category: Story **Age:** P–K

When night comes and most people are at home asleep, there is still much activity in the city. This poem tells of several people who work through the night in a bakery, observatory, hospital, post office, train, and office. [2]
CITIES AND TOWNS; NIGHT

475 *In the Night Kitchen.* Maurice Sendak. Harper & Row, 1970. Unp. $14.89. (0-06-025490-4). **Category:** Story **Age:** P–K

Characters reminiscent of Abbott and Costello blend with limited text to relate this tale about toddler Mickey, who, upon hearing a noise in the night, falls out of his clothes and into a dream about the night kitchen. Smaller-than-life Mickey refuses to be the milk in the batter and, while the cake is baking, hops out of it and the oven. After some exciting events, by morning he eventually completes his task and his dream. [1]
COOKING; DREAMS; IMAGINATION
Rev: BBC; CBK; NYT
Awards: Caldecott Honor Book; NYT Best Illustrated Book

476 *In the Night Kitchen.* Maurice Sendak. Narrated by Peter Schickele. Weston Woods Studios, 1987. Videocassette. 6 min. $100.00.

Category: Story **Age:** P–K

Mickey, a young boy, travels in the night to a bakery where he assists the bakers in the making of a cake. The use of vivid animation, lively music and song, and captivating narration brings to life Maurice Sendak's Caldecott Honor Book (Harper & Row, 1970). [1]
COOKING; DREAMS; IMAGINATION
Rev: SLJ 4/89 **Awards:** ALSC Notable Film/Video

477 *In the Tall, Tall Grass.* Denise Fleming. Henry Holt & Co., 1991. Unp. $15.95. (0-8050-1635-X). **Category:** Story **Age:** T–P

Using a unique style of illustration (pouring colored cotton pulp through hand-cut stencils), the artist/author shows creatures coming to life in the grass as they munch, dart, dip, strum, and drum through the progress of the day. Children will enjoy the sounds the words make as well as the way in which these words literally move across the page. Good for sharing. [1]
ANIMALS

478 *Ira Sleeps Over.* Bernard Waber. Houghton Mifflin, 1972. 48 pp. $13.95. (0-395-13893-0). **Category:** Story **Age:** P–K

Ira is invited to sleep over at a friend's house, and his big decision is whether or not he should take his teddy bear with him. When he finds out that he is not the only person who sleeps with a bear, he feels much better about his attachment. The conversation between the two boys is realistic and memorable. Also available in other formats from the National Library for the Blind and Physically Handicapped. [1]

SLEEP; FRIENDSHIP; TEDDY BEARS

Rev: BBC; CBK; NYT

479 *Ira Sleeps Over.* Bernard Waber. Live Oak Media, 1987. Videocassette. 14 min. $34.95. **Category:** Story **Age:** P–K

Ira is invited to sleep at a friend's house for the very first time. Does he take his teddy bear to sleep with or not? He eventually discovers that his friend Reggie has the same question. This is a good discussion starter on peer pressure for youngsters. The use of Waber's illustrations in the video makes this an appropriate supplement to the book (Houghton Mifflin, 1972). [2]

FRIENDSHIP; SLEEP; TEDDY BEARS

480 *Is Anybody Up?* Ellen Kandoian. Putnam, 1989. Unp. $14.95. (0-399-21749-5). **Category:** Concept/Counting/Alphabet **Age:** P–K

A complement to the many bedtime books available, this wake-up-time book shows breakfast rituals for children in the Eastern Time zone from Buffin Bay to Antarctica. Children, adults, and animals awaken, greet, and eat to start the new day. Soft watercolors are highlighted with ink. [2]

CONCEPTS; FOOD; MORNING

Rev: BKL 11/15/89

481 *Is It Red? Is It Yellow? Is It Blue?* Tana Hoban. Greenwillow Books, 1978. 32 pp. $13.88. (0-688-84171-6). **Category:** Concept/Counting/Alphabet **Age:** I–T–P

Handsome photographs introduce the primary colors to young children. Shape and space perception seem simple with Hoban's everyday objects. This multiethnic book can be used both by adults to introduce objects and by older children as a basis for creating stories. [1]

COLOR; CONCEPTS

482 *Is It Rough? Is It Smooth? Is It Shiny?* Tana Hoban. Greenwillow Books, 1984. Unp. $13.88. (0-688-03824-7). **Category:** Wordless **Age:** K

Color photographs of objects such as coins, cotton plants, and crumpled cans wordlessly invite the reader to consider textures. Is the object rough, or smooth, or shiny, or something else? Photos are large enough to share with a group, and they could easily engage young thinkers. [1]
SENSORY; WORDLESS
Rev: ESLC

483 *Is This a House for Hermit Crab?* Megan McDonald. Illus. by S.D. Schindler. Orchard Books, 1990. Unp. $14.99. (0-531-08455-8).

Category: Informational **Age:** P–K

After outgrowing his old shell, a hermit crab goes looking for a new one. Investigating several possibilities, the crab ultimately finds the perfect new home while eluding his enemy, the pricklepine fish. The crab moves almost lyrically across the beach ("scritch-scratch, scritch-scratch") on sand and watercolored pages. This is an excellent read-aloud book. [2]
CRABS
Rev: BKL 3/1/90

484 *It Could Always Be Worse: A Yiddish Folk Tale.* Margot Zemach. Farrar, Straus & Giroux, 1976. Unp. $11.95. (0-374-33650-4).

Category: Folklore/Folktales/Fairy tales **Age:** P–K

The old adage "count your blessings" is illustrated in this classic Jewish folktale. A poor villager, frustrated with his noisy crowded house, asks the rabbi for advice. The advice is to take the barnyard animals into the house. The resulting calamity shows the villager that things really weren't that bad before. Amusing earthtone drawings enliven the story's theme of hilarious chaos and portray a culture both humble and strong. [2]
FOLK AND FAIRY TALES; NOISE; SOUNDS
Rev: CBK; NYT **Awards:** Caldecott Honor Book

485 *It Does Not Say Meow: And Other Animal Riddle Rhymes.* Beatrice S. De Regniers. Illus. by Paul Galdone. Houghton Mifflin, 1972. Unp. $12.95. (0-395-28822-3). **Category:** Story **Age:** P–K

The rhyming text provides clues to an animal on one page, while the next shows a picture of the animal with its name in large print. A delightful way to share the book would be to read a clue to the young child before revealing the answer on the following page. [2]
ANIMALS; POETRY; RIDDLES
Rev: CBK; ESLC; NYT

486 *It Looked Like Spilt Milk.* Charles G. Shaw. Harper & Row, 1988. Unp. $11.89. (0-06-025565-X). **Category:** Story **Age:** P–K

Different things look like spilt milk but aren't. The simple story line will entice children to participate in this predictable book and will encourage the user to "read" along to discover "it" is a cloud. The pages are all dark blue, with white for the lettering and the clouds. [1]
CLOUDS; IMAGINATION
Rev: CBK

487 *It's Mine!* Illus. by Leo Lionni. Random House/Miller-Brody, 1987. Dist. by American School Publishers. Filmstrip. 4 min. $25.00.
Category: Story **Age:** P–K

Frogs Lydia, Rupert, and Milton argue selfishly over ownership of "their" air, earth, and water, until a fierce storm and a neighboring toad teach them the value of "ours." A skillful adaptation of the book (Knopf, 1986), the story conveys an ageless lesson for all. Insert material also includes an audiocassette and a guide with related science, art, and guidance activities. [3]
FABLES; FROGS; SHARING
Rev: BKL 6/1/88

488 *It's Mine! A Fable.* Leo Lionni. Alfred A. Knopf, 1986. Unp. $14.95. (0-394-97000-4). **Category:** Story **Age:** P–K

Illustrated in his familiar style of brightly distinct colors, this modern-day fable points out how difficult times and near-tragedies can erase individual differences and draw "people" together. Three quarreling frogs each maintain a selfish claim to all they encounter, until a violent storm pushes them together for survival. Good potential for discussion. A story to be enjoyed on multiple levels. Also available in other formats from the National Library for the Blind and Physically Handicapped. [2]
FABLES; FRIENDSHIP; FROGS; SHARING
Rev: CBY-87; ESLC

489 *Jack and the Beanstalk.* Retold and illustrated by John Howe. Little, Brown & Co., 1989. Unp. $14.95. (0-316-37579-9).
Category: Folklore/Folktales/Fairy tales **Age:** K

The universal theme of man's struggle to survive and his ability to overcome obstacles is captured in this favorite story about Jack climbing up the beanstalk and confronting a giant. Howe's austere, formal narrative coupled with the unique perspective of his paintings—a swaying beanstalk suspended high in the clouds and a fearsome giant who fills the page—makes this a welcome addition to any folktale collection. [2]

FOLK AND FAIRY TALES; GIANTS

Rev: BKL 10/15/89

490　*Jack Goes to the Beach.* Jill Krementz. Random House, 1986. Unp. Paper $3.95. (0-394-88001-3).　　**Category:** Story　**Age:** T

A photographic board book depicting toddler Jack's and his family's day at the beach. Activities are family centered and show Jack and Dad swimming, looking for sand treasures, building sand castles, fishing, and flying kites. Crisp, clear photos present a satisfying and realistic look at a warm-weather excursion. [3]

BOARD BOOKS; FAMILY LIFE; SEA AND SEASHORE

Rev: CBY-87

491　*Jacket I Wear in the Snow.* Shirley Nietzel. Illus. by Nancy Winslow Parker. Greenwillow Books, 1989. 32 pp. $12.88. (0-688-08030-8).

Category: Story　**Age:** T–P–K

A playful rebus-cumulative tale in which a young girl names all the items of clothing she must wear in the snow, including the zipper, which is stuck. Each piece of clothing is accompanied by a childlike complaint such as "This is the long underwear, bunchy and hot." Children will nod their head in recognition at this familiar situation, and they will sigh with relief at its satisfying ending: Mother comes to the rescue. [1]

REBUSES; CLOTHING; SNOW

Rev: BKL 9/1/89; CBY-90

492　*Jackie Torrence: Brer Rabbit Stories (The Storytelling Circle Series).* Told by Jackie Torrence. Weston Woods Studios, 1984. Audiocassette. 35 min. $9.00.　**Category:** Folklore/Folktales/Fairy tales　**Age:** P–K

Brer Rabbit is up to his usual tricks in this collection of five traditional Uncle Remus tales, including "Wonderful Tar Baby." Told in black dialect, Jackie Torrence's versions of the stories are captivating and humorous. [1]

ANIMALS; FOLK AND FAIRY TALES; RABBITS

Rev: SLJ 4/87　**Awards:** ALSC Notable Recording

493 *Jamaica's Find.* Juanita Havill. Illus. by Anne S. O'Brien. Houghton Mifflin, 1986. Unp. $12.95. (0-395-39376-0). **Category:** Story **Age:** P–K

Jamaica finds a stuffed animal at the park and struggles with keeping it or turning it in to the "Lost and Found." She finally decides to turn it in, meets the owner, and makes a friend. Outstanding watercolor illustrations enhance this story of developing self-honesty. [3]

AFRO-AMERICANS; GIRLS; HONESTY

Rev: CBY-87 **Awards:** Reading Rainbow Book; Ezra Keats New Writer Award

494 *Jamberry.* Bruce Degen. Harper & Row, 1983. Unp. $12.89. (0-06-021417-1). **Category:** Poetry/Nursery rhymes/Songs **Age:** T–P–K

Starting out simply enough with "One berry, Two berry, Pick me a blueberry" until rockets are bursting in a "cloudberry sky," a bear and a young boy romp through a fantasy world filled with berries of all kinds. Jamberry is a joyous, exuberant, poetic celebration that rolls deliciously off the lips. Drawings are just as lively and imaginative, with clever details like trees with leaves shaped like slices of bread. [3]

BEARS; FOOD; FRUIT; NURSERY RHYMES

Rev: BBC; CBK; ESLC; PP

495 *Jambo Means Hello: Swahili Alphabet Book.* Muriel Feelings. Illus. by Tom Feelings. Dial, 1974. 56 pp. $13.89. (0-8037-4350-5). **Category:** Concept/Counting/Alphabet **Age:** K

Using the standard English alphabet, Feelings offers examples of Swahili words, many within a young child's experience: baba (father), chakula (food), tembo (elephant). A short definition of each word is given along with a phonetic spelling of the proper pronunciation. Feelings presents East African scenes with authenticity and accuracy, using black ink and white tempera, which lend a soft yet solid sense to the figures. [2]

AFRICA; ALPHABET

Rev: NYT

496 *James Marshall's Mother Goose.* Illus. by James Marshall. Farrar, Straus & Giroux, 1979. 40 pp. $12.95. (0-374-33653-9). **Category:** Poetry/Nursery rhymes/Songs **Age:** T–P–K

Marshall has selected for this Mother Goose collection only those rhymes that appeal to his sense of humor: some are among the most popular verses; others are not so well-known. The classic characters—Old King Cole, Jack Sprat, etc.

—cavort through the whimsically illustrated pages. Marshall's unique comic style is perfectly suited to the simple, nonsensical rhymes. [3]
MOTHER GOOSE; NURSERY RHYMES
Rev: NYT

497 *Jen the Hen.* Colin and Jacqui Hawkins. Illus. by Colin Hawkins. Putnam, 1985. Unp. $8.95. (0-399-21207-8). **Category:** Story **Age:** K

A nonsensical story about how Jen the hen wrote a letter to Ken and Ben, the garden men. Rhyming words run through the book, which shows the ending (-en) of a word and how changing the beginning letter forms a new word: hen, den, men, and so on. The rhyming words are presented by characters talking in rhyme. Printed on heavy stock to allow pages to be turned easily. [2]
CHICKENS
Rev: BBC

498 *Jesse Bear, What Will You Wear?* Nancy White Carlstrom. Illus. by Bruce Degen. Macmillan, 1986. 32 pp. $12.95. (0-02-717350-X).
Category: Story **Age:** T–P–K

A delightful story in rhyme about Jesse Bear, who, during the course of his day, experiences "pants that dance," "sun on the run," "sand on my hand," and his chair, "cause (he's) stuck there." The pen and ink drawings along with watercolor illustrations are detailed and appealing. [1]
BEARS; FAMILY LIFE
Rev: BBC; CBK; ESLC; NYT; PP

499 *Johnny Appleseed.* Retold by Steven Kellogg. Morrow Jr. Books, 1988. Unp. $18.50. (0-688-06417-5). **Category:** Informational **Age:** P–K

Fact and fantasy are hard to distinguish in the life of well-loved John Chapman. Kellogg entertainingly illustrates Johnny Appleseed's life in its historic significance and explains how legends about him grew and continue to this day. A part of the It's in the Bag series, the book is packed inside a washable canvas bag together with a packet of spin-off games and activities. [1]
FOLK AND FAIRY TALES; SEEDS
Rev: BKL 9/1/88; SLJ 10/88

500 *Journey Cake, Ho!* Ruth Sawyer. Penguin, 1978. Unp. $3.95. (0-14-050275-0). **Category:** Folklore/Folktales/Fairy tales **Age:** –P–K

The fox ate the hens. The wolf took the sheep. The pig wandered off. And the cow fell into the brook. So the boy, with a freshly baked journey cake, is sent away to find a new home. But the cake, running ahead, entices animals to catch and eat him, and, in the process, it returns with new animals to the farmhouse. Fans of "The Gingerbread Boy" will like the happy ending to an old American mountain folktale. [2]

FOLK AND FAIRY TALES; FOOD

Rev: BBC   **Awards:** Caldecott Honor Book

501   *A Journey to Paradise.* Anne Siberell. Henry Holt & Co., 1990. 32 pp. $14.95. (0-8050-1212-5).

Category: Folklore/Folktales/Fairy tales   **Age:** K

Folktale enthusiasts will find this adaptation of an old Indian story an appropriate choice for storytelling. The colorful textured collages enhance this story of a gardener, his pet monkey, and several friends who fly away on an elephant's back to find paradise. All are surprised when they discover their true paradise. [2]

FOLK AND FAIRY TALES

Rev: BKL 4/1/90

502   *Jump Down: Songs and Rhymes for the Very Young.* Performed by Lisa Monet. Circle Sound Productions, 1987. Dist. by Music for Little People. Audiocassette. 24 min. $9.95.

Category: Poetry/Nursery rhymes/Songs   **Age:** T–P–K

A light and lively collection of songs and rhymes. Lisa Monet has arranged the music and performs a number of traditional children's favorites with a sprinkling of her own compositions. Although most of the 25 selections are set to music, several are recited as poems. Words are provided for each selection.

NURSERY RHYMES; SONGS [1]

503   *Jumpin' In a Puddle.* Performed by Kamotion. Special Things Distributing, 1987. Audiocassette. 38 min. $5.00.

Category: Poetry/Nursery rhymes/Songs   **Age:** P–K

A collection of songs unified by the notions of weather and the seasons. This one is just for fun with heavy action play. Lyric sheet included. [3]

SEASONS; SONGS; WEATHER

Rev: BKL 12/15/88

504   *Jungle Sounds.* Rebecca Emberley. Little, Brown & Co., 1989. Unp. $13.95. (0-316-23636-5).   **Category:** Informational   **Age:** I–T

Brightly colored paper cut-out animals growl, croak, hiss, and roar in this otherwise wordless jungle. To help parents point out the different animals, the creatures along with their sounds are identified in a glossary at the end of the book. The glossary ends with the question "Can you think of more animal sounds?" Appropriately, the book ends with a butterfly whispering, "Shhhhhhhhhhh." [3]

ANIMALS; JUNGLE; SOUNDS

Rev: BKL 8/89

505   *Just In Passing.* Susan Bonners. Lothrop, Lee & Shepard, 1989. Unp. $11.88. (0-688-07712-9).   **Category:** Wordless   **Age:** T–P–K

A baby's yawn is passed on and on to various passersby in this wordless look at how sleepiness is catching. Pen and ink with watercolor illustrate the different people in the baby's neighborhood, from the delivery boy to the telephone repairer to the zookeeper, as they all catch the yawn. [2]

BABIES; WORDLESS

Rev: CBY-90

506   *Just Me.* Marie Hall Ets. Viking Penguin, 1965. Unp. $13.95. (0-670-41109-4).   **Category:** Story   **Age:** P–K

A celebration of the uniqueness of each species. A little boy tries to imitate the animals around him but runs as only he can run to meet his father. Children will enjoy imitating the animals right along with the boy in this story. Also available in other formats from the National Library for the Blind and Physically Handicapped. [2]

ANIMALS; SELF-CONCEPT

Rev: ESLC   **Awards:** Caldecott Honor Book

507   *Katy and the Big Snow.* Virginia Lee Burton. Houghton Mifflin, 1973. 36 pp. $12.95. (0-395-18155-0).   **Category:** Story   **Age:** K

Katy is a big red tractor with a bulldozer and snowplow. Katy lives to work, especially on difficult jobs. One winter a heavy snow falls, and Katy is sent to clear the roads. She works hard and keeps the town of Geoppolis from shutting down. This is an exciting adventure from beginning to end. [3]

SNOW; TRACTORS

Rev: CBK; ESLC

508 *Kiddin' Around.* Music for Little People, 1980. Audiocassette. 30 min. $8.95. **Category:** Poetry/Nursery rhymes/Songs **Age:** K

Contains 13 songs from 10 different Music for Little People albums. Themes of peace, ecology, and make-believe are found in the selections. The majority of the selections have a definite rhythm and beat, but a few have a gentle, almost lullaby quality. "Crosspatch" describes the spirit of adventure that "lives in you and me." Livelier songs include "We've Got the Whole World in Our Hands" and "I Wanna Try It." [3]
ECOLOGY; IMAGINATION

509 *Kids Gardening: A Kids' Guide to Messing Around in the Dirt.* Kevin Raferty and Kim G. Raferty. Illus. by Jim M'Guinness. Klutz Press, 1989. 88 pp. $12.95. (0-932592-25-2). **Category:** Informational **Age:** P–K

"An Indoor/Outdoor All-Year Activity Guide" for the young novice. Text and illustrations explain gardening, beginning with what flowers, vegetables, herbs, and fruit trees need to grow. Chapters address the preparation of a garden, how to plant and transplant, identification of weeds, watering, and fertilizing. There are even great cooking recipes. Spiral construction and sturdy pages ensure rugged and long use. [1]
GARDENING; PLANTS

510 *Kids Get Cooking: A Celebration of Food and Cooking.* Tucker/Murphy, 1989. Dist. by KIDVIDZ. Videocassette. 25 min. $24.95. **Category:** Informational **Age:** K

A fast-paced, educational video containing 39 segments on how to do everything imaginable with the egg, from sharing jokes and riddles to cooking and safety tips. A brief activity guide is included. [3]
COOKING; EGGS
Rev: BKL 4/1/88 **Awards:** National Education Film & Video Honors

511 *A Kid's Guide to Personal Grooming.* Performed by Bill Harley. Learning Tree, 1989. Filmstrip. 6 min. $69.00. **Category:** Informational **Age:** P–K

Two filmstrips with audiocassettes teach basic skills and habits, using funny songs and rationales that kids understand. The first focuses on basic hygiene, the second on attire. Both stress the importance of morning routines and daily spot checks. Together they show children how these habits reflect our image of ourselves as well as of others. [1]
PERSONAL GROOMING
Rev: BKL 8/89

512   *A Kid's Guide to Scary Things.* Performed by Bill Harley. Learning Tree, 1988. Filmstrip. 7 min. $89.00.   **Category:** Informational   **Age:** P–K

"Everybody is afraid of something" is the message of this quick-paced, three-part program handling children's fears. Cartoons blended with songs and informative discussions provide youngsters with insights into how to manage scary situations or frightening moments, such as speaking in front of a group or being confronted by a mean dog. Accompanied with audiocassettes and guide.   [2]
FEAR
Rev: BKL 12/15/88

513   *A Kid's Guide to School Safety.* Words Inc., 1988. Dist. by Learning Tree. Filmstrip. 9 min. $69.00.   **Category:** Informational   **Age:** K

Using cartoon drawings and upbeat narration, this two-part series stresses safety rules for young viewers who must walk, bike, or take a bus to school. Asking children to take responsibility for their own safety is the basic premise. Dos and don'ts are covered in detail. Accompanied by audiocassettes and guides.   [1]
SAFETY; SCHOOL
Rev: BKL 5/15/89

514   *King Bidgood's In the Bathtub.* Audrey Wood. Illus. by Don Wood. Harcourt Brace Jovanovich, 1985. Unp. $14.95. (0-15-242730-9).
                                                                      Category: Story   **Age:** P–K

A riotous account of the day King Bidgood refused to get out of his royal bathtub. The simple lyric text is presented through magnificent, but hilarious, double-page illustrations, which give great attention to the beautiful Renaissance costuming as well as the humorous details of the story. Ample time must be afforded children to pore over the details in Wood's illustrations.   [1]
BATHS; ROYALTY
Rev: CCL; ESLC; SLJ 11/85
Awards: Caldecott Honor Book; ALA Notable Children's Book

515   *King Bidgood's In the Bathtub.* Audrey Wood. Illus. by Don Wood. Random House/Miller-Brody, 1986. Dist. by American School Publishers. Filmstrip with audiocassette. 8 min. $29.50.
                                                                      Category: Story   **Age:** P–K

Hilarious Gilbert-and-Sullivan-like operatic spoof of the Woods' Caldecott Honor book. Close-ups of Audrey Wood's attention to humorous detail and the spectacular illustrations show once again that one person's common sense is worth more than a whole court of royal pomposity. Common this filmstrip kit is not; it's a crown jewel (Harcourt, 1985). [1]
BATHS; ROYALTY
Rev: SLJ 4/88   **Awards:** ALSC Notable Filmstrip

516   *Klippity Klop.* Ed Emberley. Little, Brown & Co., 1974. Unp. $10.95. (0-316-23607-1).   **Category:** Story   **Age:** T–P–K

Prince Krispin and his horse, Dumpling, set out on an adventure (klippity klop) that takes them over a bridge (klumpity klump), across a stream (ker-plash kerplosh), and through a field (kwish kwash), until they bump into a dragon. Krispin decides "adventuring is a fine thing, but being safe at home," that's a fine thing too. Simple line drawings come to life with the sound effects as part of the illustrations. [3]
ADVENTURE; DRAGONS; KNIGHTS
Rev: ESLC

517   *The Lady and the Spider.* Faith McNulty. Illus. by Bob Marstall. Harper & Row, 1986. Unp. $12.89. (0-06-024192-6).
                                                         Category: Story   **Age:** P–K

A story that focuses on a spider and is a fine example of how to introduce science to the young child. The unusual illustrations and clear text result in a unique and very understandable narrative for a young audience. [2]
KINDNESS; SCIENCE; SPIDERS
Rev: NYT

518   *Ladybug: The Magazine for Young Children.* Carus Corp., 1989–
$29.97/yr.   **Category:** Periodical   **Age:** T–P

Combining an attractive yet simple format with picture stories, songs, poems, rhymes, games, and read-aloud stories by well-known children's authors and illustrators, this is a top priority for home or school purchase. A separate activity sheet encourages perceptional and motor skills. Inserted parents' pages provide suggestions for possible one-on-one use. Twelve issues per year. [1]
GAMES; POETRY; PUZZLES

519 **Lamb Chop's Sing-Along, Play-Along.** Performed by Shari Lewis. Original songs by Norman Martin. Harper Audio, 1988. Audiocassette. 35 min. $9.95. **Category:** Participation and manipulative **Age:** P–K

With the help of Lamb Chop, Hush Puppy, and Charlie Horse, Shari Lewis delights children with fresh and lively, original songs by Norman Martin. Each selection encourages physical participation, from hopping, jumping, and singing to answering questions. A perfectly timed combination of learning with physical movement. Songs are captivating and will engage young audiences with the clear, bright, and cheerful tunes. [1]

PARTICIPATION; SONGS

Rev: BKL 4/15/89

520 **The Lap-Time Song and Play Book.** Compiled by Jane Yolen. Illus. by Margot Tomes. Harcourt Brace Jovanovich, 1989. 32 pp. $15.95. (0-15-243588-3). **Category:** Poetry/Nursery rhymes/Songs **Age:** I–T–P

Sixteen rhymes and songs are presented here with their music, descriptions of how to play them, and brief histories of their origins. Tomes' two-page illustrations show the reader more details and add to the history of each song. Most songs are familiar, but this is a nice collection of music, history, and "how-to" all wrapped into one lovely book. [2]

GAMES; NURSERY RHYMES; SONGS

Rev: BKL 10/1/89

521 **Laura Charlotte.** Kathryn Galbraith. Illus. by Floyd Cooper. Philomel, 1990. Unp. $14.95. (0-399-21613-8). **Category:** Story **Age:** P–K

Laura Charlotte loves to hear the story of how her mother received Charlotte, a stuffed elephant, for her fifth birthday. The full-page, realistic color illustrations add warmth to this uplifting, intergenerational story. [2]

MOTHERS AND DAUGHTERS; TOYS

Rev: SLJ 4/90

522 **Lavender's Blue.** Compiled by Kathleen Lines. Illus. by Harold Jones. Oxford University Press, 1990. 180 pp. Paper $10.95. (0-19-272208-5). **Category:** Poetry/Nursery rhymes/Songs **Age:** T–P–K

Soft, pastel watercolors paint the many Mother Goose rhymes and songs in this classic collection. The poems are usefully grouped together for counting, bedtime, games, rock-a-byes, and other ways to enjoy these old nursery rhymes. Directions for playing many of the hand rhymes are included in the back. These will keep parents and young children busy for many special moments. [1]

COUNTING; MOTHER GOOSE; NURSERY RHYMES

Rev: CBK

523 *Lend Me Your Wings.* John Agard. Illus. by Adrienne Kennaway. Little, Brown & Co., 1989. 32 pp. $13.95. (0-316-02010-9).

Category: Story **Age:** P–K

In this poetic fable, a unique exchange of wings and fins enables Sister Fish to soar high into the sky and Brother Bird to glide smoothly under the sea. Later, each decides their original home is best, and they switch back. The lyrical text is accompanied by impressionistic watercolors of bright greens, yellows, blues, and purples. [3]

BIRDS; FABLES; FISH

Rev: BKL 6/15/89

524 *Leo the Late Bloomer.* Robert Kraus. Illus. by Jose Aruego. Reprint. Windmill Books/Thomas Y. Crowell, 1987. Unp. $12.89. (0-87807-043-5).

Category: Story **Age:** P–K

It is hard to see how Leo, a young tiger, can look so morose, given Aruego's cheerful illustrations, but Leo, the story's protagonist, feels he cannot do anything right. He cannot read or write or draw or even eat neatly, while all around him, others perform those tasks with ease. Even his dad is concerned, but Mother Tiger knows, "Leo is just a late bloomer." [1]

SELF-CONCEPT; TIGERS

Rev: CBK; ESLC

525 *Let Me Tell You about My Baby.* Roslyn Banish. Reprint. Harper & Row, 1988. 64 pp. $12.89. (0-06-020383-8). **Category:** Story **Age:** P–K

Through large black-and-white photos, Banish anticipates the birth of a young boy's new brother. The photographs and text are absorbing. The boy's positive and negative emotions are presented. Strong emphasis is placed on his parents' reassurance of their continuing love and concern for him. This book should satisfy the curiosity of young children and also help them cope with the arrival of a new sibling. [1]

BABIES; BROTHERS AND SISTERS; PREGNANCY

Rev: BKL 10/15/88

526   *Let's Be Friends.* Tickle Tune Typhoon, 1989. Videocassette. 50 min.
$19.98.   **Category:** Poetry/Nursery rhymes/Songs   **Age:** T–P–K

Delightful music by the singing and dancing group Tickle Tune Typhoon.
Songs are about friendship, skins, vegetables, trash, and teeth. Also included
are participation songs such as "Hokey Pokey" and "Kye Kye Lule," along
with the traditional "Twinkle, Twinkle, Little Star." Music ranges from sim-
ple ballads to waltzes to rap. Especially enjoyable is the song "Everyone Is
Differently Abled."   [1]
PARTICIPATION; SONGS
Awards: Parents' Choice Award

527   *Let's Look All Around the House.* Photos by Harold Roth. Grosset & Dunlap, 1988. Unp. $7.95. (0-448-10685-X).
                              Category: Participation and manipulative   **Age:** I–T–P

Color photographs take the child through nine rooms of a house, each room
offering a door for the reader to open in order to discover what is behind it.
Text on each two-page spread invites readers to open a door or lift a lid; text
inside these flaps encourages further discussion of the contents, such as the
closet, refrigerator, or dishwasher. Pages and flaps are made of extra-sturdy
stock to help them endure constant use.   [3]
HOUSES; PARTICIPATION
Rev: BKL 6/1/88

528   *Let's Play! An Open-and-See Flap Book.* Photos by Bob Whitfield. Warner
Books, 1988. Unp. $4.95. (1-55782-087-2).
                              Category: Participation and manipulative   **Age:** T

This board book helps children to learn the idea of "what goes where." It is
arranged in two-page spreads: the first page asks a question (What goes here?)
and provides choices; the opposite page has a flap for the child to lift to see the
correct answer. Pictures are accompanied by words. The book itself is fairly
sturdy, but the flaps may prove fragile under repeated use.   [3]
BOARD BOOKS; CONCEPTS; PARTICIPATION

529   *Let's Try.* Amy MacDonald. Illus. by Maureen Roffey. Candlewick Press/
Penguin USA, 1992. Unp. $4.95. (1-56402-022-3).
                                          Category: Informational   **Age:** T

The author encourages young readers to try to learn new but familiar tasks
such as washing your tummy, drinking milk from a cup, and patting the cat.
Illustrations resemble those by Helen Oxenbury.   [2]
BOARD BOOKS; FAMILY LIFE

530 *A Lion for Lewis.* Rosemary Wells. Dial, 1982. 32 pp. $9.89. (0-8037-4686-5). **Category:** Story **Age:** P–K

As the youngest child, Lewis always gets the lesser roles when he plays with his siblings. Lewis rebels. He discovers a large-as-life lion suit, which he puts on—and then the fun begins! Hearing Lewis's voice from inside the suit, his siblings are convinced that Lewis has been eaten. Lewis plays along, stalking George and Sophie and causing them to fear for their lives. Illustrations are reminiscent of Sendak. [3]

BROTHERS AND SISTERS; LIONS

Rev: ESLC; NYT

531 *Listen to the Rain.* Bill Martin, Jr. and John Archambault. Illus. by James Endicott. Henry Holt & Co., 1988. 32 pp. $13.95. (0-8050-0682-6). **Category:** Poetry/Nursery rhymes/Songs **Age:** P–K

One can almost hear the rain in this poetic, auditory book. Clashing and lashing, roaring and pouring, pitter and patter, dropping and stopping describe the various sounds and feelings of rain. The large, sparse text is surrounded by textured, double-page watercolor illustrations. This will surely spark young listeners' creativity and heighten their senses. [1]

POETRY; RAIN; SOUNDS

Rev: ESLC

532 *Little Bear.* Else H. Minarik. Illus. by Maurice Sendak. Harper & Row, 1957. 64 pp. $10.89. (0-06-024241-8). **Category:** Story **Age:** P–K

Mother Bear always treats Little Bear with patience and humor in this four-chapter book. Little Bear has the dreams of many children: to fly like a bird, to drive a fast car, to have an adventure. The illustrations are soft and gentle with muted tones and crosshatch shading. Also available in other formats from the National Library for the Blind and Physically Handicapped. [2]

BEARS; FAMILY LIFE; IMAGINATION

Rev: CBK; NYT

533 *Little Bear.* Else H. Minarik. Illus. by Maurice Sendak. Read by Suzanne Toren. Listening Library, 1987. Audiocassette. 72 min. $15.95. **Category:** Story **Age:** P–K

Sixteen tales on two audiocassettes about Little Bear's adventures with his loving parents and animal friends. Little Bear's imagination and curiosity will appeal to preschoolers and beginning readers. [3]

BEARS; FAMILY LIFE; IMAGINATION

534 *Little Bear Lost.* Jane Hissey. Philomel, 1989. Unp. $14.95. (0-399-21743-6). **Category:** Story **Age:** P–K

Old Bear is busily packing a picnic feast when his friends fly into the nursery for a quick game of hide-and-seek. Sadly, they discover they have once again forgotten to choose a seeker. Always ready, Old Bear volunteers. The game comes to a halt when everyone realizes that Little Bear has hidden so well he cannot be found. Hissey's superb full-color drawings of realistically frayed stuffed animals will enchant any child. [2]

BEARS; FRIENDSHIP; TOYS

Rev: BKL 11/1/89

535 *Little Bear's Trousers.* Jane Hissey. Philomel, 1987. Unp. $14.95. (0-399-21493-3). **Category:** Story **Age:** P–K

Little Bear wakes one morning to discover that his red trousers are missing. He embarks on a diligent search and finds that Camel discarded his pants in favor of pom-pom hats as humpwarmers and that Sailor had tried them out as sails for his boat before turning them over to Scottie Dog, and so on. Hissey's delectable full-color illustrations are so realistic that even adults are tempted to believe that fantasy is fact. [2]

BEARS; CLOTHING; TOYS

Rev: BKL 1/15/88

536 *Little Bunny & Her Friends.* Ulf Nilsson. Illus. by Eva Eriksson. Chronicle Books, 1988. Unp. $6.95. (0-87701-526-0).

Category: Story **Age:** P–K

Little Bunny and her friends—a frog, pig, mouse, bumblebee, and snail—gather together to play but cannot find one activity that all can do. Each tries to fly, burrow, run, or swim with humorous results, until Little Bunny finally hits upon something for them all: sharing a book. One line per page reveals this simple story with large, delicately drawn and colored pictures illustrating the sequences. [3]

PLAY; RABBITS

Rev: BKL 12/1/88

537 *The Little Engine That Could.* Retold by Watty Piper. Illus. by George Hauman and Doris Hauman. Platt & Munk, 1976. Unp. $5.95. (0-448-40520-2). **Category:** Story **Age:** P–K

This classic American childhood title appeals to all ages. The smaller engine responds to the needs of the children and does what the larger engine would not do to help. The illustrations are quite simple and one-dimensional but do

not distract from the overall appeal of the book. Adults can use the book to discuss persistence and patience, repeating "I think I can, I think I can" to encourage success. [1]
PERSEVERANCE; TRAINS
Rev: CBK; ESLC; NYT

538 *Little Fingerling.* Monica Hughes. Illus. by Brenda Clark. Kids Can Press, 1989. Unp. $12.95. (0-921103-78-6).
Category: Folklore/Folktales/Fairy tales **Age:** K

Beloved Japanese folktale of Little Fingerling, the tiny young man who leaves the protection of his parents to seek his fortune. He paints intricate designs on boxes and combs until a kind noblewoman takes him into her home. When he accompanies Plum Blossom, the noblewoman's daughter, on her journey to Kanzeon—the Goddess of Mercy—he bravely battles two monsters. [2]
BRAVERY; FOLK AND FAIRY TALES; JAPAN

539 *Little Friends for Little Folks.* Performed by Janice Buckner. A Gentle Wind, 1986. Audiocassette. 35 min. $7.95.
Category: Poetry/Nursery rhymes/Songs **Age:** P–K

A wonderful collection of active songs for the young child. Words and music are simple and easy to follow. Included are silly noises and sound effects that encourage audience participation. Songs are lively, upbeat, and not unusually long, promoting body movement and creativity. Great for use at story times.
ENTERTAINMENT; SONGS; SOUNDS [2]
Rev: BKL 9/15/87

540 *Little Hands: Songs For and About Children.* Performed by Jonathan Edwards. Phil Rosenthal, 1987. Dist. by American Melody. Audiocassette. 30 min. $9.98. **Category:** Poetry/Nursery rhymes/Songs **Age:** T–P–K

A collection of traditional and new songs written by Edwards himself, reminiscent of the folksong tradition reborn in the 1960s. The variety invites both children and adults to participate; the nostalgia will appeal to baby boomers, for example, "Children, Go Where I Send Thee" and "Stewball," both recorded by folk groups in the 1960s and 70s. [2]
SONGS
Rev: SLJ 4/88 **Awards:** ALSC Notable Recording

541   *The Little House.* Virginia Lee Burton. Reprint. Houghton Mifflin, 1942. Unp. $12.95. (0-395-18156-9).   **Category:** Story   **Age:** P–K

The classic story of a little house and the changes it goes through as time and the city close in on it. The story illustrates the concept of urbanization while showing the changing of the seasons in simple, easy-to-understand language. Children will be delighted when the house is "recycled" and put back into the country.   [1]
ECOLOGY; HOUSES; SEASONS
Rev: BBC; CBK; NYT   **Awards:** Caldecott Medal

542   *The Little Old Lady Who Was Not Afraid of Anything.* Linda Williams. Illus. by Megan Lloyd. Thomas Y. Crowell, 1986. 32 pp. $12.89. (0-690-04586-7).   **Category:** Story   **Age:** P–K

The "little old lady who was not afraid of anything" is followed home by shoes that "clomp, clomp," pants that "wiggle, wiggle," a shirt going "shake, shake," gloves that "clap, clap," and a hat going "nod, nod." At home she settles by the fire, when suddenly there is a knock on the door. The things that followed her have come to life and are making frightening sounds. Ideal for sharing at Halloween and discussing "scary" things.   [2]
FEAR; HALLOWEEN
Rev: CBY-87; ESLC

543   *The Little Pink Pig.* Barbara Dewar. Warner Books, 1989. Unp. $7.95. (1-55782-326-X).   **Category:** Participation and manipulative   **Age:** T–P

In this small, colorful board book, the little pink pig wonders what color his lunch will be. In succeeding pages, the left page is the color in question; the right features various foods of that color. The center of each page is a cutaway shape of the little pig, whose wooden form can be viewed through the hole. The form, placed on top of a drawing of the pig, can be removed for play.
BOARD BOOKS; CONCEPTS; PIGS   [3]

544   *The Little Red Hen: An Old Story.* Margot Zemach. Farrar, Straus & Giroux, 1983. Unp. $11.95. (0-374-34621-6).
                                        Category: Folklore/Folktales/Fairy tales   **Age:** K

Zemach's soft washes of color, deftly defined with pen and ink, bring a satisfying freshness to this familiar tale. The industrious hen, though smaller in stature, proves to be much larger in spirit than her three lazy friends, who steadfastly refuse to help her plant, harvest, and thresh the wheat. Poetic justice reigns supreme in the end as the hen and her chicks eat every last crumb of the much-labored-over loaf of bread. [2]

CHICKENS; FOLK AND FAIRY TALES; LAZINESS

Rev: ESLC

545 *Little Red Lighthouse & the Great Gray Bridge.* Hildegarde H. Swift and Lynd Ward. Harcourt Brace Jovanovich, 1942. Unp. $15.95. (0-15-247040-9). **Category:** Story **Age:** P–K

A little red lighthouse stands beneath the George Washington Bridge on the Hudson River, proudly sending out warnings to boats on the river, until the great gray bridge is constructed and obstructs its beacon. After the experiences of a stormy night, the lighthouse learns its true value and place as master of the river. Four-color, framed drawings powerfully illustrate the story and size comparisons between lighthouse and bridge. [2]

BOATS; LIGHTHOUSES

Rev: CCL; ESLC; NYT

546 *Little Songs of Long Ago: A Collection of Favorite Poems and Rhymes.* Illus. by Henriette W. LeMair. Philomel, 1988. 64 pp. $13.95. (0-399-21643-X). **Category:** Poetry/Nursery rhymes/Songs **Age:** I–T–P–K

This collection of nursery rhymes will captivate young and old alike. Thirty rhymes include some little-known entries as well as many old favorites. Each rhyme appears in the middle of a cream-colored page softly framed in lavender with the title in fine script at the top. The adjoining page illustrates the rhyme, using fine, precise lines and delicate colors. A nostalgic work. [3]

NURSERY RHYMES

Rev: BKL 12/1/88

547 *Little Toot.* Hardie Gramatky. Reprint. Putnam, 1967. Unp. $13.99. (0-399-60422-7). **Category:** Story **Age:** P–K

Classic story of Little Toot, who would much rather stay in the calm river and play than go into the scary ocean and work. His actions are disconcerting to his father, his grandfather, and the other hardworking tugs. One day Little Toot finds himself at the mouth of the ocean, facing a terrible storm and an ocean liner in distress. He faces the immense challenge and joins the "adult" tugboat world. Also available in other formats from the National Library for the Blind and Physically Handicapped. [3]

BOATS

Rev: CBK; ESLC

548 *Little Toot Stories.* Hardie Gramatky. Read by Hans Conried. Harper Audio, 1977. Audiocassette. 51 min. $8.98. **Category:** Story **Age:** P–K

Hans Conried's expressive voice and clear diction tell familiar tales of the frivolous little tugboat that accomplished heroic deeds. Included are "Little Toot," "Little Toot on the Grand Canal," "Little Toot on the Thames," "Little Toot Through the Golden Gate," and "Little Toot on the Mississippi." Background sound effects of water traffic and harbor activity enhance the total recording. [3]

BOATS

Rev: ESLC

549 *The Littlest Dinosaurs.* Bernard Most. Harcourt Brace Jovanovich, 1989. Unp. $12.95. (0-15-248125-7). **Category:** Informational **Age:** P–K

Starting with the 13-foot Coloradisaurus, "as long as a seesaw," and working down, the author provides details on smaller-scale prehistoric monsters. Included are pronunciation guides and comparisons with commonplace objects for those who are yet unfamiliar with inches and feet. The author makes these long-extinct monsters become 20th-century friends. [2]

DINOSAURS; SIZE

Rev: BKL 11/1/89

550 *Lizzie and Harold.* Elizabeth Winthrop. Illus. by Martha Weston. Lothrop, Lee & Shepard, 1985. 32 pp. $12.88. (0-688-02712-1).

Category: Story **Age:** –K

Lizzie sets out to make a best friend, and in the process she shuns Harold, her neighbor, because he is a boy. In the end, she discovers Harold has always been her real friend. This book realistically portrays the social dynamics of members of this age group and their desire to explore the concept of friendship. [1]

FRIENDSHIP

Rev: CBK; ESLC

551 *Look—A Butterfly.* David Cutts. Illus. by Eulala Conner. Troll Associates, 1982. Unp. $9.89. (0-89375-662-8).

Category: Informational **Age:** P–K

Striking illustrations and a few descriptive sentences detail the process by which caterpillars become butterflies and present a few common butterflies that children will recognize. The expressive title will extend a sense of discovery to very young children. An excellent ally for *The Very Hungry Caterpillar* by Eric Carle. [2]

BUTTERFLIES

Rev: CBK

552 *Look! Look! Look!* Tana Hoban. Greenwillow Books, 1988. Unp. $12.95. (0-688-07240-2). **Category:** Wordless **Age:** T–P–K

Each of nine full-color photographs is preceded by a solid black sheet with a cutout that frames a small segment of the photo, wordlessly encouraging the reader/viewer to try to guess what follows. On the back of each photograph is another of the same object, providing the child with yet another perspective.

CONCEPTS; TOY AND MOVABLE BOOKS; WORDLESS [1]

Rev: BKL 9/1/88; CBY-89

553 *Look Out, Patrick!* Paul Geraghty. Macmillan, 1990. Unp. $12.95. (0-02-735822-4). **Category:** Story **Age:** T–P–K

Patrick, a happy mouse strolling in the garden one day, does not notice all the dangers that almost befall him: a hawk tries to catch him with its claws, a snake attempts to eat him whole, a group of three rats almost kidnap him, etc. Young listeners will want to participate, shouting the warning provided for the mouse repeatedly on each page: "Look Out, Patrick!" This book should be a favorite. [1]

MICE

554 *Looking for Santa Claus.* Henrik Drescher. Narrated by Robert Sevra. Random House/Educational Enrichment Materials, 1986. Dist. by American School Publishers. Filmstrip. 7 min. $26.00.

Category: Story **Age:** P–K

It's a cossack! It's a sheik! It's ... not Santa! Drescher's zany tale of Maggie's escaping her three Scrooge-like aunts by flying away with Blossom the cow springs to life with the equally hilarious John Guth score. Accompanied with audiocassette. [1]

CHRISTMAS

Rev: SLJ 4/87 **Awards:** ALSC Notable Filmstrip

555 *Louanne Pig in the Talent Show.* Nancy Carlson. Carolrhoda Books, 1985. Unp. $9.95. (0-87614-284-6). **Category:** Story **Age:** K

Louanne the pig, a self-proclaimed "no talent dope," is miserable watching everyone else practice for the annual talent show, until a last-minute swap changes everything. Bright illustrations and a simply stated text are perfectly matched in this believable tale. [3]
CONFIDENCE; PIGS; SELF-ESTEEM
Rev: NYT

556   *Loving the Earth: A Sacred Landscape Book for Children.* Fredric Lehrman. Illus. by Lisa Tune. Celestial Arts, 1990. 47 pp. $17.95. (0-89087-603-7).   **Category:** Informational   **Age:** K

A lush combination of artwork, photographs, and informative text will instill in children the beauty of earth and the reasons why it must be protected. An appended glossary and several pages of questions and answers about the earth conclude the book. [2]
EARTH; ECOLOGY

557   *Lullabies & Good Night: A Collection of Classic Lullaby Poetry.* Musical arrangements by Stephen Elkins. Illus. by Mary Cassatt. Ideals Publishing Corp., 1989. Unp. $15.95. (0-8249-7351-8).   **Category:** Poetry/Nursery rhymes/Songs   **Age:** I–T

The publisher has combined the illustrations of Mary Cassatt's mother-and-child masterpieces with the poetry of Eugene Field, Sir Walter Scott, and Alfred, Lord Tennyson and set them to original musical arrangements by Stephen Elkins, which are sung by Ellen Musik. The result is an exquisite volume of lovely lullabies for reading and/or listening. The audiocassette has the vocals on one side and the instrumental sound track on the reverse. [1]
LULLABIES; POETRY; SONGS

558   *Lullabies for Little Dreamers: Songs and Music for the Quiet Times.* Read by Kevin Roth. CMS Records, 1985. Audiocassette. 36 min. $8.98.   **Category:** Poetry/Nursery rhymes/Songs   **Age:** T–P–K

A baker's dozen of verses, including traditional songs such as "Hush Little Baby" as well as original ones like "Leatherwinged Bat." The mountain dulcimer accompaniment provides the perfect touch. [1]
LULLABIES; SLEEP; SONGS
Rev: SLJ 4/86   **Awards:** ALSC Notable Recording

559 *Lullabies Go Jazz: Sweet Sounds for Sweet Dreams.* Jon Crosse. Jazz Cat Productions, 1987. Audiocassette. 30 min. $8.98.

       Category: Poetry/Nursery rhymes/Songs **Age:** I–T

Refreshingly unique jazz instrumentals delightfully introduce newcomers to these standard works while renewing the warm, embracing memories we may have temporarily misplaced as adults.   [2]

JAZZ; LULLABIES

Rev: SLJ 4/87 **Awards:** ALSC Notable Recording

560 *Lullaby Cradle: Soothing Lullabies for Baby's Sweet Dreams.* Sung by Sheri Huffman. Great American Audio, 1989. Audiocassette. 60 min. $24.95.   **Category:** Poetry/Nursery rhymes/Songs **Age:** I–T

The sweet, pure strains of Huffman's voice are enhanced by Gruskin's orchestral arrangements on side one of each of four audiocassettes. The reverse sides provide only the instrumental background so that listeners may sing along. The soothing sounds of "Rock-a-Bye Baby," "Twinkle, Twinkle, Little Star," "Frère Jacques," and many more will surely lull little ones into peaceful sleep. Packaged in a wooden cradle for storage.   [2]

LULLABIES; NURSERY RHYMES; SONGS

561 *Lullaby Magic.* Sung by Joanie Bartels. Discovery Music, 1985. Audiocassette. 42 min. $9.95.

       Category: Poetry/Nursery rhymes/Songs **Age:** I–T–P–K

A collection of popular lullabies with lyric sheet that will calm children without driving teachers and parents from the room. Most will recognize the popular and traditional tunes, from "Goodnight, My Someone" and "The Music Man" to "Twinkle, Twinkle, Little Star." Joanie Bartels sings vocals on one side; the flipside contains the instrumental versions. A "must purchase" for day care centers.   [1]

LULLABIES; SLEEP; SONGS

562 *Lullaby River.* Linda Danly and Mimi Danly. Narrated by Linda Danly. Danly Productions, 1984. Audiocassette. 30 min. $10.00.

       Category: Poetry/Nursery rhymes/Songs **Age:** I–T–P

Take a restful trip along Lullaby River to the soothing sounds of nine original songs just right for winding down. Introduction of the music is provided by Tucker the Turtle, and young listeners will savor the real sounds of water and birds in the background. Side one provides a tranquil respite for midday nap-time; side two offers a gently paced bedtime collection, the perfect conclusion to story time. [2]

LULLABIES; RIVERS; TURTLES

Rev: SLJ 4/86 **Awards:** ALSC Notable Recording

563 *The Lullaby Songbook.* Edited by Jane Yolen. Illus. by Charles Mikolay-cak. Harcourt Brace Jovanovich, 1986. 32 pp. $13.95. (0-15-249903-2).

Category: Poetry/Nursery rhymes/Songs **Age:** T–P–K

This collection of old and new bedtime songs from around the world has a deeply colored border with illustrations on each page. Children will find the songs easy and enjoyable. Simple piano and guitar arrangements are included, as is some history about each song. [2]

LULLABIES; SONGS

Rev: BKL 1/1/88; NYT

564 *Luxo Jr.* Direct Cinema, 1987. Videocassette. 2 min. $50.00.

Category: Wordless **Age:** P–K

A father-and-son team of Luxo desk lamps play a game of ball. Computer-animated, three-dimensional objects assume human characteristics and com-municate compassion and remorse with astounding realism. [2]

ANIMATION; ENTERTAINMENT; GAMES; WORDLESS

Rev: SLJ 4/89 **Awards:** ASLC Notable Film/Video; Academy Award Nomination

565 *Lyle, Lyle, Crocodile.* Bernard Waber. Houghton Mifflin, 1965. 48 pp. $13.95. (0-395-16995-X). **Category:** Story **Age:** P–K

One in a large series that features the lovable crocodile that resides with the Primm family in a house on New York's East 88th Street. In this one, Lyle is committed to the zoo by the nasty neighbor Mr. Grumps, only to escape by night and become a hero as he rescues Grumps and his cat, Loretta, from a house fire. *The House on East 88th Street* is available on videocassette from Ambrose Video. Also available in other formats from the National Library for the Blind and Physically Handicapped. [1]

CITIES AND TOWNS; CROCODILES; FAMILY LIFE

Rev: BBC; ESLC; NYT

566 *Lyle, Lyle, Crocodile and Other Adventures of Lyle.* Bernard Waber. Performed by Gwen Verdon. Harper Audio, 1989. Audiocassette. 55 min. $9.95. **Category:** Story **Age:** P–K

In a clear, well-modulated voice, Gwen Verdon reads four of the stories about lovable Lyle the crocodile, who lives with the Primm family in Manhattan. Selections are "The House on East 88th Street," "Lyle, Lyle, Crocodile," "Lyle and the Birthday Party," and "Lovable Lyle," all based on the books of the same titles. [2]
BIRTHDAYS; CROCODILES
Rev: ESLC

567 *Machines at Work.* Byron Barton. Thomas Y. Crowell, 1987. Unp. $12.89. (0-690-04573-5). **Category:** Story **Age:** P–K

Bright, bold pictures show a day in the life of a construction crew as they bulldoze, dig, stop for lunch, and build both a road and a building. The text is bare and simple—just right for all the activity displayed in the illustrations. [2]
MACHINES
Rev: BBC; ESLC

568 *Madeline.* Ludwig Bemelmans. Viking Penguin, 1958. Unp. $13.95. (0-670-44580-0). **Category:** Story **Age:** K

The adventures of the independent little girl who faces appendicitis while in a French school with 11 other little girls, who all wish they too could be treated as special as Madeline. The book's rhythmic flow and colorful illustrations have intrigued children for ages and endured the test of time. [3]
FRANCE; SCHOOL
Rev: BBC; CBK; ESLC; NYT **Awards:** Caldecott Honor Book

569 *Maggie and the Monster.* Elizabeth Winthrop. Illus. by Tomie dePaola. Holiday House, 1987. Unp. $13.95. (0-8234-0639-3). **Category:** Story **Age:** P–K

A little girl named Maggie has a baby monster visiting her room each night before she goes to bed. With the help of her mother, Maggie learns how to rid herself of the baby monster. DePaola's illustrations generate much of the humor in the story. [3]
BEDTIME; MONSTERS
Rev: ESLC

570 *The Magic Porridge Pot.* Paul Galdone. Houghton Mifflin, 1976. Unp. $13.95. (0-395-28805-3).

Category: Folklore/Folktales/Fairy tales **Age:** P–K

An old woman gives a hungry girl and her mother a magic pot that produces all the porridge they can eat. One day it makes too much, and the mother cannot remember the magic words to stop the pot. Children will be amused by the turn of events and want to participate in the action of the story. [2]

FOLK AND FAIRY TALES; MAGIC

Rev: ESLC

571 *The Magic Pumpkin.* Bill Martin, Jr. and John Archambault. Illus. by Robert J. Lee. Henry Holt & Co., 1989. Unp. $14.95. (0-8050-1134-X).

Category: Story **Age:** P–K

The narrator of this Halloween story is convinced by a perfect-appearing pumpkin in the patch it will make the perfect jack-o-lantern to keep away the "foolies." Although all begins well, things begin to change when the foolies creep into the yard. It turns out that the pumpkin is actually the foolies' leader, and when the frightened narrator realizes this, he quickly extinguishes its light and watches it melt away. Scary and fun. [3]

HALLOWEEN

Rev: BKL 9/1/89; SLJ 11-12/89

572 *Magical Mother Nature: The Four Seasons.* Produced by Cochran Communications. Rainbow Educational Video, 1989. Videocassette. 20 min. $89.00. **Category:** Informational **Age:** K

Beautiful scenes of the four seasons logically arranged with easy-to-follow narration make this presentation ideal for youngsters. Questions throughout encourage discussion during and after viewing. The package includes a guide.

NATURE; SEASONS [1]

Rev: BKL 1/15/90

573 *Mainly Mother Goose.* Performed by Sharon, Lois & Bram. Produced by Paul Mills. Elephant Records, 1984. Dist. by A & M Records. Audiocassette. $8.98. **Category:** Poetry/Nursery rhymes/Songs **Age:** T–P–K

A delightful collection of Mother Goose, sung by children with the help of Sharon, Lois, and Bram. A treat for young ears that children will want to play again and again. Familiar tunes are played that will be remembered quickly and sung after the cassette is turned off. [2]

MOTHER GOOSE; NURSERY RHYMES

574 *Make Way for Ducklings.* Robert McCloskey. Viking Penguin, 1941. Unp.
$12.95. (0-670-45149-5). **Category:** Story **Age:** P–K

Mr. and Mrs. Mallard are looking for a place to rear ducklings. They settle on a spot on a Boston riverbank. When the ducklings hatch, their mother teaches them to swim, dive, and walk in a straight line. Once they have learned these skills, the family marches across a busy street with the aid of a friendly police-man. A warm, nurturing story that works well with groups. Line drawings, in sepia, reflect the feel of the city. [1]
CITIES AND TOWNS; DUCKS
Rev: BBC; CBK; ESLC; NYT **Awards:** Caldecott Medal

575 *Making Friends.* Fred Rogers. Photos by Jim Judkis. Putnam, 1987. Unp.
$12.95. (0-399-21382-1). **Category:** Informational **Age:** P–K

Mr. Rogers, in his clear, straightforward manner, explains the joys and frustra-tions of making friends. The sharp, full-color photographs portray multiethnic children in all types of activities, playing together as well as disagreeing or be-ing left out. The photographs will stimulate discussion between parent and child on how to be a good friend and how to share. Also available in other formats from the National Library for the Blind and Physically Handicapped.
FRIENDSHIP; SHARING [1]
Rev: CBY-88

576 *The Man Who Kept House.* Kathleen Hague and Michael Hague. Harcourt
Brace Jovanovich, 1981. Unp. $12.95. (0-15-251698-0).
Category: Folklore/Folktales/Fairy tales **Age:** K

One of the classic Scandinavian folktales of a farmer who trades places with his wife for one day because he feels her work is easier than his. This amusing story ends with the wife coming home to find their cow hanging by a rope from the roof and her husband on the other end hanging upside down with his head in a pot over the fire. Color illustrations enhance this retelling and add to the fun of the story. [3]
FARMERS; FOLK AND FAIRY TALES
Rev: NYT

577 *Many Moons.* James Thurber. Illus. by Louis Slobodkin. Harcourt Brace
Jovanovich, 1943. Unp. $14.95. (0-15-251873-8).
Category: Folklore/Folktales/Fairy tales **Age:** P–K

Black-and-white drawings accented with watercolor and colored pencil illus-trate this tale of a 10-year-old princess who falls ill and believes she cannot be well again until the moon is hers. The court jester asks the princess to describe the moon and then has one made just for her. She recovers immediately and goes outside to play, but the king worries that the trick will be discovered when she sees the moon at night. [2]

CLOWNS, JESTERS; FOLK AND FAIRY TALES; MOON

Rev: NYT **Awards:** Caldecott Medal

578 *Marcia Berman Sings Lullabies and Songs You Never Dreamed Were Lullabies.* B B Records, 1989. Audiocassette. 30 min. $10.95.

Category: Poetry/Nursery rhymes/Songs **Age:** T–P–K

Songs originally composed for adults have been arranged to make them suitable for the young child. Berman sings the music of Johnny Mercer, Irving Berlin, John Lennon, and Paul McCartney in a soothing, gentle way. Songs such as "Lullaby of Broadway" become lullabies to soothe the spirit and help children to sleep. There is a clear, clean blend of John Bucchino's instrumental and vocal arrangements with Berman's voice. [2]

LULLABIES; SONGS

Rev: BKL 9/15/89 **Awards:** ALSC Notable Recording

579 *Marcia Berman Sings Malvina Reynolds' Rabbit Dance and Other Songs for Children.* B B Records, 1985. Record. 32 min. $9.95.

Category: Poetry/Nursery rhymes/Songs **Age:** P–K

Fifteen songs will not only entertain young children but will also help them accept and express their feelings. Some celebrate people of all races working together; others make for pure hand-clapping, finger-snapping fun. [1]

SONGS

Awards: Parents' Choice Award

580 *Martin's Hats.* Joan W. Blos. Illus. by Marc Simont. Morrow Jr. Books, 1984. Unp. $11.88. (0-688-02033-X). **Category:** Story **Age:** P–K

Martin uses his imagination and his collection of different hats as he goes through his day exploring, partying, and being an engineer, chef, traffic cop, fireman, welder, farmer, and sleepy boy. His imaginative journey is richly illustrated with watercolors that vividly portray each part of his day and introduce youngsters to a variety of occupations. [1]

CAREERS; HATS

Rev: ESLC; NYT

581   **The Marvelous Journey Through the Night.** Helme Heine. Farrar, Straus & Giroux, 1989. Unp. $14.95. (0-374-38478-9).

Category: Story   **Age:** P–K

Sleep and his sister Dream carry all living creatures, large or small, wild or tame, on the Marvelous Journey Through the Night. Surrealistic, watercolor illustrations convey the fantastic element of dreams, while the text is remarkably reassuring about the limits of that world.   [2]
DREAMS; NIGHT; SLEEP

582   **Mary Had a Little Lamb.** Sarah J. Hale. Illus. by Tomie dePaola. Holiday House, 1984. Unp. $13.95. (0-8234-0509-5).

Category: Poetry/Nursery rhymes/Songs   **Age:** T–P

DePaola's colorful illustrations bring new life to this classic nursery rhyme. Additional verses are included, as is a music score. A delightful book to be shared aloud by either reading or singing the rhyme while enjoying the pictures.   [1]
NURSERY RHYMES; SHEEP
Rev: BKL 1/1/88; NYT; PP

583   **Mary's Pets.** Clive Scruton. Lothrop, Lee & Shepard, 1989. Unp. $10.95. (0-688-08520-2).   **Category:** Participation and manipulative   **Age:** T–P–K

A little girl named Mary spends a busy day looking for her pets, all of whom are hiding under half-page flaps. Questions such as "Who suddenly pounced from the tree, with a saucy, bouncy purr?" invite the child to participate verbally, and lifting the flaps permits physical interaction with the book.   [1]
PARTICIPATION; PETS
Rev: BKL 4/1/89

584   **Maxine in the Middle.** Holly Keller. Greenwillow Books, 1989. Unp. $12.88. (0-688-08151-7).   **Category:** Story   **Age:** P–K

Maxine suffers the usual slights of middle child/rabbit: too big for baby privileges, too small to be a schoolchild, hand-me-downs, and compromises. When she goes on strike, her siblings miss her and lure her back into the family with a party in her honor. The menu includes donut holes and peanut butter and jelly without the bread. Children of any birth order will identify with Maxine's feelings of being left out.   [1]
BROTHERS AND SISTERS; RABBITS
Rev: BKL 8/89; CBY-90

585 *Max's Christmas.* Rosemary Wells. Dial, 1986. 32 pp. $8.89. (0-8037-0290-6). **Category:** Story **Age:** T–P

Ruby tries to explain Christmas Eve protocol to her younger brother Max, who is not enthusiastic about bedtime and decides to wait up for Santa. Suddenly Santa slides down the chimney practically into Max's lap. Ruby wakes Max the next morning and finds many Christmas presents hidden under Max's blanket. Wells has maintained her high level of quality in writing and illustrations. A marvelous preschool holiday book and a fun read.   [2]
CHRISTMAS; RABBITS
Rev: BBC; ESLC; PP

586 *Max's Christmas.* Rosemary Wells. Narrated by Jerry Agutter and others. Produced by Paul Gagne and Michael Sporn. Weston Woods Studios, 1988. Videocassette. 5 min. $60.00. **Category:** Story **Age:** T–P

Animated version of the story by Rosemary Wells (Dial, 1986) in which Max, a rabbit, meets Santa Claus on Christmas Eve. A delightful holiday story that young children will enjoy as they await a special visit from Santa.   [2]
CHRISTMAS; RABBITS
Rev: BKL 1/15/89

587 *Max's First Word.* Rosemary Wells. Dial, 1979. Unp. Paper $3.50. (0-8037-6066-3). **Category:** Story **Age:** T–P

Max's sister tries and tries to get him to mimic one-syllable words, but his only reply is "Bang." Finally, after biting into an apple and being asked to say "Yum," Max pronounces it "Delicious!" Simple illustrations against bright, primary backgrounds and a clever story line make this round-edged board book a winner.   [2]
BOARD BOOKS; RABBITS; WORDS
Rev: ESLC; NYT

588 *McGee.* Lawrence Productions, 1989. Software (Apple IIGS). $39.95. **Category:** Participation and manipulative **Age:** T–P

McGee, an endearing child, tries to find things to keep himself busy in this computer game and guide. Acting for McGee, the user must use a mouse to click on one of the icons across the bottom of the screen as an indication of McGee's choice of what to do next. The sound quality is excellent: Mother speaks to McGee in a clear voice, the dog barks, and a cat meows. Graphics are impressive and colorful.   [3]
PETS; PLAY; SLEEP
Rev: BKL 3/1/89

589 *The Me Book.* John E. Johnson. Random House, 1979. Unp. $2.95. (0-394-84243-X). **Category:** Informational **Age:** I–T

A sturdy cloth book that names and illustrates eyes, ears, fingers, toes, arms, nose, and tummy on a toddler boy. Several illustrations also involve counting toes and fingers. The cloth is brightly colored, and the drawings are clear and uncluttered. Nontoxic and washable. [2]

ANATOMY; TOY AND MOVABLE BOOKS

Rev: CBK

590 *Meet Your Animal Friends.* Narrated by Lynn Redgrave. Produced by J. Stein Kaplan. Never a Dull Moment Productions, 1985. Videocassette. 52 min. $29.95. **Category:** Informational **Age:** T

Children will be delighted to recognize some of their favorite animals and enchanted to see some of the less familiar ones. The script will sound as comfortable as a favorite book to the very young. Each kind of animal takes center stage for a few minutes, with spacing between each segment. A useful preview for a zoo or farm visit. [2]

ANIMALS

Rev: BKL 7/89

591 *Merry Christmas, Strega Nona.* Tomie dePaola. Harcourt Brace Jovanovich, 1986. Unp. $14.95. (0-15-253183-1).

Category: Story **Age:** P–K

Strega Nona refuses to use her magic to prepare a Christmas feast for the townspeople, despite her tired assistant's pleas. Big Anthony (her assistant) forgets to bring food, and the plans seem ruined, until the big surprise at the end of the story. A heartwarming Christmas story, beautifully illustrated, for children and their parents. [1]

CHRISTMAS; MAGIC

Rev: NYT

592 *Merry Christmas, Strega Nona.* Tomie dePaola. Listening Library, 1986. Filmstrip. 11 min. $29.95. **Category:** Story **Age:** P–K

Despite Big Anthony's repeated pleas that Strega Nona use her magic so he won't have to work so hard, she refuses. When he forgets to do his chores in preparation for the feast, all seems impossible. A surprise ending—a Christmas meal put together without the use of magic—is Anthony's gift to Strega Nona. Tomie dePaola uses soft, muted colors to depict Italian holiday foods

and traditions. Based on dePaola's book (Harcourt, 1986) and accompanied with an audiocassette and guide. [2]
CHRISTMAS; MAGIC
Rev: BKL 12/1/88

593   ***The Merry-Go-Round Poetry Book.*** Compiled by Nancy Larrick. Illus. by Karen Gundersheimer. Delacorte Press, 1989. 54 pp. $14.95. (0-385-30115-4).   **Category:** Poetry/Nursery rhymes/Songs   **Age:** T–P–K

An extremely well chosen collection of light poetry, especially for young children, that includes a variety of topics to delight young listeners. The selections encourage participation both physically and verbally. The interspersed black and white line drawings capture the flavor and lightness of the verses.
POETRY [2]
Rev: BKL 2/15/90

594   ***Mike Mulligan and His Steam Shovel.*** Virginia Lee Burton. Houghton Mifflin, 1967. Unp. Paper $3.95. (0-395-25939-8).

                   Category: Story   **Age:** P

Mike and his steam shovel, Mary Anne, have built practically everything: roads, canals, building pits. One day, Mary Anne is declared obsolete, but Mike can't bear to junk her. Determined to find work, he takes Mary Anne to a small town and offers to dig the cellar for the town hall. The solution to the problem and Mulligan's own devotion to his well-tended steam shovel point out the care necessary to maximize every resource. [1]
STEAM SHOVELS; WORKING
Rev: CBK; ESLC; NYT

595   ***Milk and Cookies.*** Frank Asch. Parents Magazine Press, 1982. Unp. $5.95. (0-8193-1088-3).   **Category:** Story   **Age:** P–K

Baby Bear dreams about feeding a dragon some cookies and milk while staying at his grandparents' house. Grandpa reassures him that it is only the wood stove and not a dragon that he fears. This story is appealing to the young child because of its simple story and clear illustrations. [2]
BEARS; DRAGONS; DREAMS
Rev: SLJ 5/83

596   ***The Milk Makers.*** Gail Gibbons. Macmillan, 1985. Unp. $13.95. (0-02-736640-5).   **Category:** Informational   **Age:** K

This clear, concise explanation of the entire dairy process begins with why cows make milk, and it proceeds to a study of cows' anatomy and digestion, use of milking machines, milk separation, tank truck delivery, mechanical processing in the dairy, packaging, and finally sale at the store. Simple color pictures accompany details of the dairy business. A chart of dairy products is included. [2]

FARMS; FOOD

Rev: NYT　**Awards:** Reading Rainbow Book

597　*Milk Shake Moustaches and Bubbly Baths: Children's Songs of Self-Esteem.* Madeline C. Nella. Performed by J. P. Nightingale. Mariposa Arts, 1986. Audiocassette. 60 min. $10.95.

Category: Poetry/Nursery rhymes/Songs　**Age:** T–P

Upbeat, original songs intended to build self-esteem point out to listeners that they are special and important, that size doesn't count, that it is all right to play alone, and that feelings constantly change. The audiocassette comes with an activities booklet for positive reinforcement of the concepts featured. [3]

SELF-ESTEEM; SONGS

598　*A Million Chameleons.* James Young. Little, Brown & Co., 1990. Unp. $11.95. (0-316-97129-4).

Category: Concept/Counting/Alphabet　**Age:** T–P–K

Fun and funny rhyming couplets invite young readers to participate in the story by guessing what color the "million chameleons" become on the next page. And there is a surprise ending guaranteed to get one and all. Bold colors and cartoon illustrations add to the fun of reading this one. [1]

CHAMELEONS; COLOR; CONCEPTS

599　*Millions of Cats.* Wanda Gag. Coward McCann, 1928. Unp. $7.95. (0-698-20091-8).　**Category:** Story　**Age:** P–K

A kindhearted old man sets out to find a cat for his lonely wife but cannot decide which of the trillion cats is the prettiest. Quarreling among themselves, the cats dispatch one another until only a modest, scraggly kitten remains. This classic tale has entranced generations of children who love the gently rounded black-and-white illustrations and delight in the refrain "millions and billions and trillions of cats." [1]

CATS

Rev: BBC; CBK; ESLC; NYT　**Awards:** Newbery Honor Book

600 *Milton the Early Riser.* Robert Kraus. Illus. by Jose Aruego and Ariane Dewey. Simon & Schuster, 1972. Unp. $13.95. (0-671-66272-4).

Category: Story **Age:** T–P

A mischievous little panda wakes early and ventures out in search of fun, but solitary play is messy and exhausting. By the time family and friends wake, the little bear is tuckered out and fast asleep. Bright, oversize illustrations add to the mayhem as little Milton tries to entertain himself with a minimum of destruction. A situation that children and adults will recognize.   [1]
BEARS; SLEEP
Rev: CBK

601 *The Mitten: A Ukrainian Folktale.* Jan Brett. Putnam, 1989. Unp. $14.95. (0-399-21920-X).   **Category:** Folklore/Folktales/Fairy tale **Age:** P–K

Nikki's grandmother knits him a pair of mittens and cautions him not to lose them in the snow. However, it isn't long until one is dropped and seemingly lost. Cumulatively, many woodland animals discover that the mitten is a snuggly place to spend cold winter days and nights. When a sneeze from Bear scatters the animals in all directions, the mitten is sent flying and is found. Watercolor with pen and ink evoke Old World scenes.   [2]
FOLK AND FAIRY TALES; MITTENS
Rev: BKL 9/15/89

602 *Molly at the Library.* Ruth S. Radlauer. Illus. by Emily A. McCully. Simon & Schuster, 1988. Unp. $8.95. (0-671-66166-3).

Category: Story **Age:** P

Molly visits the library and finds there are many books; she can even pick 10 to take home. Each day her parents read one, and then Molly can return and choose more. Genuine delight at discovering the library is clearly conveyed. The family is warm and believable, and the story simple. Colorful drawings enhance the story without clutter.   [2]
GIRLS; LIBRARIES; READING
Rev: BKL 3/1/88; SLJ 8/88

603 *Mommies at Work.* Eve Merriam. Illus. by Eugenie Fernandes. Revised. Simon & Schuster, 1955. Unp. 5.95. (0-671-64386-X).

Category: Informational **Age:** T–P

An exploration of all the kinds of things mommies do at home and at work. It starts with Mommy making cookies, then travels through a variety of jobs such as driving trucks, teaching school, counting money, and building cars. Simple drawings fit well with the book, and a diversity of ethnic groups are subtly represented. Formatted cleverly, it ends with Mommy doing what she likes best—coming home to you. [2]

CAREERS; FAMILY LIFE; MOTHERS

Rev: CBY-90

604 *Monsters in the Bathroom.* Performed by Bill Harley. Round River Productions, 1984. Audiocassette. 43 min. $9.98.

Category: Poetry/Nursery rhymes/Songs   **Age:** P–K

Absurdly funny stories and lyrics along with catchy repetitive choruses will appeal to nearly all youngsters. Recorded before a live audience, this audiocassette will draw the listener into the crowd to share in the monster stories with gleeful anticipation. Includes "The Billboard Song," "Black Sox," "Freddy the Fly-Eating Frog," "Abiyoyo," and many others. Lots of fun. [3]

HUMOR; SONGS

605 *Moo Baa La La La.* Sandra Boynton. Simon & Schuster, 1982. Unp. $3.95. (0-671-44901-X).   **Category:** Concept/Counting/Alphabet   **Age:** I–T

Bright, simple drawings and a brief text, but highly readable. Boynton takes the sounds that animals make and presents them in succession: the cow moos, the horse says neigh, the dog bowwows, and the cat meows. In the end, the book asks the listener, "What do you say?" There are no surprises in the selection of sounds, but there may be a trick or two in this humorous little board book. [1]

ANIMALS; BOARD BOOKS; CONCEPTS; SOUNDS

Rev: CBK

606 *The Moon Came Too.* Nancy W. Carlstrom. Illus. by Stella Ormai. Macmillan, 1987. 32 pp. $12.95. (0-02-717380-1).

Category: Story   **Age:** T–P

Simple rhyme that joyously conveys a toddler's excitement about a car trip to Grandma's house. Her mother readily accepts her seemingly unending amount of play paraphernalia loaded into the station wagon. She points out, "There is certainly not much room. You brought everything but the moon," but as her daughter points out from Grandma's porch, "The moon came too." [1]

GRANDMOTHERS

Rev: CBY-88

607 *Moonlight.* Jan Ormerod. Lothrop, Lee & Shepard, 1982. 32 pp. $12.88. (0-688-00847-X).   **Category:** Wordless   **Age:** T–P

Ormerod traces the classic bedtime ritual of a small child: dinner, making a boat, her bath, and her resistance to sleep are all clearly drawn. A wee night fright sends her quickly to her father's arms, but he falls asleep. She then reads with her mother, and her mother falls asleep. Typical tot's delays, but at last, sweet dreams come to all. [1]

BEDTIME; MOON; WORDLESS

Rev: BBC; CBK; ESLC; NYT

608 *Moon's Wish.* Anna G. Hines. Clarion Books, 1992. 32 pp. $14.95. (0-395-58114-1). **Category:** Story **Age:** P–K

When Molly wishes upon a dandelion, she overhears the moon making a wish. She goes to each member of her family asking if each can guess what the moon's wish was. To each she answers, "Part true, part not." As it ends, "The moon wished that all of our wishes would come true. So they did!" Soft watercolors express the individuality of each family member's interaction with Molly. [2]

FAMILY LIFE; WISHING

609 *More First Words: Every Day.* Margaret Miller. Harper & Row, 1991. Unp. $3.95. (0-694-00304-2).

Category: Concept/Counting/Alphabet **Age:** I–T

Clear, full-color photographs portray children engaged in "Every Day" activities—walk, point, eat, hug, laugh. Clean white background emphasizes each delightful child (a full range of ages and ethnicity as well as both sexes are represented). Rounded edges and little-hand-sized laminated pages are pluses for this board book. [2]

BOARD BOOKS; CONCEPTS; WORDS

610 *Morris Goes to School.* Bernard Wiseman. Directed by John Matthews. Churchill Films, 1989. Videocassette. 15 min. $305.00.

Category: Story **Age:** P–K

Learning has never been so much fun. Through the use of puppets, dance, and music, Wiseman's book comes to life. Morris struggles through learning activities at school and succeeds in a humorous, mischievous way that all ages can enjoy (Harper & Row, 1970). [1]

MOOSE; READING

Rev: BKL 4/1/89 & 1/15/90

611   ***Morris, Where Are You?*** Gillian Hulse. Oxford University Press, 1988. Unp. Paper $7.95. (0-19-520646-0).   **Category:** Story   **Age:** T–P

Where is Morris? This is the theme of Hulse's search-and-find book, and success in finding Morris will boost the child's self-esteem and encourage interaction with the story. The author-illustrator manages to convey a certain freshness to the old hunt-and-find theme. Illustrations are predominantly bright and primary colors clearly outlined in pen.   [2]

CATS

Rev: BKL 5/15/88

612   ***Moses in the Bulrushes.*** Warwick Hutton. Atheneum, 1986. 32 pp. $12.95. (0-689-50393-8).   **Category:** Story   **Age:** P–K

A retelling in simple yet dramatic text of the biblical story of the early life of Moses. Pharaoh has decreed that all boy babies born to Hebrew women must be killed. Moses' mother disobeys and devises a way to save her son's life. The watercolor paintings beautifully detail the simple life of the Hebrews, the golden opulence of the Egyptian princess who finds Moses, and the lush greenery of the Nile River valley.   [3]

BIBLE STORIES

Rev: CBY-87

613   ***Moses Supposes His Toeses Are Roses and Seven Other Silly Old Rhymes.*** Nancy Patz. Harcourt Brace Jovanovich, 1983. 32 pp. $12.95. (0-15-255690-7).

Category: Poetry/Nursery rhymes/Songs   **Age:** T–P–K

What utter nonsense and what great fun the rhymes in this hilarious book provide. The collection contains eight American and English nonsense limericks and tongue twisters that will delight both children and adults. The humorous two-color drawings add to the exuberant feeling.   [1]

HUMOR; LIMERICKS; POETRY

Rev: BKL 1/1/88

614   ***Mother Goose: A Collection of Classic Nursery Rhymes.*** Illus. by Michael Hague. Henry Holt & Co., 1984. Unp. $14.95. (0-8050-0214-6).

Category: Poetry/Nursery rhymes/Songs   **Age:** P–K

A collection of almost 50 Mother Goose rhymes is illustrated with darkly colored, Old World–style paintings. The verses are accompanied by their own picture on each page. Beginning with "Old Mother Goose," Hague's detailed paintings capture an older child's look at the nonsense poems. A useful index of first lines is also included. [2]

MOTHER GOOSE; NURSERY RHYMES

Rev: CBK

615 *Mother Goose: A Collection of Nursery Rhymes.* Illus. by Brian Wildsmith. Reprint. Oxford University Press, 1987. 80 pp. $12.95. (0-19-279611-9).

Category: Poetry/Nursery rhymes/Songs **Age:** I–T–P–K

Eighty-six well-known nursery rhymes are brought to life through Brian Wildsmith's distinctive illustrations. Each white page has a printed nursery rhyme on the bottom, with a full-color Wildsmith rendition of the scene above it. This is a must for all children, babies through kindergarteners. A first-line index is included in this ebullient collection. [2]

MOTHER GOOSE; NURSERY RHYMES

Rev: CBK

616 *Mother Goose Treasury.* Illus. by Raymond Briggs. Putnam, 1966. Unp. $16.95. (0-698-20094-2).

Category: Poetry/Nursery rhymes/Songs **Age:** I–T–P

Offering a variety of rhymes from the well-known to the obscure, this collection serves as a solid introduction to Mother Goose. Amusing scenes alternating between watercolor and pen and ink enliven the verses. Includes an index to first lines and titles. [1]

MOTHER GOOSE; NURSERY RHYMES

Rev: BBC; CBK

617 *The Mother Goose Video Treasury.* Left Coast Television, 1987. Dist. by J2 Communications. Videocassette. 30 min. $14.95.

Category: Poetry/Nursery rhymes/Songs **Age:** I–T

Favorite Mother Goose riddles and rhymes are brought to life by the use of puppets and live-action characters. The elaborate settings and costumes make "One, Two, Buckle My Shoe," "I Knew a Little Person," and "Itsy, Bitsy Spider" (to mention only a few) a real treasury for the young viewer. The video container is an action pop-up box. To date, four videocassettes are available.

MOTHER GOOSE; MUSIC; POETRY; SONGS [3]

Rev: BKL 1/15/90

618   *Mother, Mother, I Want Another.* Maria Polushkin. Illus. by Diane Dawson. Crown, 1986. Unp. Paper $3.95. (0-517-55947-1).

Category: Story   **Age:** T–P–K

At bedtime, Baby Mouse chants, "Mother, Mother, I want another." Another "what" is the mystery. Could it be another mother? Mrs. Mouse brings in all the neighborhood mothers, from Mrs. Duck to Mrs. Donkey. Finally, the reader discovers that the little mouse wants another kiss. A sweet, lyrical tale with rhyming speeches given by each of the visiting mothers.   [1]
BEDTIME; FRIENDSHIP; MOTHERS
Rev: CBK; CBY-87; NYT

619   *Mother Night.* Denys Cazet. Orchard Books, 1989. Unp. $14.95. (0-531-08430-2).   **Category:** Story   **Age:** P–K

As several young animals are lovingly put to bed by their parents, they dream a variety of dreams and are awakened the next morning in an equally loving manner. The warm, gentle tone of the book, the entertaining dreams of the animals, and the charming illustrations create a pleasant, comforting book about Mother Night, "the keeper of dreams."   [3]
ANIMALS; NIGHT; SLEEP
Rev: BKL 4/15/89

620   *The Mother's Day Mice.* Eve Bunting. Illus. by Jan Brett. Ticknor & Fields, 1986. Unp. $12.95. (0-89919-387-0).   **Category:** Story   **Age:** P–K

Littlest Mouse goes with his big brothers to find surprises for a Mother's Day gift. After gathering their own gifts, the big brothers insist on returning home before Littlest Mouse finds his gift. He has a surprise not only for his mother but also for his brothers: a song that she can keep forever. The colorful illustrations capture the tiny size of mice and the details of woodlands as they search for gifts of nature.   [3]
GIFTS; MICE; MOTHER'S DAY
Rev: CBY-87; ESLC

621   *The Mouse and the Motorcycle.* Beverly Cleary. Churchill Films, 1987. Videocassette. 41 min. $195.00.   **Category:** Story   **Age:** K

Wonderful perspective for the suspense-filled story of Ralph, an animated puppet, and his new real-life friend, Keith. This interpretation of Cleary's favorite for children is a class act from beginning to end (Morrow, 1965).   [1]
FRIENDSHIP; MICE; MOTORCYCLES
Rev: SLJ 4/88   **Awards:** ALSC Notable Film/Video

622 *Mouse Count.* Ellen Stoll Walsh. Harcourt Brace Jovanovich, 1991. Unp. $11.95. (0-15-256023-8).

Category: Concept/Counting/Alphabet **Age:** P–K

Lionni-type mice outwit a greedy snake. One by one, 10 mice are added to the snake's jar. The mice discover that they are able to work together to turn the jar over and escape. Counting forward and backward to 10 is incorporated into the simple, vibrantly colored tale. [1]

COUNTING; MICE; SNAKES

Rev: BKL 2/15/91

623 *Mouse Paint.* Ellen Stoll Walsh. Harcourt Brace Jovanovich, 1989. Unp. $11.95. (0-15-256025-4).

Category: Concept/Counting/Alphabet **Age:** P–K

White paper helps camouflage three little mice so they can hide from a cat. Then they find three jars of paint and decide to dunk themselves in the red, yellow, and blue colors. Frolicking around and mixing the paint show the reader what happens when colors are mixed. The colorful, simple collage-style artwork is perfect for young eyes. [2]

COLOR; CONCEPTS; MICE

Rev: BKL 5/15/89; CBY-90 **Awards:** Redbook Children's Picture Book Award

624 *Mouse Tales.* Arnold Lobel. Harper & Row, 1972. 64 pp. $10.89. (0-06-023942-5). **Category:** Story **Age:** P–K

Anyone familiar with Lobel's books knows his gift as a true storyteller. This early reader presents seven short tales told as bedtime stories to seven little mice by their father. Some are silly, some charming, all entertaining. Among the characters in this collection are an old mouse who holds up his pants with chewing gum and a mouse who in taking a bath has water running all over town. Also available in other formats from the National Library for the Blind and Physically Handicapped. [2]

ANIMALS; BEDTIME; MICE

Rev: NYT

625 *Mousekin's Christmas Eve.* Edna Miller. Prentice Hall, 1972. Unp. $11.95. (0-13-604454-9). **Category:** Story **Age:** T–P–K

Mousekin finds his way from an abandoned house to a home celebrating Christmas, and after dining on holiday crumbs finds safety in a miniature creche. Each mood in this book is effectively drawn: the empty house, the

bright snowy night, and winter wildlife. The illustrations are lovely and soft, and they capture faithfully the spirit of the season.   [1]
CHRISTMAS; MICE
Rev: ESLC

626 *Moving Up: From Kindergarten to First Grade.* Chuck Solomon. Crown, 1989. Unp. $12.95. (0-517-57286-9).   **Category:** Informational **Age:** K

This photo-essay can ease the transition from kindergarten to first grade by showing youngsters what they will probably find when they move up. By following first graders through a typical day of reading, gym, library, writing, lunch, art, music, and math, children can see that advancement is the fun part of growing up.   [2]
SCHOOL
Rev: BKL 10/1/89

627 *Mr. and Mrs. Pig's Evening Out.* Mary Rayner. Atheneum, 1976. Unp. $13.95. (0-689-30530-3).   **Category:** Story **Age:** P–K

Colorful illustrations blend with text in this story of 10 young pigs whose parents, planning an evening out, innocently hire Mrs. Wolf to baby-sit. Hungry for a late-night snack, she goes upstairs and picks out young Garth. Awakened by their brother's snorts and squeals, the piglets rush to Garth's rescue, working together to trap Mrs. Wolf in a blanket just as she is about to stuff Garth into the oven.   [3]
BABY-SITTING; CLEVERNESS; PIGS
Rev: BBC; ESLC; NYT

628 *Mr. Grumpy's Outing.* John Burningham. Henry Holt & Co., 1970. 32 pp. $14.95. (0-8050-0708-3).   **Category:** Story **Age:** T–P–K

Mr. Grumpy is persuaded to take two children and an assortment of animals out in his boat, but only if they promise to behave. Predictable, disastrous results ensue, and all are tipped into the water. After swimming to the bank and drying in the hot sun, Mr. Grumpy invites the menagerie home for tea and then invites them all to come again for a boat ride another day.   [1]
ANIMALS; BOATS
Rev: BBC; ESLC; NYT
Awards: ALA Notable Children's Book; Kate Greenaway Medal

629 *Mrs. Goose's Baby.* Charlotte Voake. Little, Brown & Co., 1989. 24 pp. $12.95. (0-316-90511-9).   **Category:** Story **Age:** P–K

Mrs. Goose finds an egg and keeps it safe and warm until it hatches. Unfortunately, however, her baby will not swim or eat grass like other geese, and the feathers are brown instead of white. The mother does not care about these differences and loves her baby anyway. A useful book for reinforcing the idea that all of us are different. Pen and ink crosshatch illustrations complement the story.   [2]
BABIES; GEESE
Rev: BKL 5/1/89

630   *The Mud Pony: A Traditional Skidi Pawnee Tale.* Caron L. Cohen. Illus. by Shonto Begay. Scholastic, 1988. Unp. Paper $3.95. (0-590-41526-3).
Category: Folklore/Folktales/Fairy tales   **Age:** K

This tale is part of the oral folklore of the Skidi Pawnee Indians. A Native American boy, unable to afford a horse, molds a pony from earth, which in times of need comes to life. Over the years, it guides the boy, protects him in battle, and helps him become chief. Having served its purpose, the horse returns to earth, but the power of Mother Earth remains with the chief. Hazy watercolors enchance the sense of mystic power.   [3]
FOLK AND FAIRY TALES; HORSES; INDIANS OF NORTH AMERICA
Rev: BKL 12/1/88

631   *Mufaro's Beautiful Daughters.* Illus. by John Steptoe. Narrated by Terry Alexander. Weston Woods Studios, 1988. Videocassette. 14 min. $120.00.   **Category:** Folklore/Folktales/Fairy tales   **Age:** K

Through the use of authentic-sounding dialect and music, this African folktale of the competition between two sisters is told with sensitivity and charm. Nyasha is the kind and considerate sister; Manyara is selfish and spoiled. Good wins out over evil, and in the end Nyasha becomes queen. John Steptoe's Caldecott Honor book (Lothrop, Lee & Shepard, 1987) provides the illustrations used for the video production.   [2]
AFRICA; FOLK AND FAIRY TALES
Rev: BKL 1/15/90

632   *Mushroom In the Rain.* Mirra Ginsburg. Adapted by V. Suteyev. Illus. by Jose Aruego and Ariane Dewey. Macmillan, 1988. 32 pp. $12.95. (0-02-736241-8).   **Category:** Story   **Age:** P–K

An ant crawls under a mushroom when he gets caught in the rain. Along come a butterfly, a mouse, a sparrow, and a rabbit, who crowd under the same mushroom with him. When the rain stops, they come out and discover that when it rains, mushrooms grow. An underriding theme of sharing resources among friends is also present. [3]

ANIMALS; MUSHROOMS; RAIN

Rev: ESLC

633   ***Music for Little People: 50 Playful Activities for Preschool and Early Elementary School Children.*** John M. Feierabend. Illus. by Gary M. Kramer. Sung by Luann Sanders. Boosey & Hawkes, 1989. Audiocassette. 86 min. $6.98.   **Category:** Poetry/Nursery rhymes/Songs   **Age:** P–K

A delightful collection of songs and an activity book, divided into seven sections progressing from simple finger plays and action rhymes to lyrics calling for group participation and alternating singing parts. Folksinger Luann Sanders performs songs in a clear voice, while a male voice recites the finger plays. Instructions are given throughout the tape, and actions for each lyric are illustrated. [1]

FINGER PLAY; NURSERY RHYMES; SONGS

634   ***Music for Very Little People: 50 Playful Activities for Infants and Toddlers.*** John Feierabend. Illus. by Gary Kramer. Sung by Luann Sanders. Boosey & Hawkes, 1986. Audiocassette. 46 min. $6.98.
                    Category: Poetry/Nursery rhymes/Songs   **Age:** I–T

Songs and chants to be used by parents with very small children. Accompanied by a book with words to the rhymes, music, and suggested "bouncing" actions or finger plays for each. Traditional rhymes are gleaned from folk sources such as Mother Goose. The songs and chants cover topics in a baby's life, such as animals, going places, body parts, nonsense, and food. [1]

NURSERY RHYMES; PARTICIPATION; SONGS

Rev: BKL 2/15/88

635   ***Music, Music for Everyone.*** Vera B. Williams. Greenwillow Books, 1984. Unp. $13.88. (0-688-02604-4).   **Category:** Story   **Age:** P–K

A story showing love, warmth, and caring within the family and community. Rosa and her three friends organize the Oak Street Band to cheer up Rosa's sick grandmother. Later they are asked to play at a 50th anniversary party in the neighborhood, and the four girls share the income from their performance. Vibrantly colored and bordered pictures reinforce the warm and loving relationships discussed in the text. [1]

FAMILY LIFE; GRANDMOTHERS; MUSIC

Rev: ESLC

636 *Muskrat, Muskrat, Eat Your Peas!* Sarah Wilson. Simon & Schuster, 1989. Unp. $13.95. (0-671-67515-X). **Category:** Story **Age:** P–K

Opening with a scene from the "Pea Picnic," Muskrat is surrounded by assorted animal relatives encouraging him to eat his peas. He is then forced to remember the care it took to grow the peas. But Muskrat refuses to eat because "peas make him sneeze." Much to Muskrat's joy, the animal relatives all understand, and he is then given spaghetti. [2]

FOOD; MUSKRATS

Rev: BKL 6/15/89

637 *My Baby-Sitter.* Anne Rockwell. Illus. by Harlow Rockwell. Macmillan, 1985. Unp. $8.95. (0-02-777780-4). **Category:** Story **Age:** T–P–K

A simple, straightforward accounting of a boy and his baby-sitter. A small boy relates a typical evening with his teenage baby-sitter. His easy acceptance of being left by his parents would be useful to read to a child with separation anxiety. [1]

BABY-SITTING

Rev: CBY-87

638 *My Brown Bear Barney.* Dorothy Butler. Illus. by Elizabeth Fuller. Greenwillow Books, 1989. Unp. $11.88. (0-688-08568-7).

Category: Story **Age:** P–K

As a small girl travels through her days, she enumerates all the things that go with her, including her brown bear, Barney. But when it comes time to talk of going to school, and Mother says, "Bears don't go to school," the reader glimpses Barney peeking from the girl's backpack as she remarks, "We'll see about that." Pen and watercolor illustrations capture the warmth and love of the child's world. [2]

TEDDY BEARS

Rev: BKL 9/15/89; CBY-90

639 *My Camera: At the Zoo.* Janet Perry Marshall. Little, Brown & Co., 1989. Unp. $12.95. (0-316-54687-9). **Category:** Story **Age:** T–P

This "camera" uses illustrations instead of photographs, as an unseen narrator goes on a trip to the zoo that shows animals that the viewer would see through the camera lens. First, bits of the animal are shown, and then on the next page the full animal. A short text accompanies the clever, attractive illustrations.

ANIMALS; ZOOS [3]

Rev: BKL 7/89

640 *My Daddy.* Mathew Price. Illus. by Jean Claverie. Alfred A. Knopf, 1986. Unp. Paper $3.95. (0-394-87537-0).

Category: Participation and manipulative **Age:** I–T

Board book has lift-flaps that reveal a toddler and father playing familiar games. Each page asks a question such as "Who lets me go riding?" When the flap is moved, the answer is revealed: "Daddy," with a simple color illustration of a father and child doing the activity. [2]

BOARD BOOKS; FATHERS; PARTICIPATION; PLAY

Rev: CBK

641 *My Day.* Penelope Rippon. Penguin, 1990. Unp. $12.95. (0-670-83459-9).

Category: Informational **Age:** I–T–P

Soft, realistic vignettes and charmingly simple text follow the child from waking, dressing, eating, and playing, and on through bedtime. Taken from paintings of Rippon's own daughter, the illustrations reflect the glow and serendipity of "ordinary" childhood activities. [3]

FAMILY LIFE

642 *My Dog.* Heidi Goennel. Orchard Books, 1989. Unp. $14.99. (0-531-08434-5).

Category: Informational **Age:** T–P–K

Goennel uses bold, colorful illustrations and simple, yet descriptive wording to introduce young children to the different pedigree breeds. Although the young girl's narrative explains what she likes about each dog, she ends by saying she loves her own little brown dog the best. The two-page paintings with simple line- and block-lettered text make this a good choice to read to groups. DOGS [2]

Rev: BKL 9/15/89

643 *My First Book of Sign.* Pamela J. Baker. Illus. by Patricia Bellan Gillen. Reprint. Kendall Green Publications/Gallaudet University Press, 1989. 76 pp. $12.95. (0-930323-20-3).

Category: Informational **Age:** P–K

Anyone teaching a young hearing-impaired child to communicate will find this resource invaluable. The 150 words from early vocabulary lists are oganized by initial letter in picture dictionary format. A child signs the word, and a bright, colorful drawing of the object or concept is presented. Included are instructions for proper hand shapes and an index of sign descriptions, which contains written descriptions of movements. [3]

DEAFNESS; DICTIONARIES

644 *My First Drawing Book.* Tedd Arnold. Workman, 1986. Unp. $5.95. (0-89480-350-6). **Category:** Participation and manipulative **Age:** P–K

In this small board book, readers participate by completing each illustration with the clip-on pen that accompanies the book. The surface of each page makes write-on, wipe-off easy for repeated use. Nine imaginative scenes to be completed include: a boy bear watering his . . . and carrying home a . . . and a girl bear making a. . . . Excellent for parents traveling with young children.
ART; BOARD BOOKS; PARTICIPATION   [3]

645 *My First Picture Dictionary.* Katherine Howard. Illus. by Huck Scarry. Random House, 1978. Unp. Paper $1.95. (0-394-83486-0).
Category: Informational **Age:** P–K

The title says it all. The 250 illustrations extending the definitions and the alphabet printed down the outside of each page make this slim paperback useful in two ways: as a dictionary and as an introduction to reference books in general.   [2]
DICTIONARIES
Rev: NYT

646 *My First Playhouse.* Tedd Arnold. Workman, 1987. Unp. $5.95. (0-89480-471-5). **Category:** Participation and manipulative **Age:** P–K

This wordless toy book folds into a four-room cottage for Bialosky and Suzie Bear. Reverse the house to reveal a barn and garden, then attach the notched-cover roof. A storage bag is included for the stand-up punch-out bears and play pieces. Made of heavy wipe-clean cardboard for long-term wear.   [2]
PARTICIPATION; TEDDY BEARS; TOY AND MOVABLE BOOKS; WORDLESS

647 *My First Wild Animals.* Bettina Paterson. Reprint. Harper & Row, 1991. Unp. $9.89. (0-690-04773-8). **Category:** Informational **Age:** T–P–K

Photos of torn and cut paper collages give remarkable texture, movement, and depth to these wild animals. Simple, bright colors and the black, one-word label contrast clearly against the white or primary backgrounds. Animals range from the less familiar orangutan and koala to the elephant and giraffe.   [1]
ANIMALS

648 *My Hands Can.* Jean Holzenthaler. Illus. by Nancy Tafuri. Dutton, 1978. Unp. $12.95. (0-525-35490-5). **Category:** Informational **Age:** P–K

Hands, even those of a young child, can do many important things: button, zip, tie, clap, make music, talk. They can also hurt. Even more important, they can soothe and reach out to others. Simple colors and close-ups portray little hands engaged in these important tasks. [2]

HANDS

Rev: ESLC

649 *My Mama Says There Aren't Any Zombies, Ghosts, Vampires, Creatures, Demons, Monsters, Fiends, or Things.* Judith Viorst. Illus. by Kay Chorao. Atheneum, 1973. Unp. $12.95. (0-689-30102-2).

Category: Story   **Age:** K

Sometimes even mamas make mistakes. That is why Nick still has his doubts when his mother tells him that there are no monsters. After all, didn't she say he wasn't when he said he was going to be carsick? While learning to cope with his imagination, Nick also must come to grips with the fact that sometimes parents do make mistakes. And, luckily for Nick, sometimes they don't.

FEAR; MONSTERS; MOTHERS [2]

Rev: CBK; ESLC

650 *My Mother Is Weird.* Rachna Gilmore. Illus. by Brenda Jones. Ragweed Press, 1988. Unp. (0-920304-83-4).   **Category:** Story   **Age:** K

Before coffee, Mother has horns and claws, but usually coffee returns loving ol' mom. Today though, there was no coffee AND the toilet clogged up. I left for Maria's house; her mom is always nice. Except today, she also had horns and claws—the baby had kept her up. Sure was nice to get back home to my mom, who may be weird sometimes, but at least she doesn't have hair growing out of her ears! [2]

HUMOR; MOTHERS

651 *My Mother's House, My Father's House.* C. B. Christiansen. Illus. by Irene Trivas. Atheneum, 1989. 32 pp. $12.95. (0-689-31394-2).

Category: Story   **Age:** K

A girl lives with her mother Monday through Thursday and with her father the other days. While with her mother, they take pictures and go to the zoo. When she is with her father, they go to the library and on picnics. The parents have no interaction with one another, but they are respectful. This book could be useful as a springboard to spark discussion of similar family situations. [3]

DIVORCE; FATHERS; MOTHERS

Rev: BKL 3/1/89

652 *My Pictionary.* Scott, Foresman & Co., 1990. 144 pp. $17.50. (0-673-12488-6). **Category:** Informational **Age:** P–K

Words are arranged in categories familiar to children and by parts of speech. For each word, a picture is provided to assist the user in making the word-object-meaning connection. The visual appeal makes the pictionary inviting to browse. An index arranges the words alphabetically. [1]

DICTIONARIES; WORDS

653 *My Red Umbrella.* Robert Bright. Morrow Jr. Books, 1959. Unp. $8.95. (0-688-05249-5). **Category:** Story **Age:** P

Just right for small hands, this story features a happy little girl whose umbrella grows to shelter a succession of animals. Children can join with the simple text in counting each arrival. The engaging black and white drawings are in perfect contrast to the brightness of this magical rain gear. [1]

UMBRELLAS

Rev: ESLC; NYT

654 *My Saw.* Lyn Sandow. Illus. by Jody Wheeler. Warner Books, 1988. Unp. $4.95. (1-55782-309-X). **Category:** Participation and manipulative **Age:** T–P

Each of the six thick cardboard pages of this small book is shaped like a hand-saw. The front side tells the story of two boys using a saw to build a birdhouse. The back side pictures and identifies different types of saws. *My Saw* is one in the My First Tool series and could provide the young user with hours of "reading play." [3]

BOARD BOOKS; PARTICIPATION; TOOLS

655 *My Shadow.* Robert L. Stevenson. Illus. by Glenna Lang. David R. Godine, 1989. Unp. $14.95. (0-87923-788-0). **Category:** Poetry/Nursery rhymes/Songs **Age:** P–K

A young girl travels through a dream nightscape with her shadow companion and finally returns to her bed, rising in the faint early morning light only to find "...my lazy little shadow, like an arrant sleepy-head,/ Had stayed at home behind me and was fast asleep in bed." Lang uses strong, simple shapes of pure, luscious, untextured color to create a rich visual narrative for Stevenson's classic poem "My Shadow." [1]

POETRY; SHADOWS

656 ***My Spring Robin.*** Anne Rockwell. Illus. by Harlow Rockwell and Lizzy Rockwell. Macmillan, 1989. Unp. $12.95. (0-02-777611-5).

Category: Concept/Counting/Alphabet   **Age:** P–K

While searching for the robin whose song she recalls from the summer, a little girl discovers other signs of spring in her backyard. Told with a lively text and colorful illustrations, this is a real charmer. [2]

BIRDS; CONCEPTS; SPRING

Rev: BKL 3/15/89; CBY-90

657 ***My Very First Book of Shapes.*** Eric Carle. Harper & Row, 1974. Unp. $4.95. (0-694-00013-2).

Category: Participation and manipulative   **Age:** T–P–K

Carle invites the child to match the black, silhouetted shape on the top half-page with a corresponding, full-color familiar object on the bottom half-page. Unusual shapes (half-circles, crescent, and squiggle) are shown, as are the more familiar circle, square, rectangle, and triangle. Sturdy spiral binding allows easy manipulation. [3]

PARTICIPATION; SHAPE

658 ***Nana Upstairs & Nana Downstairs.*** Tomie dePaola. Putnam, 1973. Unp. $12.95. (0-399-60787-0).   **Category:** Story   **Age:** P–K

Four-year-old Tommy shares a special closeness with his two grandmas, whom he visits each Sunday. Nana Downstairs cares for his bedridden great-grandmother, Nana Upstairs. When Nana Upstairs dies, Tommy is heartbroken but consoled on seeing a falling star in the night sky. His mother tenderly suggests it is a kiss from Nana Upstairs. As a grown man, the boy reminisces about the love they shared. [1]

DEATH; FAMILY LIFE; GRANDPARENTS

Rev: BBC; NYT

659 ***Nanny Goat and the Seven Little Kids.*** Retold by Eric A. Kimmel. Illus. by Janet Stevens. Holiday House, 1990. Unp. $14.95. (0-8234-0789-6).

Category: Folklore/Folktales/Fairy tales   **Age:** P–K

These kids (complete with headphones, skateboards, and an umbrella stroller) are smart enough not to trust the wolf (in his "Big Bad" T-shirt). After he tricks them, their mom—Nanny Goat—cleverly rescues the family. Exuberant, comical illustrations give new life to this Grimm tale. [2]

FOLK AND FAIRY TALES

Rev: BKL 3/15/90

660 **The Napping House.** Audrey Wood. Illus. by Don Wood. Harcourt Brace Jovanovich, 1984. Unp. $13.95. (0-15-256708-9).

Category: Story   **Age:** T–P–K

While Granny sleeps, she is joined by a child, a dog, a cat, a mouse, and a flea. Just as the reader, too, is almost lulled to sleep, the flea bites the mouse, who scares the cat, and the chain reaction begins. Full-color illustrations begin on a blue, rainy day, and they end in the bright sunshine. The cumulative story has a surprise element, and the superb illustrations are blended into a book well suited for story hour. [1]

CUMULATIVE TALES; FLEAS; SLEEP

Rev: ESLC; NYT; PP   **Awards:** NYT Best Illustrated Book

661 **The Napping House.** Don Wood and Audrey Wood. Narrated by Melissa Leebaert. Weston Woods Studios, 1985. Videocassette. 5 min. $60.00.

Category: Story   **Age:** T–P–K

In this cumulative story, sleeping characters are added to a bed until finally "a wakeful flea" reverses the process, and each character awakens in turn. Dark, dreamy pictures, accompanied by soft, hypnotic narration and the drizzle of rain in the background, make this particular story suited to this medium. Also available in a filmstrip/audiocassette kit with script booklet (Harcourt, 1984). CUMULATIVE TALES; FLEAS; SLEEP [1]

Rev: BKL 5/1/89

662 **Nature Walk.** Douglas Florian. Greenwillow Books, 1989. 32 pp. $12.88. (0-688-08269-6).   **Category:** Story   **Age:** T–P

The wonders of the forest are explored in simple rhyme, "Stepping stones, Pinecones," and deceptively complex crayon and pen illustrations. Although the object or activity in the text dominates each double-page spread, as in nature, there is a multitude of background details that will delight the careful observer. [2]

ECOLOGY; NATURE; WALKING

Rev: CBY-90

663 **The New Baby.** Fred Rogers. Photos by Jim Judkis. Putnam, 1985. Unp. $12.95. (0-399-21236-1).   **Category:** Informational   **Age:** P–K

Mr. Rogers explores all the contradictory feelings about having a new baby in the family and shows healthy outlets for the negative ones. Superb photos by Jim Judkis capture the warmth and magic of this special time. [1]

BABIES

Rev: CBK; ESLC

664   *The New Baby Calf.* Edith Newlin Chase. Illus. by Barbara Reid. Scholastic, 1986. 32 pp. $19.50. (0-590-36768-4).

Category: Story   **Age:** P–K

In this long-out-of-print poem, a gentle cow nurtures her calf, encouraging him in his development. Sculptured plasticine gives a three-dimensional effect to the colorful illustrations of farm life. Large type and repetition of words and phrases may encourage youngsters to read this warm tale for themselves. [3]
Cows; Farms; Poetry
Rev: CBY-88

665   *New Shoes!* Dorothy Corey. Illus. by Dora Leder. Albert Whitman & Co., 1985. Unp. $11.95. (0-8075-5583-5).   **Category:** Story   **Age:** P–K

A little girl is frustrated because everyone around her, children and adults alike, is getting new shoes. She, however, can still wiggle her toes inside of her old shoes. Finally, the day comes when she cannot, and Mother takes her downtown to buy new shoes. Both her discouragement and excitement are portrayed by both color and black-and-white illustrations.   [2]
Shoes
Rev: ESLC

666   *Nice or Nasty: A Book of Opposites.* Nick Butterworth and Mick Inkpen. Little, Brown & Co., 1987. 24 pp. $12.95. (0-316-11915-6).

Category: Concept/Counting/Alphabet   **Age:** P–K

Bright and colorful illustrations are used to teach the concept of opposites, such as nice and nasty. Many of the comparisons are distinguished by their offbeat humor such as a plate of hamburgers versus a plate of snails and slugs, a shiny new robot fixing an old rusty one, and a mouse trying to move an elephant.   [2]
Concepts; Opposites
Rev: ESLC

667   *The Night After Christmas.* James Stevenson. Greenwillow Books, 1981. Unp. $12.88. (0-688-00548-9).   **Category:** Story   **Age:** P–K

Tossed into the trash when they are supplanted by new toys, a stuffed bear and a doll are rescued from abandonment and placed in a new house. This book will reassure the tenderhearted and those let down by postholiday blues. The illustrations are full of sleet yet are warm and fuzzy.   [2]
Christmas; Toys
Rev: BBC

668   *The Night Before Christmas.* Clement Clarke Moore. Illus. by Anita Lobel. Alfred A. Knopf, 1984. Unp. Paper $3.95. (0-394-81968-3).

Category: Poetry/Nursery rhymes/Songs   **Age:** P–K

Anita Lobel's full-color paintings bring the well-known poem to life. Text is set on the left page with most of the paintings on the right page, making this a good choice for reading aloud to small groups. The illustrator used 19th-century New York for the setting and included Santa's farewell with the sleigh flying over the Brooklyn Bridge. Also available in other formats from the National Library for the Blind and Physically Handicapped.   [1]

CHRISTMAS; POETRY

Rev: NYT

669   *Night in the Country.* Cynthia Rylant. Illus. by Mary Szilagyi. Bradbury, 1986. Unp. $13.95. (0-02-777210-1).   **Category:** Story   **Age:** P–K

A quiet text in dark hues that speculates on the noises and activities that occur during a night in the country. A beautiful textual and illustrative exploration of nature.   [3]

COUNTRY LIFE; NIGHT

Rev: CBY-87; ESLC; PP

670   *Nightfeathers.* Sundaira Morninghouse. Illus. by Jody Kim. Open Hand, 1989. 32 pp. $8.95. (0-940880-27-X).

Category: Poetry/Nursery rhymes/Songs   **Age:** K

Bedtime poems offering the black experience. Selections cover such subjects as rain, nighttime, dreams, and lullabies filled with soothing musical language ready to be shared aloud. Several of the poems use traditional Mother Goose openings and then take a new direction. Soft charcoal pencil illustrations are a tender accompaniment.   [2]

AFRO-AMERICANS; NIGHT; POETRY

671   *Nighty-Night, Little One.* Katharine Ross. Illus. by Lisa McCue. Random House, 1988. Unp. Paper $2.95. (0-394-89476-6).

Category: Poetry/Nursery rhymes/Songs   **Age:** T–P

This simple introduction to day animals and nocturnal animals uses poetry and whimsical drawings to show the differences between the two groups. The day animals—the squirrel, the duckling, and the chipmunk—fall asleep when the nocturnal animals—the owl, the opossum, and the raccoon—wake up. A sturdy board book designed for little hands.   [3]

ANIMALS; BOARD BOOKS; DAY; NIGHT; POETRY

Rev: CBY-89

672 *No Nap.* Eve Bunting. Illus. by Susan Meddaugh. Houghton Mifflin, 1989. Unp. $13.95. (0-89919-813-9). **Category:** Story **Age:** K

A humorous presentation of a familiar situation: a child's refusal to take a nap. The little girl and her father engage in hilarious antics with opposite goals in mind. The book reveals good humor in a parent-child relationship, and cartoonlike illustrations enhance the fun. [1]

FAMILY LIFE; SLEEP

Rev: BKL 9/15/89; CBY-90

673 *No One Knows for Sure.* Learning Tree, 1987. Filmstrip. 6 min. $39.00. **Category:** Informational **Age:** K

This program is both witty and humorous as it addresses the issue of the imminence of death in a sincere manner children can understand. In each example, the vital importance of hope is stressed, as is the necessity to keep on trying in spite of odds or fears. "Don't quit before the miracle!" Accompanied with audiocassette and guide. [2]

DEATH

Rev: BKL 3/1/88

674 *Noah's Ark.* Pam Adams. Child's Play, 1986. Unp. $4.95. (0-85953-267-4). **Category:** Wordless **Age:** I

Infants will delight in playing with and looking at this wordless plastic bath book. Noah, his wife, and numerous animals—two of each species—are colorfully displayed in 10 brief, yet entertaining pages. Ideal for an early introduction to the biblical story. [1]

BIBLE STORIES; WORDLESS

675 *Noah's Ark (Stories to Remember).* Illus. by Peter Spier. Narrated by James Earl Jones. Joshua M. Greene for Lightyear Entertainment, 1989. Dist. by Media Home Entertainment. Videocassette. 28 min. $14.98. **Category:** Story **Age:** P–K

Based on the Caldecott Award Book by Peter Spier (Doubleday, 1977), James Earl Jones narrates this lively, animated version of the biblical tale. The viewer will enjoy seeing the animals as they board the ark, perhaps be concerned by the loss of those left behind in the flood, and marvel at the beauty of the lush landscape once the waters have receded and the ark has come to rest on Mount Ararat. [1]

BIBLE STORIES

Rev: BKL 12/15/89 & 1/15/90

676 *Nobody Asked Me If I Wanted a Baby Sister.* Martha Alexander. Dial, 1971. Unp. $10.89. (0-8037-6402-2). **Category:** Story **Age:** P–K

When everyone makes such a fuss over his new baby sister, Oliver loads her into his wagon and sets off to see if someone else will take her. Eventually, when the baby cries and Oliver is the only one who can comfort her, he concludes, "You know, Bonnie, you're a lot smarter than I thought," and takes her back home. Clever, simple illustrations and color accurately express frustrations over the arrival of a new sibling. [1]
BROTHERS AND SISTERS; FAMILY LIFE
Rev: CBK

677 *North Country.* Daniel S. Souci. Doubleday, 1990. Unp. $14.95. (0-385-41320-3). **Category:** Informational **Age:** P–K

While man sleeps, forest animals in the North Country awaken to various activities. The great horned owl, coyote, fox, mountain lion, and bobcat stalk their prey while the porcupine, beaver, cottontail, raccoon, and mule deer forage carefully. Souci's moonlight landscapes capture the predator-prey relationship of these nocturnal animals. [3]
ANIMALS; FOREST, WOODS; NIGHT

678 *A Northern Alphabet.* Ted Harrison. Tundra Books, 1982. Unp. $14.95. (0-88776-209-3). **Category:** Concept/Counting/Alphabet **Age:** K

This "Northern" alphabet is filled with terms, places, and situations familiar to children who live north of the 60th parallel, but it would also be fun for others to introduce them to a different way of life. Each full-color illustration is accompanied by a few sentences, with several words starting with the appropriate alphabet letter. Sentences can be used as the beginning of a story that the child completes. [3]
ALPHABET; CANADA

679 *Not So Fast, Songololo.* Niki Daly. Margaret K. McElderry Books, 1986. Unp. $13.95. (0-689-50367-9). **Category:** Story **Age:** K

Malusi liked doing things slowly, but he leaped at the chance to accompany his grandmother on a shopping trip to the city. The South African setting is vividly evoked in the language and the detailed, full-page watercolor illustrations while simultaneously conveying the universal appreciation of an exciting excursion and a new pair of shoes. [1]
AFRICA; GRANDMOTHERS; SHOPPING
Rev: BBC; NYT

680 *Now One Foot, Now the Other.* Tomie dePaola. Putnam, 1980. Unp.
$13.95. (0-399-20774-0). **Category:** Story **Age:** P–K

A touching, understated account of parallel experience. Bobby, whose grandfather (and best friend) Bob taught him to walk, returns the favor when Bob is
disabled by a stroke. Soft pencil drawings, highlighted with brown, green, and
blue wash, reflect the gentle tone of the story. [2]

GRANDPARENTS; ILLNESS; WALKING

Rev: CBK

681 *Numbears: A Counting Book.* Kathleen Hague. Illus. by Michael Hague.
Henry Holt & Co., 1986. Unp. $10.95. (0-03-007194-1).
 Category: Concept/Counting/Alphabet **Age:** P–K

Michael Hague has painted richly colored illustrations to accompany Kathleen
Hague's whimsical rhymes for the 12 "numbears" in this counting book. For
each "numbear," a full-color page set in white frame faces the simple text of
the opposite page. The effect is comforting, predictable, and visually satisfying. This is a "must have" for preschoolers. [2]

COUNTING; POETRY; TEDDY BEARS

682 *Numblers.* Suse MacDonald and Bill Oakes. Dial, 1988. Unp. $13.89. (0-
8037-0548-4). **Category:** Concept/Counting/Alphabet **Age:** P–K

Numbers 1 to 10 on double-page spreads are magically transformed into animals and shapes made from the same number of pieces of brightly colored
shapes as the number they represent. The visually graphic changes from number to shape are easy to identify. Descriptive text about each shape is included
on the last page. A wonderful book for story hours both for the counting aspect and for teaching visual skills. [1]

COUNTING

Rev: BKL 9/15/88

683 *Nursery Songs and Lap Games.* Text compiled by Pamela Kennedy. Ideals
Publishing Corp., 1990. Unp. $16.95. (0-8249-7351-8).
 Category: Poetry/Nursery rhymes/Songs **Age:** I–T

A mixture of the familiar and not so, the 12 rhymes and finger plays are combined with lyrics, classic artwork, and an original music score for an active and
exciting experience for both the parent and the child. Easy-to-learn tunes
were composed by Stephen Elkins and are sung by Stephanie Lippencott. On
the flipside of the 50-minute cassette is the instrumental only. [1]

GAMES; NURSERY RHYMES; SONGS

684 ***Nutshell Library.*** Maurice Sendak. Harper & Row, 1962. Unp. $10.95. (0-06-025500-5).   **Category:** Story   **Age:** P–K

Four of Maurice Sendak's most popular books are packaged together in a collection perfect for travel or reading while snuggling. "Pierre" teaches us to "care"; "One Was Johnny" is a counting book; "Chicken Soup With Rice" sets months to poetry; and "Alligators All Around" shows the reader busy alligators in alphabetical order.   [3]
ALPHABET; COUNTING
Rev: CBK; NYT

685 ***Nutshell Library.*** Maurice Sendak. Weston Woods Studios, 1987. Video-cassette. 16 min. $59.00.   **Category:** Story   **Age:** P–K

Carole King's musical versions of these four Sendak short stories (Harper & Row, 1962) are enticing and entertaining. Any young child would be intrigued. "Alligators All Around" is an alphabet adventure; "One Was Johnny" is a counting book; "Chicken Soup with Rice" describes each month of the year; and "Pierre" is the tale of a boy who learns to care.   [3]
ALPHABET; COUNTING

686 ***Oats and Wild Apples.*** Frank Asch. Holiday House, 1988. Unp. $13.95. (0-8234-0677-6).   **Category:** Story   **Age:** P–K

Calf wanted to play, but Mother Cow was not in the "M-O-O-D." Calf finds a fawn and after a day of playing in a clearing, they decide to return home. As the sun sets, each is reunited with its mother, having made a new friend. The simple, colorful drawings provide a focus for the development of this new friendship.   [1]
FRIENDSHIP

687 ***The Ocean.*** Pam Adams. Child's Play, 1984. Unp. $7.95. (0-85953-193-7).   **Category:** Participation and manipulative   **Age:** K

A wordless cardboard manipulative and panorama book that opens in zigzag fashion illustrates the various recreational, vocational, and survival functions that the ocean performs in different geographic areas around the world. As one peers around each of the many corners and sides, cutout window openings add to opportunities for exploration, allowing both interior and subterranean views.   [3]
PARTICIPATION; SEA AND SEASHORE; WORDLESS

688 ***Ocean Magic Books: My Friend the Manatee, My Friend the Sea Otter, My Friend the Polar Bear, and Others.*** Jeffery Schneider. Illus. by Wilfred Spoon. Schneider Educational Products, 1991. Unp. $4.95. (1-877779-08-3). **Category:** Story **Age:** T

Simple rhyming texts and bold graphic illustrations in bright saturated colors with black outlines follow children from a variety of cultures as they observe or cavort with the title animal in these volumes. Poetic images, striking artwork, and unusual subject matter result in superior examples of board book production. [3]
BOARD BOOKS; SEA AND SEASHORE

689 ***Oh, A-Hunting We Will Go.*** John Langstaff. Illus. by Nancy Winslow Parker. Margaret K. McElderry Books, 1974. Unp. $14.95. (0-689-50007-6). **Category:** Poetry/Nursery rhymes/Songs **Age:** T–P–K

Children will delight at the thought of catching an armadillo and putting it in a pillow or visualizing a bear in flannel underwear. Parents and teachers alike will find this work a useful way to encourage language development. The playful words and color illustrations are sure to encourage new verses, and the piano and guitar accompaniment makes this a useful addition to any music lesson. [2]
SONGS
Rev: NYT

690 ***Oh, the Places You'll Go!*** Dr. Seuss. Random House, 1990. Unp. $13.99. (0-679-90527-8). **Category:** Story **Age:** P–K

In a positive, life-affirming story, Dr. Seuss in his usual wacky way offers rhyming advice on how to succeed in life. A young pajama-clad boy sets out to make his way in life and has both negative and positive experiences. The large, colorful, cartoonlike pictures explode with zany, imaginative creatures. "You have brains in your head/You have feet in your shoes/You can steer yourself/Any direction you choose." [2]
POETRY; SUCCESS
Rev: BKL 1/1/90

691 ***Oh, What a Mess.*** Hans Wilhelm. Crown, 1988. Unp. $12.95. (0-517-56909-4). **Category:** Story **Age:** P–K

Franklin is the only neat pig in the family and is embarrassed to live in such a messy home. One day he wins an award for a rainbow drawing. This picture changes the whole household, as the family cleans up both the house and themselves. [1]

CLEANLINESS; PIGS

Rev: BKL 6/1/88

692 *Old Bear.* Jane Hissey. Philomel, 1986. Unp. $14.95. (0-399-21401-1).

Category: Story **Age:** P–K

Enchanting story of four nursery friends who are worried that their playmate, Old Bear, has been left in the attic far too long. They make several ingenious albeit unsuccessful attempts to rescue Old Bear before hitting upon a heroic plan. Hissey's text will stimulate young imaginations, and her illustrations will entice small hands to "feel" the fuzzy textures of the stuffed animals. Also available in other formats from the National Library for the Blind and Physically Handicapped. [1]

BEARS; BRAVERY; FRIENDSHIP; TOYS

Rev: CBY-87; ESLC   **Awards:** BKL Editors' Choice 1986

693 *Old MacDonald Had a Farm.* Illus. by Glen Rounds. Holiday House, 1989. Unp. $14.95. (0-8234-0739-X).

Category: Poetry/Nursery rhymes/Songs **Age:** T–P

Large print and the characteristic broad humor of Rounds' drawings enchance this old classic. Joining the usual cows, sheep, dogs, roosters, turkeys, horses, geese, and pigs is the skunk, who ends the book with a PEE-YOO here and a PEE-YOO there and everywhere a PEE-YOO! Good smelly fun! [1]

ANIMALS; FARMERS; SONGS

Rev: CBY-90

694 *Old MacDonald Had a Farm.* Illus. by Nancy Hellen. Orchard Books, 1990. Unp. $13.95. (0-531-05872-7).

Category: Poetry/Nursery rhymes/Songs **Age:** T–P

One of the most original renditions of the familiar, well-loved song for children. The song begins with an illustration of Old MacDonald waving and facing a cut-out barnyard scene. When the page is turned, the animals appear one by one from behind a barrel, haystack, basket, etc. Youngsters will want this one sung and shared again and again. The music is on the end pages.

ANIMALS; FARMS; SONGS [1]

695   *Oliver Jones.* Produced and directed by Lillian Spina. Coronet MTI Film & Video, 1989. Videocassette. 10 min. $250.00.

Category: Story   **Age:** K

Oliver Jones is proud of his very blue skin, too proud actually. In serious, sensitive, yet humorous and poetic ways, Oliver learns that skin color does not mean that one is "less or more, better or worse"; in fact, it "doesn't change what is you." He learns that people are all different colors, sizes, and shapes and that it is what's inside, not outside, a person that really counts. Accompanied with a guide.   [2]

PREJUDICE; PRIDE; SKIN COLOR

Rev: BKL 8/89

696   *On Market Street.* Arnold Lobel. Illus. by Anita Lobel. Greenwillow Books, 1981. 40 pp. $13.88. (0-688-84309-3).

Category: Concept/Counting/Alphabet   **Age:** P–K

An imaginary adventure down Market Street yields apples, books, clocks, doughnuts, and more, all represented by people composed of the actual items. Vivid and imaginative, the illustrations invite children to identify the objects in their new surroundings.   [1]

ALPHABET; SHOPPING

Rev: CBK; ESLC; NYT

697   *One Bear at Bedtime.* Mick Inkpen. Little, Brown & Co., 1988. Unp. $12.95. (0-316-41889-7).

Category: Concept/Counting/Alphabet   **Age:** P–K

Imagination takes a flight of fantasy as a little boy prepares for bedtime. This counting book will delight young children and will encourage them to look for the nine elusive caterpillars throughout the book. Each page has engaging artwork of the animals to be counted. The art also shows the little boy's attachment to his favorite bear, which he realizes is all he needs at bedtime.   [2]

BEDTIME; COUNTING; TEDDY BEARS

Rev: BKL 3/15/88

698   *One Fine Day.* Nonny Hogrogian. Macmillan, 1971. Unp. $12.95. (0-02-744000-1).   **Category:** Folklore/Folktales/Fairy tales   **Age:** P–K

"One fine day a fox traveled through the great forest. When he reached the other side he was very thirsty." So begins a humorous retelling of the favorite American folktale about the fox who, after stealing milk from an old woman, loses his tail to her knife. During the rest of the day, the fox displays a variety of emotions as he must bargain to get his tail back. A story that children will

follow with ease and anticipation. Also available in other formats from the National Library for the Blind and Physically Handicapped.   [3]
FOLK AND FAIRY TALES; FOXES
Rev: BBC; CBK; ESLC; NYT   **Awards:** Caldecott Medal

699   *One Fish, Two Fish, Red Fish, Blue Fish.* Dr. Seuss. Beginner Books, 1960. 64 pp. $5.95. (0-394-80013-3).   **Category:** Story   **Age:** T–P–K

A beginning reader using nonsense and made-up words offers a rhyming story that covers flying things from here to there and everywhere and also provides a comical outlet for the silliness that preschoolers absolutely love. Wild and comical illustrations are typical of the Seuss style.   [2]
POETRY
Rev: ESLC; NYT

700   *101 Things to Do with a Baby.* Jan Ormerod. Lothrop, Lee & Shepard, 1984. 32 pp. $11.75. (0-688-03801-8).   **Category:** Story   **Age:** P–K

A charming list of 101 things that an older sister can do to entertain, to nurture, and to have fun with a baby brother. Mom and Dad also get involved. From morning to night, the emphasis is on family time spent together in typical and loving activities.   [2]
BABIES
Rev: BBC; CBK; ESLC; NYT

701   *One Hungry Monster: A Counting Book In Rhyme.* Susan Heyboer O'Keefe. Illus. by Lynn Munsinger. Little, Brown & Co., 1989. Unp. $12.95. (0-316-63385-2).   **Category:** Story   **Age:** K

Details the arrival of first one, then two, then three hungry monsters, and so on. The uninvited guests display "monstrous" manners as they wreak havoc in a young boy's house. They smear peanut butter on their faces, braid spaghetti into wigs, and wear pumpkins for hats. Both the repetitive pattern used in counting the monsters and the colorful pictures of their mayhem are sure to bring giggles from young audiences.   [2]
COUNTING; MANNERS; MONSTERS
Rev: BKL 6/1/89

702   *1 Hunter.* Pat Hutchins. Greenwillow Books, 1982. 24 pp. $12.88. (0-688-00615-9).   **Category:** Concept/Counting/Alphabet   **Age:** P–K

A determined hunter strides myopically through the jungle, unaware of two elephants, three giraffes, and so on. Colorful and funny, this counting book offers young readers the chance to find a clue on each page, which leads to the action that follows on the next page.   [2]
COUNTING; HUNTING
Rev: NYT

703 *One Light, One Sun.* Raffi. Shoreline, 1985. Dist. by A & M Records. Audiocassette. 34 min. $8.98.
                              Category: Poetry/Nursery rhymes/Songs   **Age:** T–P–K

Using a variety of songs, Raffi takes listeners to many parts of the world to show how all people are under the same sun. Simple but catchy vocal and instrumental pieces; good for group or independent listening.   [2]
SONGS; SUN; WORLD
Rev: SLJ 4/86   **Awards:** ALSC Notable Recording

704 *One Morning in Maine.* Robert McCloskey. Viking Penguin, 1952. Unp. $13.95. (0-670-52627-4).   **Category:** Story   **Age:** P–K

Sal and her family live on the Maine seacoast among the boats, gulls, clams, and seals. This quiet story chronicles a typical morning when Sal awakens with a loose tooth, sees a loon, runs on the shore, helps her father dig clams, and takes a boat ride to a nearby grocery store. The blue-toned, award-winning drawings capture the feel of seacoast life. Also available in other formats from the National Library for the Blind and Physically Handicapped.   [2]
FAMILY LIFE; SEA AND SEASHORE
Rev: CBK   **Awards:** Caldecott Honor Book

705 *1 One-Year-Old: Counting Children 1 to 10.* Juliet Bawden. Photos by Helen Pask. Henry Holt & Co., 1989. Unp. $9.95. (0-8050-1257-5).
                              Category: Concept/Counting/Alphabet   **Age:** P

Full-color photographs show children from one year old to 10 engaged in a variety of activities: playing ball, walking in the rain, riding a tricycle, painting, etc. The young child will enjoy seeing how children grow as the numbers increase.   [3]
COUNTING
Rev: BKL 5/15/90; SLJ 9/90

706 *One Sun: A Book of Terse Verse.* Bruce McMillan. Holiday House, 1990. Unp. $14.95. (0-8234-0810-8).

Category: Poetry/Nursery rhymes/Songs **Age:** T–P–K

High-quality pictures capture the activities of a little boy who spends a day at the beach. Terse verse (two monosyllabic words that sound alike) briefly describes events as the boy and his friends explore their surroundings. Good minority representation. [1]

POETRY

707 *One, Two, Buckle My Shoe: A Book of Counting Rhymes.* Rowan Barnes-Murphy. Simon & Schuster, 1988. Unp. $10.95. (0-671-63791-6).

Category: Poetry/Nursery rhymes/Songs **Age:** T–P–K

Lighthearted watercolor illustrations bring alive many familiar and some not-so-familiar counting rhymes. This collection features both American and British rhymes, and it goes beyond counting to three or ten. As with most nursery rhymes, rhythm and rhyme portray nonsense and fun. This collection offers colorful counting fun. [1]

COUNTING; NURSERY RHYMES

Rev: BKL 3/15/88; ESLC

708 *1 2 3 for Kids.* The Chenille Sisters. Red House Records, 1989. Audiocassette. 30 min. $10.00.

Category: Poetry/Nursery rhymes/Songs **Age:** I–T–P–K

Performed by a harmonious female trio, which has been featured on "A Prairie Home Companion," the selections include traditional favorites ("Hokey Pokey," "At the Codfish Ball"), contemporary favorites (Shel Silverstein's "I'm Being Swallowed by a Boa Constrictor"), original songs, and a few less well known songs by other artists. All are guaranteed to entertain children of all ages. [1]

DANCING; HUMOR; SONGS

Awards: Parents' Choice

709 *1 2 3 I Can Count.* Illus. by Lynn N. Grundy. Ladybird Books, 1980. Unp. $3.95. (0-7214-5053-9).

Category: Concept/Counting/Alphabet **Age:** P–K

Numbers one to 10 are each given a double-page spread. An arabic numeral is enlarged on the left page, with the number's name printed along with the appropriate number of pink circles. On the right page, each number is brightly

illustrated with pictures of familiar objects arranged in their correct numerical pattern. Last five pages provide practice in matching, sorting, and counting.
COUNTING [3]

710 **_One, Two, Three to the Zoo: A Counting Book._** Eric Carle. Putnam, 1990. Unp. Paper $5.95. (0-399-21970-6).

Category: Concept/Counting/Alphabet   Age: T–P

From the engine to the caboose, Carle has created a counting masterpiece. From the colorful numbers covering the endpapers to the bold menagerie of bright, colorful animals riding in the various cars, this book is an imaginative game. Illustrations are large with a little mouse in each to add to the humor.
COUNTING [1]

711 **_One Wide River._** American Melody, 1988. Audiocassette. 41 min. $9.98.

Category: Poetry/Nursery rhymes/Songs   Age: P–K

The musical arrangements for this collection of traditional songs and stories are entertaining and delightful. The banjo, fiddle, mandolin, and harmonica along with clear and distinct voices provide uplifting music for young people.
ANIMALS; SONGS [3]
Awards: Parents' Choice Award

712 **_Oonga Boonga._** Frieda Wishinsky. Illus. by Suçie Stevenson. Little, Brown & Co., 1990. Unp. $13.95. (0-316-94872-1).   Category: Story   Age: K

No one could make Baby Louise stop crying. Finally, brother Daniel comes in and with the words "Oonga boonga" causes Baby Louise to smile. These words work well for all until Daniel leaves, but he returns to save the day with new words: "Bonka wonka." Cartoon-style color illustrations depict the family and neighborhood trials with Baby Louise. Nonsense words are very appealing when read aloud. [1]
BABIES; BROTHERS AND SISTERS
Rev: SLJ 5/90

713 **_Opposites._** Rosalinda Kightley. Little, Brown & Co., 1986. 32 pp. $6.95. (0-316-49931-5).   Category: Concept/Counting/Alphabet   Age: T–P

Twelve vividly colored pairs of opposites using large simple designs invite the toddler's attention. Whether shared one-on-one or by a large group, the bold colors and familiar subjects (train, frog, book, bunny, child, chair, and more) easily illustrate such concepts as open/shut, full/empty, up/down, and dry/wet.
CONCEPTS; OPPOSITES [2]
Rev: CBY-88

714 *Oranges and Lemons.* Compiled by Karen King. Illus. by Ian Beck. Oxford University Press, 1985. 48 pp. $12.95. (0-19-279796-4).
Category: Poetry/Nursery rhymes/Songs **Age:** P–K

Forty-six different singing games are included to use with preschoolers. Both written and illustrated directions are given for each game. A good resource tool for preschool teachers to use with their students. [2]
GAMES; SONGS
Rev: BKL 2/15/88

715 *The Orchard Book of Nursery Rhymes.* Edited by Zena Sutherland. Illus. by Faith Jaques. Orchard Books, 1990. 88 pp. $21.95. (0-531-05903-0).
Category: Poetry/Nursery rhymes/Songs **Age:** I–T–P

Favorite rhymes, songs, lullabies, finger plays, tales, nonsense verse, and more are cumulated by an established expert in children's literature. Richly colored and detailed illustrations placed in an 18th-century setting grace each page.
NURSERY RHYMES; SONGS [1]

716 *Our World, Parts I, II, and III.* National Geographic Society, 1989. Filmstrip. 16 min. $67.00. **Category:** Informational **Age:** P–K

This multicultural and global approach to families, schools, neighborhoods, communities, countries, and the earth is culturally expansive. Each section explores similarities and differences. As expected, the photography is colorful and captivating. An excellent means of vocabulary development. Accompanied with audiocassettes and guide. [1]
COMMUNITIES, NEIGHBORHOODS; FOREIGN LANDS; SCHOOL
Rev: BKL 8/89

717 *Out and About.* Shirley Hughes. Lothrop, Lee & Shepard, 1988. 48 pp. $12.88. (0-688-07691-2).
Category: Poetry/Nursery rhymes/Songs **Age:** T–P–K

Rhyming text celebrates the seasons through the eyes of a small girl. The pages address important topics such as "Mudlarks," "Wind," and "Seaside" as they progress through a year. Hughes's illustrations depict a lively neighborhood enriched by ethnic diversity. [2]
NATURE; POETRY; WEATHER
Rev: BKL 3/15/88

718   *Outside-In: A Lift-the-Flap Body Book.* Clare Smallman and Edwina Riddell. Barron's Educational Series, 1986. Unp. $12.95. (0-8120-5760-0).
Category: Informational   **Age:** P–K

Simple text and lift-the-flap illustrations explain the functions of the body. Topics include the skin, muscles, keeping cool and warm, breathing, bones and teeth, the digestive system, blood, and the heart, and there are easy-to-do experiments. Questions are asked with visual clues in full-color illustrations. An excellent introduction for preschoolers. [2]
ANATOMY; PARTICIPATION; TOY AND MOVABLE BOOKS
Rev: SLJ 5/87

719   *Over in the Meadow.* John Langstaff. Illus. by Feodor Rojankovsky. Harcourt Brace Jovanovich, 1957. Unp. $14.95. (0-15-258854-X).
Category: Poetry/Nursery rhymes/Songs   **Age:** T–P–K

Ten meadow creatures and their families are introduced in this version of the old counting rhyme. Detailed colorful illustrations and a text that includes variety and repetition provide information and entertainment. Music score with the complete text is included on the last page. [3]
ANIMALS; SONGS
Rev: ESLC

720   *Over the River and Through the Wood.* Lydia Marie Child. Illus. by Brinton Turkle. Coward McCann, 1974. Unp. $14.95. (0-698-20301-1).
Category: Poetry/Nursery rhymes/Songs   **Age:** T–P–K

Turkle has done an excellent job of capturing the excitement of an old-fashioned Thanksgiving holiday filled with family and good food. Black-and-white illustrations framed by an orange border are paired with the pages containing the text. Double pages of full-color illustrations depict such scenes as the sleigh ride, the woods, and children sledding. The song with music score is included at the end. [2]
FAMILY LIFE; SONGS; THANKSGIVING DAY
Rev: BBC

721   *The Owl and the Pussycat.* Edward Lear. Illus. by Lorinda B. Cauley. Putnam, 1986. Unp. $12.95. (0-399-21254-X).
Category: Poetry/Nursery rhymes/Songs   **Age:** T–P–K

Lear's classic tale of how the owl courts the pussycat at sea and of their eventual marriage is exquisitely illustrated by Cauley. The audience will easily take in every detail, from the fish that dance while the owl sings, to the lavishness of a tropical island wedding celebration. The color of the moon reflecting on the nighttime waters illuminates romance, and the costumes of the animal wedding guests radiate joy. [1]

ANIMALS; NURSERY RHYMES; POETRY

Rev: BKL 1/1/88

---

722 *Owl Moon.* Jane Yolen. Illus. by John Schoenherr. Philomel, 1987. Unp. $14.95. (0-399-21457-7). **Category:** Story **Age:** P–K

Warm, personal tale set on a winter's evening when a family tradition of love leads a father and his young daughter on a late-night owling expedition. Their patiently silent hope is rewarded as the father's repeated calls are eventually answered by the owl. Illustrations strike a perfect balance between accurate representation of the natural world and expression of the emotional nuances experienced by father and child. [1]

FATHERS; OWLS; WINTER

Rev: CBY-88; ESLC **Awards:** Caldecott Medal

---

723 *Ox-Cart Man.* Donald Hall. Illus. by Barbara Cooney. Viking Penguin, 1979. Unp. $14.95. (0-670-53328-9).

Category: Informational **Age:** P–K

Taking the listener back to early 19th-century New England, this story portrays the activities of one family throughout a year. By beginning with the selling of the family's goods in October, the story presents the concept of seasons and work as cyclical. Text and illustrations combine to reflect a time and a life-style otherwise unknown to most readers. [2]

FARMS; SEASONS; WORKING

Rev: BBC; NYT **Awards:** Caldecott Medal; NYT Best Illustrated Book

---

724 *"Paddle," Said the Swan.* Gloria Kamen. Atheneum, 1989. Unp. $12.95. (0-689-31330-6).

Category: Poetry/Nursery rhymes/Songs **Age:** T–P–K

Soothing bedtime rhymes show rural animals' sounds and movements. The swan tells her babies to paddle; a mare urges her colt to run. The sounds of crickets and owls tell that nighttime is approaching as the warm illustrations show the sunset. At the end of the day, the mother encourages her baby to sleep. Soft, colorful illustrations combine with the gentle, simple text to make this good bedtime reading. [3]

ANIMALS; BEDTIME; NURSERY RHYMES

Rev: BKL 3/15/89; CBY-90

725 *Pair of Red Clogs.* Masako Matsuno. Illus. by Kazue Mizumara. Listening Library, 1976. Filmstrip. 13 min. $24.95.   **Category:** Story   **Age:** K

Using Japanese culture as a backdrop, the author and illustrator relate the story of a little girl and her adventures with a pair of red clogs. Her excitement over her new shoes is tainted when she breaks one playing the weather-telling game. In an effort to find a way to get them replaced, she gets her shoes dirty, but her mother makes her clean and dry them herself. The girl's efforts are rewarded in the end (Collins, 1960). Accompanied with audiocassette and guide.   [2]

JAPAN; SHOES

Rev: ELSC

726 *Pajamas.* Livingston Taylor and Maggie Taylor. Illus. by Tim Bowers. Harcourt Brace Jovanovich, 1988. Unp. $13.95. (0-15-200564-1).

          Category: Story   **Age:** T–P

Bright acrylic drawings leap off every page in this rhythmic bedtime story that captures the fun and warmth of pajama time. Taken from the authors' song, the bouncy text will invite parents to sing along as they ready little ones for bed.   [1]

BEDTIME; SLEEP

Rev: BKL 9/1/88

727 *The Pancake Boy: An Old Norwegian Folk Tale.* Retold and illustrated by Lorinda B. Cauley. Putnam, 1988. Unp. $14.95. (0-399-21505-0).

          Category: Folklore/Folktales/Fairy tales   **Age:** P–K

This version of the Norwegian gingerbread boy contains picturesque language. The pancake greets everyone by saying, "I have given the slip to . . ." Additional interest and involvement on the part of listeners are elicited by the question "And what do you think happened next?" Full-color illustrations show expressions of surprise and dismay, anticipation and delight, and finally, contentment.   [2]

FOLK AND FAIRY TALES; NORWAY

Rev: BKL 10/1/88

728 *The Park in the Dark.* Martin Waddell. Illus. by Barbara Firth. Lothrop, Lee & Shepard, 1989. Unp. $11.88. (0-688-08517-2).

          Category: Story   **Age:** P–K

Three stuffed toys escape the nursery to play in the park at night until they are frightened by the train. They flee back to the safety of the sleeping child's

bed. Appealing stuffed animal characters take part in this adventure, illustrated in soft, nighttime colors. Facial expressions depict the changing mood of the story, which is told in repetitive, rhyming verse. [2]
NIGHT; TOYS

729   *Passover.* Miriam Nerlove. Albert Whitman & Co., 1989. Unp. $10.95. (0-8075-6360-9).   **Category:** Informational   **Age:** P–K

A simple description of the celebration of Passover, beginning with a brief Bible history and ending with the seder meal. The young boy narrator selects incidents with which young readers can identify. A page of notes offers further information. [3]
PASSOVER
Rev: BKL 1/15/90

730   *Pat the Bunny.* Dorothy Kunhardt. Western, 1987. Unp. (0-307-14000-8).
                    Category: Participation and manipulative   **Age:** I–T

This classic baby's activity book invites the youngest hands to feel the fuzzy bunny and Daddy's scratchy beard, the tiniest noses to sniff the flowers, and the most innocent eyes to look into the shiny mirror. This small, cardboard book comes with a plush bunny. An excellent choice for encouraging connections between words and the senses. [2]
PARTICIPATION; RABBITS; TOY AND MOVABLE BOOKS
Rev: CBK; NYT

731   *Patrick and Ted Ride the Train.* Geoffrey Hayes. Random House, 1988. Unp. $4.95. (0-394-89872-9).   **Category:** Story   **Age:** P–K

An exciting adventure unfolds for bears Patrick and Ted when they ride the train to visit Grandpa Poopdeck. When two weasel bandits board the train, Patrick and Ted help save the day. This title is part of the Just Right for 4s and 5s series. The soft, rounded illustrations portray a host of friendly looking animal characters. [1]
TRAINS
Rev: BKL 2/1/89; ESLC

732   *Paul Bunyan.* Steven Kellogg. Morrow Jr. Books, 1988. Unp. $7.95. (0-688-08397-8).   **Category:** Folklore/Folktales/Fairy tales   **Age:** K

In this splendid retelling of the traditional tall tale, Kellogg's illustrations jump from the pages in humorous, copious detail. Along with Babe—his big blue ox —and his lumbering crew, Paul Bunyan journeys across the United States.

The legendary heroes fight the wild Gumberoos in the Appalachians, scalp the tops of the Rocky Mountains, and dig a trench later known as the Grand Canyon. [2]

FOLK AND FAIRY TALES

Rev: NYT

733 *The Paw Paw Patch: Favorite Children's Songs.* Performed by Phil Rosenthal. Phil Rosenthal, 1987. Dist. by American Melody. Audiocassette. 30 min. $9.98. **Category:** Poetry/Nursery rhymes/Songs **Age:** T–P–K

Phil Rosenthal sings traditional songs, such as "Six Little Ducks," "Looby Loo," and "Polly Wolly Doodle," accompanied by bluegrass instrumentals. Clear vocalization and lively use of instruments such as banjos, fiddles, and mandolins make this a must for sing-alongs. [2]

NURSERY RHYMES; SONGS

Rev: SLJ 4/88 **Awards:** ALSC Notable Recording

734 *The Pea Patch Jig.* Thacher Hurd. Crown, 1986. Unp. $11.95. (0-517-56307-X). **Category:** Story **Age:** P–K

The title, taken from an old fiddle tune, features three related stories of the adventures of Baby Mouse and her family. Large, bright vegetables on the endpapers give just a taste of the delightful color and action inside, where the irrepressible little mouse gets into much mischief in Farmer Clem's garden but redeems herself by saving her family from a fox. [2]

GARDENING; MICE

Rev: BKL 4/15/89; CBY-87 **Awards:** SLJ Best Books of the Year

735 *A Peaceable Kingdom: The Shaker Abecedarius.* Illus. by Alice Provensen and Martin Provensen. Viking Penguin, 1978. Unp. $13.95. (0-670-54500-7). **Category:** Concept/Counting/Alphabet **Age:** I–T–P

Originally published as "Animal Rhymes" in the *Shaker Manifesto* of July 1882, this illustrated alphabet rhyme uses Shaker sayings to present creatures of all kinds in a Shaker environment. Each written in 26 lines of "creature" words, the rhyme presents the alphabet as the first letter of each line, allowing any three creatures to finish the set. This allows inclusion of such unusual creatures as bobolink and dragonfly. [3]

ALPHABET; ANIMALS; POETRY

Rev: NYT **Awards:** NYT Best Illustrated Books

736   *Penguin Moon.* Annie Mitra. Holiday House, 1989. Unp. $13.95. (0-8234-0749-7).   **Category:** Story   **Age:** P–K

Penguin passes the long, lonely nights sitting on an iceberg and wishing desperately that the moon could talk to him. Beluga the whale grants him five wishes. Through the use of his wishes, his dream finally comes true. The story is told with simplicity and use of bright colors that will quickly catch the attention of young children.   [3]
MOON; PENGUINS
Rev: BKL 11/15/89; SLJ 10/89

737   *People from Mother Goose: A Question Book.* Lee Bennett Hopkins. Illus. by Kathryn Hewitt. Gulliver Books/Harcourt Brace Jovanovich, 1989. Unp. $6.95. (0-15-200558-7).
Category: Poetry/Nursery rhymes/Songs   **Age:** P–K

Questions are asked about well-known characters from Mother Goose, and rhymed answers are provided on each page of this small book. Attractive watercolors and having the reader turn the page to discover the answer make the book appealing. The contents are ideal for sharing by a caregiver but are also appropriate for browsing by the independent youngster.   [2]
MOTHER GOOSE; NURSERY RHYMES; TOY AND MOVABLE BOOKS
Rev: BKL 11/1/89

738   *Perfect the Pig.* Susan Jeschke. Henry Holt & Co., 1981. 40 pp. $10.95. (0-8050-0704-0).   **Category:** Story   **Age:** K

Perfect wished for wings, and a good deed granted him his wish. Treated as a misfit by both pigs and birds, he flies to the city and into the life of Olive, an artist. Olive earns money for them by painting pictures of Perfect. Lost while flying in a fog, Perfect is captured and enslaved by an evil man who forces him to perform as The Great Flying Oink. The story does end happily when Perfect is rescued by Olive.   [2]
PIGS
Rev: NYT

739   *Pet Food.* Jan Pienkowski. Doubleday, 1990. Unp. $5.95. (0-385-41344-0).   **Category:** Concept/Counting/Alphabet   **Age:** T–P

Five little monsters feed their pet various-shaped objects that reappear in silhouette inside him. A companion to an equally clever, versed subtraction book, *Eggs for Tea.*   [3]
CONCEPTS; MONSTERS; SHAPE

740 *Pet Show!* Ezra Jack Keats. Macmillan, 1972. Unp. $14.95. (0-02-749620-1). **Category:** Story **Age:** P–K

On the day of the pet show, Archie's cat disappears. Determined to participate, Archie uses his imagination and wins a ribbon for the quietest pet, an invisible pet germ he calls Al. An elderly woman finds his cat and returns it in time to win another ribbon, which Archie generously allows her to keep. Bold illustrations with the occasional appearance of collage reproduce the inner-city setting of the text. [1]
FRIENDSHIP; IMAGINATION; PETS
Rev: CBK; ESLC **Awards:** Reading Rainbow Book

741 *Peter, Good Night.* Alison Weir. Illus. by Deborah K. Ray. Dutton, 1989. 24 pp. $11.95. (0-525-44464-5). **Category:** Story **Age:** T–P

A young boy gets into his bed for the night and looks out the window. All the things he sees give him comfort and encourage him to sleep. The clouds whisper, "May your pillow be fluffy," and the moon, trees, stars, and fog have messages as well. Finally, a breeze says, "May your sleep be peaceful," and Peter's is. Beautiful illustrations enhance this bedtime tale. [2]
BEDTIME; NIGHT; SLEEP
Rev: BKL 4/1/89; CBY-90

742 *Peter Lippman's Numbers: A Pull-Tab Surprise Book.* Peter Lippman. Grosset & Dunlap, 1988. Unp. $8.95. (0-448-19105-9).
Category: Concept/Counting/Alphabet **Age:** T–P

The pull-tabs on this number book are very sturdy and should hold up well. Each page features a bright object illustrating the numbers one through 10; each tab reveals a coordinated object. A nicely designed selection that children will enjoy over and over again. [2]
COUNTING; GAMES; PARTICIPATION
Rev: BKL 11/15/88

743 *Peter Rabbit and Friends.* Beatrix Potter. Read by Pauline Brailsford. Weston Woods Studios, 1986. Audiocassette. 37 min. $9.00.
Category: Story **Age:** T–P–K

Reading in a British accent, the narrator follows the exact text of Beatrix Potter's tales. This collection includes: "The Tale of Peter Rabbit," "The Tale of Jeremy Fisher," "The Tale of Tom Kitten," "The Tale of Two Bad Mice," and "The Tale of Benjamin Bunny." [2]
ANIMALS
Rev: SLJ 4/87 **Awards:** ALSC Notable Recording

744 *Peter Rabbit's ABC.* Beatrix Potter. Warne, 1987. Unp. $6.95. (0-7232-3423-X).   **Category:** Concept/Counting/Alphabet **Age:** T–P

A wonderful way to learn the alphabet and experience Potter's illustrations at their best. Each letter is coordinated by both color and text with the illustrations and their captions. For example, the letter C is shown in uppercase and lowercase in an orange box. It is represented by a picture of a carrot with the phrase "C is for Carrot." On the facing page is a wonderful illustration of a rabbit eating a carrot.   [2]
ALPHABET; RABBITS
Rev: CBY-88

745 *Peter Rabbit's 1 2 3.* Beatrix Potter. Warne, 1988. Unp. $6.95. (0-7232-3424-8).   **Category:** Concept/Counting/Alphabet **Age:** T–P

Counting was never so much fun as in this wonderfully coordinated collection of illustrations. In each offering of 1 through 12, a question is answered by both the side-by-side illustrations and the text. As in its companion book, *Peter Rabbit's ABC*, the source of each illustration is given under the accompanying caption. Bold numerals on the endpapers carry out the theme and add interest.   [2]
COUNTING; RABBITS
Rev: BKL 3/15/88

746 *Peter Spier's Christmas.* Peter Spier. Doubleday, 1983. 40 pp. $13.95. (0-385-131844).   **Category:** Wordless **Age:** T–P–K

This wordless book details the many activities of a family with three youngsters prior to Christmas, during Christmas, and in the first week after. Spier's illustrations are rich in detail and are so complete that young children will love supplying the words for this story.   [1]
CHRISTMAS; WORDLESS
Rev: ESLC

747 *Peter Spier's Rain.* Peter Spier. Doubleday, 1981. Unp. $12.95. (0-385-15484-4).   **Category:** Wordless **Age:** T–P–K

A brother and sister enjoy a rainy afternoon when they put on their gear and wander around their neighborhood. This wordless book captures many adventures and discoveries in vivid, detailed illustrations. Two drenched youngsters return home to a warm bath and dry clothes. The nighttime scenes, while the

storm continues, as well as the bright, sunshiny morning scenes are extremely
effective. [1]

PLAY; RAIN; WORDLESS
Rev: CBK; ESLC; NYT

748 *Peter Spier's Rain.* Peter Spier. Music and narration by Michael Barber
and Family. Spoken Arts, 1984. Filmstrip. 10 min. $39.95.

Category: Story **Age:** T–P–K

Just the right amount of narration has been added to this wordless book to
make the filmstrip version truly enjoyable. Natural sounds and music bring to
life the experiences of a young brother's and sister's walk in the rain as they
investigate their neighborhood, then return home for a hot bath and a cozy
dinner. Since the book itself is difficult to share with a large group, the film
version with accompanying audiocassette and guide is a valuable addition
(Doubleday, 1981). [1]

PLAY; RAIN

749 *Peter's Chair.* Ezra Jack Keats. Harper & Row, 1967. Unp. $13.89. (0-06-
023111-4). **Category:** Story **Age:** P–K

Peter feels threatened by his new baby sister when he finds his father painting
all his baby furniture "pink." Peter and his dog, Willie, run away from home
and establish residence on the sidewalk in front of their house. Mother coaxes
Peter back home with "something special for lunch," and upon realizing he
cannot fit into his baby chair anymore, Peter helps his father to paint the chair
for baby Susie. [2]

AFRO-AMERICANS; FAMILY LIFE; SIBLING RIVALRY
Rev: CBK; ESLC **Awards:** Reading Rainbow Book

750 *Pets and Their Wild Relatives.* National Geographic Society, 1989. Dist.
by Karol Media. Videocassette. 15 min. $59.95.

Category: Informational **Age:** P–K

Although lacking in transition from one scene to another, the program has
merit for the information it provides on the origin of pets and their place in
the home environment. The viewer is shown rabbits, guinea pigs, parrots,
goldfish, cats, and dogs. The characteristics that make for a good pet as well as
the pets' counterparts in the wild are displayed. [2]

ANIMALS; PETS
Rev: SLJ 11/89

751 *Petunia.* Roger Duvoisin. Alfred A. Knopf, 1950. Unp. $8.99. (0-394-90865-1).
                                  Category: Story   **Age:** P–K

Petunia the silly goose thinks that she can become wise just by carrying a book under her wing. After a series of humorous near-disasters, she learns that in order to be truly wise, she must learn what is in the book.   [2]
GEESE; PRIDE; READING
Rev: NYT

752 *Petunia the Silly Goose Stories.* Roger Duvoisin. Alfred A. Knopf, 1987. 145 pp. $15.95. (0-394-98292-4).
                                  Category: Story   **Age:** P–K

A collection of five tales featuring Petunia and the animals of Pumpkin Farm and its environs. Both a monetary and literary bargain, in one volume are brought together, unabridged and in full color, "Petunia," "Petunia Beware," "Petunia's Treasure," "Petunia's Christmas," and "Petunia Takes a Trip." Good-natured, silly fun; a lengthier text makes this more suitable for older preschoolers.   [1]
ANIMALS; FARMS; GEESE
Rev: BBC; CBY-88

753 *Picnic.* Emily Arnold McCully. Harper & Row, 1984. 32 pp. $12.89. (0-06-024100-4).
                                  Category: Wordless   **Age:** P–K

A beautiful day beckons the large mouse family to enjoy a picnic in the country. After frolicking about playing ball, swimming, and taking some pictures, the mouse family realizes one member is missing. All ends well. Enchanting, colorful pictures tell this wordless story.   [3]
MICE; PICNICKING; WORDLESS
Rev: BBC; ESLC; NYT   **Awards:** ALA Notable Books; Christopher Award

754 *Pig Pig Grows Up.* David McPhail. Live Oak Media, 1985. Unp. $19.95. (0-941078-96-5).
                                  Category: Story   **Age:** T–P–K

Pig Pig plays to the hilt his role as the baby of the family, until the day he is catapulted into action and maturity to save a real baby in the path of his careening stroller. Large, expressive watercolor and ink illustrations are set against a solid white background and aptly capture the humorous relationship between the long-suffering mother and her petulant piglet.   [2]
GROWING UP; PIGS
Rev: BBC; CBK; ESLC

755 *Pig Pig Rides.* David McPhail. Live Oak Media, 1988. Audiocassette. 3 min. $12.95. **Category:** Story **Age:** P–K

Lively music accompanies the introduction to Pig Pig's adventurous plans for the day. Sound effects of trains, rockets, horses, and race cars bring the accompanying book to life as Pig Pig drives a train to China and a rocket to the moon, jumps elephants with a motorcycle, makes a delivery by truck, breaks a racing car speed record, and jockeys his own horse (Dutton, 1982). [3]
PIGS; TRAVEL
Rev: BKL 12/15/88

756 *Piggies.* Audrey Wood and Don Wood. Illus. by Don Wood. Harcourt Brace Jovanovich, 1991. Unp. $13.95. (0-15-256341-5).
Category: Concept/Counting/Alphabet **Age:** T–P

Five pairs of piggies—fat, smart, long, silly, and wee ones—frolic on a young child's corresponding fingers. All the gleeful imagination of the child's activities—making snowballs, mudpies, and soap bubbles as well as tromping across the bed covers—is shown through the child's eyes as views of the elfin creatures are displayed. Backlighted oil illustrations add to the magical air as these "piggies" take on a life and will of their own. [1]
COUNTING; FINGER PLAY; PIGS

757 *The Pigs' Picnic.* Keiko Kasza. Putnam, 1988. Unp. $13.95. (0-399-21543-3). **Category:** Story **Age:** T–P–K

Mr. Pig puts on finery borrowed from his friends Fox, Lion, and Zebra on his way to ask Miss Pig to go on a picnic. By the time he knocks on her door, he has a bushy tail, a shaggy mane, and gray stripes. His strange appearance leads Miss Pig to slam the door in his face. When he returns the borrowed items and goes to her door again, this time she is happy to see him. Being oneself is okay, Mr. Pig discovers. [2]
ANIMALS; PICNICKING; PIGS
Rev: BKL 10/15/88; CBY-90

758 *Pippo Gets Lost.* Helen Oxenbury. Macmillan, 1989. 14 pp. Paper $5.95. (0-689-71336-3). **Category:** Story **Age:** T–P

Tom the toddler is unable to locate Pippo, his toy monkey and closest companion. Told from the boy's point of view, the story makes readers identify with his feelings of desperation, which quickly turn to panic at the monkey's loss. A mixture of simple line drawings with text and full-color illustrations on reinforced heavy-duty paper adds to the book's usefulness. One in a series of 12 Pippo titles. [1]

LOSING THINGS; MONKEYS; TOYS

Rev: BKL 10/15/89

759 *Planting a Rainbow.* Lois Ehlert. Harcourt Brace Jovanovich, 1988. Unp. $14.95. (0-15-262609-3). **Category:** Story **Age:** T–P–K

A mother and child share in the joy of the annual gardening cycle, from planting seeds, seedlings, and bulbs to picking a dazzling bouquet. Vibrant double-page collages allow children to see the growth process above and below the ground until all is in glorious bloom. All plants are labeled, and a flip-page design creates a rainbow display of flowers. A botany lesson has never been so appealing. [1]

COLOR; FLOWERS; GARDENING

Rev: BKL 5/15/88; CBY-89

760 *The Please Touch Cookbook.* Please Touch Museum. Silver Burdett Press, 1990. 64 pp. Paper $6.95. (0-671-70558-X).

Category: Informational **Age:** K

Simplified recipes organized by mealtime are illustrated by black and white line drawings and accompanied by riddles, poems, stories, or activities to do while the meal is cooking. Some are directly related to children's literature, such as the recipe for stone soup that suggests reading the book. Recipes will require a little adult supervision and assistance. [3]

COOKING

761 *Plunk's Dreams.* Helen V. Griffith. Illus. by Susan Condie Lamb. Greenwillow Books, 1990. Unp. $12.88. (0-688-08813-9).

Category: Story **Age:** P–K

While observing his dog, Plunk, who wiggles and woofs in his sleep, John imagines what Plunk is dreaming. Simple dreams of chasing rabbits or eating dinner are not adventurous enough for his fertile imagination. The reader is treated to visions of Plunk the Indian dog traveling in a canoe, the brave dog scaring off alien dogs from outer space, etc. But John is certain, when Plunk's tail wags, that he is dreaming of him. [3]

DOGS; DREAMS; IMAGINATION

Rev: BKL 3/15/90

762 *Poems to Read to the Very Young.* Selected by Josette Frank. Illus. by Eloise Wilkin. Random House, 1982. 48 pp. $6.95. (0-394-95188-3).

Category: Poetry/Nursery rhymes/Songs **Age:** T–P

Reissue of a classic collection of short poems with just the sort of clear-colored illustrations children like. This familiar art often fills the whole page along with real poems and real authors, going beyond traditional nursery rhymes. Works by contemporary poets as well as poets of generations ago have been selected. Acknowledgments and an index of first lines are included. [2]
NURSERY RHYMES
Rev: CBK

763 *Polar Bear, Polar Bear, What Do You Hear?* Bill Martin, Jr. and Eric Carle. Henry Holt & Co., 1991. Unp. $13.95. (0-8050-1759-3).

Category: Story **Age:** T–P–K

A colorful, rhythmic approach to learning zoo animals and the sounds they make. Includes unusual animals such as flamingoes, walruses, peacocks, and leopards. Great for groups and sure to encourage assistance from your audience. The closing illustration shows children dressed in masks for all the animals shown in the book. [1]
ANIMALS; SOUNDS; ZOOS

764 *The Polar Express.* Chris Van Allsburg. Houghton Mifflin, 1985. 32 pp. $16.95. (0-395-38949-6). **Category:** Story **Age:** P–K

A young boy is taken aboard the *Polar Express* on Christmas Eve en route to the North Pole, where he is chosen by Santa Claus to receive the first gift of Christmas. Although he loses the bell, on Christmas morning he finds it under the tree in a small box with the admonition to fix the hole in his pocket. Not only is this a story filled with wonder, but also the Van Allsburg illustrations are a wonder unto themselves. [1]
CHRISTMAS; DREAMS; TRAINS
Rev: NYT **Awards:** Caldecott Medal; NYT Best Illus. Book

765 *The Polar Express.* Chris Van Allsburg. Narrated by Mandy Patinkin. Random House/Miller-Brody, 1988. Dist. by American School Publishers. Filmstrip. 12 min. $29.50. **Category:** Story **Age:** P–K

Instead of sleigh bells, a young boy hears the hiss of the *Polar Express* waiting to transport him to the North Pole, where he receives the first gift of Christmas from Santa. Through Tony winner Mandy Patinkin's superb narration and Rosemary Killen's haunting, mysterious production, we can hear the bell's

magical ringing. Curricular connections for literature, social studies, drama, and art provided (Houghton Mifflin, 1985). Accompanied with audiocassette.
CHRISTMAS; DREAMS; TRAINS [1]
Rev: SLJ 4/88   **Awards:** ALSC Notable Filmstrip

766   *The Porcelain Cat.* Michael Patrick Hearn. Illus. by Leo Dillon and Diane Dillon. Little, Brown & Co., 1987. 32 pp. $12.95. (0-316-35330-2).
Category: Story   **Age:** K

When an old sorcerer decides to bring a china cat to life and rid his library of rats, he sends his apprentice to find the missing ingredient for the spell. Thus begins Nickon's adventure into a world of mystical creatures. The artists' illustrations are full of surprises to delight the eye. Readers will revel in one discovery after another. [2]
CATS; MAGIC
Rev: NYT

767   *A Porcupine Named Fluffy.* Helen Lester. Illus. by Lynn Munsinger. Houghton-Mifflin, 1986. 32 pp. Paper $13.95. (0-395-36895-2).
Category: Story   **Age:** P–K

A humorous narrative about a porcupine named Fluffy, who realizes that he definitely does not fit his name. How he goes about trying to become fluffy will delight and amuse children. Musinger captures these moments through a continuous array of hilarious illustrations. [1]
NAMES; PORCUPINES
Rev: CBY-87

768   *Prehistoric Animals.* Gail Gibbons. Holiday House, 1988. Unp. $13.95. (0-8234-0707-1).   **Category:** Informational   **Age:** K

A simple overview of the dinosaur era. Gibbons provides interesting facts about many curious animals, including the ancestors of the horse and the elephant. A time line and clear, scale-sized color illustrations add to the information. [2]
ANIMALS; SCIENCE
Rev: BKL 9/1/88

769   *The Princess and the Frog.* Rachel Isadora. Greenwillow Books, 1989. 32 pp. $12.95. (0-688-06374-8).
Category: Folklore/Folktales/Fairy tales   **Age:** P–K

The Grimm tale of a princess who promises friendship to the frog who will rescue her ball but then revokes the promise once the ball is retrieved. Her father insists she honor her promise when the frog appears at their door. After three nights, the frog turns into a handsome prince, an evil spell broken. Isadora has lavished her retelling with rich watercolors that make this story special. [3]

FOLK AND FAIRY TALES
Rev: BKL 3/15/89

---

770   ***The Princess and the Pea.*** Hans Christian Andersen. Translated by Anthea Bell. Illus. by Eve Tharlet. Picture Book Studio, 1987. Unp. $13.95. (0-88708-052-9).

Category: Folklore/Folktales/Fairy tales   **Age:** P–K

A queen devises a test to prove a princess's authenticity before marrying her young son. After sleeping on a pea hidden under 20 mattresses and 20 eiderdown quilts, the princess complains about the terrible night due to lying on something hard. Of course, only a real princess could have detected a pea. Humorous text combined with soft, watercolor illustrations makes for a perfect story. [2]

FOLK AND FAIRY TALES; ROYALTY
Rev: BKL 1/1/88; ESLC; SLJ 2/88

---

771   ***The Pudgy Book of Make-Believe.*** Illus. by Andrea Brooks. Putnam, 1984. Unp. $2.95. (0-448-10209-9).

Category: Participation and manipulative   **Age:** T

This sturdy board book illustrates the world of make-believe in humorous everyday scenes. A baby blanket becomes a teepee, a box becomes "your very own little house," a chair becomes a train, and a full bathtub becomes a sailing ship. Illustrations depict both boy and girl toddlers in soft pastel tones. Excellent for one-to-one sharing. [3]

BOARD BOOKS; MAKE-BELIEVE
Rev: CBK

---

772   ***The Pumpkin Blanket.*** Deborah Turney Zagwyn. Fitzhenry & Whiteside, 1990. Unp. $18.95. (0-88902-741-2).   **Category:** Story   **Age:** P–K

Clee's colorful quilt, a gift from the Northern Lights when she was born, warmed her soul as well as her body. But when Clee was "just-past-small, on-her-way-to-big," she lovingly yet painfully sacrificed each of the 12 beautiful

patches to keep the 12 garden pumpkins warm. A tender story of letting go and growing up, richly illustrated in warm, harvest-toned watercolors.   [2]
BLANKET; GROWING UP; HALLOWEEN

773   *The Puppy Who Wanted a Boy.* Jane Thayer. Illus. by Lisa McCue. Morrow Jr. Books, 1986. Unp. Paper $3.95.   **Category:** Story   **Age:** K

A warm, sentimental story of a puppy named Petey, who asks his mother for only one Christmas present: a boy. Unfortunately, his mother cannot find a boy for him. He searches all over the town but can find no dog who is willing to give up a boy. Just when he is ready to give up, Petey ends up outside a boys' orphanage, where he finds not one but many boys to love. Also available in other formats from the National Library for the Blind and Physically Handicapped.   [2]
CHRISTMAS; DOGS
Rev: CBY-87

774   *Push, Pull, Empty, Full: Book of Opposites.* Tana Hoban. Macmillan, 1972. 32 pp. $12.95. (0-02-744810-X).
     Category: Concept/Counting/Alphabet   **Age:** T–P

Interesting, clear, black-and-white photographs illustrate opposites. Photos of animals, objects, and people are familiar to young readers and are selected to demonstrate these concepts effectively.   [1]
CONCEPTS; OPPOSITES; WORDS
Rev: CBK; ESLC

775   *Puss in Boots.* Illus. by John S. Goodall. Margaret K. McElderry Books, 1990. Unp. $14.95. (0-689-50521-3).
     Category: Folklore/Folktales/Fairy tales   **Age:** P–K

This favorite tale of a clever cat pleasing his poor master with his ability to find food and a beautiful princess, who soon becomes a wife, will delight young children. Goodall uses watercolor paintings without text to show the adventures of the cat and his master through the countryside. Half-pages used between the full-page spreads reveal the sequential events.   [1]
CATS; FOLK AND FAIRY TALES; WORDLESS

776   *The Quarreling Book.* Charlotte Zolotow. Illus. by Arnold Lobel. Harper & Row, 1963. Unp. $11.89. (0-06-026976-6).
     Category: Story   **Age:** P–K

The story follows a chain of events that illustrate what can happen with feelings and tempers on a gray rainy day. The ending, which includes the sun's coming out, leads to resolution for all. Also available in other formats from the National Library for the Blind and Physically Handicapped. [2]
FAMILY LIFE; FEELINGS
Rev: CBK

777 *The Raffi Singable Songbook.* Raffi. Illus. by Joyce Yamamoto. Crown, 1987. 104 pp. $15.95. (0-517-56638-9).
Category: Poetry/Nursery rhymes/Songs   **Age:** T–P–K

The rhyme, rhythm, and pure delight of famed folksinger Raffi's first three albums are available in printed form. Lyrics, music score, and chord changes are included for over 50 songs. Arrangements are simple enough to be mastered by even beginning musicians. The spirit of these engaging tunes is echoed in the illustrations: children's original crayon and marker drawings.
SONGS [1]
Rev: NYT

778 *Raffi's Christmas Treasury: Fourteen Illustrated Songs and Musical Arrangements.* Raffi. Illus. by Nadine Bernard Westcott. Crown, 1988. 84 pp. $17.95. (0-517-56806-3).
Category: Poetry/Nursery rhymes/Songs   **Age:** T–P–K

A delightful holiday treasury comes alive in this illustrated collection of 15 songs. Traditional carols like "Deck the Halls" and "The First Noel," children's favorites including "Frosty" and "Rudolph," and Raffi's own "Every Little Wish" are combined with other selections from various artists to add sparkle to the story hour. Lyrics are brightly illustrated in the first half, and musical arrangements in the second. [2]
CHRISTMAS; MUSIC; SONGS
Rev: BKL 11/15/88

779 *The Raggy Taggy Toys.* Joyce Dunbar. Illus. by P. J. Lynch. Barron's Educational Series, 1988. Unp. $10.95. (0-8120-4130-5).
Category: Story   **Age:** K

Hannah loves to rescue old stuffed animals and dolls, but her mother, who is getting annoyed by the clutter, has forgotten what it's like to be a little girl and love old toys, until one day something changes her mind. Lively watercolor illustrations in full color add to the magic of this tender story. [2]
MAGIC; TOYS
Rev: BKL 2/1/89

780 *Rain.* Robert Kalan. Illus. by Donald Crews. Greenwillow Books, 1978. 24 pp. $12.88. (0-688-84139-2).

Category: Concept/Counting/Alphabet **Age:** I–T

In a bright blue sky, the clouds gather, and the rain begins. It falls on everything—black road, green grass, orange flowers, brown fence, and red car. Finally, the rain stops, and a rainbow appears and gathers together all the colors the young readers have seen. [2]

COLOR; CONCEPTS; RAIN

Rev: BBC

781 *Rain Makes Applesauce.* Julian Scheer. Illus. by Marvin Bileck. Holiday House, 1964. 36 pp. $13.95. (0-8234-0091-3).

Category: Poetry/Nursery rhymes/Songs **Age:** P–K

". . . And rain makes applesauce" is the only phrase that makes any sense in this whimsical nonsense book. Delicate, detailed drawings colorfully pull the reader into imaginatively thinking about the world. Occasionally, little friends in the corners remind the reader that this is "just talking silly talk," but a child can play with the words and images long after the book is closed. [1]

IMAGINATION; POETRY; RAIN

Rev: ESLC

782 *A Rainbow of My Own.* Don Freeman. Live Oak Media, 1987. Videocassette. 5 min. $34.95. **Category:** Story **Age:** P–K

After a rainstorm, a young boy tries to catch the rainbow. Although he is disappointed, he pretends he has a rainbow as a playmate. When he arrives home, he discovers a rainbow "of my own" made from the sun shining through his fishbowl. Includes a guide with suggested activities. Based on the book by Don Freeman (Viking, 1966). [1]

IMAGINATION; RAINBOWS

783 *The Random House Book of Mother Goose: A Treasury of 306 Timeless Nursery Rhymes.* Selected and illustrated by Arnold Lobel. Random House, 1986. 176 pp. $14.95. (0-394-86799-8).

Category: Poetry/Nursery rhymes/Songs **Age:** T–P–K

Large, colorful pictures that match the nursery rhymes ranging from just one to several related rhymes on each page. The book includes favorite childhood rhymes as well as others not so well-known. For those who like Arnold Lobel's illustrations, this is a must for a Mother Goose collection. [1]

MOTHER GOOSE; NURSERY RHYMES

Rev: BBC; BKL 1/1/88; NYT

784 *The Random House Book of Poetry for Children.* Selected by Jack Prelutsky. Illus. by Arnold Lobel. Random House, 1983. 248 pp. $16.95. (0-394-85010-6).

Category: Poetry/Nursery rhymes/Songs   **Age:** T–P–K

A fine anthology of poems and nursery rhymes for every occasion, with a nice balance of the traditional and the new. The poems include selections by Silverstein, Belloc, and Livingston as well as traditional poets like Frost, Sandburg, and Hughes. The ample paintings and drawings by Lobel enhance the excitement generated by the selections. A must for every child's collection.   [1]

POETRY

Rev: NYT

785 *Read-Aloud Rhymes for the Very Young.* Selected and narrated by Jack Prelutsky. Illus. by Marc Brown. Alfred A. Knopf, 1986. 98 pp. $19.95. (0-394-87218-5).   **Category:** Poetry/Nursery rhymes/Songs   **Age:** T–P–K

Prelutsky has selected for younger children more than 200 poems about animals, the weather, everyday experiences, the seaside, holidays, etc. Brown's humorous, softly colored illustrations add to the enjoyment of this well-balanaced anthology. The book is accompanied by a 40-minute audiocassette with an introduction discussing the positive impact of reading poetry aloud to young children.   [1]

NURSERY RHYMES; POETRY

Rev: BKL 1/1/88; CBY-88; NYT

786 *Ready . . . Set . . . Read! The Beginning Reader's Treasury.* Compiled by Joanna Cole. Illus. by Anne Burgess & others. Doubleday, 1990. 144 pp. $17.95. (0-385-41416-1).

Category: Poetry/Nursery rhymes/Songs   **Age:** P–K

The beginning reader will find many hours of fun in this extensive anthology. From Dr. Seuss to Maurice Sendak, from "Stories" and "Poems" to "Fun and Games," the compilation is an exemplary collection of children's literature at the beginner's level. Table of contents, title index, and author and artist index included.   [1]

CONCEPTS; POETRY; READING

787 *The Real Mother Goose: Picture Word Rhymes.* Illus. by Blanche Fisher Wright. Reprint. Checkerboard, 1987. 128 pp. $9.95. (0-02-689038-0).

Category: Poetry/Nursery rhymes/Songs   **Age:** P–K

Traditional Mother Goose favorites are presented in a rebus picture/word format. The picture words are shown at the bottom of each page along with the correct spelling of the words they represent. Framed, old-fashioned illustrations reminiscent of Kate Greenaway adorn each left-hand page; the text, in large black type with colored rebus pictures, is on the right.   [2]

MOTHER GOOSE; NURSERY RHYMES; PUZZLES

Rev: NYT

788   *The Rebus Treasury.* Jean Marzollo. Illus. by Carol D. Carson. Dial, 1986. 64 pp. $12.89. (0-8037-0255-8).

Category: Poetry/Nursery rhymes/Songs   **Age:** P–K

Varied collection of 41 well-loved rhymes and songs uniquely presented in rebus form. Includes introduction explaining what a rebus is as well as a key to some of those used in the book. Large, well-spaced letters and colored rebuses make the selections easy to read. Young children will appreciate being able to "read," while older children will enjoy the novelty of each rebus.   [2]

NURSERY RHYMES; REBUSES; WORDS

Rev: BBC; CBK; ESLC; SLJ 8/86

789   *Red, Blue, Yellow Shoe.* Tana Hoban. Greenwillow Books, 1986. Unp. Paper $4.95. (0-688-06563-5).

Category: Concept/Counting/Alphabet   **Age:** T

Ten basic colors are presented in this glossy board book. Each page features a single color presented three ways: in a swatch of that color, spelled out in writing, and illustrated by an item in that color. Familiar objects, such as a leaf, a mitten, and an orange, are used to exemplify the color.   [2]

BOARD BOOKS; COLOR; CONCEPTS

Rev: CBY-87

790   *Red Riding Hood.* James Marshall. Dial, 1987. unp. $10.89. (0-8037-0345-7).   **Category:** Folklore/Folktales/Fairy tales   **Age:** P–K

Contemporary version of the favorite fairy tale including a smiling Red Riding Hood and a cunning, yet polite wolf. Bright, uncluttered illustrations in primary colors coordinate nicely with the lively text. Details vary slightly from more familiar versions (Red Riding Hood's basket contains custard; Granny is annoyed when the wolf interrupts her reading; etc.), but the story will be enjoyed nevertheless.   [2]

FOLK AND FAIRY TALES; WOLVES

Rev: CBY-88

791 **Redbird.** Patrick Fort. Orchard Books, 1988. 18 pp. $19.95. (0-531-05746-1). **Category:** Participation and manipulative **Age:** T–P–K

Redbird, a small plane, has to overcome bad weather and other obstacles before it can land at the airport. Raised illustrations and a braille translation of the simple text invite the sighted child to use his or her sense of touch. [1]
AIRPLANES; BLINDNESS; PARTICIPATION
Rev: BKL 8/88

792 **Reuben Runs Away.** Richard Galbraith. Orchard Books, 1989. Unp. $12.95. (0-531-08390-X). **Category:** Story **Age:** P–K

Reuben, a neglected teddy bear, decides to run away from home and try life in the city. He boards a train, walks the streets, sleeps in a garbage can, and is finally rescued by an old lady who sells him along with her other "junk." A grandfather buys him for his granddaughter, who happens to be the same little girl the bear left. It is a happy reunion. Children will sympathize with Reuben's troubles and the comforting resolution. [2]
RUNNING AWAY; TEDDY BEARS
Rev: BKL 3/15/89

793 **Rhythms on Parade.** Words and music by Hap Palmer. Educational Activities, 1989. Audiocassette. 30 min. $10.50.
Category: Poetry/Nursery rhymes/Songs **Age:** T–P–K

Introduces young children to the musical concepts of tempo, dynamics, and meter in a fun and inviting way. A variety of adults and children perform the vocals. A useful guide outlines the objectives of each song and describes activities children can do with the music. [3]
SONGS
Rev: BKL 6/15/89

794 **Richard Scarry's ABC Word Book.** Richard Scarry. Random House, 1971. Unp. $8.95. (0-394-82339-7).
Category: Concept/Counting/Alphabet **Age:** P–K

Little animal people, illustrated in clear, bright colors, populate the pages. Curly Pig, Farmer Fox, Huckle Cat, and others are busily involved in a variety of exciting activities. In brief stories for each letter, the letter is printed in red whenever it appears in the text or in the labels for the many objects depicted. [3]
ALPHABET; ANIMALS
Rev: CBK

795 *Richard Scarry's Best Counting Video Ever!* Emily P. Kingsley and Sharon Lerner. Illus. by Richard Scarry. Jerry Lieberman Productions, 1989. Dist. by Random House Home Video. Videocassette. 30 min. $14.95.

Category: Concept/Counting/Alphabet   **Age:** T–P

Busytown is bustling with all the children's favorite characters: Huckle Cat, Lowly Worm, Bananas Gorilla, and many more. Everyone is looking for things to count from 1 to 20. Lily Bunny invites the viewer to assist in their efforts and adventure. The slow pace enables those watching to participate and feel a sense of accomplishment as they keep up with and even outwit the animals.   [3]

COUNTING

Rev: BKL 1/15/90

796 *Richard Scarry's Best Word Book Ever.* Richard Scarry. Revised. Western, 1963. 71 pp. $8.95. (0-307-15510-2).

Category: Informational   **Age:** T–P–K

An encyclopedic approach to the naming of a child's first realities, this book is quite possibly a toddler's first reference book. From boats and ships to breakfast, school, bedtime, useful tools, and circus performers, Scarry presents an ever-cheerful world of information for tiny fingertips—and far beyond.   [1]

CONCEPTS; WORDS

Rev: NYT

797 *Ride a Purple Pelican.* Jack Prelutsky. Illus. by Garth Williams. Greenwillow Books, 1986. 64 pp. $13.00. (0-688-04031-4).

Category: Poetry/Nursery rhymes/Songs   **Age:** K

Like Greenaway, Caldecott, and Lear, Prelutsky and Williams team up in the 20th century to present U.S. children with Mother Goose–like rhymes. The two-page illustrations of zany people and animals continue a time-honored tradition for children, updated and rejuvenated.   [3]

POETRY

Rev: BKL 1/1/88

798 *Rock & Read.* Tamar Simon Hoffs. Narrated by Pauly Shore. MCA Home Video, 1989. Videocassette. 29 min. $14.95.

Category: Poetry/Nursery rhymes/Songs   **Age:** P–K

A combination of live-action and computer animation invites young children to sing and dance to traditional songs in this video, which also teaches them to recognize key words that appear in each song. Some of the songs included are

"Twinkle, Twinkle, Little Star," "I'm a Little Teapot," and "Eensy Weensy Spider." [2]
PARTICIPATION; READING; SONGS

799 Rockabye Bunny. Linda Danly. Danly Productions, 1987. Audiocassette. 38 min. $11.00. **Category:** Poetry/Nursery rhymes/Songs **Age:** I–T–P

Join Rockabye Bunny on his wonderful day, from waking and exploring the garden to mealtime, bath time, and finally snuggling into mother's arms at day's end. A tender collection of six original songs are woven through the baby bunny's story on side one. Side two offers "Bunny Dream," a sweet instrumental reprise of the melodies, perfect for slumber. Includes lyrics. [2]
LULLABIES; RABBITS; SONGS
Rev: SLJ 4/88 Awards: ALSC Notable Recording

800 Rooster's Off to See the World. Eric Carle. Picture Book Studio, 1972. Unp. $15.95. (0-88708-042-1).
Category: Concept/Counting/Alphabet **Age:** P–K

Carle, a master of strikingly simple, brilliantly colored collage, has written the counting book of which no young child should be deprived. He subtly blends the story of the lonely rooster, who collects and later loses two cats, three frogs, four turtles, and five fish during his quest to see the world, with such mathematical concepts as counting, number sets, and addition. Also available in other formats from the National Library for the Blind and Physically Handicapped. [2]
ANIMALS; COUNTING; MATH
Rev: ESLC

801 Rosie's Walk. Pat Hutchins. Macmillan, 1968. 32 pp. $13.95. (0-02-745850-4).
Category: Story **Age:** T–P

Rosie the hen takes a leisurely stroll through her own territory, unaware of a fox who hungrily follows her every step. Predictably, the fox is thwarted at every step. The concepts of over, under, through, and around are presented in this nearly wordless book. [1]
CHICKENS; CONCEPTS; FOXES
Rev: BBC; CBK; ESLC; NYT

802   *Round and Round the Garden: Play Rhymes for Young Children.* Compiled by Sarah Williams. Illus. by Ian Beck. Oxford University Press, 1988. 48 pp. $12.95. (0-19-279766-2).

Category: Poetry/Nursery rhymes/Songs   **Age:** T–P

Forty nursery rhymes, including old favorites such as "I'm a Little Teapot" and "Here's the Lady's Knives and Forks," as well as some new lyrics such as "Piggy on the Railway," compose this collection. Instructions for finger plays are included for each rhyme. The illustrations are large enough to share with a group, and bright colors enhance each page.   [2]

FINGER PLAY; NURSERY RHYMES; SONGS

Rev: BKL 2/15/88

803   *Round Trip.* Ann Jonas. Greenwillow Books, 1983. 32 pp. $13.88. (0-688-01781-9).   **Category:** Story   **Age:** K

From sunup to moonlight, the book is a journey to the city and back, which the reader must follow by reading the book first right side up and then upside down. Striking black-and-white graphic skylines capture the eye in both directions, and require a patient or practiced interpreter.   [2]

TRAVEL

Rev: CBK

804   *Rumpelstiltskin.* Jacob Grimm and Wilhelm K. Grimm. Retold and illustrated by Paul O. Zelinsky. Dutton, 1986. Unp. $13.95. (0-525-44265-0).

Category: Folklore/Folktales/Fairy tales   **Age:** K

A familiar Grimm tale retold in a medieval setting. The elaborately detailed illustrations tell the story of the fear and despair of a poor miller's daughter who bargains with a little man to turn her spinning into gold in exchange for her first-born child. The book would be most successfully shared one-on-one to allow time for explanation of unfamiliar subjects.   [1]

FEAR; FOLK AND FAIRY TALES

Rev: NYT   **Awards:** Caldecott Honor Book

805   *Rumpelstiltskin.* Illus. by Paul O. Zelinsky. Random House/Miller-Brody, 1987. Dist. by American School Publishers. Filmstrip. 11 min. $29.50.

Category: Folklore/Folktales/Fairy tales   **Age:** K

Zelinsky's Caldecott Honor Book (Dutton, 1986) is charmingly brought to life via Robert Stattel's superior narration and John Guth's mystical sound track. Rich, vibrant color and texture reflect the medieval trappings of this classic.

Spin-off activities in literature, guidance, and history are suggested in the insert. [1]

FEAR; FOLK AND FAIRY TALES

Rev: SLJ 4/89   **Awards:** ALSC Notable Filmstrip

806   *The Runaway Bunny.* Margaret Wise Brown. Illus. by Clement Hurd. Harper & Row, 1972. 40 pp. $11.95. (0-06-020765-5).

Category: Story   **Age:** T–P

A loving tale of how a little bunny seeks his independence with the comforting thought that his mother will always be close by. Black and white drawings are used on the pages with the text; then, to help emphasize to what lengths his mother would go to find him, the fantasy illustrations are in beautiful, vibrant colors for a notable shift in mood and emotion. [2]

RABBITS

Rev: CBK; ESLC; NYT

807   *Runaway Ralph.* Beverly Cleary. Churchill Films, 1988. Videocassette. 40 min. $225.00.   **Category:** Story   **Age:** K

A sequel to Cleary's *Mouse and the Motorcycle.* This production is first-rate. The hilarious, fast-paced episodes, the lively music, and the animated puppet, Ralph, keep the viewer captivated (Morrow, 1970). [1]

MICE

Rev: BKL 5/1/89; SLJ 4/89   **Awards:** ALSC Notable Film/Video

808   *Ruth's Bake Shop.* Kate Spohn. Orchard Books, 1990. Unp. $13.95. (0-531-05889-1).   **Category:** Story   **Age:** P

Ruth, an octopus, avoids housework by doing what makes her truly happy: baking everything from cookies to bread to chocolate eclairs to sauerkraut, and on and on. In order to sell her goodies, she opens a bakery and immediately becomes popular with all her underwater friends. Youngsters will enjoy counting the items on each page but will probably become hungry in the process.

BAKERS; OCTOPUSES [2]

809   *Sam.* Ann Herbert Scott. Illus. by Symeon Shimin. McGraw-Hill, 1967. Unp. $14.95. (0-07-055803-5).   **Category:** Story   **Age:** P

Warm, touching story of a universal childhood experience set in the context of middle-class black family life. Everyone in preschooler Sam's family is too busy to play with him or accept his primitive overtures of either friendship or task involvement. His tears begin to flow, and the realization of his need for a task hits his family. Beautifully illustrated with charcoal pencil on sepia and coppertones. [2]

AFRO-AMERICANS; BOREDOM; FAMILY LIFE

Rev: CBK; ESLC

810 *Samuel Todd's Book of Great Colors.* E. L. Konigsburg. Atheneum, 1990. Unp. $13.95. (0-689-31593-7).

Category: Concept/Counting/Alphabet **Age:** P–K

Samuel Todd looks at colors in a certain order: orange, green, purple, yellow, brown, red, blue, gray, pink, black, and white because that is the order in which they appear in his book of great colors. Vibrant illustrations highlight some rather unusual objects that depict our multicultural world as a good place to be. [2]

COLOR; CONCEPTS

Rev: BKL 1/15/90

811 *Sarah's Bear.* Marta Koci. Picture Book Studio, 1987. Unp. $14.95. (0-88708-038-3). **Category:** Story **Age:** P–K

Unloved, Bear is washed overboard a ship and lands on an island, where he is discovered by Sarah and her dog. Sarah and her other animals show Bear what it means to be part of a family that really loves him. Soft, watercolor illustrations effectively portray the happy family members and their pleasant surroundings to help reinforce readers' and listeners' feelings of warmth, security, and a sense of belonging. [3]

FAMILY LIFE; TEDDY BEARS

Rev: ESLC

812 *The Saucepan Game.* Jan Ormerod. Lothrop, Lee & Shepard, 1989. Unp. $10.95. (0-688-08519-9). **Category:** Story **Age:** I–T

A baby and a cat play with a saucepan, discovering its many wonders: they can look in it, chew on its handle, sit on it, and even put the cat inside. Simple illustrations capture the infant's inquisitive expressions as well as those of the cat. The essence of the event is accurately displayed by this talented author-illustrator. [3]

BABIES; CATS; PLAY

Rev: SLJ 10/89

813 *Scholastic Let's Find Out.* Scholastic, 1966– . $8.50/yr.
Category: Periodical **Age:** P–K

Children are exposed monthly to events, people, stories, games, posters, animals, and more. Organized by weeks, each four-page newsletter has implications across curricula in language arts, social studies, science, math, art, music, and dance as pointed out in the teachers' edition. A letter to parents in both English and Spanish that may be photocopied contains directions for using the publication at home. [1]
READING

814 *School Bus.* Donald Crews. Greenwillow Books, 1984. Unp. $13.88. (0-688-02808-X). **Category:** Concept/Counting/Alphabet **Age:** T–P–K

Shows a typical day for a school bus as it goes from the fleet parking lot in the morning across town to pick up children to take them to school. This simple book shows what a bus does each day and that buses come in all shapes and sizes, from very large to very small. [3]
CONCEPTS; SCHOOL; SIZE
Rev: CBK; ESLC; PP

815 *Scienceland: To Nurture Scientific Thinking.* Scienceland, 1977– . $13.95/yr. **Category:** Periodical **Age:** K

Intended to "nurture scientific thinking," this full-color nature periodical provides information via pictures accompanied by concise narrative appropriate for kindergarten through second grade. Thick pages add to its durability. A student edition along with a detailed teacher's guide packed with objectives, background, and activities for each issue makes this a high priority for classroom collections. Eight issues per year. [1]
SCIENCE

816 *The 2nd Raffi Songbook: 42 Songs from Raffi's Albums Baby Beluga, Rise and Shine and One Light, One Sun.* Piano arrangements by Catherine Ambrose. Illus. by Joyce Yamamoto. Crown, 1986. 104 pp. $15.95. (0-517-56638-9). **Category:** Poetry/Nursery rhymes/Songs **Age:** P–K

A collection of songs from three ever-popular Raffi albums with the words set to piano accompaniment, along with guitar and rhythm instrument notes appended where appropriate. Attractive white-line designs against colored backgrounds introduce each tune. Binding is a helpful feature: spiral inside for keeping pages open and reinforced outside for strength. [3]
SONGS

817   *The Sesame Street ABC Book of Words.* Sesame Street Editors. Illus. by Harry McNaught. Random House, 1988. 48 pp. $9.95. (0-394-88880-4).

Category: Concept/Counting/Alphabet   Age: T–P

Bert, Ernie, Big Bird, and the rest of the Muppets romp across the pages of this alphabet book. Each page features a letter in an upper corner and printed again in a white box, with the remainder of the page filled with items beginning with that letter. Each item is clearly labeled, and most will be familiar to preschoolers. Pictures are bright and colorful. Children's familiarity with and love for these characters constitute the big appeal.   [2]

ALPHABET; WORDS

Rev: ESLC

818   *Sesame Street Magazine.* Children's Television Workshop, 1971– .
$13.97/yr.   Category: Periodical   Age: T–P

Familiar characters from the series tell stories, play games, sign, and offer challenging activities. Children have an opportunity to practice skills viewed on TV and have fun while learning. Users are exposed to pictures of children from many cultures. Ten issues per year.   [2]

ENTERTAINMENT; READING

Rev: ESLC

819   *Seven Chinese Brothers.* Margaret Mahy. Illus. by Jean Tseng and Mousien Tseng. Scholastic, 1990. Unp. $12.95. (0-590-42055-0).

Category: Folklore/Folktales/Fairy tales   Age: K

Despite their identical appearances and mannerisms, each of the seven brothers has a unique and extraordinary power. When the emperor orders the execution of Third Brother, the brothers take turns using their unusual skills to dupe the evil ruler and save themselves. A spirited and skillful retelling coupled with evocative watercolors creates a sense of drama and respect for a culture void of stereotypes.   [3]

CHINA; FOLK AND FAIRY TALES

Rev: BKL 4/1/90

820   *17 Kings and 42 Elephants.* Margaret Mahy. Illus. by Patricia MacCarthy. Dial, 1987. Unp. $11.95. (0-8037-0458-5).   Category: Story   Age: P–K

On "a wild wet night," kings and elephants meet many animals such as "hippopotomums" and "gorillicans" as they make their way through the jungle. Brilliant batik illustrations and nonsense words spice up this rhymed journey

as the cheerful monarchs disappear into the "deep dark jungle." Lilting rhythm makes this a great read-aloud story. [2]
ANIMALS; JUNGLE; RHYMES
Rev: BBC; ESLC; NYT   **Awards:** NYT Best Illustrated Book

821   Shadows and Reflections. Tana Hoban. Greenwillow Books, 1990. Unp. $12.95. (0-688-07089-2).   **Category:** Wordless   **Age:** P–K
Hoban shows the imagery of reflections and shadows as they appear around the city. From the reflection in a fun house mirror to the shadow made by children's hands playing a string game, the color photographs capture a moment and a mood as only this photographer can. [2]
SHADOWS; WORDLESS
Rev: BKL 2/15/90

822   Shake My Sillies Out. Raffi. Illus. by David Allender. Crown, 1987. Unp. $9.95. (0-517-56646-X).
                                    Category: Poetry/Nursery rhymes/Songs   **Age:** T–P–K
Exhuberant, childlike artwork combines with the text of the song by Raffi to exhort young audiences to "Shake My Sillies Out" and "Wiggle My Waggles Away." Music and song verses are included on the last two pages. [1]
SONGS
Rev: CBY-88

823   Shapes, Shapes, Shapes. Tana Hoban. Greenwillow Books, 1986. Unp. $11.88. (0-688-05833-7).   **Category:** Wordless   **Age:** T–P–K
Begins with "some shapes to look for," followed by pages of photographs. The full-color stills, framed in white, give a formal, static look at some action scenes in which distinct colors emphasize dominant shapes. No words, simply close observation guides the reader-viewer. The familiarity of the subjects invites close attention. [1]
CONCEPTS; SHAPE; WORDLESS
Rev: PP

824   Sharon, Lois & Bram: The Elephant Show. Sharon, Lois & Bram. Cambium Films & Video Productions, 1984. Dist. by Bullfrog Films. Videocassette. 28 min. $95.00.
                                    Category: Poetry/Nursery rhymes/Songs   **Age:** T–P–K

Designed to teach values, social skills, and reading readiness by involving children in making music, recording artists Sharon, Lois, and Bram enthusiastically stroll through a zoo singing various songs about animals. Not intended to teach facts about animals, the songs instead concentrate on having fun with music and stress participation. The zoo is simply a background. Teacher's guide included. [2]

ANIMALS; MUSIC; VALUES

Rev: BKL 1/15/89   **Awards:** Parents' Choice Award; Silver Award, Intn'l Film

825   ***Sharon, Lois & Bram's Mother Goose.*** Sharon, Lois & Bram. Illus. by Maryann Kovalski. Atlantic Monthly Press, 1986. 96 pp. $16.95. (0-316-78282-3).   **Category:** Poetry/Nursery rhymes/Songs   **Age:** T–P–K

While popular children's recording artists Sharon, Lois, and Bram lend their names to this book, it is Eddie Grap's simple piano arrangements and Maryann Kovalski's illustrations that set this collection of songs, nursery rhymes, finger games, and tickling verses apart from other collections. A helpful index lists contents by title and first line. [3]

MOTHER GOOSE; NURSERY RHYMES; SONGS

Rev: BKL 1/1/88

826   ***Sheep In a Jeep.*** Nancy Shaw. Illus. by Margot Apple. Houghton Mifflin, 1986. Unp. $12.95. (0-395-41105-X).   **Category:** Story   **Age:** T–P–K

Apple's colored pencil illustrations accentuate the humor and antics of this escapade in rhyme about four sheep in a jeep. Sparse text in bold print makes this ideal for both young listeners and beginning readers. [1]

HUMOR; SHEEP

Rev: BBC; NYT

827   ***Shella Rae, the Brave.*** Kevin Henkes. Greenwillow Books, 1987. 32 pp. $11.88. (0-688-07156-2).   **Category:** Story   **Age:** P–K

Sheila Rae the mouse is so brave that she growls at stray dogs and bares her teeth at stray cats. But when she gets lost, it is her quiet little sister, Louise, who rescues her. Gentle, funny illustrations bring these mouse sisters to life.

COURAGE; SISTERS [3]

Rev: CBY-88; ESLC

828   ***Shopping Trip.*** Helen Oxenbury. Dial, 1982. Unp. Paper $3.50. (0-8037-7939-9).   **Category:** Wordless   **Age:** T–P–K

Without words and in board-book format, this title presents all the events encountered by a mother and her child in a shopping trip to several stores. Simple illustrations are uncluttered yet contain sufficient color and detail to retain children's interest and attention. Excellent source for discussing shopping and mother-child relations. [1]

BOARD BOOKS; SHOPPING; WORDLESS

Rev: CBK

---

829 *Sick In Bed.* Anne Rockwell and Harlow Rockwell. Macmillan, 1982. 24 pp. $8.95. (0-02-777730-8). **Category:** Story **Age:** P–K

A little boy describes having a sore throat and fever, being cared for by concerned parents, going to the doctor (a woman), having a throat culture, bravely getting a shot, getting better, and returning to school, where his teacher (a man) assures him he was missed. This comforting little book will help remove the anxiety that children experience when they are sick. [1]

FAMILY LIFE; ILLNESS; MEDICINE

Rev: ESLC

---

830 *Side by Side: Poems to Read Together.* Collected by Lee Bennett Hopkins. Illus. by Hilary Knight. Revised. Simon & Schuster, 1988. 80 pp. $14.95. (0-671-63579-4).
Category: Poetry/Nursery rhymes/Songs **Age:** T–P–K

These poems are meant for sharing. Selections include traditional, well-known works by Robert Louis Stevenson, Edward Lear, and Langston Hughes, as well as refreshing verses by contemporary poets. Poems are grouped into sections compatible with children's interests such as "Seasons," "ABCs & 123s," "Playtime," and "Birds and Beasts." Playful, detailed, and spirited watercolors enliven each page. [1]

POETRY

Rev: BKL 11/1/88

---

831 *Silent Night.* Joseph Mohr. Illus. by Susan Jeffers. Dutton, 1988. Unp. $14.95. (0-525-44144-1).
Category: Poetry/Nursery rhymes/Songs **Age:** P–K

A pictorial account, in soft, nighttime colors, of a favorite Christmas carol. Joy and devotion are evident on the faces of angels, animals, shepherds, and people. The text of three verses and the music are included on the last page of the

slightly oversize picture book. Useful in presenting the Christmas story as well as in discussion of the hymn.   [2]
CHRISTMAS; SONGS
Rev: BKL 1/1/88

832   *Sing a Song of Popcorn: Every Child's Book of Poems.* Edited by Beatrice De Regniers. Illus. by Marcia Brown and others. Scholastic, 1988. 142 pp. $16.95. (0-590-40645-0).
Category: Poetry/Nursery rhymes/Songs   **Age:** P–K

A celebration of the best in poetry and in children's book illustration. Nine Caldecott award winners illustrate over 100 poems, which are arranged in loose subject areas: animals, spooky, weather, etc., that are perfectly suited to each illustrator's unique style. A book for all ages.   [1]
POETRY
Rev: BKL 8/88

833   *Singing Bee! A Collection of Favorite Children's Songs.* Compiled by Jane Hart. Illus. by Anita Lobel. Lothrop, Lee & Shepard, 1982. 160 pp. $17.95. (0-688-41975-5).
Category: Poetry/Nursery rhymes/Songs   **Age:** I–T

Lullabies, finger games, and Mother Goose rhymes set to music are joyously illustrated by Lobel's soft-toned pictures. Old favorites and less familiar rhymes are included. The addition of guitar chords to match the piano accompaniments helps to make this a useful songbook for early childhood educators.
NURSERY RHYMES; SONGS   [2]
Rev: CBK

834   *Six Crows: A Fable.* Leo Lionni. Alfred A Knopf, 1988. Unp. $12.95. (0-394-89572-X).   **Category:** Folklore/Folktales/Fairy tales   **Age:** P–K

Lionni has deftly combined sparingly worded text with bold collage. When the farmer builds increasingly menacing scarecrows to keep the crows away, the ingenious crows fight back by making a ferocious bird kite. When the frightened farmer neglects his crop, the owl plays peacemaker, convincing the farmer and crows to talk over their differences. Young children can readily understand the moral of this fable.   [1]
BIRDS; FABLES; FARMERS; OWLS
Rev: BKL 6/1/88; CBY-89; ESLC

835   *Skip to My Lou.* Adapted and illustrated by Nadine B. Westcott. Little, Brown & Co., 1989. Unp. $12.95. (0-316-93137-3).

Category: Story   **Age:** P–K

A menagerie of animals wreaks havoc on a boy's house while his parents are away, giving the reader a rhyming look at the story behind the familiar song "Skip to My Lou." Colorful, playful illustrations in watercolor frolic across the pages, emphasizing the book's carefree atmosphere.   [1]

FAMILY LIFE; HUMOR; SONGS

Rev: BKL 5/1/89

836   *Sky All Around.* Anna G. Hines. Houghton Mifflin, 1989. Unp. $13.95. (0-89919-801-5).

Category: Story   **Age:** P–K

Daddy's night to take care of his small daughter begins in the late afternoon with a push in the swing and ends on the hillside looking at the night sky. Hines teaches about the constellations by use of beautiful hues and patterns of the stars, which resemble objects we know. Help is provided in the band of text beneath each large illustration. Clever way to teach both children and adults about this subject.   [3]

FATHERS; STARS

Rev: BKL 3/15/89

837   *Sky Full of Babies.* Richard Thompson. Illus. by Eugenie Fernandes. Annick Press, 1987. Unp. Paper $4.95. (0-920303-92-7). Dist. by Firefly Books.

Category: Story   **Age:** P–K

Jesse builds a spaceship and takes her father for a ride in space to see the sky full of babies and their loving parents. The adventure begins again at the end as mother is invited aboard. The family story is full of love and understanding and will entice children to use their imagination. The large, softly colored drawings offer interesting perspectives of the voyage. A variety of multiethnic characters are illustrated.   [2]

BABIES; FATHERS; SPACE AND SPACESHIPS

838   *The Sleeping Beauty.* Retold and illustrated by Trina Schart Hyman. Little, Brown & Co., 1983. Unp. $14.95. (0-316-38702-9).

Category: Folklore/Folktales/Fairy tales   **Age:** P–K

With colorful, detailed, realistic drawings and limited text, the illustrator retells the traditional story of a princess who is cursed to sleep for 100 years, to be awakened only by a charming prince. Illustrations are bright, musty, foreboding, sinister, frightening, and uplifting as appropriate to the text.   [1]

FOLK AND FAIRY TALES; ROYALTY; SLEEP

Rev: NYT

839 *Sleepy Book.* Charlotte Zolotow. Illus. by Ilse Plume. Reprint. Harper & Row, 1988. Unp. $12.95. (0-06-026968-5).

Category: Concept/Counting/Alphabet **Age:** T–P–K

Zolotow's text and Plume's exquisite illustrations draw the reader into an appreciation of the infinite variety and beauty of nature. The wintry bears in their den, the silky cocoons of caterpillars, and the watery home of goldfish are each shown, leading up to young children who are sleeping "warm under their blankets in their beds." For naptime or bedtime, a gentle hug of a book. [2]
ANIMALS; CONCEPTS; SLEEP

Rev: BKL 5/15/88

840 *Sleepytime Serenade.* Performed by Linda Schrade. A Gentle Wind, 1988. Audiocassette. 40 min. $8.95.

Category: Poetry/Nursery rhymes/Songs **Age:** I–T–P

Linda Schrade performs 15 bedtime songs, including a variety of traditional and modern tunes accompanied by flute and acoustic guitar. The soothing, pleasant tones have a calming and relaxing effect on listeners and entice children to sing along. Lyrics are provided. [2]
LULLABIES; SONGS

Rev: BKL 5/15/89

841 *A Snake Is Totally Tail.* Judith Barrett. Illus. by Lonni S. Johnson. Atheneum, 1983. Unp. $12.95. (0-689-30979-1).

Category: Concept/Counting/Alphabet **Age:** K

Alliteration is cleverly used to describe one outstanding feature of each animal in this unique concept book. A snake is totally tail, a porcupine is piles of prickles, and a crocodile is mostly mouth. The amusing text is accompanied by illustrations that alternate between bright, soft colors and bold black and white. [2]
ANIMALS; CONCEPTS; SNAKES

Rev: NYT

842 *Snow Day.* Betsy Maestro. Illus. by Giulio Maestro. Scholastic, 1989. Unp. $12.95. (0-590-41283-3). **Category:** Informational **Age:** P–K

When a winter storm blankets a town, a snow day is declared. Schools, businesses, airports, and even harbors are closed down until people and machines working together clear away the snow. By evening, things are back to normal

until the next snowfall. Watercolor illustrations with plenty of blue and white highlight the activities and machinery important in a snow emergency.   [2]
MACHINES; SNOW
Rev: BKL 11/1/89

843   *The Snowman.* Raymond Briggs. Random House, 1978. Unp. $12.95. (0-394-93973-5).   **Category:** Wordless **Age:** P–K

A modern classic that depicts a young boy's snowman come to life and the adventures they experience. The boy shares with his chilly friend the wonders of modern conveniences inside his home, and in turn the snowman takes him on an unforgettable night flight above magnificent cities and strange, faraway lands. Preparatory discussion of the scientific principle of changes of state might avoid a jarring shock at story's end.   [1]
DREAMS; SNOW; SNOWMEN; WORDLESS
Rev: ESLC; NYT   **Awards:** Boston Globe–Horn Book Award

844   *The Snowy Day.* Ezra Jack Keats. Viking Penguin, 1962. 34 pp. $11.95. (0-670-65400-0).   **Category:** Story **Age:** P–K

Peter spends a solitary day in the snow making a snowman, climbing and sliding down snow hills, and making a snow angel. The collage illustrations, with their bright colors, stand in contrast to the ever-present white of the snow, creating a feeling of isolation as Peter goes through numerous adventures. At the end of the day, he returns to a warm bath and bed. Also available in other formats from the National Library for the Blind and Physically Handicapped.
SNOW   [1]
Rev: BBC; CBK; ESLC; NYT   **Awards:** Caldecott Medal

845   *Some of the Days of Everett Anderson.* Lucille Clifton. Illus. by Evaline Ness. Henry Holt & Co., 1970. Unp. $10.95. (0-8050-0290-1).
                                                        Category: Story **Age:** K

Each day of the week is a backdrop for a short poem celebrating a part of six-year-old Everett Anderson's life. Simple pleasures such as a rainy day, being in a candy store, bedtime routines, playing with Mom and Dad, and nighttime stargazing, as well as fear of the dark and loneliness are explored. Double-page illustrations capture the feelings offered by this heartwarming book.   [3]
BOYS; POETRY
Rev: CBK

846 *Some Things Go Together.* Charlotte Zolotow. Illus. by Karen Gundersheimer. Harper & Row, 1983. Unp. $11.89. (0-690-04328-7).

Category: Concept/Counting/Alphabet **Age:** P–K

The rhythmic text and gentle illustrations clearly show a wonderful relationship between a mother and her son. "Things" that go together are woven in with the times that mother and son share with one another. [1]
CONCEPTS; LOVE; MOTHERS
Rev: PP

847 *Somebody's Sleepy.* Paul Rogers. Illus. by Robin B. Corfield. Atheneum, 1989. 24 pp. $10.95. (0-689-31491-4). **Category:** Story **Age:** T–P

Vivid, charming watercolors suit the activities of a preschooler warding off bedtime and finally succumbing to sleep. A short book just the right size for small hands, with contents perfect for a young child's empathic identification with the main character. [2]
BEDTIME; SLEEP
Rev: CBY-90

848 *The Something.* Natalie Babbitt. Farrar, Straus & Giroux, 1970. Unp. $6.95. (0-374-37137-7). **Category:** Story **Age:** K

Subtle humor is used to portray the fear of night by having a young beasty creature afraid of "something" that might come in his window. Children will be amused to find out that this "something" is only a little girl. Illustrations are depicted in ink-line drawings on yellow paper for day and gray paper for night. Text is written in a narrative style that shows the concerns of both mother and child beasty for the problem. [3]
DREAMS; MONSTERS; NIGHT
Rev: NYT

849 *Something Is Going to Happen.* Charlotte Zolotow. Illus. by Catherine Stock. Harper & Row, 1988. Unp. $12.89. (0-06-027029-2).

Category: Story **Age:** P–K

Beautiful, softly shaded drawings suggest the hushed beginning of a new day as each family member awakens on a cold November morning with the same thought: "Something is going to happen today." The magical happening, which each individual welcomes with amazement, is softly falling snow. [3]
MORNING; SNOW
Rev: BKL 10/1/88; CBY-89

850 *Something Special.* David McPhail. Little, Brown & Co., 1988. Unp. $10.95. (0-316-56324-2). **Category:** Story **Age:** P–K

Sam the raccoon is disheartened because everyone in his family seems to have a unique talent except for him. But he finally discovers his own special gift as he begins to paint pictures. Simple, boldly outlined illustrations in primary colors highlight this delightful story of self-discovery. [1]
ARTISTS; FAMILY LIFE; SELF-CONCEPT
Rev: BKL 11/15/88

851 *Sometimes I Like to Be Alone.* Heidi Goennel. Little, Brown & Co., 1989. 32 pp. $14.95. (0-316-31842-6). **Category:** Story **Age:** P–K

A girl likes to do things when she is alone, such as make a cake, read a book, teach her dog tricks, or fish for supper. The theme is simple and uncomplicated; the illustrations are bright and simply shaped. This book suggests a number of activities that can be done by a child who is alone, mixing active things, such as dancing or teaching a dog tricks, with quiet things, such as reading or looking for shooting stars. [3]
SOLITUDE
Rev: BKL 10/1/89

852 *Song and Dance Man.* Karen Ackerman. Illus. by Stephen Gammell. Alfred A. Knopf, 1988. 32 pp. $11.95. (0-394-89330-1). **Category:** Story **Age:** K

Grandpa, a former song-and-dance man, dons his bowler hat and tap shoes and entertains his grandchildren, who are suitably impressed. Afterward, even though Grandpa affectionately insists he would not "trade a million good old days" for the time he spends with his grandchildren, they suspect he really misses his vaudeville days. Engaging watercolor illustrations wonderfully capture Grandpa's sparkle and the children's delight. Also available in other formats from the National Library for the Blind and Physically Handicapped.
GRANDFATHERS [1]
Rev: BKL 10/1/88; CBY-89 **Awards:** Caldecott Medal

853 *Songs from Mother Goose: With the Traditional Melody for Each.* Compiled by Nancy Larrick. Illus. by Robin Spowart. Harper & Row, 1989. 70 pp. $16.89. (0-06-023714-7). **Category:** Poetry/Nursery rhymes/Songs **Age:** I–T–P–K

Larrick provides a wonderful selection of rhymes presented with simple musical notation for their traditional melodies. The handsomely designed book is large enough for lap sharing, with numerous golden-colored, soft-edged drawings sprinkled throughout for added interest. From "Baa Baa, Black Sheep" to "Pat-a-Cake," each selection invites involvement through singing, dancing, or clapping. [1]

MOTHER GOOSE; NURSERY RHYMES; SONGS

Rev: BKL 9/1/89

854 **_Sounds My Feet Make._** Arlene Blanchard. Illus. by Vanessa Julian-Ottie. Random House, 1989. 24 pp. $4.95. (0-394-89648-3).

Category: Concept/Counting/Alphabet **Age:** T–P

Children are invited to imitate the sounds their feet make during familiar activities: splashing in a rain puddle, strolling through autumn leaves, wearing new shoes, taking a bath, and tiptoeing to bed. Anchored by corner illustrations of objects repeated from the scene, each two-page spread is outlined in black pen. Featuring sturdy pages, this title will inspire children to participate in noise-making merriment. [2]

CONCEPTS; FEET; SOUNDS

Rev: BKL 6/15/89; CBY-90

855 **_Spectacles._** Ellen Raskin. Atheneum, 1988. Unp. Paper $4.50. (0-689-71271-5). **Category:** Story **Age:** P–K

Iris Fogel did not always wear glasses, but perhaps she should have. What she saw before she got glasses will delight readers and listeners alike as they try to guess by the illustration what Iris was seeing. Unique and imaginative illustrations make this work fun and involving for either group or individual sharing.

GIRLS; GLASSES; HUMOR [1]

Rev: CBK

856 **_Spinky Sulks._** William Steig. Farrar, Straus & Giroux, 1988. Unp. $13.95. (0-374-38321-9). **Category:** Story **Age:** P–K

Spinky thinks no one loves him—he is angry and hurt. He'll show them; he'll just sulk. His sister, brother, mother, father, grandma, and friends all try to cheer him up; after all, they do love him, each one in his or her own way. Once Spinky begins to understand this, he then has to figure out a way to give up sulking and not hurt his pride. Truly sulky illustrations make readers/viewers laugh as they relate. [2]

FAMILY LIFE; LOVE; PRIDE

Rev: BKL 1/15/89

857 **Splash! All About Baths.** Susan Kovacs Buxbaum and Rita Golden Gelman. Illus. by Maryann Cocca-Leffler. Little, Brown & Co., 1987. Unp. $14.95. (0-316-30726-2). **Category:** Informational **Age:** P–K

A first science book for picture book readers that answers questions such as "Why do some soaps float and why does skin wrinkle in the tub?" A penguin and his animal friends are featured in humorous illustrations, as the questions that a young child might ask at bath time are answered in simple, clear terms.
BATHS; SOAP; WATER [2]
Rev: ESLC

858 **Spot Sleeps Over.** Eric Hill. Putnam, 1990. Unp. $3.75. (0-399-21815-7).
Category: Participation and manipulative **Age:** T–P

Spot the dog is invited to sleep over at his friend Steve's house. This sturdy, lift-the-flap book humorously chronicles Spot's preparation. He packs his toys but forgets his most important possession: a teddy bear. Luckily, his mom saves the day. Hill's bold drawings in bright, primary colors will attract young readers. [1]
BEDTIME; FRIENDSHIP; PARTICIPATION

859 **Spot's Big Book of Words.** Eric Hill. Putnam, 1988. Unp. $9.95. (0-399-21563-8). **Category:** Concept/Counting/Alphabet **Age:** T–P

Eric Hill's playful puppy introduces the young child to words for familiar objects. Each oversize, two-page spread shows Spot, his friends, and his family engaged in various activities (housecleaning, going to the beach, being at school, etc.). A short paragraph explains the activities, and various objects are identified. [2]
CONCEPTS; WORDS
Rev: BKL 10/1/88

860 **Spots, Feathers, and Curly Tails.** Nancy Tafuri. Greenwillow Books, 1988. 32 pp. $11.95. (0-688-07536-3). **Category:** Story **Age:** T–P

This vivid farmyard identification tour introduces farm animals and their important individual characteristics: spots, manes, feathers, and curly tails. [2]
ANIMALS; FARMS
Rev: BKL 8/88; CBY-90

861 **Spot's First Words.** Eric Hill. Putnam, 1986. Unp. $3.50. (0-399-21348-1).
Category: Concept/Counting/Alphabet **Age:** T–P

Inquisitive Spot introduces the child to objects familiar in the child's world. Each page shows Spot involved with an object and names that object at the page top. Each two-page spread of this small board book has a sentence at the bottom explaining Spot's relationship to the two objects (e.g., "Spot picks up a shoe and hides under the table."). [1]

BOARD BOOKS; CONCEPTS; DOGS; WORDS

Rev: CBY-87

862 *Spot's Toys.* Eric Hill. Putnam, 1984. 8 pp. $2.95. (0-399-21067-9).

Category: Concept/Counting/Alphabet **Age:** I–T

On each vinyl page of this soft tub book, the popular dog is featured with some toys. Infants will delight in the simple, brightly colored pictures. This work can serve as an introduction to other titles about Spot, such as those in a lift-the-flap format. [2]

CONCEPTS; DOGS; TOY AND MOVABLE BOOKS

Rev: CBK

863 *Spring.* Ron Hirschi. Photos by Thomas D. Mangelsen. Dutton, 1990. Unp. $13.95. (0-525-65037-7). **Category:** Informational **Age:** P–K

Large, exquisite photographs present the panorama of spring. Flora and fauna provide a continuum of this rebirth—a special period that must occur between winter and summer. Hirschi's afterword adds information on the process of the earth's reawakening. [1]

SPRING

Rev: SLJ 11/90

864 *Spring Is Here.* Taro Gomi. Chronicle Books, 1989. Unp. $11.95. (0-87701-626-7). **Category:** Story **Age:** T–P–K

Gomi presents the unending cycle of the seasons via the world of the newborn calf. As the spring snows melt, black spots appear on the white calf's back. The calf blends into the foreground, and the black spots become the earth, ripe with new life that unfolds, season by season, until the calf reappears, a year older. The deceptively simple text and illustrations are rich with multi-layered meanings. [1]

SEASONS; SPRING

Rev: BKL 8/89

Awards: Graphic Prize Winner–Children's Book Fair, Bologna

865 ***Squiggles, Dots & Lines.*** Produced and directed by Jane Murphy and Karen Tucker. Tucker/Murphy, 1989. Dist. by KIDVIDZ. Videocassette. 25 min. $24.95. **Category:** Concept/Counting/Alphabet **Age:** K

Ed Emberley narrates while children demonstrate his picture book art that combines squiggles, dots, and lines from the drawing alphabet. His drawing books should be available for examination as well. Includes instructional guide. [3]

ART; CONCEPTS

Rev: BKL 7/89

866 ***Stamp Your Feet: Action Rhymes.*** Chosen by Sarah Hayes. Illus. by Toni Goffe. Lothrop, Lee & Shepard, 1988. 32 pp. $12.88. (0-688-07695-5). **Category:** Poetry/Nursery rhymes/Songs **Age:** P–K

Action nursery rhymes and songs suitable for preschoolers are presented with illustrations that literally encourage movement. Comical drawings of children interpreting the rhymes help the reader to know how to respond to a wide variety of selections. This collection should prove particularly helpful to parents and professionals who are new to the field of action rhymes and songs. [1]

NURSERY RHYMES; RHYTHM

Rev: BKL 8/88

867 ***Star Dreamer: Nightsongs and Lullabies.*** Sung by Priscilla Herdman and others. Produced by Alcazam!, 1988. Dist. by Alcazar Records. Audiocassette. 44 min. $9.98. **Category:** Poetry/Nursery rhymes/Songs **Age:** P–K

New and old bedtime songs with a folk touch, enhanced with soft, melodic vocals. Combinations of various instruments, such as mandolin, accordion, fiddle, and cello, add a rich-textured sound. At times, the music has the flavor of seafaring ballads and Gaelic tunes. This collection instills soothing, calm feelings just right for naps and bedtimes. [2]

BEDTIME; MUSIC; SONGS

Rev: BKL 4/15/89; SLJ 4/89 **Awards:** ALA Notable Children's Recording

868 ***Staying Up.*** Special Things Distributing, 1988. Audiocassette. 40 min. $8.98. **Category:** Poetry/Nursery rhymes/Songs **Age:** P–K

The melodies in this collection address topics common to all children: the desire to avoid bedtime, an inquisitive nature, the fun of riding escalators, and eating ice cream. Another invites listeners to make noises like a train. The final song celebrates the smile as having universal meaning in all languages. [3]

SONGS

Rev: BKL 11/1/89

869 *Steppin' to the Music.* Written and performed by Linda Saxton Brown. Linda Saxton Brown, 1987. Dist. by Tahoe Crafts Printing. Audiocassette. 40 min. $9.95. **Category:** Poetry/Nursery rhymes/Songs **Age:** P–K

Fourteen original songs simply orchestrated and clearly sung for youngsters' enjoyment. Accompanying booklet provides lyrics and suggests activities for classroom use. Included are quiet, contemplative songs and active, lively numbers that deal with a variety of subjects to appeal to this young audience.
SONGS [3]
Rev: BKL 11/1/89

870 *Stevie.* John Steptoe. Harper & Row, 1969. Unp. $12.89. (0-06-025764-4). **Category:** Story **Age:** K

Robert's world changes when his mother agrees to care for a friend's young son, Stevie. He has to share his toys and look after little Stevie, much to his chagrin when his friends taunt him. As time passes, Robert begins to enjoy the time spent with Stevie, being his playmate, teacher, and brother. A thoughtful look at foster care and sibling relationships. [3]
BROTHERS; FAMILY LIFE; FOSTER HOME CARE
Rev: NYT

871 *Still as a Star: A Book of Nighttime Poems.* Selected by Lee Bennett Hopkins. Illus. by Karen Milone. Little, Brown & Co., 1989. 32 pp. $14.95. (0-316-37272-2). **Category:** Poetry/Nursery rhymes/Songs **Age:** P–K

Fourteen short poems on the theme of nighttime and sleep by noted children's poets such as Nikki Giovanni, Nancy Willard, and Aileen Fisher are superimposed on double-page watercolor paintings. Tones of purple, blue, and pink dominate the appealing illustrations, which are filled with whimsical details and which feature a fine cross section of multiethnic children. [3]
NIGHT; POETRY; SLEEP
Rev: BKL 5/15/89

872 *Stone Soup.* Marcia Brown. Scribner's, 1947. 48 pp. $12.95. (0-684-92296-7). **Category:** Folklore/Folktales/Fairy tales **Age:** P–K

Three hungry soldiers who are returning from war trick a village into making stone soup flavored with plenty of vegetables. The villagers are amazed at the magic the soldiers have created. A fine lesson in cooperation is offered, which is worthy of discussion by youngsters. [2]

FOLK AND FAIRY TALES; FRANCE

Rev: CBK; NYT   **Awards:** Caldecott Honor Book

873   ***Stop Go.*** Jan Pienkowski. Simon & Schuster, 1992. Unp. $2.95. (0-671-74519-0).   **Category:** Concept/Counting/Alphabet   **Age:** I–T

This multicultural nursery board book, small enough for the littlest of hands, explores the relationship of opposites. Examples include standards such as push/pull, shout/whisper, and start/finish, as well as more challenging concepts such as make/break and leave/return. [1]

BOARD BOOKS; OPPOSITES

874   ***The Story about Ping.*** Marjorie Flack. Illus. by Kurt Wiese. Viking Penguin, 1933. Unp. $10.95. (0-670-67223-8).   **Category:** Story   **Age:** P–K

Ping, a young duck who lives with his large, extended family on the Yangtze River, spends a night and a day away from home. He swims down the river looking for the "wise-eyed" houseboat and is almost cooked for dinner instead. Fortunately, a little boy sets him free. Ping is reunited with his family, more than likely never to stray again. Soft, pastel illustrations capture the beauty and peacefulness of the river. [2]

CHINA; DUCKS

Rev: BBC; CBK; ESLC; NYT

875   ***The Story of Babar: The Little Elephant.*** Jean De Brunhoff. Reprint. Random House, 1984. 48 pp. $18.95. (0-394-86823-4).

Category: Story   **Age:** P–K

This oversize book is written in script and tells the story of a baby elephant, Babar, who is cruelly orphaned when a hunter shoots his mother. The frightened baby elephant runs away to the city, where he meets a splendid old lady who gives him everything he wants. Babar eventually returns to the forest along with his little cousins, Arthur and Celeste. There Babar agrees to be king of the elephants. Also available in other formats from the National Library for the Blind and Physically Handicapped. [1]

ELEPHANTS; ORPHANS; ROYALTY

Rev: BBC; ESLC; NYT

876   ***The Story of Ferdinand.*** Munro Leaf. Illus. by Robert Lawson. Viking Penguin, 1936. Unp. $11.95. (0-670-67424-9).

Category: Story   **Age:** P–K

While all the other bulls run around snorting and butting, leaping and jumping so that they will be picked for the bullfight, Ferdinand just sits quietly and smells the flowers. Because he refuses to fight, Ferdinand is returned home and allowed to sit under his favorite cork tree, quietly partaking of the smells around him. Also available in other formats from the National Library for the Blind and Physically Handicapped. [2]

BULLS; SELF-CONCEPT; SPAIN

Rev: BBC; NYT   **Awards:** Caldecott Honor Book

877   *The Story of Ferdinand.* Munro Leaf. Illus. by Robert Lawson. Live Oak Media, 1985. Filmstrip. 9 min. $22.95.   **Category:** Story   **Age:** P–K

Lightly colored illustrations and softly played Spanish music enchance the gentle and loving story of Ferdinand the bull. This classic story teaches children the importance of being happy with themselves (Viking, 1936). [3]

BULLS; SELF-CONCEPT; SPAIN

878   *Strega Nona's Magic Lessons.* Tomie dePaola. Read by Tammy Grimes. Harper Audio, 1989. Audiocassette. 62 min. $9.95.

Category: Story   **Age:** K

Seven stories, ranging from the humorous magic of "Strega Nona" to the gentleness of "Nana Upstairs & Nana Downstairs," are presented clearly and expressively. The others are "Oliver Button Is a Sissy," "Now One Foot, Now the Other," "Helga's Dowry," "Big Anthony & the Magic Ring," and "Strega Nona's Magic Lessons." [1]

FOLK AND FAIRY TALES; GRANDPARENTS; MAGIC

Awards: ALSC Notable Recording

879   *The Sun, the Wind & the Rain.* Lisa Westberg Peters. Illus. by Ted Rand. Henry Holt & Co., 1988. Unp. $13.95. (0-8050-0699-0).

Category: Story   **Age:** K

A narrative about two mountains: the earth made one, and young Elizabeth, playing at the beach, made the other. Each double-page spread explains the story of geological evolution by comparing and contrasting the earth's mountain with the child's wet sand construction. The simple text and bold, colorful illustrations are very effective in presenting a complex subject simply. [3]

MOUNTAINS; NATURE

Rev: BKL 10/15/88

880 *The Sun's Day.* Mordicai Gerstein. Harper & Row, 1989. Unp. $12.89. (0-06-022405-3).   **Category:** Story   **Age:** P–K

Gerstein poetically describes and shows the changing hours and activities of a day. The sun is not a static round shape but changes through the day from a new chick emerging from an egg at sunrise to a little baby sinking into the night sky ready for its evening bath. Much detail and imagination are highlighted in this enchanting picture book.   [2]

Day; Sun; Time

Rev: BKL 11/1/89

881 *Sunshine.* Jan Ormerod. Lothrop, Lee & Shepard, 1981. Unp. $12.88. (0-688-00553-5).   **Category:** Wordless   **Age:** T–P

A wordless picture book relating the story of a small girl who is awakened by the sun and is responsible for rousing her parents to see that the family members all leave the house on time. The step-by-step progress of a waking family is clearly depicted through detailed illustrations.   [2]

Family life; Morning; Sun; Wordless

Rev: BBC; ESLC

882 *Super, Super, Superwords.* Bruce McMillan. Lothrop, Lee & Shepard, 1989. 32 pp. $11.88. (0-688-08099-5).

                                    Category: Counting/Concept/Alphabet   **Age:** P–K

Each double-page spread features three crisp, colorful photographs of multiethnic children in a kindergarten class engaged in activities that illustrate comparative degrees of 13 adjectives. The author-photographer captures the spontaneity of the playful situations and offers variety in his compositions while presenting the concept creatively and clearly.   [1]

Concepts; Words

Rev: BKL 5/1/89

883 *Superbabe!* Deborah van der Beek. Putnam, 1988. Unp. $9.95. (0-399-21507-7).   **Category:** Story   **Age:** P–K

Able to leap small cats with a single bound, under tables, through chairs, it's ... Superbabe! Written in clever verse from the older sister's point of view, *Superbabe* humorously and lovingly illustrates the havoc that one small toddler can wreak on an otherwise very normal household.   [1]

Babies; Brothers and sisters

Rev: CBY-89

884 *Supposes.* Dick Gackenbach. Harcourt Brace Jovanovich, 1989. Unp. $12.95. (0-15-200594-3). **Category:** Story **Age:** P–K

Humorous watercolor illustrations depict the often silly and sometimes clever suppositions of two well-fed children (a la Campbell Kids style) dealing with animals and word plays. Children may appreciate this more than adults do and are certain to enjoy conjuring up their own supposes. [2]
ANIMALS; HUMOR
Rev: BKL 4/1/89

885 *Surprises.* Edited by Lee Bennett Hopkins. Illus. by Megan Lloyd. Harper & Row, 1984. 64 pp. $10.89. (0-06-022585-8).
Category: Poetry/Nursery rhymes/Songs **Age:** P–K

A collection of 38 poems by well-known poets, including Marchette Chute, Myra Cohn Livingston, Aileen Fisher, and Lee Bennett Hopkins, deals with everyday experiences of young children. Simple illustrations and text make this an easy beginning reader. [3]
POETRY
Rev: NYT; PP

886 *Swan Sky.* Keizaburo Tejima. Philomel, 1988. Unp. $13.95. (0-399-21547-6). **Category:** Story **Age:** K

A serious subject handled simply, this story about a young swan's death is stark, yet elegant. Tejima writes many stories that border on being folktales; this is one. The swan family has a young member who cannot join them for their annual migration. They depart and then return to stay the night with her while she dies. The swans go on to their destination sadly; then they believe they see her in the rising sun of springtime. [3]
DEATH; FAMILY LIFE; SWANS
Rev: BKL 11/1/88

887 *Sweet Sleep: A Collection of Lullabies, Poems and Cradle Songs.* Christopher Headington. Clarkson N. Potter, 1989. 88 pp. $14.95. (0-517-57321-0). **Category:** Poetry/Nursery rhymes/Songs **Age:** I–T

Children can be crooned to sleep with this collection of over 30 mostly Western European lullabies and poems. Each song has music notation for the melody, a brief explanation of origin, and complete lyrics as well as a beautiful illustration. A contents page and an index of first lines aid in locating the many familiar titles as well as the lesser known ones. [2]
BABIES; LULLABIES; SONGS

888 *Swimmy.* Leo Lionni. Alfred A. Knopf, 1987. Unp. Paper $2.95. (0-317-53621-4).   **Category:** Story **Age:** P–K

Enchanting story of how a small, lonely fish uses instinct to outsmart the bigger fish. Unique multimedia illustrations depict Swimmy and the various sea creatures encountered on the journey. The text describes various underwater sea life and environments. Great for large or small groups as well as with a classroom.   [1]
FISH; FRIENDSHIP
Rev: CBY-88; NYT

889 *Sylvester and the Magic Pebble.* William Steig. Simon & Schuster, 1988. Paper $6.95. (0-671-67144-8).   **Category:** Story **Age:** K

When a small donkey meets a fierce lion, he uses his magic pebble to turn himself into a rock. Now unable to hold the wishing pebble, he is imprisoned inside. As seasons pass, his parents coincidentally visit the spot where their Sylvester lies trapped. They find the red pebble and they place it atop the large rock nearby. Hearing his parents' tearful reminiscence, Sylvester awakens and wishes himself a donkey once again. Also available in other formats from the National Library for the Blind and Physically Handicapped.   [1]
DONKEYS; MAGIC; WISHING
Rev: BBC **Awards:** Caldecott Medal

890 *Tail Toes Eyes Ears Nose.* Marilee Robin Burton. Harper & Row, 1988. Unp. $11.89. (0-06-020874-0).
                                Category: Concept/Counting/Alphabet **Age:** P–K

Bright, primary colors show an animal's tail, eyes, and nose on every other page. Children will eagerly try to decide what animal these parts belong to and then turn the page to see if they guessed correctly. The visual discrimination needed to make this decision helps children get ready to read. This clever, simple book will delight them.   [1]
ANIMALS; PUZZLES
Rev: BKL 9/15/88; CBY-89; ESLC

891 *The Tale of Mr. Jeremy Fisher.* Beatrix Potter. Illus. by David Jorgensen. Picture Book Studio, 1989. 32 pp. $19.95. (0-88708-095-2). Harper Audio, 1989. Audiocassette. 62 min. min. $9.95.
                                Category: Story **Age:** T–P–K

Jorgensen's softly textured and colored illustrations infuse new life into this classic tale. Mr. Jeremy Fisher's fishing expedition turns out to be more of an adventure than he bargained for, but his friendly good humor remains intact.

Instead of minnows, he and his friends enjoy roasted grasshopper with lady-bird sauce for dinner. Audiocassette is brilliantly narrated by Meryl Streep against whimsical background music. Also available in other formats from the National Library for the Blind and Physically Handicapped. [2]

FISHING; FRIENDSHIP; FROGS

892 *The Tale of Peter Rabbit.* Beatrix Potter. Warne, 1987. 60 pp. $4.95. (0-7232-3460-4). **Category:** Story **Age:** T–P–K

This is a rephotographed edition of the original 1902 edition, but it retains Potter's original watercolors and small size. Impatient for adventure, Peter goes into Mr. McGregor's garden, where he is caught and barely escapes. Also available in other formats from the National Library for the Blind and Physically Handicapped. [1]

RABBITS

Rev: BBC; CBK; ESLC; NYT

893 *The Tale of Peter Rabbit.* Beatrix Potter. Narrated by Meryl Streep. Windham Hill and Rabbit Ears Productions, 1988. Dist. by Alcazar Records. Compact disc. 31 min. $16.00.

Category: Story **Age:** T–P–K

Potter's "Tale of Peter Rabbit," "The Tale of Mr. Jeremy Fisher," and "The Tale of Two Bad Mice" are lovingly ushered into the 1990s in this lyrical offering. Streep's lilting voice and carefully metered telling is a delightful match to the new-age accompaniment by jazz artist Lyle Mays and musician Art Lande. A splendid production that will appeal to all. [1]

FROGS; MICE; RABBITS

Rev: BKL 12/15/88

894 *The Tale of Three Trees: A Traditional Folktale.* Retold by Angela E. Hunt. Illus. by Tim Jonke. Lion, 1989. Unp. $13.95. (0-7459-1743-7).

Category: Folklore/Folktales/Fairy tales **Age:** K

A retelling of a gentle American folktale. Three trees on a mountaintop long for greatness. Each assumes a surprising role in the life of Jesus: the first, cut down and formed into a feed box, eventually becomes his cradle; the second, a boat, carries him on Galilee; the last becomes his cross. The careful telling and beautiful illustrations of God's love are given in a simple way that the child can understand. [2]

CHRISTMAS; FOLK AND FAIRY TALES

Rev: BKL 11/1/89

895 *Talking Schoolhouse Series.* Orange Cherry Software, 1989. Software.
$59.00.   **Category:** Concept/Counting/Alphabet **Age:** K

The Talking Schoolhouse Series provides the user with sequential developmental activities for learning various concepts. With "Animal Sounds" and "ABC's," looking and listening come first; gradually, the child is provided with opportunities for interaction. Colorful and lively graphics, a user-friendly format, and digitized speech enhance the presentation (Apple IIGS disks).
ALPHABET; ANIMALS   [3]
Rev: BKL 1/1/90

896 *Tasting.* Henry Pluckrose. Photos by Chris Fairclough. Franklin Watts, 1986. Unp. $9.40. (0-531-10173-8).
                                           Category: Informational **Age:** T–P–K

The full-color, full-page, close-up photographs are so suggestive that the impressionable reader has the sensation of tasting. Posed as a series of preferences—do you prefer this or that—the book's pacing is pleasing and purposeful.   [1]
FOOD

897 *Taxi: A Book of City Words.* Betsy Maestro. Illus. by Giulio Maestro. Ticknor & Fields, 1989. Unp. $13.95. (0-89919-528-8).
                                           Category: Informational **Age:** P–K

A day in the life of a big-city taxi introduces words common to a big city, such as bridge, apartment, building, and tunnel. The taxi's customers include people trying to catch a train, children going to the zoo, passengers arriving on a cruise ship, and people going to the theater, to the museum, and shopping. The bright, watercolor illustrations help give a feel of the hustle and bustle of a big city.   [2]
CITIES AND TOWNS; WORDS
Rev: BKL 4/1/89

898 *The Teddy Bear ABC.* Laura R. Johnson. Illus. by Margaret L. Sanford. Green Tiger Press, 1982. Unp. $7.95. (0-914676-86-5).
                                           Category: Story **Age:** P–K

The story transcends time, remaining appealing with the help of Teddy Bear Frolicking. Original ink-line illustrations are uniquely colored with watercolor washes to give a classic look for children's books. Each letter with rhyming text is incorporated into the story. Children will enjoy hearing the adventures brought on by the next letter.   [3]
ALPHABET; POETRY; TEDDY BEARS

899 ***Teddy Bears 1 to 10.*** Susanna Gretz. Reprint. Four Winds, 1986. 24 pp. $13.95. (0-02-738140-4).

Category: Concept/Counting/Alphabet **Age:** T–P

Expressive teddy bears are used to introduce the concept of numbers from 1 to 10. The dirty, old teddy bears are laundered, dyed, and dried but finish in time for tea. Gretz's bears are done in autumn colors on a white background, giving a distinctive look. Large, simple pictures make this book useful for young children individually or in groups. [3]
COUNTING; TEDDY BEARS
Rev: ESLC

900 ***Teddy Bears ABC.*** Susanna Gretz. Four Winds, 1986. Unp. $13.95. (0-02-738130-7). **Category:** Concept/Counting/Alphabet **Age:** P–K

The antics of five small teddy bears and their animal guests are aptly captured in this madcap adventure, which includes everything from arriving in an airport, mucking in the mud, and tickling in a tent, to, finally, in desperation, zipping off to the zoo. The bright illustrations are large enough for group use, and the text stimulates vocabulary development. [3]
ALPHABET; TEDDY BEARS
Rev: ESLC

901 ***The Teddy Bears' Picnic.*** Jimmy Kennedy. Illus. by Alexandra Day. Green Tiger Press, 1983. Unp. $14.95. (0-88138-010-5).

Category: Poetry/Nursery rhymes/Songs **Age:** P–K

Full-page, soft-colored illustrations are used in this oversize book about a boy and girl who disguise themselves as teddy bears to attend a picnic of bears. The picnic ends when the parents take all the tired little teddy bears home to bed. Along with the book is a four-minute recording of "The Teddy Bears' Picnic," sung by Bing Crosby. [1]
PICNICKING; SONGS; TEDDY BEARS
Rev: SLJ 8/84

902 ***Teeny Tiny.*** Jill Bennett. Illus. by Tomie dePaola. Putnam, 1986. Unp. $9.95. (0-399-21293-0). **Category:** Story **Age:** P

The teeny tiny woman finds a teeny tiny bone for her supper, which she puts in her teeny tiny pocket and takes back to her teeny tiny house. When the ghostly owners of the bone appear and demand that the woman give back the bone, she is very brave. Children will love the gentle spookiness and repetition in the story. The colorful, stylized dePaola illustrations are perfect for this old tale. [2]

CUMULATIVE TALES; GHOSTS; HALLOWEEN

Rev: CBY-87

---

903 *Teeny Tiny.* Illus. by Tomie dePaola. Retold by Jill Bennett. Listening Library, 1987. Audiocassette. 5 min. $29.95.

Category: Story **Age:** P–K

Teeny Tiny, the main character in this delightful retelling of a well-known tale, searches for a bone to make soup. While sleeping, she is awakened by the ghostly cupboard demanding: "GIVE ME MY BONE." DePaola's illustrations coupled with the orchestral background make this a perfect selection for youngsters (Putnam, 1986). [1]

CUMULATIVE TALES; GHOSTS; HALLOWEEN

Rev: BKL 11/15/88; SLJ 4/89 **Awards:** ALSC Notable Recording

---

904 *Tell Me a Story, Featuring Beauty & the Beast.* Kartes Video Communications, 1986. Videocassette. 30 min. $9.95.

Category: Folklore/Folktales/Fairy tales **Age:** P–K

Husband and wife team Mitch Weiss and Martha Hamilton, known as the storytellers "Beauty" and "The Beast," perform well-known stories together before a group of young children. Included are both traditional tales and works of modern authors. [2]

FOLK AND FAIRY TALES

---

905 *Tell Me a Story, Mama.* Angela Johnson. Illus. by David Soman. Orchard Books, 1989. 32 pp. $13.99. (0-531-08394-2).

Category: Story **Age:** K

At bedtime, a young black girl asks her mother to tell her a story. As the mother recalls incidents from her own girlhood, the daughter contributes details, since she is obviously familiar with the stories. Soft, watercolor scenes convey realistic portraits of a loving family as they move through the course of time. [3]

AFRO-AMERICANS; FAMILY LIFE

---

906 *10 Bears in My Bed: A Goodnight Countdown.* Stan Mack. Pantheon Books, 1974. Unp. $10.99. (0-394-92902-0).

Category: Poetry/Nursery rhymes/Songs **Age:** T–P–K

Based on a familiar counting rhyme, the book whimsically reduces the number of bears in a little boy's bed from 10 to zero, except for a comfortable teddy bear. As the bears "roll over" and go out the window, they each use a different method. One rides a tricycle, another a toy train, so that by the time all are gone, the bedroom is cleaned, too. The final pages find the boy dreaming about ... what else? ... 10 bears. [2]

COUNTING; NURSERY RHYMES; TEDDY BEARS
Rev: ESLC

907   *Ten Black Dots.* Donald Crews. Revised. Greenwillow Books, 1986. Unp. $12.88. (0-688-06068-4).

Category: Concept/Counting/Alphabet   **Age:** T–P–K

Shows what can be done with 10 black dots: ONE can make a sun, TWO a fox's eyes, and EIGHT the wheels of a train. Simple rhyming text combined with brightly colored, uncomplicated pictures make this a delightful counting book for young children. Illustrations are large enough for group story use.

COUNTING [1]
Rev: ESLC

908   *Ten In a Bed.* Adapted and illustrated by Mary Rees. Little, Brown & Co., 1988. Unp. $12.95. (0-316-73708-9).

Category: Counting/Concept/Alphabet   **Age:** P–K

A familiar counting-out rhyme receives fresh treatment from the deftly humorous hand of the illustrator. Fun begins as each slumber party guest is pushed from bed, only to wander about the house and garden engaged in play and mischief. Chaos mounts until the deposed nine pull the "little ones' " hostess from her bed. A multicultural cross section represented in the expressive frenzy of pastel watercolor and ink illustrations. [2]

BEDTIME; COUNTING; PARTIES
Rev: BKL 3/15/88

909   *Ten Little Babies.* Debbie MacKinnon. Illus. by Lisa Kopper. Dutton, 1990. Unp. $9.95. (0-525-44643-5).

Category: Concept/Counting/Alphabet   **Age:** T–P

Ten bouncy toddlers sitting in a row, devouring cookies, painting red and blue are "bumped" from the play, one by one, until only one baby is left, ready to be snuggled into bed. Each two-page spread reveals the antics of delightful babies on the left, with the appropriate numeral on the flap of the right page.

BABIES; COUNTING; PARTICIPATION [2]
Rev: SLJ 2/91

910 ***Ten, Nine, Eight.*** Molly Bang. Greenwillow Books, 1983. Unp. $13.88. (0-688-00907-7).   **Category:** Concept/Counting/Alphabet **Age:** I–T–P

A father lovingly counts down from 10 to 1 as he prepares his daughter for bedtime in this peaceful counting book. This Caldecott Honor book is illustrated with soft pastels that evoke a gentle and tender mood, capturing the special relationship between parent and child.   [1]
BEDTIME; COUNTING; LULLABIES
Rev: BBC; CBK; ESLC; NYT; PP   **Awards:** Caldecott Honor Book

911 ***Ten Potatoes in a Pot and Other Counting Rhymes.*** Selected by Michael Jay Katz. Illus. by June Otani. Harper & Row, 1990. Unp. $12.89. (0-06-023107-6).   **Category:** Concept/Counting/Alphabet **Age:** P–K

In his first book for children, the author captures the cadence of counting rhymes, some of which are familiar, others little known. These are combined within the framework of 1920s-style watercolor illustrations to present a lilting concept book for the very youngest child.   [3]
COUNTING; NURSERY RHYMES
Rev: BKL 4/1/90

912 ***The Tenth Good Thing about Barney.*** Judith Viorst. Illus. by Erik Blegvad. Atheneum, 1971. 32 pp. $12.95. (0-689-20688-7).

                    Category: Story **Age:** T–P–K

When a child's cat dies, his family and friends help him "talk through" his grief. His mother suggests listing "10 good things about Barney" to tell at the funeral. The child is able to list only nine. Not until he and his father are gardening does he think of the tenth: "Barney is in the ground and he's helping grow flowers." The child's acceptance of the cat's death is tenderly shown. The book is most appropriate for sharing with young children when they have had a similar experience.   [3]
CATS; DEATH; FAMILY LIFE
Rev: NYT

913 ***Thanksgiving Treat.*** Catherine Stock. Bradbury, 1990. Unp. $11.95. (0-02-788402-3).   **Category:** Story **Age:** P–K

The entire family is busily preparing for the Thanksgiving meal at the grandparents' house, so much so that the youngest, a little boy, is left out of the activities because of his size and inexperience. Finally, after having been rejected by everyone, he is encouraged by his grandfather to find chestnuts for

roasting in the fire. Watercolor scenes highlighted by colored pencil capture
the holiday spirit. [2]
FAMILY LIFE; HOLIDAYS; THANKSGIVING DAY

914   *Theodore.* Edward Ormondroyd. Illus. by John M. Larrecq. Houghton Mifflin, 1984. 40 pp. Paper $4.95. (0-395-36610-0).

Category: Story   **Age:** P–K

Theodore, a cuddly and lovable bear, is sometimes forgotten by Lucy. But, being an old and experienced bear, he does not mind too much. After a harrowing experience at the washateria, Theodore becomes a clean, new-looking bear that is a stranger to Lucy. The charming ways Theodore becomes himself again will captivate young children. The pen and ink drawings with a soft touch of color help to make the story very special. [2]
GIRLS; TEDDY BEARS
Rev: BBC

915   *There's a Horse In My Pocket.* Performed by Laura Simms. Kids Records, 1987. Dist. by Alcazar Records. Audiocassette. 45 min. $9.98.

Category: Poetry/Nursery rhymes/Songs   **Age:** K

Combining talents as a storyteller and musician, Laura Simms tells stories with instrumental accompaniment. The original stories are in the style of folktales. The tape is balanced with both humorous and serious stories, such as "Rabbit in the Moon" and "Two Brothers." Simms' vocal ability will captivate listeners. [2]
HUMOR; SONGS
Rev: BKL 6/15/88

916   *There's a Nightmare In My Closet.* Mercer Mayer. Dial, 1968. Unp. $11.89. (0-8037-8683-2).   **Category:** Story   **Age:** P–K

Mayer's illustrations and text bring together a sense of control that the main character develops to get over the fear of the "nightmare" in the closet. As the young boy identifies and confronts the frightening creature, he begins to realize his ability to control his own fears. This title proves an excellent opportunity to discuss fear in general with any child experiencing such trauma. [1]
FEAR; MONSTERS; NIGHTMARES
Rev: CBK

917   *There's a Nightmare In My Closet.* Illus. by Mercer Mayer. Produced by Phillip J. Marshall and Susan Osborne. Phoenix BFA Films & Videos, 1987. Videocassette. 14 min. $265.00.   **Category:** Story   **Age:** P–K

Goodness! Christopher does have a nightmare in his closet! But does anyone believe him? Finally, he must confront his fears on his own. This video is both an entertaining and a sensitive adaptation of Mercer Mayer's picture book (Dial, 1968). [1]
FEAR; MONSTERS; NIGHTMARES
Rev: BKL 3/1/88

918   ***Things That Go.*** Anne Rockwell. Dutton, 1986. 24 pp. $10.95. (0-525-44266-9).   **Category:** Concept/Counting/Alphabet   **Age:** T–P–K

On the road, in the air, to work, in the yard, in the house, Rockwell's animals propel "things that go." From fire engines to roller skates, from water skis to hobby horses, each brightly colored spread is packed with "going" items for the child to look up and classify. Includes table of contents. [2]
CONCEPTS; TRANSPORTATION

919   ***Things to Play With.*** Anne Rockwell. Dutton, 1988. 24 pp. $11.95. (0-525-44409-2).   **Category:** Concept/Counting/Alphabet   **Age:** T–P

Various animals are at play in many different settings: in the yard, at the beach, in the child's room, etc. A table of contents lists each of these places in words and pictures, giving the child a first opportunity to learn the skill of locating information in a book. Active, bright, and colorful illustrations make this a visually attractive book. [1]
CONCEPTS; PLAY; WORDS
Rev: BKL 10/1/88

920   ***This Little Pig Went to Market.*** Illus. by Denise Fleming. Random House, 1985. 14 pp. Paper $2.95. (0-394-87030-1).
                                Category: Poetry/Nursery rhymes/Songs   **Age:** I–T

Familiar nursery poem depicted in a board-book format featuring flip tabs. Pastel watercolors portray lovable pigs in the market, at home, and so on. The cover shows a mother playing "piggy" with her baby's toes. The final spread pictures the baby playing "piggy" with its own toes while smiling at a toy pig. A charming version of an old favorite. [3]
BOARD BOOKS; NURSERY RHYMES; PIGS
Rev: CBK

921 ***This Old Man: The Counting Song.*** Illus. by Robin M. Koontz. Putnam, 1988. Unp. $12.95. (0-396-09120-2).

Category: Poetry/Nursery rhymes/Songs   **Age:** P–K

Wonderfully illustrated version of the Old English counting song. A young girl watches as 10 old men play knick-knack on everything from a drum to a clothesline. Along with the old men and the girl, the action is enhanced by a dog, a cat, cows, and a chicken. The book includes sheet music and suggestions for play actions.   [3]

COUNTING; GAMES; SONGS

Rev: BKL 11/15/88

922 ***The Three Bears.*** Illus. by Paul Galdone. Houghton Mifflin, 1972. 32 pp. $13.95. (0-395-28811-8).

Category: Folklore/Folktales/Fairy tales   **Age:** P–K

Galdone can always be relied on to supply faithful renditions of traditional tales with appealing illustrations. This may be his best. A hulking family of bears is first shown in a blissful house in the woods. Soon they are eye-poppingly outraged at the antics of that young trespasser, Goldilocks. The type size varies according to the size of the bear speaking. A storytime must. [1]

BEARS; FOLK AND FAIRY TALES

Rev: CBK

923 ***The Three Billy Goats' Gruff.*** Retold and illustrated by Paul Galdone. Houghton Mifflin, 1973. Unp. $13.95. (0-395-28812-6).

Category: Folklore/Folktales/Fairy tales   **Age:** P–K

The troll in this large-format version of the familiar folktale is quite scary looking. The three billy goats, however, are fearless as they trot over the bridge and toss the troll into the river. Their journey ends in the meadow full of sweet grass and bright daisies. The large, colorful illustrations make this an excellent version to read aloud.   [1]

FOLK AND FAIRY TALES; GOATS

Rev: NYT

924 ***The Three Billy Goats' Gruff and The Three Little Pigs.*** Illus. by David Jorgensen. Narrated by Holly Hunter. Directed by David Jorgensen and Mark Sottnick. Mark Sottnick/Rabbit Ears Productions, 1989. Dist. by Teacher's Discovery. Videocassette. 30 min. $14.95.

Category: Folklore/Folktales/Fairy tales   **Age:** P–K

Another outstanding production by Mark Sottnick. Storyteller Holly Hunter rejuvenates these favorites in contemporary versions. The detailed illustrations by Jorgensen and the jazzy music of Art Lande add their own visual and audio delight. [1]

FOLK AND FAIRY TALES; GOATS; PIGS
Rev: BKL 2/1/90

925 *The Three Jovial Huntsmen: A Mother Goose Rhyme.* Susan Jeffers. Aladdin, 1989. 32 pp. Paper $3.95. (0-689-71309-6).

Category: Poetry/Nursery rhymes/Songs **Age:** K

Softly colored illustrations finished in pen and ink enrich this adaptation of the traditional Mother Goose rhyme. Rabbits, deer, and raccoons hide deftly among tree trunks, branches, and bushes. To the three huntsmen, however, the forest appears empty. Children will delight in discovering the camouflaged animals, which play a relentless joke on the huntsmen. [2]

HUNTING; MOTHER GOOSE; NURSERY RHYMES
Rev: NYT **Awards:** Caldecott Honor Book

926 *Three Little Pigs.* James Marshall. Dial, 1989. Unp. $11.89. (0-8037-0594-8). **Category:** Folklore/Folktales/Fairy tales **Age:** P–K

This retelling of the familiar tale portrays one of the three brother pigs surviving the wolf's attacks by using his head and planning well. The bright ink and watercolor illustrations present the characters in a humorous fashion. The action in the illustrations would encourage dramatic play. [1]

FOLK AND FAIRY TALES; PIGS; WOLVES
Rev: BKL 9/1/89; CBY-90

927 *The Three Sillies and 10 Other Stories to Read Aloud.* Anne Rockwell. Reprint. Harper & Row, 1986. 87 pp. $7.95. (0-06-443093-6).

Category: Folklore/Folktales/Fairy tales **Age:** K

Anne Rockwell's retelling of 11 classic tales and fables is accompanied by amusing watercolor illustrations on almost every page. Some of the longer tales, for example, "The Three Sillies," have quite a bit of text, but the lively writing style should hold a youngster's interest. [2]

FOLK AND FAIRY TALES
Rev: ESLC

928 *Through Grandpa's Eyes.* Patricia MacLachlan. Illus. by Deborah Ray. Harper & Row, 1980. 38 pp. $12.89. (0-06-024043-1).

Category: Story **Age:** P–K

A young boy learns from his blind grandfather a very different way of seeing the world. This slight volume provides a thoughtful, gentle opportunity for discussions about blindness. Its text is manageable for older readers. Younger audiences will find comfort and reassurance in the soft tones of the evocative watercolor illustrations. [3]

BLINDNESS; GRANDFATHERS

Rev: CBK

929 *Thumbelina.* Hans Christian Andersen. Adapted and illustrated by Demi. Dodd Mead/Putnam, 1988. Unp. $13.95. (0-396-09241-1).

Category: Folklore/Folktales/Fairy tales **Age:** K

A tiny little girl is so small she can easily sleep in a walnut shell. After numerous adventures with animal friends and enemies, she comes across a transparent little man who offers her his crown of gold. The retelling of this Hans Christian Andersen story is enhanced through flowing illustrations in clear, bold, and bright colors. [2]

FOLK AND FAIRY TALES; GIRLS

Rev: BKL 3/1/89

930 *Thump, Thump, Rat-a-Tat-Tat.* Gene Baer. Illus. by Lois Ehlert. Harper & Row, 1989. Unp. $11.89. (0-06-020362-5).

Category: Story **Age:** T–P–K

What child does not delight in a parade? Here vibrant colors and shapes, word sounds, even the type size combine to create the building excitement of a marching band. A deceptively simple and effective presentation that will be fun to read and hear. [1]

PARADES; SOUNDS

Rev: BKL 11/1/89

931 *Thunder Cake.* Patricia Polacco. Philomel, 1990. Unp. $14.95. (0-399-22231-6). **Category:** Story **Age:** K

A young girl visits her Russian grandmother in Michigan. She fears the sound of summer storm thunder, but her grandmother helps her, in a very unusual way, to overcome this fear. Detailed illustrations, full of color and expression, add to the heartwarming tale. The recipe for "thunder cake" is included.

FEAR; GRANDMOTHERS; THUNDER [1]

Rev: BKL 2/15/90

932 *Tidy Titch.* Pat Hutchins. Greenwillow Books, 1991. Unp. $13.95. (0-688-09964-5). **Category:** Story **Age:** P–K

Upon seeing how tidy Titch's room is, Mother tells Peter and Mary to tidy their rooms. Titch offers to help, taking the broken, ignored, and outgrown toys from their rooms to his own. Now their rooms are tidy, but his is not. Detailed, full-page illustrations provide much of the story's amusement and delight. [2]

BROTHERS AND SISTERS; CLEANLINESS

933 *Tim and the Cat and the Big Red Hat.* Hartley Courseware, 1988. Software. $39.95. **Category:** Informational **Age:** K

Ideal for beginning readers, this animated color program contains 10 sequenced stories about a mischievous cat and his friend. Optional sound using an Echo speech synthesizer or a Ufonic reinforces the vocabulary. After each story, the child is asked to answer both literal and inferential comprehension questions (Apple II disk). [3]

WORDS

Rev: BKL 6/1/89

934 *Time for Bed, the Babysitter Said.* Peggy P. Anderson. Houghton Mifflin, 1987. Unp. $12.95. (0-395-41851-8). **Category:** Story **Age:** P–K

The babysitter is unsuccessful in getting young Joe to go to bed until she finally says, "Please." This simple story is told in conversation and in humorous cartoon-style drawings of the frog characters. Most animal book characters are furry or feathered; frog characters make a refreshing change. With humor, the author-illustrator demonstrates the power of the word "please." [3]

BEDTIME; FROGS; HUMOR

Rev: ESLC

935 *Time to ....* Bruce McMillan. Lothrop, Lee & Shepard, 1989. Unp. $13.88. (0-688-08856-2). **Category:** Story **Age:** K

Time passes in a kindergartner's day, marked by the changing hands on a clock from hour to hour and photographed as the light changes throughout the day. On one page is the digital display of the hour; on the next is accompanying kindergarten activity—painting, waking, sleeping, eating. Details such as different clothes changing on the hooks next to the clock, toys changing on the shelf, etc., help to establish context. [1]

CLOCKS; TIME

Rev: BKL 9/15/89; CBY-90

936 *Tin Toy.* Directed by John Lasseter. Direct Cinema, 1988. Videocassette. 5 min. $75.00.   **Category:** Wordless   **Age:** P–K

A wind-up toy encounters a boisterous baby as it seeks amusement. Using superb computer animation, the director captures the inquisitive baby, the frightened toys, and the game of pursuit in a brief, realistic moment. Preschool and kindergarten youngsters will delight in seeing and remembering their crawling years and the abuse they gave to their own toys.   [1]
ANIMATION; BABIES; TOYS
Rev: BKL 6/1/89   **Awards:** 1989 Academy Award; American Film and Video

937 *The Tiny Seed.* Eric Carle. Picture Book Studio, 1987. Unp. $15.95. (0-88708-015-4).   **Category:** Informational   **Age:** K

Large, colorful collages illustrate the life story of a tiny seed, which is compared to other, larger seeds in a series of adventures reflecting the many reasons seeds fail to grow (lack of water, etc.). This is an interesting and creative way to teach children about the life cycle of plants, with a happy ending.
PLANTS; SEEDS   [2]
Rev: BKL 4/15/87

938 *To Sleep.* James Sage. Illus. by Warwick Hutton. Margaret K. McElderry Books, 1990. Unp. $12.95. (0-689-50497-7).   **Category:** Story   **Age:** T

A mother makes the statement to her small child as they prepare for bedtime: "We have reached the end of the day." And the child asks: "Where is the end, Mother?" What follows is her explanation and a pictorial flight of fantasy as the bed, containing both of them, flies out the window and over the scenes she describes: the garden, the town, the city, the sea, the stars, and finally dreamland. A comforting read-aloud before sleep.   [2]
BEDTIME; DREAMS

939 *Toddlers on Parade: Musical Exercises for Infants and Toddlers.* Carol Hammett and Elaine Bueffel. Musical arrangements by Dennis Buck. Kimbo Educational, 1985. Audiocassette. 30 min. $10.95.
                      Category: Poetry/Nursery rhymes/Songs   **Age:** I–T

Familiar songs such as "Gifts for Mommy," "Wheels on the Bus," and "Little Bunny Foo Foo" are accompanied by a piano and flute. Also included are two holiday songs: one for Halloween, one for Thanksgiving. A lively, uplifting collection, perfect for "exercise" routines with the assistance of a parent or caregiver.   [2]
GAMES; MUSIC; SONGS
Awards: Parents' Choice Award

940 *Together.* George-Ella Lyon. Illus. by Vera Rosenberry. Orchard Books, 1989. Unp. $14.95. (0-531-08431-0).

Category: Poetry/Nursery rhymes/Songs   **Age:** P–K

A ponytailed black girl and her braided-blonde-haired friend engage in joyful cooperative activities in this delightful poem. "You cut the timber and I'll build the house. You bring the cheese and I'll fetch the mouse. You salt the ice and I'll crank the cream." Each stanza ends with the refrain, "Let's put our heads together and dream the same dream." Framed watercolors stretch the imagination and heighten the excitement.   [1]

FRIENDSHIP; POETRY

Rev: BKL 9/15/89

941 *Tom and Pippo Make a Friend.* Helen Oxenbury. Aladdin, 1989. Unp. $5.95. (0-689-71339-8).   **Category:** Story   **Age:** P

When Mommy takes Tom and his toy monkey, Pippo, to the park, Tom learns a lesson in sharing. A little girl shares her sandbox bucket, and Tom shares Pippo. Half of the illustrations are black and white sketches, and half are done in colorful pastels. All are realistic and full of expression.   [1]

FRIENDSHIP; PLAY; SHARING

Rev: CBY-89

942 *Tomie dePaola's Book of Poems.* Tomie dePaola. Putnam, 1988. 96 pp. $17.95. (0-399-21540-9).

Category: Poetry/Nursery rhymes/Songs   **Age:** P–K

With the opening poem by Emily Dickinson, "There's No Frigate Like a Book," and illustrations of children sailing off while engrossed in reading a book, dePaola has gathered a variety of poems from classics to modern-day verses covering every mood from nonsense to serious. His illustrations colorfully animate the verses and capture the imagination of all ages.   [2]

POETRY

Rev: BKL 11/1/88

943 *Tomie dePaola's Favorite Nursery Tales.* Selected and illustrated by Tomie dePaola. Putnam, 1986. 128 pp. $17.95. (0-399-21319-8).

Category: Folklore/Folktales/Fairy tales   **Age:** T–P–K

DePaola has created a distinctive volume of over 25 nursery tales, chosen from among the fairy and folk tales, fables, and poems he loved as a boy. The works

of Hans Christian Andersen, the Brothers Grimm, Aesop, and poets Stevenson, Longfellow, and Lear are represented here. Children of all ages will respond to dePaola's humorous, brilliantly colored illustrations.   [2]
FOLK AND FAIRY TALES; NURSERY RHYMES; POETRY
Rev: NYT

944   *Tomie dePaola's Mother Goose.* Illus. by Tomie dePaola. Putnam, 1985. 127 pp. $17.95. (0-399-21258-2).
Category: Poetry/Nursery rhymes/Songs   Age: T–P–K

Tomie dePaola has compiled an exhaustive collection of over 200 Mother Goose rhymes. In his humorous, stylized fashion, dePaola gives us all the old favorites like "Simple Simon," "Little Bo Peep," and "Jack and Jill" as well as the not-so-familiar "Taffy Was a Welshman" and "Jerry Hall." Index of first lines is included.   [1]
MOTHER GOOSE; NURSERY RHYMES
Rev: BKL 1/1/88; CBK; NYT

945   *The Tomorrow Book.* Doris Schwerin. Illus. by Karen Gundersheimer. Pantheon Books, 1984. 32 pp. $10.95. (0-394-85459-4).
Category: Story   Age: P–K

In this bedtime storybook, the author uses the concept of "night" to explain the concept of future time—tomorrow—and portrays a child's bedtime, then the awakening to a new day and participation in typical daytime activities. Tiny, bright, but expressive and appealing drawings are on each page of this large-format book. The story ends with a guarantee of continuous love: "Kisses for today and tomorrow ... all for you."   [3]
TIME
Rev: ESLC

946   *The Tomten and the Fox.* Astrid Lindgren. Illus. by Harald Wilerg. Coward McCann, 1966. Unp. $5.95. (0-698-20644-4).
Category: Folklore/Folktales/Fairy tales   Age: P–K

The tomten is a Swedish troll who guards farm animals at night. When Reynard, the fox, slinks around the farm at night hoping to catch a hen in the hen house, the tomten provides another solution. He fills a bowl with porridge for the fox, convincing him to leave the farm animals alone. Full-page illustrations of snowy winter nights on the farm make the book memorable.   [3]
FOLK AND FAIRY TALES; FOXES
Rev: NYT

947   ***Too Many Eggs: A Counting Book.*** M. Christina Butler. Illus. by Meg Rutherford. David R. Godine, 1988. Unp. $12.95. (0-87923-741-4).

Category: Story   **Age:** P–K

Mrs. Bear is absentminded and cannot count. When she bakes a birthday cake
for Mr. Bear, she uses "too many eggs," and the results are delightful for
young children. Readers participate with Mrs. Bear by counting the eggs for
her from the basket in the cupboard on the inside back cover of the book.
Cardboard pages make turning back and forth easier for little fingers and will
extend the life of the book.   [2]
BEARS; COUNTING; EGGS

948   ***Tortillitas para Mama: And Other Nursery Rhymes, Spanish and English.***
Margaret C. Griego, et al. Illus. by Barbara Cooney. Henry Holt & Co.,
1981. Unp. $14.95. (0-8050-0285-5).

Category: Poetry/Nursery rhymes/Songs   **Age:** T–P–K

Latin American nursery rhymes are offered in Spanish and English transla-
tions. Simple and charming, they feature parents and children performing the
everyday activities of dressing, playing, eating, etc., with suggested finger
movements. Cooney's earth-toned illustrations, with their strong molded
figures, convey perfectly the folk quality of the verses.   [2]
NURSERY RHYMES; SPANISH LANGUAGE
Rev: NYT

949   ***Totally Teddy.*** Melody House, 1988. Record. 22 min. $9.95.

Category: Poetry/Nursery rhymes/Songs   **Age:** T–P–K

Several pleasant-sounding male and female voices sing a delightful collection
of songs about teddy bears. Young children seem to have a special relationship
with their bears, and these songs validate their feelings. The words of the
songs are printed inside the album cover. The 10 songs can be used with dramatic play or listened to and sung just for pleasure.   [1]
SONGS; TEDDY BEARS
Rev: BKL 2/15/90   **Awards:** Parents' Choice Award

950   ***Touch Me Book.*** Eve Witte and Pat Witte. Illus. by Harlow Rockwell. Western, 1961. Unp. $5.95. (0-307-12146-1).

Category: Participation and manipulative   **Age:** I–T–P

Bold black outlines of nine simple objects are supplemented with additional
materials to provide a range of tactile experiences: fur feels soft, a feather feels

ticklish, rubber is stretchy, etc. The simple text reinforces the concepts through questions and repetition. Spiral binding. [3]
PARTICIPATION; TOUCHING
Rev: CBK

951 *Town and Country.* Alice Provensen and Martin Provensen. Crown, 1985. 32 pp. $9.95. (0-517-55594-8).

Category: Informational **Age:** P–K

Readers and viewers sample the bustling excitement of the big city and savor the quiet pleasures of life on the farm. Wonderfully detailed illustrations in this oversize volume highlight the colorful differences between urban and rural settings. All the children play and go to school, yet their surroundings differ in many interesting ways. [2]
CITIES AND TOWNS; FARMS
Rev: NYT

952 *The Town Mouse and the Country Mouse.* Lorinda B. Cauley. Putnam, 1984. 32 pp. $11.95. (0-399-21123-3).

Category: Folklore/Folktales/Fairy tales **Age:** P–K

Country Mouse begins to view his simple life differently when cousin Town Mouse tells him he works too hard for his supper and his days are dull compared with city life. When Country Mouse accompanies him to his Victorian home, he discovers that Town Mouse eats a lavish supper—but under threat of discovery by two huge dogs. Country Mouse returns home, confident that a life of luxury is not worth living in constant fear. [1]
FOLK AND FAIRY TALES; MICE
Rev: NYT

953 *Town Mouse and Country Mouse.* Lorinda B. Cauley. Narrated by Donald Davis. Weston Woods Studios, 1987. Filmstrip. 9 min. $26.00.

Category: Folklore/Folktales/Fairy tales **Age:** P–K

With guitar music in the background, Cauley's retelling of this traditional tale of two cousins and the very different lives they lead is told with a distinct flavor of country. Illustrations from the book (Putnam, 1984) are detailed and lively. Script included. [1]
FOLK AND FAIRY TALES; MICE
Rev: SLJ 4/89 **Awards:** ALSC Notable Filmstrip

954   Traffic: A Book of Opposites. Betsy Maestro and Giulio Maestro. Crown, 1981. Unp. $10.95. (0-517-54427-X).

Category: Concept/Counting/Alphabet   **Age:** P–K

While a little car travels from city to country, a number of concepts are covered: over/under, left/right, stop/go, slow/fast, big/little, empty/full, closed/open, narrow/wide, dark/light, long/short, far/near, high/low, front/back, and day/night. Bright colors and the simple shapes of familiar sights make these opposites easy to grasp.   [2]

CONCEPTS; OPPOSITES; TRAFFIC

Rev: BBC; CBK

955   Transitions 2: Music to Help Baby Sleep. Produced by Fred J. Schwartz. Placenta Music, 1990. Compact Disc. 60 min. $10.98.

Category: Participation and manipulative   **Age:** I–T

Designed to encourage sleep, using the digitally recorded sound of a "maternal placental pulse" and the breathing sounds of a pregnant woman as a backdrop for soft female vocals and instrumentals. Approximating the sound of tides breaking at an accelerated pace, the pulse and breathing serve as a constant. Developed for use during labor and delivery, for calming "agitated" infants, and for stress reduction for the parent.   [1]

BEDTIME; SLEEP

956   Treasure Nap. Juanita Havill. Illus. by Elivia Savadier. Houghton Mifflin, 1992. Unp. $13.95. (0-395-57817-5).   **Category:** Story   **Age:** P–K

It's too hot to sleep, so Mama tells a story which is "to be told when it's too hot to nap." The story is about great-grandmother visiting her grandfather in his Mexican village. After the nap it's time to rediscover the many treasures belonging to Rita's grandfather.   [2]

MEXICO; SLEEP

957   A Tree Is Nice. Janice May Udry. Illus. by Marc Simont. Harper & Row, 1956. 32 pp. $11.89. (0-06-026156-0).

Category: Informational   **Age:** P–K

This book discusses the merits of trees, and, with accompanying watercolor illustrations, readers learn how trees improve life and the environment. Various types of trees and settings are featured. Although published in 1956, this book will maintain its universal appeal for years to come.   [3]

TREES

Rev: CBK; NYT   **Awards:** Caldecott Medal

958   *Treeful of Pigs.* Arnold Lobel. Illus. by Anita Lobel. Greenwillow Books, 1979. 32 pp. $12.88. (0-688-84177-5).   **Category:** Story   **Age:** P–K

The exasperated wife of a lazy farmer tries several ploys to get her husband to help take care of a barnyard of pigs. Colorful illustrations that are distinctly Lobel and delightful humor will appeal to young listeners as they anticipate which of the wife's tactics will finally motivate the farmer to help.   [2]
Laziness; Pigs
Rev: ESLC

959   *Tricky Tortoise.* Mwenye Hadithi. Illus. by Adrienne Kennaway. Little, Brown & Co., 1988. Unp. $13.95. (0-316-33724-2).

Category: Story   **Age:** P–K

Clever Tortoise is tired of being stepped on by big old Elephant, so he decides it is time to teach Elephant a lesson. By enlisting the help of his brother, Tortoise wins the day, showing again that size is not everything. A witty text and dramatically vivid jungle illustrations are aptly combined in this wonderful tale of wisdom and humor.   [3]
Africa; Elephants; Turtles
Rev: BKL 12/1/88

960   *The Trip.* Ezra Jack Keats. Greenwillow Books, 1978. Unp. $12.88. (0-688-84123-6).   **Category:** Story   **Age:** P–K

Brightly colored, collagelike illustrations add depth to Louis's adventures as he imaginatively takes himself back for a visit to his old neighborhood friends. His day ends happily as he goes out to trick or treat with new friends.   [3]
Afro-Americans; Halloween; Loneliness
Rev: CBY-88

961   *A Trip in a Hot Air Balloon.* Lancit Media, 1989. Dist. by Churchill Films. Videocassette. 14 min. $195.00.   **Category:** Informational   **Age:** P–K

Accompanied by Yoyo the clown, viewers are shown the process of setting up, riding in, and bagging a hot air balloon. The music and bright colors complement the perspective and excitement of flight.   [3]
Ballooning; Clowns, jesters
Rev: BKL 09/1/89

962 *Trot, Trot to Boston: Play Rhymes for Baby.* Compiled by Carol F. Ra. Illus. by Catherine Stock. Lothrop, Lee & Shepard, 1987. 32 pp. $12.88. (0-688-06191-5).　**Category:** Poetry/Nursery rhymes/Songs　**Age:** I–T

Besides "This Little Piggy Went to Market" and "Pat-a-Cake, Pat-a-Cake," several other less familiar nursery rhymes are included with simple instructions about how they are played. The emphasis is on rhythm, play, touch, and fun. Colorful watercolor scenes and characters complete this treat.　　[2]
BABIES; NURSERY RHYMES
Rev: BKL 1/1/88

963 *The Trouble with Babies.* Chris Sage. Illus. by Angie Sage. Viking Penguin, 1989. Unp. $11.95. (0-670-82392-9).

Category: Informational　**Age:** P–K

The actual trouble with babies is that they cry, are messy, and get all the attention. But they do have a few redeeming features, even to big brothers or sisters. Uniquely illustrated in pastels, this is a very useful tool for the older sibling learning to cope with the threat of a new baby.　　[1]
BABIES; BROTHERS AND SISTERS; SIBLING RIVALRY
Rev: BKL 2/15/90

964 *The Trouble with Tyrannosaurus Rex.* Lorinda B. Cauley. Harcourt Brace Jovanovich, 1988. Unp. $13.95. (0-15-290880-3).

Category: Story　**Age:** P–K

Tyrannosaurus Rex is the bully of the neighborhood, always looking for smaller dinosaurs to eat. Duckbill and Ankylosaurus were afraid to enjoy the clear lake and the afternoon sunshine unless Rex was away. Then Duckbill thinks of a way for all of the smaller dinosaurs to gang up on him, causing Rex to leave the neighborhood. This fanciful fantasy and the color pencil illustrations will delight dinosaur lovers.　　[2]
BULLYING; DINOSAURS
Rev: BKL 4/1/88

965 *Truck.* Donald Crews. Greenwillow Books, 1980. Unp. $12.88. (0-688-84244-5).　**Category:** Wordless　**Age:** P–K

With no words but with bright, colorful illustrations, this is the story of a big red truck, loaded with tricycles, that leaves a loading dock, travels on city streets, and goes through a tunnel, down superhighways, and across a bridge to its final destination. Perfect for even the youngest truck lovers.　　[1]
TRUCKS; WORDLESS
Rev: BBC; CBK; ESLC　**Awards:** Caldecott Honor Book

966   ***Trucks.*** Gail Gibbons. Harper & Row, 1981. Unp. Paper $12.95. (0-690-04118-7).   **Category:** Informational   **Age:** P–K

Many kinds of trucks go everywhere and help the community in different ways all day long. The illustrations will capture the attention of the listener and elicit questions about the various types of trucks shown.   [2]
MACHINES; TRUCKS
Rev: CBK; ESLC

967   ***The True Story of the Three Little Pigs.*** Alexander Wolf as told to Jon Scieszka. Illus. by Lane Smith. Viking Penguin, 1989. 32 pp. $13.95. (0-670-82759-2).   **Category:** Story   **Age:** P–K

The retelling of the story of the "Three Little Pigs" from the wolf's point of view with a tongue-in-cheek tone. Accompanied by sophisticated and surreal illustrations that appear at times somewhat menacing, this unique rendition will delight viewers and listeners, especially those who have heard the original from the pigs' point of view.   [1]
PIGS; WOLVES
Rev: BKL 9/1/89

968   ***Tubtime.*** Elvira Woodruff. Illus. by Suçie Stevenson. Holiday House, 1990. Unp. $14.95. (0-8234-0777-2).   **Category:** Story   **Age:** K

The dirty, mud-loving O'Mally sisters are just beginning "tubtime" when their mother gets a phone call from long-winded Aunt Minnie. The sisters discover that their new bubble pipes have extraordinary powers, and they blow giant bubbles encasing chickens, frogs, and a hungry alligator. Stevenson's wacky drawings add to the merriment.   [3]
BATHS; BROTHERS AND SISTERS
Rev: BKL 4/1/90

969   ***Turn on the Music!*** Written and sung by Hap Palmer. Produced by Amy Weintraub and Brooks McEwen. Media Home Entertainment, 1988. Videocassette. 30 min. $14.98.
                                    Category: Poetry/Nursery rhymes/Songs   **Age:** P–K

Use of boys and girls to act out Hap Palmer's songs is a definite plus as gender stereotyping is laid to rest. In an especially lively number called "Hurry Up Blues," Dad has the job of getting the kids off to school. Another effective number, from both an instrumental and a vocal point of view, is "Amanda Schlupp." Hap Palmer wrote and performed the songs. Clay animation ties the selections together.   [2]
SELF-CONCEPT; SONGS
Rev: BKL 2/1/90

970 *The Turnip: An Old Russian Folktale.* Illus. by Pierr Morgan. Philomel, 1990. Unp. $13.95. (0-399-22229-4).

Category: Folklore/Folktales/Fairy tales **Age:** P–K

This variation of the Russian folktale uses brief text, authentic names, and simple illustrations to tell the story of a turnip seed that grew not only quite large but also very stubborn as harvest time arrived. Colorful illustrations, using gouache and india ink, clearly present the characters' facial expressions, a realistic turnip, and the tremendous effort required to extract the great vegetable from the earth.   [3]

FOLK AND FAIRY TALES; RUSSIA

Rev: BKL 4/1/90

971 *Twelve Dancing Princesses.* Marianna Mayer. Illus. by Kinuko Y. Craft. Morrow Jr. Books, 1989. 40 pp. $14.88. (0-688-02026-7).

Category: Folklore/Folktales/Fairy tales **Age:** K

The well-known fairy tale in which a king worries over his dozen daughters who suffer from an enchantment that causes them to dance each evening until dawn. Richly retold and lavishly illustrated with detailed paintings.   [3]

DANCING; FOLK AND FAIRY TALES; ROYALTY

Rev: BKL 3/15/89

972 *The Twelve Days of Christmas.* Illus. by Jan Brett. Putnam, 1986. Unp. $13.95. (0-396-08821-X).

Category: Poetry/Nursery rhymes/Songs **Age:** T–P–K

Beginning with the music arrangement for this traditional English Christmas carol, each day is framed by lush illustrations of the activities both inside and out in preparation for the holiday. In addition to the characters in the song, Brett shows a courtship between a gentleman and a lady, a family decorating the tree, and "Merry Christmas" in 11 languages across the bottom of the pages.   [1]

CHRISTMAS; MUSIC; SONGS

Rev: NYT

973 *26 Letters and 99 Cents.* Tana Hoban. Greenwillow Books, 1987. 32 pp. $14.88. (0-688-06362-4).

Category: Concept/Counting/Alphabet **Age:** P–K

The first half of this cleverly formatted book contains photos of brightly colored uppercase and lowercase soft touch letters with appropriately corresponding objects. By turning the book upside down and beginning again, it becomes a 1–99 counting book with pennies, nickels, dimes, and quarters. Although higher numerical concepts may be beyond the understanding of kindergarten children, the actual-size photos are helpful. [1]

ALPHABET; COUNTING; MONEY

Rev: BKL 3/1/87; PP

974 *Twenty-six Rabbits Run Riot.* Cara L. Smith. Little, Brown & Co., 1990. Unp. $12.95. (0-316-80185-2). **Category:** Story **Age:** P–K

Nice Mrs. Fitzwarren has 26 naughty little rabbit children, who run rampant through the park, woods, beach, restaurant, and home. All 26 have distinctive personalities, costumes, and names. The child is constantly on the lookout for the baby rabbit's black-tipped ears to see where he may be hiding this time.

RABBITS [2]

975 *Two New Sneakers.* Nancy Tafuri. Greenwillow Books, 1988. Unp. Paper $3.95. (0-688-07462-6). **Category:** Story **Age:** T–P

Beginning with sneakers on the cover, each page of this board book features a richly colored piece of clothing that finds itself on one little child. At times, the puppy helps by bringing sneakers and scarf. Simple shapes on a white background make an attractive and easy-to-identify book for the very young.

BOARD BOOKS; CLOTHING; SHOES [2]

Rev: BKL 5/1/88

976 *Two Orphan Cubs.* Barbara Brenner and May Garelick. Illus. by Erika Kors. Walker & Co., 1989. Unp. $12.95. (0-8027-6868-7).

Category: Informational **Age:** P–K

When a wildlife scientist discovers black bear cubs whose mother has been shot by a poacher, he devises a plan to try to save the two orphans. He transfers them to another bear's cave, where he hopes they will be adopted. Black-and-white sketches gently portray this true story. An additional informational page follows the story and tells about a wildlife scientist's work with black bears. [2]

BEARS; ORPHANS

Rev: BKL 6/1/89; CBY-90; SLJ 6/89

977 *Tyrannosaurus Was a Beast.* Jack Prelutsky. Illus. by Arnold Lobel. Greenwillow Books/Library Learning Resources, 1988. $18.50. (0-688-06443-4). **Category:** Poetry/Nursery rhymes/Songs **Age:** K

In Prelutsky's poems, 14 dinosaurs glide, plod, amble, or swim as they engage in appropriate dinosaur pursuits, accompanied by Lobel's accurate, chubby illustrations. Activities included in this kit encourage adults and children to work together on art projects, in measuring dinosaur sizes, or in writing their own poems. [2]
DINOSAURS; POETRY
Rev: BKL 8/88

978 *The Ugly Duckling.* Hans Christian Andersen. Narrated by Cher. Illus. by Robert Van Nutt. Alfred A. Knopf, 1986. Unp. $13.95. (0-394-88403-5). **Category:** Folklore/Folktales/Fairy tales **Age:** P–K

An award-winning edition of the classic tale of an ugly duckling who suffers cruelty and rejection before growing into a beautiful swan. Van Nutt's skillfully executed paintings are characterized by muted colors and a close-up focus on the animals. Cher's distinctive voice narrates the accompanying audiocassette, which is enhanced by a gentle musical score composed and performed by Patrick Ball. [1]
DUCKS; FOLK AND FAIRY TALES; SWANS
Rev: NYT **Awards:** NYT Best Illustrated Book

979 *The Umbrella Day.* Nancy Evans Cooney. Illus. by Melissa B. Mathis. Philomel, 1989. Unp. $14.95. (0-399-21523-9). **Category:** Story **Age:** P–K

After her mother's admonition, Missy reluctantly drags the dusty old umbrella from the closet and sets off. As big fat drops begin to fall, she is thankful for the umbrella, but its stuffiness prompts her command, "Be a toadstool." From this point on, the story enters the realm of fantasy. The plot reaches a dangerous climax but is quickly brought to a safe conclusion. Luminous, luscious, and lacy illustrations throughout. [3]
ANIMALS; RAIN; UMBRELLAS
Rev: BKL 5/1/89

980 *Unbearable Bears.* Kevin Roth. Marlboro Records, 1986. Audiocassette. 35 min. $9.98. **Category:** Poetry/Nursery rhymes/Songs **Age:** T–P–K

Captivating collection of 10 songs, many of which are originals about bears and self-esteem. One song, "The Garden," is from the Arnold Lobel story. Others include "Teddy Bear's Picnic"; "The Bear You Loved," about keeping and loving your teddy bear; a humorous song, "The Bear That Snores"; and an old standby, "I Know an Old Lady Who Swallowed a Fly." [2]

SONGS; TEDDY BEARS

Rev: SLJ 4/87   **Awards:** ALSC Notable Recording

981   *Under the Big Top.* Melody House, 1989. Record. 41 min. $9.95.

Category: Participation and manipulative   **Age:** P–K

A rollicking good time! The record includes original circus songs and activities plus the most familiar of all circus tunes, "The Grand March." The album jacket provides the lyrics as well as suggested activities to accompany each song. Side one contains vocals; side two is instrumental only. A "find" for teachers and others who play with very young children. [2]

CIRCUS

Rev: BKL 1/15/90

982   *Under the Blanket.* Madelaine Gill Linden. Little, Brown & Co., 1987. Unp. $12.95. (0-316-52626-6).   **Category:** Story   **Age:** T–P

A rhyming story of hide-and-seek played by a young girl and three stuffed toys: a lion, a mouse, and a bear. The soft colors and small scale of the illustrations limit this book to one reader, but the rhyme and rhythm tell a sweet story of a little girl's make-believe game with her toys. [3]

IMAGINATION; PLAY; TOYS

Rev: ESLC

983   *Under the Moon.* Joanne Ryder. Illus. by Cheryl Harness. Random House, 1989. Unp. $5.99. (0-394-91960-2).   **Category:** Story   **Age:** P–K

A little mouse knows only that he lives under the moon. Mama Mouse wants to teach him how to recognize his home by the way it smells, sounds, and feels. A warm, reassuring tale with illustrations that come alive with the depiction of abundant wildlife. [3]

MICE; MOTHERS

Rev: BKL 6/1/89; CBY-90

984   *Underwear!* Mary E. Monsell. Illus. by Lynn Munsinger. Albert Whitman & Co., 1988. Unp. $10.95. (0-8075-8308-1).   **Category:** Story   **Age:** P–K

Unlike Zachary Zebra and Orfo the Orangutan, who simply love underwear and think it grand fun, Bismark the Buffalo sees no purpose in it, refuses to

wear it, in fact refuses to have any fun at all, and just gets grumpier and lonelier all by himself. Munsinger's perfect illustrations dance, prance, and tickle readers silly.   [1]
ANIMALS; FRIENDSHIP; UNDERWEAR
Rev: BKL 4/1/88

985 *Up and Down on the Merry-Go-Round.* Bill Martin, Jr. and John Archambault. Illus. by Ted Rand. Henry Holt & Co., 1988. Unp. $12.95. (0-8050-0681-8).   **Category:** Story   **Age:** T–P–K

A sing-songy rhyming text conveys the breathless motion and enjoyment of a merry-go-round. Children of all ages and races ride bright ponies and other exotic animals. As the ride slows, the disappointment is palatable. A little girl decides, when she grows up, she will run a merry-go-round that never stops. The bright watercolor illustrations exhibit multiple perspectives and blurred edges, which convey perfectly the dizzy motion.   [2]
MERRY-GO-ROUNDS
Rev: BKL 6/15/88

986 *The Velveteen Rabbit.* Margery Williams. Illus. by David Jorgensen. Narrated by Meryl Streep. Rabbit Ears, 1985. Dist. by Random House Home Video. Videocassette. 27 min. $49.95.   **Category:** Story   **Age:** K

Jorgensen's softly colored and textured illustrations fade gently in and out to create an illusion of motion in this lovely retelling of Williams' fantasy about a little toy rabbit who longs to become real. The velveteen rabbit learns from the skin horse that "real is a thing that happens to you when a child loves you for a very long time." Streep's gentle, expressive narration adds an extra touch of class to this classic tale.   [1]
MAGIC; RABBITS; TOYS
Rev: SLJ 4/87   **Awards:** ALSC Notable Film/Video

987 *The Very Busy Spider.* Eric Carle. Philomel, 1984. Unp. $16.95. (0-399-21166-7).   **Category:** Story   **Age:** T–P–K

Each day a spider spins her web on a fence post. As each page progresses, nine different barnyard animals try to distract her. She stays with the task, and the finished product is beautiful and helps her catch flies. The rhythmic, repetitive text allows for audience participation in making the sound for each animal. Raised lines in the spider web make this story accessible to both sighted and blind children. A multisensory delight.   [1]
PARTICIPATION; SPIDERS; TOY AND MOVABLE BOOKS
Rev: BBC; CBK; CBY-90; ESLC; NYT; PP

988 **The Very Hungry Caterpillar.** Eric Carle. Putnam, 1989. Unp. $15.95. (0-399-21933-1). **Category:** Concept/Counting/Alphabet **Age:** T–P–K

Over the course of a week, a tiny caterpillar eats its way through an amazing quantity of food, wraps itself into a cocoon, and goes to sleep. It awakens to discover it has been transformed into a beautiful butterfly. Holes are punched through the brightly colored fruits and other foods, large enough for a caterpillar and for small fingers. *La Oruga muy Hambrienta* is the title of the Spanish version. [1]

BUTTERFLIES; CONCEPTS; TOY AND MOVABLE BOOKS

Rev: CBK; NYT

989 **A Very Special Friend.** Dorothy Hoffman Levi. Illus. by Ethel Gold. Kendall Green Publications/Gallaudet University Press, 1989. 40 pp. $8.95. (0-930323-55-6). **Category:** Story **Age:** K

Frannie is lonely because she has no friend. When Laura moves next door, Frannie eagerly greets her only to learn Laura is deaf. Disappointed, Frannie seeks solace from her mother, who helps her overcome her confusion regarding deafness. Soon, Frannie begins to learn basic signing, and the two become best friends. Included are the illustrated American manual alphabet and descriptions of nine basic signs. [2]

DEAFNESS; DISABLED; FRIENDSHIP

Rev: BKL 6/15/89

990 **A Visit to the Zoo.** Nancy Hellen. Peter Bedrick, 1990. Unp. $5.95. (0-87226-431-9). **Category:** Participation and manipulative **Age:** T

A pop-up book just the right size to be held in a small child's hands. The animals and backgrounds are drawn with simple lines, and the pictures are colorful and uncluttered. There is a simple command or question on each page, which points out a main characteristic of each animal. For example, "See the snake's long, shiny body." [2]

TOY AND MOVABLE BOOKS; ZOOS

991 **Visiting Granny.** Kim Fernandes. Annick Press, 1990. Unp. Paper $4.95. (1-55037-084-7). Dist. by Firefly Books. **Category:** Story **Age:** T–P

Steven and Jenny visit Granny's house and discover all its wonders. Among the activities there, they count the animals, listen to stories, and share in the baking of cookies. The carefully sculpted children and animals are eye appealing, but it is Granny, with an abundance of curly, white hair, who lovingly dominates each scene. [3]

COOKING; COUNTING; GRANDMOTHERS

992 **Waiting for Jennifer.** Kathryn O. Galbraith. Illus. by Irene Trivas. Margaret K. McElderry Books, 1987. 32 pp. $12.95. (0-689-50430-6).

Category: Story **Age:** P–K

A fresh telling of the six-month wait for the birth of a sibling. Nan and Thea are believable characters, who think the baby will never come and have a surprise when the baby is born. Realistic dialogue, good humor, and colorful pastel drawings add to the book's appeal. [2]

BABIES; BIRTH; GIRLS

Rev: CBY-88; ESLC

993 **A Walk in the Rain.** Ursel Scheffler. Illus. by Ulises Wensell. Putnam, 1986. Unp. $7.95. (0-399-21267-1). **Category:** Story **Age:** P

Josh's and Grandma's rainy day walks and nature excursions with faithful canine Barney feature a fun-loving, chance-taking duo who truly enjoy each other's company. Pleasingly pastel watercolor-wash illustrations create a realistic backdrop for this intergenerational love story in which the simple pleasures of companionship create lasting memories. [2]

GRANDMOTHERS; GRANDPARENTS; RAIN

Rev: CBY-87

994 **Wally Whale and His Friends.** Pam Adams. Child's Play, 1986. Unp. $4.95. (0-85953-268-2). **Category:** Participation and manipulative **Age:** I–T

Brightly colored nontoxic plastic bathtub title that invites child participation. A one-liner directs the youngster to squeeze the first of four dual-sided accordion panels each time a new friend is met, resulting in Wally's squeak and a spurt of water from a top "blowhole" opening. The squeaker-manipulative seems firmly and safely anchored. [2]

SEA AND SEASHORE; TOY AND MOVABLE BOOKS; WHALES

995 **Walter's Tail.** Lisa Campbell Ernst. Bradbury, 1992. Unp. $14.95. (0-02-733564-X). **Category:** Story **Age:** P–K

Walter has a tail that wags non-stop. As a pup he's cute, but as he and his tail grow, they create one accident after another, which leads to animosity from Mrs. Tully's friends and neighbors. However, when Mrs. Tully needs help, it is Walter's tail to the rescue. Young readers will certainly identify with the "accident-proneness" of Walter. [3]

ACCIDENTS; DOGS

996 *Watermelon! And Other Stories.* Told by Betty Lehrman. Tales for the Telling, 1987. Audiocassette. 60 min. $9.00. **Category:** Story **Age:** K

An upbeat collection of eight stories and songs. Many center on food and eating, including "Banana Song" and "Watermelon!" One noticeable story is "Concoctions," in which a young boy drinks a strange mixture of beverages and turns into a dinosaur. The narration is relaxed and natural, with sound effects and children's voices adding texture to the music and stories. Useful for story times and story telling. [3]
FOOD
Rev: BKL 2/15/88

997 *We Are Best Friends.* Aliki. Greenwillow Books, 1982. 32 pp. $11.88. (0-688-00823-2). **Category:** Story **Age:** P–K

Peter and Robert are best friends, but Peter's family moves away. The boys write to each other, sharing misery and loneliness. Then each makes a new friend and begins to accept the changed, long-distance friendship. This positive, reassuring book is complemented by cheery, bright watercolor illustrations. [2]
FRIENDSHIP; MOVING
Rev: CBK

998 *We Keep a Store.* Anne Shelby. Illus. by John Ward. Orchard Books, 1990. Unp. $14.99. (0-531-08456-6). **Category:** Story **Age:** P–K

A young black girl tells a story about her family and its ownership of a grocery store. The reader quickly comes to understand that there are many reasons why "that's another good thing about keeping a store," such as working together, free candy, visiting with customers, and playing with other children. A simple story with a positive family message. [2]
AFRO-AMERICANS; FAMILY LIFE; STORES

999 *We Play.* Phyllis Hoffman. Illus. by Sarah Wilson. Harper & Row, 1990. Unp. $12.89. (0-06-022558-0). **Category:** Story **Age:** T–P–K

For any child new to the day care or school scene, this book introduces the delights of the school day, from arrival through lunch and naptime to departure. The simple rhyming format is combined with the multicultural classroom full of objects and activities. Short metrical lines speed readers through the text, while the illustrations slow with the busy fullness of each scene.
DAY CARE CENTERS; SCHOOL [1]

1000 *Weather Words and What They Mean.* Gail Gibbons. Holiday House, 1990. Unp. $13.95. (0-8234-0805-1). **Category:** Informational **Age:** K

Packed with facts about words used to describe the weather, this book can be used best in pieces with this age group for a discussion of the environment and the changes that take place daily outdoors. Just enough information is shared along with the pictures to make the concepts clear and understandable. A page of unusual weather trivia is included. [3]
WEATHER

1001 *We're Going on a Bear Hunt.* Michael Rosen. Illus. by Helen Oxenbury. Margaret K. McElderry Books, 1989. 40 pp. $14.95. (0-689-50476-4).
Category: Story **Age:** T–P–K

A father and four children set off on an exuberant search for a bear. Undaunted by any obstacle, they face each hindrance head-on and brave their way through long grass, a cold river, thick mud, a dark forest, and a swirling snowstorm, until they reach a narrow, gloomy cave in which they find: a bear! Onomatopoeic patterning combines with the pell-mell action to invite audience participation. [1]
BEARS; FATHERS; HUNTING
Rev: BKL 8/89; CBY-90

1002 *A Wet and Sandy Day.* Joanne Ryder. Illus. by Donald Carrick. Harper & Row, 1977. Unp. $10.89. (0-06-025159-X).
Category: Story **Age:** P–K

Although it promises to be a gloomy day, a little girl finds that there is still much to enjoy on the sandy beach. With dribbles of blue watercolor on each page, the weather is evoked, but the "rain" does not interfere with the basic pleasures of going off alone to play in the sand and water—even on a rainy day. Also available in other formats from the National Library for the Blind and Physically Handicapped. [3]
RAIN; SEA AND SEASHORE
Rev: BBC

1003 *What a Good Lunch!* Shigeo Watanabe. Illus. by Yasuo Ohtomo. Reprint. Putnam, 1981. 32 pp. $8.95. (0-399-20811-9).
Category: Story **Age:** P–K

A very young bear faces the challenge of sitting at the table to eat lunch without supervision. The almost slapstick humor in the situation will appeal to young children as they relate both to the bear's "success" and to his desire to "do it all by myself." [2]

BEARS; FOOD

Rev: CBK

1004 *What Am I? Very First Riddles.* Stephanie Calmenson. Illus. by Karen Gundersheimer. Harper & Row, 1989. 32 pp. $11.89. (0-06-020998-4).

Category: Concept/Counting/Alphabet **Age:** P–K

"Reader" is asked to solve simple riddles involving everyday objects and occurrences that are described in four-line verses. Answers appear in full-page illustrations on the reverse side. Preschoolers will enjoy these attractive guessing games. [2]

CONCEPTS; RIDDLES

Rev: CBY-90; ESLC

1005 *What Can You Do?* Angela Littler. Illus. by Maureen Galvani. Julian Messner, 1988. Unp. $3.95. (0-671-67230-4).

Category: Concept/Counting/Alphabet **Age:** I–T–P

A concept book that uses few words and simple, colorful pictures to illustrate activities a small child can perform. The text is simple poetry, the illustrations contain a large amount of white space, and the binding and pages are sturdy. A game of "find the teddy bear" may also be played on each page. [3]

CONCEPTS; POETRY; SELF-CONCEPT

Rev: SLJ 3/87

1006 *What Did Mommy Do Before You?* Abby Levine. Illus. by DyAnne DiSalvo-Ryan. Albert Whitman & Co., 1988. Unp. $12.95. (0-8075-8819-9).

Category: Informational **Age:** P–K

Answering a question asked by most young children, this softly illustrated book shows how Mommy grew from a baby herself through childhood, adolescence, and young womanhood. Convincingly, it expresses that even Mommy needed help and made mistakes, helping a child understand this often difficult concept. An endearing book that would be ideal for mother and child to share together. [2]

GROWING UP; MOTHERS; SIZE

Rev: BKL 3/1/88 & 9/1/88

1007 ***What Do Toddlers Do?*** Photographs selected by Debby Slier. Random House, 1985. Unp. Paper $1.95. (0-394-87280-0).

Category: Informtional **Age:** I–T

Part of a series entitled Cuddle Books, this board book features photographs of toddlers engaging in everyday activities: climbing, playing, drinking, etc. Infants and toddlers will delight in seeing children like themselves taking part in similar daily routines. [1]

BOARD BOOKS; TODDLERS

Rev: CBK

1008 ***What Do You Do with a Kangaroo?*** Mercer Mayer. Scholastic, 1973. Unp. $2.95. (0-590-41436-4). **Category:** Story **Age:** P–K

What do you do when an opossum uses your toothbrush or a raccoon eats your cereal? A resourceful young girl has all the answers until she is outnumbered. The cartoon characters as well as their playful antics are typical of Mercer Mayer's style. [3]

ANIMALS; KANGAROOS

Rev: CBY-88

1009 ***What Does Baby See?*** Denise Lewis Patrick. Illus. by Kathy Cruickshank. Golden Press, 1990. Unp. $2.98. (0-307-06130-2).

Category: Informational **Age:** I–T

Baby is taken visually through an active day of seeing Mommy upon waking, a duck when bathing, a dog sleeping, Daddy in the mirror, and much more, until finally falling asleep and seeing "sweet dreams." This board book with cartoonlike drawings and simple, predictable text will withstand repeated readings. Ideal to familiarize the infant or toddler with things and people encountered daily. [2]

BABIES; BOARD BOOKS; SIGHT

1010 ***What I Can Be: Creative Aerobics for Early Childhood.*** Melody House, 1983. Record. 15 min. $9.95.

Category: Participation and manipulative **Age:** K

One side provides music and narration for aerobic exercise activities, including warm-up and cool-down routines. The record album centerfold has details for each workout, plus teacher notes. Ballet, yoga, rhythmic games, and aerobic dance are included in the routines, which increase to a challenging pace and then decrease to prepare for cool down. Reverse side features the same music, without the words. [3]

EXERCISE

1011 **What Is a Bird?** Ron Hirschi. Photos by Galen Burrell. Walker & Co., 1987. Unp. $10.95. (0-8027-6720-6). **Category:** Informational **Age:** T–P–K

Hirschi explores the world of birds, using a simple, single line of text for each double-page color photograph. Each spread features a large picture with a smaller picture insert. Lines of the text, though imparting information, are somewhat poetic in their phrasing. The photographs are exceptionally clear. Many perspectives are explored, and action is depicted throughout. [2] BIRDS; WILDLIFE

1012 **What Is a Girl? What Is a Boy?** Stephanie Waxman. Reprint. Thomas Y. Crowell, 1989. Unp. $10.89. (0-690-04711-8).

Category: Informational **Age:** P–K

Designed to help children and adults feel comfortable with sexuality. Simple text and photographs, some nude, explore ideas of male and female behavior and appearance. Breaking down the stereotypes, the book concludes that it is differences in anatomy that make one a boy or girl, a man or woman. [3] ANATOMY; SEX INSTRUCTION

Rev: BKL 3/15/89

1013 **What Is It?** Tana Hoban. Greenwillow Books, 1985. Unp. Paper $3.95. (0-688-02577-3). **Category:** Concept/Counting/Alphabet **Age:** I–T

Colorful photographs in a wordless board book provide the answers to "What is it?" Objects a baby might see every day are shown isolated against a white background. A red bib, a blue cup, and a set of keys are some of the familiar objects for parents and babies to guess. [2] BOARD BOOKS; CONCEPTS; WORDLESS

Rev: CBK

1014 **What the Moon Saw.** Brian Wildsmith. Oxford University Press, 1978. Unp. $12.95. (0-19-279724-7).

Category: Concept/Counting/Alphabet **Age:** T–P–K

The Sun tells the Moon of all the wonders she sees in the world, using examples of opposite pairs—large cities and small villages, patterned and plain animals, etc. She believes she has seen it all, until the Moon tells her she will never see the "Dark." Brilliant and unique illustrations supplement the sparse text. [2] CONCEPTS; MOON; SUN

Rev: ESLC

1015 *Whatever Happened to the Dinosaurs?* Bernard Most. Harcourt Brace Jovanovich, 1984. Unp. $13.95. (0-15-295295-0).

Category: Informational   **Age:** P–K

Some delightful answers are provided for the eternal question of what ever happened to the dinosaurs. The bright colors and humorous pictures invite children to come up with their own solutions. [3]

DINOSAURS

Rev: NYT

1016 *What's in the Deep Blue Sea? A Lift-the-Flap Pop-up Book.* Peter Seymour. Illus. by David A. Carter. Henry Holt & Co., 1990. Unp. $10.95. (0-8050-1450-0).   **Category:** Informational   **Age:** T–P

Exciting and colorful illustrations beautifully re-create the splendor and wonder of the aqua world as sea creatures seemingly come to life and pop out of the book. [1]

FISH; SEA AND SEASHORE; TOY AND MOVABLE BOOKS

1017 *What's Inside.* Photos by Anthea Sieveking. Dial, 1990. Unp. 9.95. (0-8037-0719-3).   **Category:** Informational   **Age:** T–P

Each two-page spread shows a delightful toddler exploring the "insides" of a familiar container: clothes drawer, toy box, kitchen cupboard. The right page then reveals clearly labeled objects commonly found in that container. Bright, primary colors and clean layout are definite attractions in this sturdy book.

CONCEPTS [3]

1018 *What's Inside? The Alphabet Book.* Satoshi Kitamura. Farrar, Straus & Giroux, 1985. Unp. $12.95. (0-374-38306-5).

Category: Concept/Counting/Alphabet   **Age:** P–K

The full-color paintings on each page make hunting the alphabet letters and the words in which they appear a real treat. Clever puzzles introduce the next two letters. There are a flying iguana and a literature rat, a musical hippo and a sensible vampire bat in this imaginative journey through the alphabet. [2]

ALPHABET; PUZZLES

Rev: NYT

1019 *What's Missing?* Niki Yektai. Illus. by Susannah Ryan. Ticknor & Fields, 1989. Unp. $12.95. (0-89919-510-5).

Category: Concept/Counting/Alphabet   **Age:** P–K

Two children, their parents, and a dog are shown involved in various daily activities, such as walking the dog, playing in the park, eating meals, and bathing. However, each picture has something important missing, such as the slide on the page where the child is sliding. Children will enjoy the simple text and humorous illustrations as they use visual discrimination to answer the recurring question "What's missing?" [1]
CONCEPTS; QUESTIONING
Rev: CBY-88

1020 *The Wheels on the Bus: An Adapation of the Traditional Song.* Maryann Kovalski. Little, Brown & Co., 1987. Unp. $11.95. (0-316-50256-1).

Category: Poetry/Nursery rhymes/Songs **Age:** P

Large illustrations capture all the antics of the riders on a crowded city bus as it heads uptown. Based on the familiar song, the people on the bus go up and down as babies go waaa, waaa, waaa, and parents go shhh, shhh, shhh—as more and more passengers crowd into the bus aisles. The surprise ending to the familiar song will amuse young listeners. A good read-aloud selection.
BUSES; SONGS [2]
Rev: BKL 12/15/87; CBY-88; ESLC; SLJ 11/87

1021 *When a Pet Dies.* Fred Rogers. Photos by Jim Judkis. Putnam, 1988. Unp. $12.95. (0-399-21504-2). **Category:** Informational **Age:** T–P–K

Realistic photos and sensitive text help both the child and the adult find constructive ways to deal with the death of a well-loved pet. Also available in other formats from the National Library for the Blind and Physically Handicapped. [2]
DEATH; PETS
Rev: BKL 6/1/88; CBY-89

1022 *When I See My Doctor.* Susan Kuklin. Bradbury, 1988. 32 pp. $12.95. (0-02-751232-0). **Category:** Informational **Age:** P–K

Thomas is four years old and visiting the doctor for a routine checkup. Color photographs accompany simple text to explain the many aspects of the annual visit. Photographs and pronunciation guides are also included for some key terms, such as "stethoscope." The doctor's examination of Thomas, from checking the ears for elephants to a prick on the finger to check blood for iron, reveals a healthy, active little boy. [2]
DOCTORS
Rev: CBY-89

1023 When I Was Young In the Mountains. Cynthia Rylant. Illus. by Diane Goode. Dutton, 1982. Unp. $12.95. (0-525-42525-X).

Category: Story   **Age:** P–K

Rylant recalls her childhood with her grandparents in the mountains of West Virginia. Childhood events and activities include Grandfather coming home from the coal mine, Grandmother's country cooking, sitting on the porch shelling beans, and baptism in the swimming hole. Soft-hued illustrations complement the text and reinforce the author's perception that life in the mountains "was always enough."   [3]
Country life; Family life; Mountains
Rev: BBC

1024 When Sheep Cannot Sleep: The Counting Book. Satoshi Kitamura. Farrar, Straus & Giroux/Putnam, 1986. Unp. $9.95. (0-374-38311-1).

Category: Concept/Counting/Alphabet   **Age:** P–K

An unusual counting book. No numerals are printed on the page as the number concepts from 1 to 22 are sequentially developed. Rather, the reader discovers the number for each page by using clues from text and illustrations, then confirms the number by counting the animals or objects in the illustrations. Number concepts and inferential thinking can be developed in a clever and imaginative way.   [2]
Counting; Sheep
Awards: NYT Notable Book of the Year

1025 When Summer Ends. Susi Gregg Fowler. Illus. by Marisabina Russo. Greenwillow Books, 1989. Unp. $11.88. (0-688-07606-8).

Category: Concept/Counting/Alphabet   **Age:** P–K

A girl tells her mother she does not want summer to end, but her mother gently reminds her of the excitement of other seasons and the numerous holidays that occur. Russo's clear drawings with strong colors make this an appropriate choice for a unit on seasons.   [2]
Concepts; Mothers and daughters; Seasons; Summer
Rev: BKL 3/1/89; CBY-90

1026 When the Dark Comes Dancing: A Bedtime Poetry Book. Compiled by Nancy Larrick. Illus. by John Wallner. Philomel, 1983. 79 pp. $17.95. (0-399-20807-0).   **Category:** Poetry/Nursery rhymes/Songs   **Age:** I–T–P–K

A multicultural representation of poems, lullabies, and lyrics—some traditional and some contemporary, but all for preparing children for bedtime. Larrick points out, "The bedtime hour can provide the warmth, the intimacy, the

reinforcement so often missing in the day's activities." Wallner's detailed and haunting paintings will be remembered in children's dreams.   [1]
BEDTIME; POETRY; SLEEP
Rev: NYT

1027   *When the New Baby Comes, I'm Moving Out.* Martha Alexander. Dial, 1979. Unp. $8.89. (0-8037-9558-0).   **Category:** Story   **Age:** T–P–K

The baby is taking Oliver's high chair, his crib, and even his mother's lap, and it is not even born yet. Oliver decides to run away, but his mother convinces him that being an older brother could be lots of fun. In a candid and humorous manner, Oliver expresses the jealousy and fear of every child when a new sibling arrives.   [1]
BABIES; SIBLING RIVALRY
Rev: CBK; NYT   **Awards:**

1028   *When We Went to the Park.* Shirley Hughes. Lothrop, Lee & Shepard, 1985. Unp. $4.95. (0-688-04204-X).
                    Category: Concept/Counting/Alphabet   **Age:** T–P–K

Within the framework of a grandfather's and a little girl's trip to the park, Hughes counts items from 1 to 10: three ladies chatting on a bench, four babies in buggies, etc. The book's small size and animated drawings will appeal to small children. The affectionate relationship portrayed between grandfather and grandchild adds an extra dimension to this counting book.   [3]
COUNTING; GRANDFATHERS; PARKS
Rev: CBK; ESLC

1029   *When We Were Very Young.* A. A. Milne. Illus. by Ernest H. Shepard. Dutton, 1988. 102 pp. $9.95. (0-525-44445-9).
                    Category: Poetry/Nursery rhymes/Songs   **Age:** T–P

Charming, old-fashioned verses are filled with witty observations from a child's perspective. Some are rather dated, but most still convey the essence of a young child's endearing logic and sensibility. Shepard's lovely line drawings accompany each verse. Also available in other formats from the National Library for the Blind and Physically Handicapped.   [1]
POETRY
Rev: NYT

1030   *When You Were a Baby.* Ann Jonas. Greenwillow Books, 1982. Unp. $13.88. (0-688-00864-X).   **Category:** Story   **Age:** T–P

Told from the point of view of a toddler soon to be preschooler, the child looks back on all the things that could not be done as a baby. Large, uncluttered, colorful pictures complement the simple text. A reassuring story for both child and parent, showing that growth brings about rewarding changes.
BABIES; GROWTH   [1]
Rev: BBC; CBK; ESLC; NYT

1031 **Where Are You Going, Little Mouse?** Robert Kraus. Illus. by Jose Aruego and Ariane Dewey. Greenwillow Books, 1986. Unp. $13.95. (0-688-04295-3).   **Category:** Story **Age:** T–P

The lyrical tale of a young mouse who, feeling unloved, runs away in search of a new family. His search proves fruitless, and he soon misses his real family. By the end of one day, the little mouse calls home and asks his parents to come for him. The large illustrations and rhythmic text make this a joy to share with one child or a roomful of children.   [2]
MICE; RUNNING AWAY
Rev: BBC; NYT

1032 **Where Do Birds Live?** Ron Hirschi. Photos by Galen Burrell. Walker & Co., 1987. Unp. $10.95. (0-8027-6722-2).
                                    Category: Informational **Age:** P–K

Magnificent color photographs matched with sparse yet lilting descriptions glorify a variety of birds in flight, at rest, and during every season. Including an afterword that identifies each page, this companion to *What Is a Bird?* reveals the joys of the natural world to children of all ages.   [1]
BIRDS; NATURE

1033 **Where Does the Sun Go at Night?** Mirra Ginsburg. Illus. by Jose Aruego and Ariane Dewey. Morrow Jr. Books, 1980. 32 pp. $10.88. (0-688-84245-3).   **Category:** Folklore/Folktales/Fairy tales **Age:** T–P–K

The question-and-answer format of this adaptation of an Armenian song becomes a playful catechism of nature's family relationships. Though music is not included, the comfortable, rounded figures of the animal participants and the clear, innocent colors are melody itself.   [1]
FOLK AND FAIRY TALES; SUN
Rev: NYT

1034 *Where Is Everybody? An Animal Alphabet.* Eve Merriam. Illus. by Diane de Groat. Simon & Schuster, 1989. Unp. $14.95. (0-671-64964-7).

Category: Concept/Counting/Alphabet **Age:** P–K

Animal lovers will enjoy the giraffe who gets out his lawn mower or the rabbit's ears that fly back while it rides the roller coaster. Listeners will learn that Quail is on the quarterdeck, and they will be amused by the antics of Mole and his camera. [3]

ALPHABET; ANIMALS

Rev: BKL 6/15/89; CBY-90

1035 *Where Is the Bear at School?* Bonnie Larkin Nims. Illus. by Madelaine Gill. Albert Whitman & Co., 1989. Unp. $10.95. (0-8075-8935-7).

Category: Concept/Counting/Alphabet **Age:** P

This rhymed puzzle asks one to find a bear in each bustling school setting. Soft watercolors portray multiethnic, able, and disabled children in many detailed activities. Not only a puzzler, the book shows a variety of early school experiences. Fun for children who love to find and point. [3]

BEARS; CONCEPTS; SCHOOL

Rev: BKL 1/1/90

1036 *Where the Wild Things Are.* Maurice Sendak. Reprint. Harper & Row, 1988. 48 pp. $12.89. (0-06-025493-9). **Category:** Story **Age:** T–P–K

Wild behavior gets Max sent to his room without supper. His imagination leads him and the viewer on a wonderful and wild romp with other wild things. Upon his return, Max finds supper waiting. Vivid illustrations coupled with Sendak's mastery of the language bring the story to life and make the event memorable. Children will want this book read again and again. [1]

DREAMS; IMAGINATION

Rev: BBC; ESLC; NYT **Awards:** Caldecott Medal

1037 *Where the Wild Things Are.* Maurice Sendak. Narrated by Peter Schickele. Produced by Morton Schindel. Weston Woods Studios, 1988. Videocassette. 8 min. $60.00. **Category:** Story **Age:** P–K

After being banished to his room for misbehaving, Max fantasizes about becoming the king of "all Wild Things." The vivid, color animation and adventure-filled story will entice and amuse young audiences (Harper, 1988). [1]

DREAMS; IMAGINATION

Rev: BKL 12/1/89

1038 *Where the Wild Things Are, In the Night Kitchen, Outside over There: And Other Stories.* Maurice Sendak. Performed by Tammy Grimes. Harper Audio, 1977. Audiocassette. 42 min. $9.95.

Category: Story **Age:** P–K

Grimes exhibits the power and awe of storytelling as she reads eight stories by Maurice Sendak, including "In the Night Kitchen," "Where the Wild Things Are," "Alligators All Around," and "The Sign on Rosie's Door." Selections are short enough for even younger listeners and ideal as read-alongs.   [1]
ADVENTURE; ANIMALS
Rev: ESLC

1039 *Where's Spot?* Eric Hill. Putnam, 1980. Unp. $10.95. (0-399-20758-9).

Category: Story **Age:** T–P

Spot must be hiding somewhere in the house, because he has not eaten his dinner, so Sally goes looking behind a door, in the clock, inside the piano, and under the stairs and bed, until she finally locates him in a basket. Lift-tabs form a game of peek-a-boo that will enable the child to solve the mystery and assist in locating Spot. Sturdy binding and pages make this a book that will last after repeated tellings.   [1]
ADVENTURE; DOGS; GAMES; TOY AND MOVABLE BOOKS
Rev: BKL 2/15/88; CBK; ESLC; NYT

1040 *Which One Would You Choose?* Edith Kunhardt. Greenwillow Books, 1989. 24 pp. $11.88. (0-688-07908-3).

Category: Participation and manipulative **Age:** P

Maggie and Will make choices throughout the day. After they have made theirs, then the listener gets a chance: "Which one do you choose?" Familiar objects—shirts, food, clothing, flowers, kittens, toys—entice the young child to participate. Small, distinct drawings surrounded by plenty of white space add appeal to the book.   [2]
PARTICIPATION
Rev: BKL 4/15/89

1041 *Whistle for Willie.* Ezra Jack Keats. Viking Penguin, 1964. Unp. $12.95. (0-670-76240-7).   **Category:** Story **Age:** T–P

Although Peter is a happy child, he wants to learn how to whistle. He tries everything—even putting on his father's hat—but still no whistle. A classic, simple tale, illustrated in Keats' recognizable collage style.   [2]
BOYS; DOGS; WHISTLING
Rev: BBC; CBK; ESLC

1042 *Who Am I?* Faith Hubley. Pyramid Film & Video, 1990. Videocassette. 4 min. $250.00.   **Category:** Informational   **Age:** P–K

Faith Hubley has created and produced an imaginative and captivating sensory flow through sight, sound, smell, touch, and taste. *Who Am I?* is fun. It puts a smile on a child's face and makes the child think about all the things the senses can do.   [1]
ENTERTAINMENT; SENSORY

1043 *Who Said Red?* Mary Serfozo. Illus. by Keiko Narahashi. Margaret K. McElderry Books, 1988. 32 pp. $12.95. (0-689-50455-1).
                                        Category: Concept/Counting/Alphabet   **Age:** P–K

Unusual because it includes a story line, this concept book introduces primary colors through a combination of rhythmic text and vivid watercolor illustrations. Helping her younger brother find his lost red kite, the sister asks in a teasing voice a series of questions dealing with color concepts. Small children will recognize colors from familiar surroundings and want to return to this memorable work again and again.   [1]
COLOR; CONCEPTS
Rev: BKL 9/1/88

1044 *Who Sank the Boat?* Pamela Allen. Coward McCann, 1982. Unp. $12.99. (0-698-30755-0).   **Category:** Story   **Age:** T–P–K

The animals—a cow, a donkey, a sheep, a pig, and a mouse—board a boat. One by one, they decide to take a row on the lake. Naturally, the overcrowding results in a sinking, and readers are kept on edge throughout with the title question. The joke of the story is unmistakable and will delight even the youngest of audiences.   [1]
ANIMALS; BOATS
Rev: NYT

1045 *Who's Afraid of the Dark?* Crosby Bonsall. Harper & Row, 1980. 32 pp. $9.89. (0-06-020599-7).   **Category:** Story   **Age:** P–K

Bonsall offers a bit of reassurance for those nighttime fears that can creep up on a child. A young boy is telling an older girl how Stella, his dog, is afraid of the dark. As he tells how Stella shivers, shakes, and hears scary sounds, the pictures on the opposite page reveal it is he who hides under his pillow at night. The older girl offers some helpful advice. Final pictures show the boy and dog snuggled together asleep.   [2]
FEAR; NIGHT
Rev: CBK; ESLC

1046 *Who's Counting?* Nancy Tafuri. Greenwillow Books, 1986. 24 pp. $11.88.
(0-688-06131-1). **Category:** Concept/Counting/Alphabet **Age:** T–P

A brightly colored, action-filled counting book showing a playful puppy investigating his surroundings. From the first page to the last, children will engage in identifying the animals and counting the objects that gain the dog's attention. [1]
COUNTING; DOGS
Rev: ESLC

1047 *Who's Hiding Here?* Yoshi. Picture Book Studio, 1987. Unp. $15.95. (0-88708-041-3). **Category:** Concept/Counting/Alphabet **Age:** P–K

The white rabbit, snake, and more all seem to disappear into their surroundings. Yoshi's striking illustrations, combining paint with batik technique on silk, show various examples of animals in camouflage. Young children will enjoy peeking through die-cut holes to discover "Who's hiding?" on the next page. The gamelike format and rhyming text combine to make this an outstanding introduction to our environment. [1]
ANIMALS; CAMOUFLAGE; CONCEPTS; TOY AND MOVABLE BOOKS
Rev: ESLC

1048 *Whose Baby?* Masayuki Yabuuchi. Philomel, 1985. 30 pp. $9.95. (0-399-21210-8). **Category:** Informational **Age:** P–K

Elaborately detailed animal illustrations show baby animals, and the question "Whose baby is it?" is asked. When the page is turned, the baby is shown with its mother and father. Text is simple yet informative as all the names are given. Basic for the younger child to start learning about wildlife but also wonderful for small groups and study corners. [1]
ANIMALS; BABIES; CONCEPTS
Rev: PP

1049 *Whose Hat?* Margaret Miller. Greenwillow Books, 1988. Unp. $11.95. (0-688-06906-1). **Category:** Informational **Age:** T–P–K

Using bright, vibrant photographs, Miller answers the question "Whose hat?" The question is posed on one page and answered on the following two pages. Hats featured include those of a chef, construction worker, magician, and fire fighter. Even the youngest hat lover will soon be "reading" this book. [2]
HATS
Rev: BKL 4/1/88; CBY-89

1050 *Whose Mouse Are You?* Robert Kraus. Illus. by Jose Aruego. Macmillan, 1970. Unp. $12.95. (0-02-751190-1).   **Category:** Story   **Age:** T–P

A little mouse is lonely because he thinks he belongs to nobody. This attitude quickly changes when he rescues his father from a trap, his mother from a cat, and his sister from a mountaintop, and then ends up with a new brother. Rhyming text in a question-and-answer format with bright, bold illustrations. MICE   [1]

Rev: BBC; CBK; ESLC

1051 *Whose Shoe?* Margaret Miller. Greenwillow Books, 1991. Unp. $13.95. (0-688-10009-0).   **Category:** Participation and manipulation   **Age:** P–K

Colorful, multicultural, and non-sexist photographs of children and families wearing different kinds of shoes. Good guessing fun for sharing one-on-one or with groups. The last page gives the proper name of each shoe, for instance, baseball cleat, flipper, hip wader, and ballet slipper.   [3]

PARTICIPATION; SHOES

1052 *Why Is Baby Crying?* Ryerson Johnson. Illus. by DyAnne DiSalvo-Ryan. Albert Whitman & Co., 1989. Unp. $12.95. (0-8075-9084-3).

Category: Story   **Age:** P–K

A mother tells her daughter the story of the time when the daughter was a baby and was crying in the night. She and Daddy tried and tried but could not figure out what was wrong. Finally, they discovered it was cuddling and loving that she wanted, and they all then fell asleep. Warm, cozy illustrations portray the love of a mother and father for their baby.   [2]

BABIES; BEDTIME

Rev: BKL 11/15/89; CBY-90

1053 *Why Mosquitoes Buzz In People's Ears: A West African Tale.* Verna Aardema. Illus. by Leo Dillon and Diane Dillon. Dial, 1975. Unp. $14.89. (0-8037-6087-6).   **Category:** Folklore/Folktales/Fairy tales   **Age:** K

This African legend tells of a chain reaction started innocently by the mosquito, which eventually ends with Mother Owl so sad that she cannot hoot to wake the sun. Thus night is extended longer than normal, to all the animals' dismay. The bold, striking watercolor illustrations are sure to entertain as this tale is read to preschoolers.   [2]

AFRICA; ANIMALS; FOLK AND FAIRY TALES

Rev: NYT   **Awards:** Caldecott Medal; SLJ Best Book of the Year

1054 *Why the Crab Has No Head: An African Folktale.* Barbara Knutson. Carolrhoda Books, 1987. Unp. $9.95. (0-87614-322-2).

Category: Folklore/Folktales/Fairy tales   **Age:** K

Using dramatic black on white illustrations and a storyteller's natural rhythms, Knutson artfully retells this African tale of Crab, who "lost" his head because of his own conceit. This is no ordinary creation story: the creator is a strong-armed goddess, not a god, and the consequence of pride is not punishment but continued embarrassment for Crab.   [2]

CRABS; FOLK AND FAIRY TALES

Rev: BKL 2/1/88

1055 *Will I Have a Friend?* Miriam Cohen. Illus. by Lillian Hoban. Macmillan, 1967. Unp. $12.95. (0-02-722790-1).   **Category:** Story   **Age:** P–K

Young Jim is anxious about his first day in kindergarten. He yearns for a friend and, eventually, finds one. This warm, comforting book helps relieve children's worries about starting school. Other books in this author's series also cover familiar situations encountered during the school year.   [1]

FRIENDSHIP; SCHOOL

Rev: CBK; NYT

1056 *Will You Come Back for Me?* Ann Tompert. Illus. by Robin Kramer. Albert Whitman & Co., 1988. Unp. $12.95. (0-8075-9112-2).

Category: Story   **Age:** P–K

This story deals with fears of being left at a day care center and of parents' not returning. The family is of Japanese origin, and children from other racial groups are pictured. This is a good story to read to a child before beginning to attend day care, especially if the child has been staying at home. Different sizes and placement of the illustrations add to interest in a heartfelt interchange between mother and daughter.   [2]

DAY CARE CENTERS; FEAR

Rev: BKL 11/1/88

1057 *William's Doll.* Charlotte Zolotow. Illus. by William P. Du Bois. Harper & Row, 1972. 32 pp. $12.89. (0-06-027048-9).

Category: Story   **Age:** P–K

William's determination to have a doll is finally satisfied by his understanding and sensible grandmother. He shows that being good at sports and playing with electric trains with Dad and brother are fine but not enough to meet all his needs. This book has become a classic and was one of the first to show that boys and girls have multiroles. [2]

Boys; Dolls; Feelings

Rev: CBK; ESLC; NYT

1058 *Will's Mammoth.* Rafe Martin. Illus. by Stephen Gammell. Putnam, 1989. Unp. $14.95. (0-399-21627-8). **Category:** Story **Age:** K

Will's parents assure him that there are no mammoths around anymore, but he determines that there are. This launches him into an imaginary adventure in which he rides on the back of the woolly mammoth and encounters all sorts of prehistoric animals. Although he must return home for dinner, his belief is not shaken. Sparse text incorporated with Gammell's unique illustrative style make this an exciting and memorable book. [1]

Imagination; Mammoth

1059 *Winnie-the-Pooh.* A. A. Milne. Illus. by Ernest H. Shepard. Dutton, 1988. 176 pp. $9.95. (0-525-44443-2). **Category:** Story **Age:** P–K

Winnie-the-Pooh, the Bear of Very Little Brain, has been entertaining parents and their children for generations. Some of Milne's best is in this volume: "The Heffalump," "Eeyore and His Broken Balloon," "Empty Honey Pot," and of course, Pooh getting stuck in Rabbit's house. The "decorations" by Shepard are classics. [1]

Folk and fairy tales; Teddy bears

Rev: NYT

1060 *The Witch's Hat.* Tony Johnston. Illus. by Margot Tomes. Putnam, 1984. Unp. $10.99. (0-399-61223-8). **Category:** Story **Age:** P–K

A skinny witch was concocting a magic potion when her hat fell into the vat. When she tried to retrieve it, the hat turned into a bat, then a rat, next a cat. Finally, after poking and prodding, she had her hat back, until it changed again. The humorous word play of the text is accompanied by scratchy earth-tone illustrations with a comical feel. [2]

Hats; Witches

Rev: ESLC

1061 *With the Wind.* Liz Damrell. Illus. by Stephen Marchesi. Orchard Books, 1991. Unp. $14.99. (0-531-08482-5). **Category:** Story **Age:** K

A young boy experiences freedom and power when he rides a horse. Movement is captured on the canvaslike pages. Bold color abounds. Enlarged insets

focus on the immediate action of the thought-provoking story. The reader discovers that the young boy cannot walk but does feel strengthened in spirit as a result of the horseback ride. [2]
DISABLED; HORSES

1062 *The Wolf's Chicken Stew.* Keiko Kasza. Putnam, 1987. Unp. $13.95. (0-399-21400-3). **Category:** Story **Age:** P–K

A wolf plans on having chicken stew after fattening a particular hen. Humorous watercolor illustrations depict the wolf while he cooks pancakes, donuts, and cake to enlarge his future dinner. Children will be amused with the outcome. Text is quick and simple. [3]
CHICKENS; HUMOR; WOLVES
Rev: CBY-88; ESLC

1063 *A World of Stories.* Collected and retold by Andrea Spalding. Illus. by Gillian Campbell. Red Deer College Press, 1989. 71 pp. $19.95. (0-88995-044-X). **Category:** Folklore/Folktales/Fairy tales **Age:** P–K

A collection of folklore stories that represent the various cultural groups that settled in Canada. Includes some well-known tales from Germany, France, China, the Ukraine, and England, as well as little known tales from Canada and the United States. Selections are short, yet lively enough to read aloud. Large, colorful illustrations are worth sharing once the narrative is complete.
FOLK AND FAIRY TALES [3]
Awards: Canadian Children's Book Centre Choice

1064 *Wynken, Blynken and Nod.* Eugene Field. Illus. by Susan Jeffers. Dutton, 1982. 32 pp. $11.95. (0-525-44022-4). **Category:** Poetry/Nursery rhymes/Songs **Age:** P–K

Jeffer's enchanting artwork captures the mood set by this wonderfully imaginative classic. Faces show delight and wonder with each adventure befalling them. Bold outlines and rich late-night colors bring life to the double-page, pastel-colored illustrations. Fantasy and imagery abound as the viewer sails in a wooden shoe across the star-laced evening sky. A version of this poem that should not be missed. [1]
BEDTIME; DREAMS; POETRY
Rev: BBC; BKL 1/1/88

1065 *A Year of Beasts.* Ashley Wolff. Dutton, 1986. Unp. $11.95. (0-525-44240-5) **Category:** Concept/Counting/Alphabet **Age:** P–K

The double-block prints in primary colors are simple and effective in illustrating the animals found during various seasons around Ellie's and Peter's house. Each month depicts the changes in nature with an appropriate family activity. These relationships—of nature, seasons, and family life—are the focus of this concept book. [1]

CONCEPTS; COUNTRY LIFE; SEASONS

Rev: ESLC

1066 *A Year of Birds.* Ashley Wolff. Putnam, 1984. Unp. $13.95. (0-399-21697-9). **Category:** Informational **Age:** P–K

Through a setting in the Vermont countryside, Ellie, the main character, is displayed with her activities against seasonal backdrops containing pictures of 25 species of birds. Exquisite hand-colored linoleum block prints evoke a mood for each month. Ideal for bird-watching together. [2]

BIRDS; MONTHS OF THE YEAR; TIME

Rev: CBK; PP

1067 *Yonder.* Tony Johnston. Photography by Lloyd Bloom. Directed by Sara Kurtz. McGraw-Hill Media, 1989. Dist. by American School Publishers. Videocassette. 11 min. $30.00.

Category: Poetry/Nursery rhymes/Songs **Age:** K

"Yonder, where the hills go on forever, a farmer on a jet black horse" marries, becomes a father and grandfather, and commemorates each event by planting a tree. Passing seasons in the poem symbolize the patchwork continuity of family. Artful camera handling and John Guth's folklike score skillfully extend Tony Johnston's poetic text and Lloyd Bloom's impressionistic illustrations. A guide is included with the program. [3]

DEATH; FAMILY LIFE; POETRY; SEASONS

Rev: BKL 2/15/90

1068 *You Hold Me and I'll Hold You.* Jo Carson. Illus. by Annie Cannon. Orchard Books, 1992. Unp. $14.95. (0-531-08495-7).

Category: Story **Age:** K

A sensitive and nurturing single father comforts his daughter when his Aunt Ann dies. This heartfelt experience teaches that death is natural, that it is all right for everyone to cry when sad, and that it's comforting to all to be held and to hold. [1]

DEATH; FATHERS; SADNESS

1069 *A Young Children's Concert with Raffi.* Shoreline Records/Divine Video-works, 1984. Dist. by A & M Records. Videocassette. 50 min. $19.95.

Category: Poetry/Nursery rhymes/Songs   **Age:** T–P

Children and adults will delight in and swing to the upbeat, familiar tunes this master artist shares during one of his musical concerts. Raffi plays his guitar as he sings and interacts with his audience, encouraging them and the viewer to join in. A video that will be played and replayed. Teacher-parent notes and a lyrics booklet accompany the video.   [2]

ENTERTAINMENT; MUSIC; SONGS

1070 *Your Big Backyard.* National Wildlife Federation, n.d. $8.50/yr.

Category: Periodical   **Age:** P–K

A monthly "discovery" magazine designed to teach word recognition and number identification "while expanding the preschooler's understanding of the world." Photographs of animals abound. A minimum of text is used, with one exception, a "Read to me" story. A parent's guide is attached to each issue. This periodical should be in every young child's library collection.   [1]

CONCEPTS; NATURE; READING

1071 *Zoo.* Gail Gibbons. Live Oak Media, 1988. Filmstrip. 8 min. $24.95.

Category: Informational   **Age:** P

Listeners take a trip through the zoo and learn about the opening and closing routines as well as the responsibilities of the keeper and veterinarian. Gibbons's simple line drawings in primary colors and her enthusiastic narrative provide orientation for a first-time zoo visit (Crowell, 1987).   [3]

ANIMALS; CAREERS; ZOOS

Rev: BKL 8/88

1072 *Zoo Song.* Barbara Bottner. Illus. by Lynn Munsinger. Scholastic, 1987. Unp. $12.95. (0-590-41005-9).   **Category:** Story   **Age:** P–K

Gertrude the hippo is a singer with a terrible voice. Herman the lion plays a screechy violin. Fabio the bear tap-dances with great noise and energy. These three try to drown out each others' noise while practicing their craft at the highest decibels all night long. Come morning, Gertrude begins a soft harmony, Herman finds a lovely melody, and Fabio begins to dance the rhythm. Cooperation becomes the key to their success.   [2]

SONGS; ZOOS

Rev: ESLC

1073 *Zoobables.* Carolyn Fireside. Photos by Michael O'Neill. Villard Books/ Random House, 1991. Unp. $17.00. (0-679-40698-0).

Category: Informational   **Age:** P–K

Full-page, unique portraits capture the "personality" and "character" of 25 zoo animal babies from around the world including a giraffe, wolf, koala, armadillo, oryx, rhino, goblin, and alligator. Each facing page tells the animal's name, age, diet, habits, and geographic origin.   [2]

ANIMALS; ENDANGERED ANIMALS; ZOOS

1074 *Zoom at Sea.* Tim Wynne-Jones. Illus. by Ken Nutt. Douglas & McIntyre Ltd., 1983. Unp. $9.95. (0-88899-021-9).   **Category:** Story   **Age:** P–K

Zoom the cat loved water and sailed all night in his bathtub. When Zoom finds his uncle's diary with an address and map to the sea, he takes the bus to the address. The fantasy of the small cat's adventure is enhanced by Nutt's imaginative pencil sketches with watercolor washes. His use of shade and light add to the magic.   [2]

CATS; SEA AND SEASHORE

Rev: EL 11/84

Appendixes

Appendix 1
Professional Resources

by Betty Kay Seibt

The items listed in this section have been culled from an initial gathering of over 300. The criteria for selection have been simple: retain only those materials that are practical and that will be immediately useful to the reader, whether educator, parent, care provider, or librarian. The aim has been to strive for a blend of materials—some that provide background knowledge, some that have immediate application in a classroom or day-care environment, and some that provide continuing self-education for the adults who work with very young children.

P1   *A to Zoo: Subject Access to Children's Picture Books, 3rd ed.* Carolyn W. Lima and John A. Lima. R. R. Bowker, 1989. 939 pp. $44.95. (0-8352-2599-2).

Third edition of this popular and helpful guide to informational and fictional picture books. Over 8,500 titles are divided into five sections: subject headings, subject guide, bibliographic guide, titles, and illustrators. Useful for libraries as a help in collection development and for teachers and caregivers who need ready access to "what's out there."

P2   *An Activities Handbook for Teachers of Young Children.* Doreen J. Croft. Houghton Mifflin, 1990. 447 pp. $26.36. (0-395-43207-3).

Activities for preprimary children in the areas of language arts, science, math, art, and cooking. Annotated bibliographies suggest further material for both teachers and children. Materials needed for the activities are readily available. Format is full-page size and spiral-bound.

P3 *Adventuring with Books: A Booklist for Pre-K—Grade 6, 9th ed.* Edited by Mary Jett-Simpson. National Council of Teachers of English, 1989. 549 pp. $16.50. (0-8141-0078-3).

An annotated bibliography listing some of the best books for children from infancy through the elementary school years. Titles for the very young are divided by type (board books, wordless books, picture books, etc.). Books for older children are divided by genres such as historical fiction, science fiction, etc. Both fiction and nonfiction are discussed in the school subject area (science, math, etc.) listings.

P4 *Ages and Stages: Developmental Descriptions and Activities—Birth Through Eight Years.* Karen Miller. Telshare Publishing, 1985. 153 pp. $10.95. (0-910287-05-8).

Besides an outline of developmental stages through age eight, Miller provides hints, activities, and skill builders, many in list form for ease of use. She also gives lists of safety tips for each stage, which would be especially helpful for first-time parents. Clear and user friendly, the author speaks in a straightforward manner that many will appreciate.

P5 *The All New Elephant Jam.* Sharon, Lois & Bram. Illus. by David Shaw. Lorraine Greey Pubs/McGraw-Hill Ryerson, 1989. 128 pp. $12.95. (0-07-549709-3).

Presents songs from "The Elephant Show" TV program, both old favorites and new. Accompanying words and music are finger plays and whole-body actions that children will enjoy. Music for piano and chords for guitar and ukulele are provided. Rich in songs from other cultures (and languages other than English). The book assumes the ability to play one of the instruments.

P6 *American Folk Songs for Children in Home, School and Nursery School: A Book for Children, Parents and Teachers.* Ruth C. Seeger. Illus. by Barbara Cooney. Reprint. Doubleday, 1980. 190 pp. $8.95. (0-385-15788-6).

Over 150 pages of traditional American folk songs along with finger or whole-body plays that can accompany each tune. The almost 50 pages of introductory material are significant and helpful. Titles and first lines are indexed, as are subjects. Songs are also indexed by rhythms, tunes, and types of play. Bass and treble piano accompaniment are provided, as are chords for guitar and harmonica.

P7 *Appraisal: Science Books for Young People.* Children's Science Book Review Committee, 1967– . $24/yr.

Believing that science books for children should receive the same careful attention as literature, the Children's Science Book Review Committee prepares this quarterly gathering of reviews of science books. Each book is reviewed by a librarian and a subject specialist; reviews are signed and graded from excellent to unacceptable (if there is misleading information).

P8 *As a Child Grows.* Rosanne Keller. Illus. by Mark Fingar. New Readers Press, 1989. 32 pp. $2.25. (0-88336-511-1).

Useful for caregivers or professionals who work with parents with a limited command of vocabulary. Gives a loving look at discipline and developmental stages from birth to five years. The text is simple but direct and includes safety tips and encouraging words for parents.

P9 *Becoming a Nation of Readers: What Parents Can Do.* Edited by Marilyn R. Binkley. D. C. Heath & Co./What Parents Can Do, 1988. 30 pp. $0.50.

Drawn heavily from the Report of the Commission on Reading, *Becoming a Nation of Readers* outlines ways that parents can influence their children to be better readers (and writers). Topics include reading to and with children, talking with preschoolers, beginning to read, developing good reading programs, and encouraging children to do well with their schoolwork.

P10 *Best Games: 188 Active and Quiet, Simple and Sophisticated Games for Preschoolers Through Adults.* Linda Jennings, Mary L. Lamp, and Jerome Stenberg. McFarland & Co., 1985. 135 pp. $13.95. (0-89950-159-1).

A "rule book" for 188 games that can be played by those of all ages. Each game is rated for age level, activity level, number of players, and whether it is an indoor or outdoor activity. Instructions are clearly and briefly written (none take more than half a page), and equipment needed is minimal.

P11 *Bibliography of Books for Children.* Association for Childhood Education International, 1989. 128 pp. $11.00. (0-87173-118-5).

A bibliography of recommended books for children divided by picture books, fiction, and nonfiction by Dewey number. A selected list of reference books for an elementary school library is also included, as is a list of magazines and newspapers for children and young adults. Title and author index are included.

P12 ***Bibliography on Disabled Children: A Guide to Materials for Young People Aged 3 to 17.*** Canadian Library Association, 1981. 50 pp. $4.00. (0-88802-159-3).

Brief but helpful annotations of materials (primarily books) on a wide range of topics dealing with the disabled. Both fiction and nonfiction are included, as are a variety of formats. Divided by types of conditions and graded for children aged 3–17.

P13 ***Booklist.*** American Library Association, 1905– . $56/yr.

Provides a current buying list of recent books and nonprint media with annotations that can assist librarians with collection development. Only recommended books are included; the section on children's books includes grade levels. Once each month the children's book section includes reviews of easy reading material. All formats and all types of materials are reviewed.

P14 ***Books and Children in Pediatric Settings: A Guide for Caregivers and Librarians.*** Marcella F. Anderson. Illus. by Ky Wilson. Photos by Colin Klein. Rainbow Babies and Childrens Hospital, 1988. 103 pp. $7.95.

Aimed at librarians and caregivers who work with children in medical settings. Includes theories for having libraries in such settings, selection of materials, read-aloud programs (including bibliotherapy and reading to the comatose patient), and the role of the library as part of the hospital team.

P15 ***Booksharing: 101 Programs to Use with Preschoolers.*** Margaret Read MacDonald. Illus. by Julie Liana MacDonald. Library Professional Publications Shoe String Press, 1988. 250 pp. $2.50. (0-208-02159-0).

Each program is based on a stated theme and includes opening activities; suggested books, films, and songs; and possible craft or worksheet activities. Includes an extensive bibliography and the music for some of the songs. Although no library or school will have every resource mentioned, this is still a versatile and worthwhile purchase.

P16 ***Bulletin of the Center for Children's Books.*** University of Chicago Press, 1948– . $25/yr.

Review journal of books for children aged 4–14. Covers about 75 titles each month, and titles are evaluated by both educators and librarians on the university faculty. Reviewers make recommendations that are both favorable and negative.

P17 *Buy Me! Buy Me! The Bank Street Guide to Choosing Toys for Children.* Joanne F. Oppenheim. Pantheon Books, 1987. 311 pp. $11.95. (0-394-75546-4).

Investigates many facets of toys and toy buying, including developmental levels, toy and play safety, and violence in toys. After a considerable overview of toys, the book is divided by stages of growth from infancy to 11 years, and some of the better choices are discussed. How toys can aid in intellectual, social, and physical development is discussed in each section.

P18 *CBC Features.* The Children's Book Council. $25.00.

The Children's Book Council—a sponsor of National Children's Book Week—produces this newsletter, which is full of information of interest to those who work with children and their books. A one-time handling (not subscription) fee places a name on the mailing list forever. Recipients are mailed *Features* as well as information about Book Week materials and other promotions.

P19 *Children Today.* Office of Human Development Services, 1954– $7.50/yr.

A publication of the U.S. government, covering a wide range of child care, development, and education issues. The reasonable price makes it accessible to libraries, schools, and day care centers as well as parents who want to keep informed on key issues.

P20 *Children's Books in Print.* R. R. Bowker, 1969– . $62.95.

Lists over 40,000 paper and hardcover books currently for sale by U.S. publishers. No textbooks, "toybooks," or workbooks are reviewed. Books are indexed by author, title, and illustrator; vital bibliographic and ordering information are provided, as is availability of library bindings.

P21 *Children's Books of the Year.* Child Study Children's Book Committee, 1943– . 58 pp. $4.00.

The committee reviews over 3,000 books each year and chooses approximately 700, which are annotated and listed by subject and/or type. An award book is chosen each year. Selection criteria are given in each year's issue. A helpful guide for those who select books for children from birth to age 14.

P22 *Children's Catalog, 16th ed.* Edited by Juliet Yaakov. H. W. Wilson, 1991. 1370 pp. $72.00. (0-8242-0805-6).

A basic bibliography of materials for K–6 that is useful for building collections. The analytical index makes finding material on special subjects easier. Contents: Pt. 1—Classified catalog; Pt. 2—Author, title, subject, and analytical index; and Pt. 3—Directory of publishers and distributors.

P23 *Children's Library Services Handbook.* Jane G. Connor. Oryx Press, 1990. 128 pp. $27.50. (0-89774-489-6).

Pulls a great diversity of material into one book for children's librarians. Covering the fundamentals of children's librarianship from selection to public relations, this would be an auxiliary text, a "primer" for a new children's librarian, or a source of reference for seasoned librarians. The bibliographies at the end of each chapter are especially helpful resources.

P24 *Children's Media Market Place, 3rd ed.* Edited by Dolores B. Jones. Neal-Schuman Publishers, 1988. 397 pp. $45.00. (1-55570-007-1).

An invaluable resource for suppliers of materials and computer software for children's needs as well as for publishers and bookstores specializing in children's books. The fact that this is a third edition suggests that it will be kept up-to-date. Of special note is the month-by-month calendar of events and conferences of interest to those who work with children of all ages.

P25 *Children's Video Review Newsletter.* Children's Video Review Newsletter, 1986–   . $36/yr.

A newsletter reviewing videotapes for children. Each program is examined for literacy and educational and recreational content based on professional library and instructional criteria. Reviews are designed to help both as a purchasing guide and as a guide to programming.

P26 *The Child's Concept of Story: Ages Two to Seventeen.* Arthur N. Applebee. Reprint. University of Chicago Press, 1989. 209 pp. $12.95. (0-226-02120-3).

Looks at how story is a representation of experience and how it can be used to help children accept and process new information (experiences) of their own. Beginning with the theories of Piaget, the cognitive development of small children is discussed progressing to the child at the age of 17. Interesting and important for teachers and librarians or anyone who wants to use story to its best effect.

P27 *The Childwise Catalog: A Consumer Guide to Buying the Safest and Best Products for Your Children.* Jack Gillis and Mary Ellen R. Fise. Pocket Books, 1986. 370 pp. $6.95. (0-671-55410-7).

A handy and usable consumer guide that evaluates products used with children up to five years of age in order to recommend the safest and best. The authors leave no area unexamined, from baby furniture to crayons and modeling clay. Products are mentioned by name. The size, price, and ease of use make it a good home purchase, but libraries, preschools, day-care centers—even religious schools—will want to own one.

P28 *Choosing Books for Children: A Commonsense Guide.* Betsy Hearne. Revised. Dell Publishing/Delacourt Press/Delta, 1990. 228 pp. $9.95. (0-385-30108-1).

Hearne's book differs from other "mass market" guides for introducing children to books in that it is given over wholly to the theory behind book selection and a discussion of what makes a good choice in each of the areas discussed. Deals with such topics as sex and violence in books, books for teens, matching books to developmental stages, and selection aids. Brief lists of recommended books are included in each chapter.

P29 *Choosing Books for Kids: Choosing the Right Book for the Right Child at the Right Time.* Joanne F. Oppenheim, Barbara Brenner, and Betty D. Boegehold. Ballantine Books, 1986. 345 pp. $9.95. (0-345-32683-0).

Combines an annotated list of over 1,500 books with a section on developmental stages and the theory behind selecting books for children. Arranged by ages and themes. At the end of each age unit are special tips on selection for that age. Price and ease of use make this a good resource for schools, libraries, day-care centers, and parents.

P30 *Day One: A Positive Beginning for Parents and Their Infants.* Dee Dickinson. New Horizons for Learning, 1986. Videocassette. 32 min. $225.00.

Looks at developmental stages with an emphasis on what babies can do immediately after birth. Stresses that babies' brains grow at a fantastic rate during the first year and the importance of positive, loving, and encouraging stimulation. Useful for prenatal classes and for expectant or new parents. Libraries, day-care centers—even hospitals and doctors—will find this a useful purchase.

P31 *Early Childhood Special Education: Birth to Three.* Edited by June B. Jordan. Council for Exceptional Children, 1988. 257 pp. $24.00. (0-86586-179-X).

A look at how schools can best meet the challenges and mandates of caring for physically and mentally handicapped youth. This could be an invaluable source of information for those concerned with the educational needs of children with disabilities.

P32 *Early Childhood Teacher.* Edgell Communications, 1986– . Free.

A quarterly journal aimed at primary school professionals (according to the masthead) but useful for parents and children at home as well. Activities are simple, and most do not require special equipment or materials. Activities in each issue are geared to the three-month period covered and tie into holidays, seasonal changes, etc. Each quarterly issue averages about 40 pages.

P33 *The Elementary School Library Collection: A Guide to Books and Other Media, 18th ed.* Edited by Laureen K. Lee. Brodart, 1992. 1254 pp. $99.95. (0-87272-095-0).

A classified catalog of recommended print and audiovisual materials for preschool to sixth-grade. Reference materials, fiction, periodicals, and professional materials are covered. Full bibliographic and purchasing data are given, along with reading and interest level and annotations that often give suggestions for use. The latest edition of a standard and time-tested selection tool. Also provides a "Media for Preschool Children" listing of recommended titles.

P34 *Emerging Literacy: Young Children Learn to Read and Write.* Edited by Dorothy Stickland and Lesley Morrow. International Reading Association, 1989. 161 pp. $9.00. (0-87207-351-3).

This book focuses on the theory and practice of teaching literacy for children 2–8 years in classroom settings including day-care and prekindergarten. The basic theory is one of reading-writing integration, and good exercises and tips are given throughout. Each chapter is written by an expert in that area.

P35 *Environmental Hazards to Young Children.* Dorothy N. Kane. Oryx Press, 1985. 246 pp. $35.00. (0-89774-221-4).

A technical book for libraries and day-care centers rather than one to recommend for home purchase. Discusses children and all types of environmental safety hazards: fire and burns, falls, noise, radiation, toxic substances, and more. Prevention, protective devices, evaluation of protective devices, and more are covered. Extensive bibliographic material and tips for safety management are included.

P36 *ERIC EECE Newsletter.* ERIC Clearinghouse on EECE, 1989– . Free.

A newsletter devoted to early childhood materials filed with the Educational Resources Information Center (ERIC). Its four-page format includes lists of ERIC documents of note and provides ERIC numbers, ordering information, and brief reviews. Many of the publications listed are available free, especially digests and catalogs of further materials.

P37 *Exceptional Children.* Council for Exceptional Children, 1934– . $35/yr.

A professional journal for those who deal with exceptional children. Covers a multitude of issues in the field through in-depth essays. Averages 80 pages with little advertising; most space carries information. A useful resource for teachers in this area, for librarians, and for concerned parents.

P38 *For Love of Reading: A Parent's Guide to Encouraging Young Readers from Infancy Through Age 5.* Masha K. Rudman and Anna M. Pearce. Consumers Union, 1988. 399 pp. $15.00. (0-89043-209-0).

About half of the book carries bibliographies and lists of recommended books that should prove helpful to parents and caregivers. The other half shows adults how to work with children's literature, beginning with the earliest books for infants. The authors mention specific titles in each chapter and show clearly how books may be used to encourage the love of reading and the link between literature and life.

P39 *Freedom to Grow: A Day by Day Guide for Rearing Emotionally Healthy Preschoolers.* Angie Rose and Lynn Weiss. Humanics Ltd, 1984. 115 pp. $12.95. (0-89334-046-4).

A series of developmentally graded exercises and games that help children come to grips with their world. Works with a five-stage approach, helping the child develop self-control, self-awareness, self-esteem, a sense of power, and, finally, a sense of control over his or her own environment. Useful for parents or caregivers.

P40 *From Kids with Love: Gifts Preschoolers Can Make and Give.* Janis Hill and Laure Patrick. Fearon Teacher Aids, 1987. 90 pp. $8.95. (0-8224-3166-1).

What makes this special is its focus on crafts that younger children can make for gifts. While most of the craft projects are old standbys, some are new, and many have a unique twist. Since all of these projects are destined to be gifts, special care has been taken to "finish" each project appealingly. This factor makes it worthwhile for preschools, religious schools, and even perhaps adaptable for kindergarten classrooms.

P41 *Fun for Kids: An Index to Children's Craft Books.* Marion F. Gallivan. Scarecrow Press, 1981. 340 pp. $21.00. (0-8108-1439-0).

Indexes over 300 commonly found titles by title and author, by type of craft project, and by type of material used. An ideal resource for public libraries or school libraries—especially when teachers have access to a good craft book collection.

P42 *Guide to Videocassettes for Children.* Edited by Diana H. Green. Consumers Union, 1989. 270 pp. $13.95. (0-89043-240-6).

Lists videos in a variety of categories (drama, science fiction and fantasy, folktales, etc.) suitable for children and gives basic production information as well as a signed annotation. Videos are graded by ages, and a few suggested books that might be coupled with each video are listed. Criteria for selection are given in the introduction. A helpful resource for public and school libraries.

P43 *Happy Hands and Feet: Art Projects for Young Children.* Cindy Mitchell. Illus. by Susan Eaddy. Incentive Publications, 1989. 79 pp. $7.95. (0-86530-062-3).

Suggests art projects using—literally—hands, feet, fingers, and toes to create the pictures. Results, while slightly messy, are highly individualistic projects that children will enjoy making and parents will find entertaining and dear. A good book for day-care centers, religious schools, vacation Bible schools, or early grades in public schools.

P44 *Helping Your Child Become a Reader.* Nancy L. Roser. International Reading Association, 1989. 18 pp. $1.75. (0-87207-161-8).

Covers a wide range of reading situations, including letting children read to adults, reading to children, selecting books in bookstores and libraries, and controlling the TV. A bibliography and list of resources give further suggestions for guides. The approach is positive, and the aim is to encourage reading as a pleasurable experience for both parent (or caregiver) and child.

P45 *The Horn Book Guide to Children's and Young Adult Books.* Edited by Ann A. Flowers. Horn Book, 1989– . 176 pp. $50.00.

Twice-yearly guide to all children's books published, reviewed with Horn Book's unfailing critical standards. Bibliographic information, reading level, and Dewey number are provided; fiction is ranked by genre. All reviews are signed, and each book is also given a quality ranking. A useful selection tool for libraries and schools.

P46 *Horn Book Magazine.* Horn Book, 1924– . $32/yr.

A journal well respected for the quality of its book reviews. Publishes the text of the Caldecott, Newbery, and Laura Ingalls Wilder award acceptance speeches. A must for libraries and schools with significant collections. Published six times a year.

P47 *How to Raise a Reader: Sharing Books with Infants and Toddlers.* Edited by Floyd C. Dickman and Janice D. Smuda. American Library Association, 1990. Unp. 50 cents.

A pamphlet, in brief annotated form, giving the basic information that parents need to encourage a love of reading in their children. Brevity and a reasonable price suggest this as a handout for parents' night or as a ready reference for parents who are wondering how to beat the TV monster.

P48 *Hug a Tree: And Other Things to Do Outdoors with Young Children.* Robert E. Rockwell, Elizabeth A. Sherwood, and Robert A. Williams. Illus. by Laurel J. Sweetman. Gryphon House, 1986. 103 pp. $8.95. (0-87659-105-5).

A group of highly experiential outdoor projects that stimulate children's senses and teach them to appreciate the out-of-doors while teaching scientific concepts. Many of the projects assume access to ponds or "woods" plus a willingness to get wet, dirty, or both. Some projects require more than one day or one "step." Geared to ages 2+ to 5+.

P49 *Is the Left Brain Always Right? A Guide to Whole Child Development.* Clare Cherry, Douglas Godwin, and Jesse Staples. Fearon Teacher Aids, 1989. 372 pp. $13.95. (0-8224-3911-5).

Basic information on brain hemisphere research and development in young children. Exercises and tasks help children develop both the left side of the brain, which controls language and logic, and the right side, which controls imagination and emotion.

P50 *Know Your Child: An Authoritative Guide for Today's Parents.* Stella Chess and Alexander Thomas. Basic Books, 1987. 397 pp. $12.95. (0-465-03731-3).

An authoritative guide to child development, covering important areas such as cognitive development, self-esteem, and temperament. Also moves ahead to the problems of the teen years. Easy to read, yet not at all in the "pop" psychology mold. Information is professionally presented. Valuable for teachers and caregivers as well as parents.

P51 *Learning Games for Infants and Toddlers: A Playtime Handbook.* J. Ronald Lally and Ira J. Gordon. Illus. by Bill Finch. New Readers Press, 1977. 80 pp. $4.75. (0-88-336565-0).

Activities are aimed at the youngest children to stimulate their awareness of themselves and their environment. Some games build coordination, muscle strength, and reflexes. Games are divided by ages, and each has an annotation describing its particular aim. Good for all who work with the very young.

P52 *Literature for the Young Child, 2nd ed.* Eileen M. Burke. Allyn and Bacon, 1990. 316 pp. $23.00. (0-205-12144-6).

Looks at all children's books as literature. The author uses a tactile approach to helping children truly experience books—the sounds, textures, and sights. Burke deals with fairy tales, folktales, humor books for children, and Bible stories. Includes helpful lists, charts, and booklists as well as many good examples.

P53 *Literature for Young Children, 2nd ed.* Joan I. Glazer. Charles E. Merrill, 1986. 282 pp. $19.95. (0-675-20398-8).

Looks at the theory as well as the practice of selecting materials for young children. Read-aloud and sharing programs are well covered. Contains good sections on how literature aids a child's development at all levels, including social, literacy, aesthetic, and intellectual. The main vehicle used is the picture book, and good titles are recommended, although the bibliographic function is not primary.

P54 *Look at Me: Creative Learning Activities for Babies and Toddlers.* Carolyn B. Haas. Illus. by Jane B. Phillips. Chicago Review Press, 1987. 228 pp. $8.95. (1-55652-021-2).

Filled with acitivities especially geared to very young children. Required materials are readily available and safe for even the tiniest child. All activities stimulate children's awareness of texture, color, and shape or of themselves in some purposeful and exciting way, including language development, coordination, social interaction skills, and more. For a wide variety of situations.

P55 *Materials for Adults to Use with Children from Birth to Three: A Selected Resource List.* Frank Self, Nancy DeSalvo, and Faith Hektoen. Farmington Library, 1983. 47 pp. $4.50.

An annotated list of resources for both children and the adults who work with children. Although the list is not meant to be comprehensive, each title is recommended. Organized by categories: formats (cloth, board, etc.), types (Mother Goose, counting, picture), nonprint materials, and toys. An introduction for each section gives information on that type of material.

P56 *Medical Toys & Books.* Pediatric Projects, 1989– . $14/yr.

A buyer's guide to medically oriented playthings for toddlers through teens. Some materials are as simple as character bandages; others are as sophisticated as disabled dolls and animals. Most toys and equipment are shown in black and white pictures. Another section lists suggested book titles covering a range of health-related subjects, from teen sexuality to AIDS.

P57 *More Than the ABCs: The Early Stages of Reading and Writing.* Judith A. Schickedanz. NAEYC, 1986. 147 pp. $6.00. (0-912674-95-4).

Based on her own realization that children are often ready to make the reading-writing-talking link before the adults in their lives, Schickedanz has created a guide for teachers' efforts to prepare the young child to write. Begins with children's natural orality and moves to the connection between what is on the printed page and what is read to them. Includes the first attempts to "write" by themselves.

P58 *Mother Goose Comes First: An Annotated Guide to the Best Books and Recordings for Your Preschool Child.* Lois Winkel and Sue Kimmel. Henry Holt & Co., 1990. 194 pp. $14.95. (0-8050-1001-7).

Specializes in books, tapes, and records for children up to five years. The guide is easy to use and will be a boon for parents, teachers, and caregivers as well as librarians. Because it describes 700 items, it is not so large as to be overwhelming, and all are recommended titles. Complete bibliographic information, age level, format, and a brief annotation are given for each.

P59 *Move Over, Mother Goose! Finger Plays, Action Verses & Funny Rhymes.* Ruth I. Dowell. Illus. by Concetta C. Scott. Gryphon House, 1987. 126 pp. $9.95. (0-87659-113-6).

Contains over 100 short rhymes that can be used as either finger plays or action verses. Each rhyme has directions for movements for one or both formats. Divided by subject (animals, seasons, food, home and family, etc.). Does not shy away from "hard" words or "tricky" rhyme patterns. These are not the familiar or the "tried and true," but they are fun and will vary any preschool program.

P60 *Mudluscious: Stories and Activities Featuring Food for Preschool Children.* Jan Irving and Robin Currie. Illus. by Robert B. Phillips. Libraries Unlimited, 1986. 259 pp. $21.50. (0-87287-517-2).

Includes activities, rhymes, lists of books, and suggestions for programs with food as the theme. Although smaller children may not be able to do some of the crafts, they would enjoy seeing the easily crafted puppets used in a story or finger play. Material is adaptable for most preschoolers and would work well in a variety of settings. Be aware: not all the food mentioned is strictly "high nutrition," but it is all fun.

P61 *Mudpies to Magnets: A Preschool Science Curriculum.* Robert A. Williams, Robert E. Rockwell, and Elizabeth A. Sherwood. Illus. by Laurel J. Sweetman. Gryphon House, 1987. 157 pp. $12.95. (0-87659-112-8).

A multitude of science projects for children 2–5 and up, most of which can be accomplished with readily available materials. Activities are indexed by broad types. Each set of instructions is explicit and cross-referenced to lead the teacher to other "like" activities. Emphasizes appeal to all the senses. The aim is for children to experience science rather than to gain specific facts.

P62 *Mudworks: Creative Clay, Dough, and Modeling Experiences.* MaryAnn F. Kohl. Illus. by Kathleen Kerr. Bright Ring/Gryphon House, 1989. 150 pp. $14.95. (0-935607-02-1).

Every possible type of play "dough" mixture is detailed for use in a school or child-care environment. Handy symbols tell if the mix is edible, requires baking, or needs special adult supervision, as well as offer a suggested age range for each project. Recipes are clear, the illustrations helpful, and the projects fun. Dough art is popular with kids of all ages, and this makes it easy as well.

P63 *Music for Ones and Twos: Songs and Games for the Very Young Child.* Tom Glazer. Illus. by Karen A. Weinhaus. Reprint. Doubleday, 1983. 96 pp. $9.95. (0-385-14252-8).

A collection of easy-to-sing songs for younger children. Although music for piano and guitar is provided, most tunes are familiar and could be sung unaccompanied. Simplest instructions for finger or body games are given for some songs: "Shoo Fly"—the baby waves away the fly. These songs and games can extend the teaching of the concept of numbers of fingers and toes, up and down, etc., in a fun way for baby and adult.

P64 *Musical Story Hours: Using Music with Storytelling and Puppetry.* William M. Painter. Library Professional Publications/Shoe String Press, 1989. 158 pp. $27.50. (0-208-02205-8).

Aimed primarily at libraries and other institutions with the resources for staging fairly elaborate puppet plays. However, the basic idea of introducing children to classical music along with stories of "their own" is a good one and worthy of being adapted for small productions. Story and music suggestions are extensive, yet not prescriptive, and material is generally adaptable.

P65 *The New Read-Aloud Handbook.* Jim Trelease. Penguin, 1989. 290 pp. $9.95. (0-14-046881-1).

Although a classic in its first edition, this collection is not without its problems. The selections are wholly Trelease's, and he does not consider nonfiction exciting reading. Otherwise, the basic aim—encouraging family reading aloud—is a good one, and the titles are solid if egocentric.

P66 *The New York Times Parent's Guide to the Best Books for Children.* Eden R. Lipson. Revised. Times Books, 1991. 508 pp. $15.00. (0-812-91889-4).

Designed to assist parents and teachers in selecting books for children, this book's currency is a particular selling point. Thirty-four indexes include access by age appropriateness, levels for listening and reading aloud, author, illustrator, and subject. The annotated section is arranged by broad type of book. ISBN is not given in bibliographic information.

P67 *Once upon a Storytime: A Workbook for Planning and Presenting Creative Storytimes for Children Two–Six Years of Age.* Carolyn Booth Stanson. Minnesota Association of Library Friends, 1989. 252 pp. $15.00.

For anyone who intends to present story time programs; helps in the preparation and planning phases of the process. Suggestions are highly flexible, so the book is "good" for more than one year. Oversized with a spiral binding so that it lies flat and plenty of white space on the pages, which invites users to add their own suggestions. A treasure.

P68 *Once upon a Time ... An Encyclopedia for Successfully Using Literature with Young Children.* Carol O. Hurst et al. DLM, 1990. 360 pp. $54.95. (1-55924-324-4).

Uses a variety of approaches, including author-illustrator and thematic entries, suggested activities, and good cross referencing to expand the uses of children's literature. Composed primarily of lists, but this does not limit usefulness, especially for those new to programming or the reader's advisory function. Many teachers will be glad to see the activity suggestions and to know which authors answer mail.

P69 *Parents and Children Together: Discipline and Learning.* Family Literacy Center at Indiana University, 1990. 62 pp. $9.00.

One of the monthly publications from the Family Literacy Center, whose aim is to promote literacy for both parents and children. Each publication is accompanied by an audiotape, and each discusses a problem such as discipline, reluctant readers, etc. One side of each tape (and part of each booklet) is given over to stories that reinforce the general theme of the publication.

P70 *Parents' Choice: A Review of Children's Media.* Parents' Choice Foundation, 1978– . $15/yr.

A newspaper-format, tabloid-size magazine offering reviews of books, movies, and records as well as articles and essays. Especially helpful for teachers and librarians, but parents who are concerned about encouraging their children's reading will find it useful as well.

P71 *Playground Equipment: Do-It-Yourself, Indestructible, Practically Free.* Lloyd Marston. Illus. by Gerlinder Henn. McFarland & Co., 1984. 147 pp. $14.95. (0-89950-104-4).

Contains building plans for over 150 pieces of playground equipment. Basic materials are wood (posts and boards) and old tires. Some but not all of this equipment would be suitable for very young children. A good do-it-yourselfer could probably follow most of the plans, and the materials needed are low cost or even free.

P72 *Pre-School Storytimes.* Ken Roberts. Canadian Library Association, 1987. 15 pp. $7.50. (0-88802-225-5).

A pamphlet covering the basic considerations involved with a preschool story time in the public library. Goals, organization, formats, and methods for using various types of materials are discussed. Specific issues (should parents participate?) are also discussed. Most material could be adapted to nonlibrary settings.

P73 *The Preschool Handbook: Making the Most of Your Child's Education.* Barbara Brenner. Pantheon Books, 1990. 276 pp. $11.95. (0-679-72551-2).

Aimed at parents of children 3–5, but information could be appropriate and useful for parents of younger children. Its purpose is to help parents judge and select preschools and to ease the transition from home to preschool. The general goal is to help children make the most of the preschool years.

P74 *Primaryplots: A Book Talk Guide for Use with Readers Ages 4–8.* Rebecca L. Thomas. R. R. Bowker, 1989. 392 pp. $39.95. (0-8352-2514-3).

Aimed to serve as a guide for adults who give book talks or serve as reader's advisors for children. Provides plot summaries for 150 recent picture and early reading books. Suggested grade level is given along with a brief summary of plot, theme, and characters. Divided by subject, but indexes to subject, author, title, and illustrator are given. Summaries also include references for material on authors.

P75 *Puppetry In Early Childhood Education.* Tamara Hunt and Nancy Renfro. Nancy Renfro Studios, 1982. 258 pp. $17.95. (0-931044-04-9).

Nancy Renfro is a well-known expert in creating and using puppets, so this, along with *Bags Are Big* (on paper bag craft) and *Pocketful of Puppets* (short stories to act out), are good additions to any puppetry collection. This basic book offers bibliographic material, books to use with puppets, and material on collecting and making puppets.

P76 *Read to Me: Libraries, Books and Your Baby.* Greater Vancouver Library Federation, 1986. Videocassette. 15 min. $50.00.

A 15-minute "encourager" for parents and caregivers who want to begin reading to very young children. Centered on the library-home relationship, it promotes the idea of singing to and reading to babies as good ways to promote language development and love of reading. While the emphasis is on starting young, it does not suggest pushing children; the producers want reading to be fun for babies.

P77 *Read to Me Too! Libraries, Books and Your Child.* Greater Vancouver Library Federation, 1989. Videocassette. 15 min. $50.00.

Encourages parents of early-school-age children to continue reading aloud to them and to present children with opportunities for reading and being read to outside the classroom. Another aim is to build the home-library connection so that parents look to public libraries and librarians as helpers in promoting children's reading.

P78 *Reading Is Fundamental: Guide to Encouraging Young Readers.* Edited by Ruth Graves. Doubleday, 1987. 336 pp. $9.95. (0-385-23632-8).

Contains, first, a large collection of reading and book-related activities for infants and children to age 11. Second, it provides an annotated list of suggested titles. A third list gives further resources (books, organizations, book sources) that can help parents encourage reading. Useful in school as well as home-based, reading-encouragement programs.

P79 *Reading Is Fundamental: Publications.* RIF.

RIF (Reading Is Fundamental) has added four new titles to its list of pamphlets that give parents tips and activities to encourage reading: *Encouraging Your Writers, Building a Family Library, Family Storytelling,* and *Summertime Reading* join many other fine and helpful titles. Available singly or in bulk, these brochures would make good additions to libraries as well as good giveaways to encourage parent participation in learning.

P80   *Reading Together: Sharing Books with Children, Infancy Through Age Eight.* Barbara N. Taylor and Dianne L. Monson. GoodYear Books, 1991. 168 pp. $9.95. (0-673-38969-3).

This book, focused on infancy through grade two, is aimed at parents, but this should not preclude professional use. The annotated book list is a good "core collection" that parents or day-care providers may want to include in a beginning library. The book's compactness is its special feature.

P81   *Ready, Set, Read: Best Books to Prepare Preschoolers.* Ellen Mahoney and Leah Wilcox. Scarecrow Press, 1985. 348 pp. $22.50. (0-8108-1684-9).

The goal here is to help parents or caregivers select literature for sharing with prereaders. Divided into progressive stages of growth and development, dealing with children's interests at each stage, and suggesting a theory behind book choice as well as titles. Title and author indexes are included.

P82   *Scholastic Pre-K Today.* Scholastic, 1986– . $32/yr.

A monthly magazine for teachers, day-care operators, librarians, or anyone who works with pre-K children. Each issue averages about 100 pages of articles for teachers, suggested activities, advertisements for materials and equipment, and more. One issue looks at dealing with feelings, teaching children to solve problems, and teaching through open-ended questioning. A valuable and attractive resource.

P83   *School Library Journal.* Cahners/R.R. Bowker, 1954– . $56/yr.

Journal most widely used by school librarians (and many teachers) for its numerous book reviews and articles on books and librarianship. A must for any library; a publication teachers should be aware of and use.

P84   *A Song Is a Rainbow: Music, Movement and Rhythm Instruments in the Nursery School and Kindergarten.* Patty Zeitlin. Scott, Foresman & Co./ Good Year Books, 1982. 259 pp. $16.95. (0-673-16460-8).

A highly integrated approach to teaching young children music appreciation. Includes a great deal of pedagogical rational and supplemental material for preschool and elementary school teachers. If a serious commitment to music is part of the school's program, this is a first selection. Format is full-page size, spiral-bound.

P85 ***STORY S-T-R-E-T-C-H-E-R-S: Activities to Expand Children's Favorite Books.*** Shirley C. Raines and Robert J. Canady. Gryphon House, 1989. 251 pp. $14.95. (0-87659-119-5).

Eighteen chapters, each built around a common theme or unit taught in preschools, kindergartens, etc. Five books are dealt with under each theme, for a total of 90 books. The stretchers provide activities such as music, art, and science projects that extend children's participation with the theme being taught. Old favorites as well as new titles are recommended. Two new editions supplement the original.

P86 ***Storytelling with Puppets.*** Connie Champlin and Nancy Renfro. American Library Association, 1985. 293 pp. $19.95. (0-8389-0421-1).

Gives a wide variety of useful information, including why and how to use puppets, how to adapt stories, how to make simple puppets, and techniques that work well with different age groups. Stories and puppet-based activities are included, as are bibliographies of selected materials for use with puppets. Most patterns provided are full size.

P87 ***Storytimes for Two-Year-Olds.*** Judy Nichols. Illus. by Lora Sears. American Library Association, 1987. 141 pp. $20.00. (0-8389-0451-3).

Aimed at beginning storytellers working with two-year-olds. Begins with the most basic ideas such as seating dynamics, finger plays, music, and puppetry. Each unit has suggested books, finger plays, and follow-ups. Some of the crafts may be beyond story time environments, but probably not beyond day-care centers or schools. Patterns are not full size.

P88 ***Strategies for Teaching Young Children, 3rd ed.*** Judith A. Schickedanz et al. Prentice Hall, 1990. 384 pp. $39.67. (0-13-850561-6).

Aimed at teachers, beginning with a theoretical framework and covering subjects such as working with handicaps, discipline, and the classroom as social context. Each subject area (math, science, performing arts, language arts, social science, visual arts) is given a chapter, and the book concludes with a sample unit. Charts, lists, and illustrations are helpful.

P89 ***Teaching Pre K–8.*** Early Years, 1970– . $18/yr.

Contains some exciting and even striking suggestions for teaching children in pre-K through grade eight. While the focus may be more on the post-K grades, this is a useful journal for teachers at all levels. Many articles, lists, etc., in each issue are aimed directly at classroom use.

P90 **Tell Me a Story.** Charley Orbison. Texas Woman's University, 1990. Videocassette. 30 min. Free loan.

An encouraging "tutorial" in story telling that could be useful to any parent, teacher, caregiver, or librarian who wants to become a storyteller or a better storyteller. Featuring such storytellers as Elizabeth Ellis and Augusta Baker, the tape discusses selection, presentation, and techniques, and, best of all, it promotes story telling as an important factor in children's language and literacy growth.

P91 **Time for Tots: Library Service to Toddlers.** Virginia Van Vliet. Canadian Library Association, 1987. 20 pp. $7.50. (0-88802-224-7).

A booklet giving excellent theoretical support for and advice about starting story time programs for two-year-olds. Although aimed at public libraries, the material is useful for all situations in which group read-aloud programs might take place. Brief descriptions of basic services and resources are given, as is practical advice for starting such a program and ensuring its success.

P92 **Totline.** Warren Publishing House, 1979– . $15/yr.

For those who work with very young children, this is a mixed bag of activities, games, ideas, and holiday celebrations. Most activities could be accomplished by the very young child, and the rest could be adapted.

P93 **The Uses of Enchantment: The Meaning and Importance of Fairy Tales.** Bruno Bettelheim. Vintage Books, 1989. 327 pp. $10.95. (0-679-72393-5).

Bettelheim's classic on the meaning and symbols in fairy tales should be required reading for anyone working with this genre. Although some of Bettelheim's theories have come under question since his death, this book is still of importance and should have a place in any professional collection.

P94 **Using Picture Storybooks to Teach Literary Devices: Recommended Books for Children and Young Adults.** Susan Hall. Oryx Press, 1990. 168 pp. $24.95. (0-89774-582-5).

Makes the link between literature for children and all literature. Hall begins with brief discussions of types of children's literature, then moves to literary terms. Most of the book is an annotated book list suggesting titles that are examples of each literary device. For beginning teachers or for those who want to use a more literary approach to children's literature.

P95 *What to Expect the First Year.* Arlene Eisenberg, Heidi E. Murkoff, and Sandee E. Hathaway. Workman, 1989. 671 pp. $10.95. (0-89480-577-0).

A comprehensive step-by-step guide through the critical first year, discussing social and physical development, diseases, medical terms, eating habits and problems, and almost anything that can or might happen in the first year. Good illustrations and charts; well indexed. Advice is helpful and common-sense, and text is readable and accessible. Wonderful resource for first-time parents.

P96 *When a Baby Is New.* Rosanne Keller. Illus. by Mark Fingar. New Readers Press, 1989. 48 pp. $2.45. (0-88336-517-0).

Helpful to caregivers or professionals in dealing with parents who have a limited command of vocabulary. Shows a simple but loving approach to working with very new babies. Includes holding, feeding, diapering, burping—all the basic skills.

P97 *You Can Help Your Child with Writing.* Marcia Baghban. International Reading Association, 1989. 13 pp. $1.75. (0-87207-160-X).

A short pamphlet aimed at helping parents encourage their small children to begin to write—both in the sense of penmanship and in the sense of authorship. Methods suggested are positive and encouraging rather than pushy or competitive. Could be used carefully with younger children especially to encourage their efforts to draw and make stories. A bibliography and a list of resources are provided.

Appendix 2
Print Publishers and Nonprint Suppliers

Print Publishers

Aladdin, Div. of Macmillan, 866 Third Ave., New York, NY 10022

Albert Whitman & Co., 5747 W. Howard St., Niles, IL 60648

Alfred A. Knopf, Div. of Random House, 225 Park Ave. S., New York, NY 10003

Allyn and Bacon, 160 Gould St., Needham Heights, MA 02194-2310

American Library Association, 50 E. Huron St., Chicago, IL 60611

Annick Press, 15 Patricia Ave., Toronto, ON M2M 1H9 Canada

Association for Childhood Education International, 11141 Georgia Ave., Ste. 200, Wheaton, MD 20902

Atheneum, Div. of Macmillan, 866 Third Ave., New York, NY 10022

Atlantic Monthly Press, 19 Union Sq. W., New York, NY 10003

Ballantine Books, 201 E. 50th St., New York, NY 10022

Barron's Educational Series, P.O. Box 8040, 250 Wireless Blvd., Hauppauge, NY 11788-8040

Basic Books, Subs. of HarperCollins, 10 E. 53rd St., New York, NY 10022

Bedrick see Peter Bedrick

Beginner Books, Div. of Random House, 201 E. 50th St., New York, NY 10022

Bowker see R. R. Bowker

Bradbury, Div. of Macmillan, 866 Third Ave., New York, NY 10022

Bright Ring, P.O. Box 5768-B, Bellingham, WA 98227

Brodart, 500 Arch St., Williamsport, PA 17705

Canadian Children's Book Centre, 229 College St., 5th Floor, Toronto, ON M5T 1R4 Canada

Canadian Library Association, 200 Elgin St., Ste. 602, Ottawa, ON K2P 1L5 Canada

Candlewick Press, Div. of Walker Books, 2067 Massachusetts Ave., Cambridge, MA 02140

Carolrhoda Books, 241 First Ave. N., Minneapolis, MN 55401

Carus Corporation, *Ladybug,* 315 Fifth St., Peru, IL 61354

Celestial Arts, 231 Adrian Rd., Millbrae, CA 94030

Charles E. Merrill, Div. of Macmillan, 866 Third Ave., New York, NY 10022

Charlesbridge, 85 Main St., Watertown, MA 02172

Checkerboard, Div. of Macmillan, 866 Third Ave., New York, NY 10022

Chicago Review Press, 814 N. Franklin, Chicago, IL 60610

Child Study Children's Book Committee, Bank Street College, 610 W. 112th St., New York, NY 10025

Children's Better Health Institute, Benjamin Franklin Literary & Medical Society, P.O. Box 567, Indianapolis, IN 46206-0567

Children's Book Council, 67 Irving Place, New York, NY 10003

Children's Science Book Review Committee, Boston Univ. Sch. of Educ./Sci. Educ. Dept., 605 Commonwealth Ave., Boston, MA 02215

Children's Television Workshop, One Lincoln Plaza, New York, NY 10023

Children's Video Review Newsletter, 110 Lena Ct., Grass Valley, CA 95949

Child's Play, 310 W. 47th St. #3D, New York, NY 10036

Chronicle Books, 275 Fifth St., San Francisco, CA 94103

Clarion Books, 215 Park Ave. S., New York, NY 10003

Clarkson N. Potter, Div. of Random House, 225 Park Ave. S., New York, NY 10003

Consumers Union, 256 Washington St., Mount Vernon, NY 10553

Council for Exceptional Children, 1920 Association Dr., Reston, VA 22091-1589

Coward McCann, Div. of Putnam, 390 Murray Hill Pkwy., East Rutherford, NJ 07073-2185

Crowell see Thomas Y. Crowell

Crown, Div. of Random House, 225 Park Ave. S., New York, NY 10003

D. C. Heath & Co., Distribution Center, 2700 N. Richardt Ave., Indianapolis, IN 46219

David R. Godine, Horticulture Hall, 300 Massachusetts Ave., Boston, MA 02115

Delacorte Press, 1 Dag Hammarskjold Plaza, 245 E. 47th St., New York, NY 10017

Dell Publishing, 666 Fifth Ave., New York, NY 10103

Dial, Div. of Penguin, 375 Hudson St., New York, NY 10014

DLM, One DLM Park, Allen, TX 75002

Dog Ear Press, 19 Mason St., Brunswick, ME 04011

Doubleday, 666 Fifth Ave., New York, NY 10103

Douglas & McIntyre Ltd., 1615 Venables St., Vancouver, BC V5L 2H1 Canada

Dover Publications, 31 E. Second St., Mineola, NY 11501

Dutton, Div. of Penguin, 375 Hudson St., New York, NY 10014

Early Years, Subs. of Highlights for Children, 40 Richards Ave., Norwalk, CT 06854

Edgell Communications, 7500 Old Oak Blvd., Cleveland, OH 44130

ERIC Clearinghouse on EECE, University of Illinois at Urbana-Champaign, 805 W. Pennsylvania Ave., Urbana, IL 61801

Family Literacy Center at Indiana University, 2805 E. 10th St., Ste. 150, Bloomington, IN 47408-2698

Farmington Library, P.O. Box 407, 6 Monteith Dr., Farmington, CT 06034-0407

Farrar, Straus & Giroux, 19 Union Sq. W., New York, NY 10003

Fearon Teacher Aids, Div. of David S. Lake, 19 Davis Dr., Belmont, CA 94002

Fitzhenry & Whiteside, 195 Allstate Pkwy., Markham, ON L3R 4T8 Canada

Four Winds, Div. of Macmillan, 866 Third Ave., New York, NY 10022

Franklin Watts, Subs. of Grolier, 387 Park Ave. S., New York, NY 10016

Gallaudet University Press, 800 Florida Ave. NE, Washington, DC 20002-3625

Godine see David R. Godine

Good Year Books, Department GYB, 1900 E. Lake Ave., Glenview, IL 60025

Green Tiger Press, 435 E. Carmel St., San Marcos, CA 92069-4362

Greenwillow Books, Div. of William Morrow, 105 Madison Ave., New York, NY 10016

Grossett & Dunlap, Div. of Putnam, 200 Madison Ave., New York, NY 10016

Gryphon House, P.O. Box 275, Mt. Rainier, MD 20712-0275

Gulliver Books, Imprint of Harcourt Brace Jovanovich, 1250 Sixth Ave., San Diego, CA 92101

H. W. Wilson Co., 950 University Ave., Bronx, NY 10452

Harcourt Brace Jovanovich, 1250 Sixth Ave., San Diego, CA 92101

Harper & Row see HarperCollins

HarperCollins, 10 E. 53rd St., New York, NY 10022

Heath see D. C. Heath & Co.

Henry Holt & Co., 115 W. 18th St., New York, NY 10011

Highlights for Children, P.O. Box 269, Columbus, OH 43216-0269

Holiday House, 40 East 49th St., New York, NY 10017

Holt see Henry Holt & Co.

Horn Book, 14 Beacon St., Boston, MA 02108

Houghton Mifflin, 2 Park St., Boston, MA 02108

Humanics Ltd., P.O. Box 7447, Atlanta, GA 30309

Ideals Publishing Corp., Nelson Place at Elm Hill Pike, P.O. Box 14800, Nashville, TN 37214-8000

Incentive Publications, 3835 Cleghorn Ave., Nashville, TN 37215

International Reading Association, P.O. Box 8139, 800 Barksdale Rd., Newark, DE 19714-8139

Julian Messner, Div. of Silver Burdett Press, Prentice Hall Bldg., Englewood Cliffs, NJ 07632

Kar-Ben Copies, 6800 Tildenwood Ln., Rockville, MD 20852

Kids Can Press, 585 1/2 Bloor St. W., Toronto, ON M6G 1K5 Canada

Klutz Press, 2170 Staunton Ct., Palo Alto, CA 94306

Knopf see Alfred A. Knopf

Ladybird Books, P.O. Box 1690, 49 Omni Circle, Auburn, ME 04210-1690

Libraries Unlimited, P.O. Box 3988, Englewood, CO 80155-3988

Lion, 1705 Hubbard Ave., Batavia, IL 60510

Lippincott, Div. of HarperCollins, 10 E. 53rd St., New York, NY 10022

Little, Brown & Co., 34 Beacon St., Boston, MA 02108

Lothrop, Lee & Shepard, Div. of William Morrow, 105 Madison Ave., New York, NY 10016

McFarland & Co., P.O. Box 611, Jefferson, NC 28640

McGraw-Hill, 1221 Avenue of the Americas, New York, NY 10020

McGraw-Hill Ryerson, 330 Progress Ave., Scarborough, ON M1P 2Z5 Canada

Macmillan, 866 Third Ave., New York, NY 10022

Macmillan of Canada, 29 Birch Ave., Toronto, ON M4V 1E2 Canada

Margaret K. McElderry Books, Div. of Macmillan, 866 Third Ave., New York, NY 10022

Merrill see Charles E. Merrill

Messner see Julian Messner

Minnesota Association of Library Friends, 1417 28th St. SW, Rochester, MN 55902

Modern Curriculum Press, Div. of Simon & Schuster, 13900 Prospect Rd., Cleveland, OH 44136

Morrow Jr. Books, Div. of William Morrow, 105 Madison Ave., New York, NY 10016

NAEYC, 1834 Connecticut Ave. NW, Washington, DC 20009-5786

Nancy Renfro Studios, P.O. Box 164226, Austin, TX 78716-4226

National Council of Teachers of English, 1111 Kenyon Rd., Urbana, IL 61801

National Wildlife Federation, 1412 16th St. NW, Washington, DC 20036-2266

Neal-Schuman Publishers, 23 Leonard St., New York, NY 10013

New Readers Press, P.O. Box 131, Syracuse, NY 13210

North-South Books, 1123 Broadway, Ste. 600, New York, NY 10010

Office of Human Development Services, U.S. Dept. of Health and Human Services, 200 Independence Ave. SW, Washington, DC 20201

Open Hand, P.O. Box 22048, Seattle, WA 98122-2048

Orchard Books, Div. of Franklin Watts, 387 Park Ave. S., New York, NY 10016

Oryx Press, 40–41 N. Central, Phoenix, AZ 85012-3397

Oxford University Press, 200 Madison Ave., New York, NY 10016

Pantheon Books, Div. of Random House, 201 E. 50th St., New York, NY 10022

Parents' Choice Foundation, P.O. Box 185, Waban, MA 02168-0185

Parents Magazine Press, 685 Third Ave., New York, NY 10017

Pediatric Projects, P.O. Box 1880, Santa Monica, CA 90406

Penguin, 375 Hudson St., New York, NY 10014

Peter Bedrick, 2112 Broadway, Ste. 318, New York, NY 10023

Philomel, Div. of Putnam, 390 Murray Hill Pkwy., East Rutherford, NJ 07073-2185

Picture Book Studio, P.O. Box 9139, 10 Central St., Saxonville, MA 01701-9139

Platt & Munk, Div. of Putnam, 390 Murray Hill Pkwy., East Rutherford, NJ 07073-2185

Pocket Books, Div. of Simon & Schuster, 1230 Avenue of the Americas, New York, NY 10020

Potter see Clarkson N. Potter

Prentice Hall, Div. of Simon & Schuster, 190 Sylvan Ave., Englewood Cliffs, NJ 07632

Puffin Books, Div. of Penguin, 375 Hudson St., New York, NY 10014

Putnam, 390 Murray Hill Pkwy., East Rutherford, NJ 07073-2185

R. R. Bowker, Div. of Reed Publishing (USA), Inc., 121 Chanlon Rd., New Providence, NJ 07974

Ragweed Press, P.O. Box 2023, Charlottetown, PE C1A 7N7 Canada

Rainbow Babies and Childrens Hospital, 2101 Adelbert Rd., Rm. 340, Cleveland, OH 44106

Random House, 225 Park Ave. S., New York, NY 10003

Red Deer College Press, 56th Ave. & 32nd St., P.O. Box 5005, Red Deer, AB T4N 5H5 Canada

RIF, 600 Maryland Ave. SW, Ste. 500, Smithsonian Institution, Washington, DC 20560

Scarecrow Press, P.O. Box 4167, 52 Liberty St., Metuchen, NJ 08840

Schneider Educational Products, 2880 Green St., San Francisco, CA 94123

Scholastic, 730 Broadway, New York, NY 10003

Scienceland, 501 Fifth Ave., Ste. 2108, New York, NY 10017-6165

Scott, Foresman & Co., 1900 E. Lake Ave., Glenview, IL 60025

Scribner's, Div. of Macmillan, 866 Third Ave., New York, NY 10022

Shoe String Press, P.O. Box 4327, 925 Sherman Ave., Hamden, CT 06514

Silver Burdett Press, Subs. of Simon & Schuster, 190 Sylvan Ave., Englewood Cliffs, NJ 07632

Silver Press, Subs. of Silver Burdett Press, 190 Sylvan Ave., Englewood Cliffs, NJ 07632

Simon & Schuster, 1230 Avenue of the Americas, New York, NY 10020

Telshare Publishing, P.O. Box 679, Marshfield, MA 02050

Thomas Y. Crowell, Div. of HarperCollins, 10 E. 53 St., New York, NY 10022

Ticknor & Fields, Subs. of Houghton Mifflin, 215 Park Ave. S., New York, NY 10003

Troll Associates, 100 Corporate Dr., Mahwah, NJ 07430

Tundra Books, 1434 St. Catherine St. W., Ste. 308, Montreal, PQ H3G 1R4 Canada

University of Chicago Press, 5801 Ellis Ave., Chicago, IL 60637

Viking Kestrel, Div. of Penguin, 375 Hudson St., New York, NY 10014

Viking Penguin, Div. of Penguin, 375 Hudson St., New York, NY 10014

Villard Books, Div. of Random House, 201 E. 50th St., New York, NY 10022

Vintage Books, Div. of Random House, 201 E. 50th St., New York, NY 10022

Walker & Co., 720 Fifth Ave., New York, NY 10019

Warne, Div. of Viking Penguin, 375 Hudson St., New York, NY 10014

Warner Books, 666 Fifth Ave., New York, NY 10103

Warren Publishing House, P.O. Box 2250, Everett, WA 98203

Western, 850 Third Ave., New York, NY 10022

Whitman see Albert Whitman & Co.

Wilson see H. W. Wilson

Workman, 708 Broadway, New York, NY 10003

Young Naturalist Foundation, P.O. Box 11314, Des Moines, IA 50340

Nonprint Suppliers

A & M Records, 1416 N. La Brea Ave., Hollywood, CA 90028

Agency for Instructional Technology, P.O. Box A, Bloomington, IN 47402

Alcazar Records, P.O. Box 429, Waterbury, VT 05676-0429

American Melody, P.O. Box 270, Guilford, CT 06437-0270

American School Publishers, P.O. Box 408, Hightstown, NJ 08520-0408

Audio Outings, Children's Imagination Tapes, 16 All Souls Crescent #3, Asheville, NC 28803

B B Records, 570 N. Arden Blvd., Los Angeles, CA 90004

Barr Films, P.O. Box 7878, Irwindale, CA 91706-7878

Boosey & Hawkes, 52 Cooper Sq., New York, NY 10003

Britannica Software, 345 Fourth St., San Francisco, CA 94107

Brown & Associates see J. Aaron Brown & Associates

Bullfrog Films, P.O. Box 149, Oley, PA 19547-0149

Churchill Films, 12210 Nebraska Ave., Los Angeles, CA 90025

CMS Records, 4685 Manhattan College Pkwy., Ste. 120, Bronx, NY 10471

Coronet MTI Film & Video, Film Service Center, 420 Academy Dr., Northbrook, IL 60062

Danly Productions, 7250 S. Santa Fe Dr., Hodgkins, IL 60525

Direct Cinema, P.O. Box 69589, Los Angeles, CA 90069-9589

Discovery Music, 4130 Greenbush Ave., Sherman Oaks, CA 91423

Earth Mother Productions, P.O. Box 43204, Tucson, AZ 85733-3204

Educational Activities, P.O. Box 392, Freeport, NY 11520-0392

Educational Graphics Press, P.O. Box 180476, Austin, TX 78718-0476

Family Express Video, P.O. Box 609, Farmington, MI 48332-0609

Gemini, 2000 Penncraft Ct., Ann Arbor, MI 48103

A Gentle Wind, P.O. Box 3103, Albany, NY 12203-3103

Great American Audio, 33 Portman Rd., New Rochelle, NY 10801

Great American Music, 17 Arlington Rd., Natick, MA 01760

Harper Audio, 10 E. 53rd St., New York, NY 10022

Hartley Courseware, 133 Bridge St., Dimondale, MI 48821

High Windy Audio, P.O. Box 553, Fairview, NC 28730-0553

J. Aaron Brown & Associates, 1508 16th Ave. S., Nashville, TN 37212

J2 Communications, 10850 Wilshire Blvd., Ste. 1000, Los Angeles, CA 90024

Jazz Cat Productions, 345 S. McDowell Blvd., Ste. 203, Petaluma, CA 94954

Karol Media, 350 N. Pennsylvania Ave., P.O. Box 7600, Wilkes-Barre, PA 18773-7600

Kartes Video Communications, 7225 Woodland Dr., Indianapolis, IN 46278

KIDVIDZ, 618 Centre St., Newton, MA 02158

Kimbo Educational, P.O. Box 477, 10 N. Third Ave., Long Branch, NJ 07740

Learning Tree, P.O. Box 4116, Englewood, CO 80155

Listening Library, One Park Ave., Old Greenwich, CT 06870-9990

Live Oak Media, P.O. Box 34, Ancramdale, NY 12503

Mariposa Arts, P.O. Box 83695, Los Angeles, CA 90083

Marlboro Records, 845 Marlboro Springs Rd., Kennett Square, PA 19348

MCA Home Video, 70 University City Plaza, Universal City, CA 91608

Media Home Entertainment, 5730 Buckingham Pkwy., Culver City, CA 90230

Media Inc., P.O. Box 384-B, Media, PA 19063

Melody House, 819 NW 92nd St., Oklahoma City, OK 73114

Moose School Records, P.O. Box 960, Topanga, CA 90290-0960

Music for Little People, P.O. Box 1460, Redway, CA 95560

National Geographic Society, Educational Services, Washington, DC 20036

Never a Dull Moment Productions, 1406 N. Topanga Canyon Blvd., Topanga, CA 90290

Orange Cherry Software, P.O. Box 390, Pound Ridge, NY 10576-0390

Phoenix BFA Films & Videos, 468 Park Ave. S., New York, NY 10016

Placenta Music, 2675 Acorn Ave. NE, Atlanta, GA 30305

Pyramid Film & Video, P.O. Box 1048, Santa Monica, CA 90406

Rainbow Educational Video, 170 Keyland Ct., Bohemia, NY 11716

Random House Home Video, 225 Park Ave. S., New York, NY 10003

Red House Records, P.O. Box 4044, St. Paul, MN 55104-4044

Round River Productions, 301 Jacob St., Seekonk, MA 02771

Roundup Records, P.O. Box 154, North Cambridge, MA 02140-0154

RS Records, P.O. Box 651, Brattleboro, VT 05301

Society for Visual Education, 1345 Diversey Pkwy., Chicago, IL 60614

Special Things Distributing, P.O. Box 844, Bala Cynwyd, PA 19004-0844

Spoken Arts, 310 North Ave., New Rochelle, NY 10801

Tahoe Crafts Printing, 589 N. Lake Blvd., Tahoe City, CA 95730

Tales for the Telling, 99 Arlington St., Brighton, MA 02135

Teacher's Discovery, P.O. Box 7048, 1130 E. Big Beaver, Troy, MI 48083

Tickle Tune Typhoon, P.O. Box 15153, Seattle, WA 98115-5153

United Learning, 6633 W. Howard St., Niles, IL 60648

Valentine Productions, 3856 Grand Forest Dr., Norcross, GA 30092

Weston Woods Studios, Weston, CT 06883

Appendix 3
Organizations

Academy of Family Films and Family Television
334 W. 54th St.
Los Angeles, CA 90037
213-752-5811
Sponsors seminars and conferences in order to improve the quality of children's motion pictures and television; holds annual awards for achievement.

Action for Children's Television
20 University Rd.
Cambridge, MA 02138
For information, send a self-addressed stamped envelope to ACT.

American Association of School Librarians
Division of American Library Association
50 E. Huron St.
Chicago, IL 60611
312-280-2163
800-545-2433
Interested in the general improvement and extension of library media services for children and young people; specifically the planning of programs of study and services related to library media services in schools as a means of strengthening the educational program, and the evaluation, selection, interpretation, and utilization of media as they are used in the context of the school program.

American Federation of Teachers
555 New Jersey Ave. NW
Washington, DC 20001
202-879-4400
800-238-1133
Represents the professional, economic, and social concerns of teachers, school-related personnel, public-sector employees, higher education faculty members, and health-care professionals; an AFL-CIO international union.

American Foundation for the Blind, Inc.
15 W. 16th St.
New York, NY 10011
212-620-2000
800-AFBLIND (232-5463)
A national nonprofit organization that advocates, develops, and provides programs and services to help blind and visually impaired people to achieve independence with dignity in all sectors of society.

American Home Economics Association
1555 King St.
Alexandria, VA 22314
703-706-4600
800-424-8080
703-706-HOME fax
Mission is to improve the quality and standards of individual and family life through education, research, cooperative programs, and public information.

Association for Library Service to Children
Division of American Library Association
50 E. Huron St.
Chicago, IL 60611
312-280-2163
800-545-2433 x2163
Advocates the rights of children within and beyond the library profession, evaluates materials for children, promotes international exchange of materials and professional knowledge, conducts and evaluates research projects, and recommends program plans for library service to children.

Association for the Care of Children's Health
7910 Woodmont Ave., Ste. 300
Bethesda, MD 20814
301-654-6549
Mission is to ensure that all aspects of children's health are family centered, psychosocially sound, and developmentally appropriate; believes that healthcare systems and practices are most effective when they are planned, coordinated, delivered, and evaluated through meaningful collaboration among families and professionals across all disciplines.

Braille Institute
741 N. Vermont Ave.
Los Angeles, CA 90029
213-663-1111

A private, nonprofit organization providing training, education, and assistance for those who are blind or visually impaired; publishes *Expectations*, an annual anthology in braille of children's literature that is distributed free of charge to blind children in grades 3–6 or to their parents, teachers, or guardians, and to libraries and organizations that serve blind children.

Child Welfare League of America, Inc.
440 First St. NW, Ste. 310
Washington, DC 20001-2085
202-638-2952
202-638-4004 fax
A federation of public and voluntary child welfare agencies, working with children and their families on critical issues such as child abuse, day care, adolescent pregnancy, adoption, foster care, and homelessness.

Children's Book Council
568 Broadway
New York, NY 10012
212-966-1990
A nonprofit organization encouraging the reading and enjoyment of books for children and young adults; works with other national and international organizations to that end; sponsors National Children's Book Week.

Children's Defense Fund
122 C St. NW
Washington, DC 20001
202-628-8787
Mission is to provide a strong and effective voice for the children of America, who cannot vote, lobby, or speak out for themselves, paying particular attention to the needs of poor, minority, and disabled children. One goal is to educate the nation about the needs of children and to encourage preventive investment

in children before they become ill, drop out of school, or get into trouble.

Children's Literature Association
22 Harvet Ln.
Battle Creek, MI 49017
616-965-8180
Goals are to encourage serious scholarship and research in children's literature, to enhance the professional stature of the graduate and undergraduate teaching of children's literature, and to encourage high standards of criticism in children's literature by awarding fellowships and prizes and by sponsoring conferences and workshops in the field.

Children's Literature Center
Library of Congress
First and Independence St. SE
Washington, DC 20540
202-707-5535
Serves organizations and individuals who study, produce, collect, interpret, and disseminate children's books, films, television programs, or other forms of materials destined for children's information and recreation.

Church and Synagogue Library Association
P.O. Box 19357
Portland, OR 97219-9357
503-244-6919
Purpose is to provide educational guidance in the establishment and maintenance of library service in churches and synagogues.

Council for Children with Behavioral Disorders
Division of Council for Exceptional Children
1920 Association Dr.
Reston, VA 22091-1589
703-620-3660

An international professional organization committed to promoting and facilitating the education and general welfare of children and youth with behavioral and emotional disorders. Actively pursues high-quality educational services and program alternatives for persons with behavioral disorders, advocates for the needs of such children and youth, emphasizes research and professional growth as vehicles for better understanding of behavioral disorders, and provides professional support for those involved with and who serve children and youth with behavioral disorders. Publishes a quarterly journal, *Behavioral Disorders*, a quarterly newsletter, and *Beyond Behavior* magazine, three times a year.

Council for Exceptional Children
1920 Association Dr.
Reston, VA 22091-1589
703-620-3660 (voice & TDD)
703-264-9494 fax
Dedicated to improving the quality of education for all exceptional children and youth and to supporting the professionals who serve them, with particular focus on teacher advocacy, recruitment and retention, professional collaboration, and high-quality instruction.

Council for Indian Education
P.O. Box 31215
Billings, MT 59107-1215
406-252-7451
A nonprofit organization publishing culturally oriented reading materials for use in teaching Native American children from preschool through high school age.

Direction Sports, Inc.
600 Wilshire Blvd., Ste. 320
Los Angeles, CA 90017
213-627-9861

Purpose is to use the magnetism of team membership to develop specific academic and attitudinal skills; emphasizes reading and mathematics, group dynamics, and academic competition over sports; enhances self-esteem by empowering participants to teach, coach, and counsel their younger peers.

ERIC Clearinghouse on Elementary and Early Childhood Education
College of Education
University of Illinois
805 W. Pennsylvania Ave.
Urbana, IL 61801-4897
217-333-1386
217-333-5847 fax

For further information, user may wish to contact:
Educational Resources Information Center
U.S. Department of Education
Office of Education Research and Improvement
555 New Jersey Ave. NW
Washington, DC 20208-5720
202-219-2289
202-219-1859 fax
Develops a database of significant educational materials on the physical, cognitive, social, educational, and cultural development of children from birth through early adolescence; prenatal factors; parental behavior factors; learning theory research and practice related to the development of young children, including the preparation of teachers for this educational level; educational programs and community services for children; and theoretical and philosophical issues pertaining to children's development and education.

Family Service America
11700 W. Lake Park Dr.
Milwaukee, WI 53224
414-359-1040
414-359-1074 fax
Mission is to influence society and its institutions to encourage, protect, and promote healthy family life in North America by cultivating formal and informal working relationships with organizations in the common cause of enhancing family life, ensuring a level of excellence in providing services for families through programs directed to the needs of its constituent membership, maintaining research programs that help develop a growing body of knowledge that is recognized and utilized in improving service to families, influencing public- and private-sector policy to support healthy family life, and increasing public awareness of the importance of healthy family life for a healthy society.

High/Scope Educational Research Foundation
600 N. River St.
Ypsilanti, MI 48198
313-485-2000
Goals are to promote the learning and development of children from infancy through adolescence and to support parents and teachers as they help children to learn and grow.

International Reading Association
P.O. Box 8139
Newark, DE 19711-8139
302-731-1600
302-731-1057 fax
A nonprofit, professional organization that encourages study of the reading process, research, and better teacher education; promotes the development of reading proficiency to the limit of each person's ability; and works to develop an

awareness of the need and importance of reading as a lifetime habit.

Jewish Book Council
15 E. 26th St.
New York, NY 10010
212-532-4949, x297
To promote interest in Jewish books through a variety of programs such as Jewish Book Month, National Jewish Book Awards, Jewish Books in Review syndicated review service, and Jewish Book World.

Kids on the Block, Inc.
9385 C. Gerwig Ln.
Columbia, MD 21046
800-289-6566
800-368-KIDS
An international performing company that prepares children and adults to accept, understand, appreciate, and interact with persons who have a disability, emphasizing the issues surrounding disabilities, differences, and social concerns.

Learning Disabilities Association of America
4156 Library Rd.
Pittsburgh, PA 15234
412-341-1515
A national organization devoted to defining and finding solutions for the broad spectrum of learning problems: visual, auditory, motor control, communication, logic, etc., and emphasizing a total approach to the educational, physiological, psychological, and medical needs of the individual child.

National Art Education Association
1916 Association Dr.
Reston, VA 22091-1590
703-860-8000
Purpose is to contribute to the advancement of high-quality visual art education at all levels of instruction, from preprimary levels through university and continuing education.

National Association for the Education of Young Children
1834 Connecticut Ave. NW
Washington, DC 20009
202-232-8777
800-424-2460
202-328-1846 fax
A nonprofit professional organization dedicated to improving the quality of services offered to young children and their families by providing educational opportunities and resources to promote the professional development of those working for and with young children and by working to increase public knowledge and support for high-quality early childhood programs.

National Association for Visually Handicapped
22 W. 21st St.
New York, NY 10010
212-889-3141
Offers counsel and guidance, information, and referral for partially seeing people (not totally blind) and their families, the professionals and paraprofessionals who work with them, and the business community that employs them. Provides informational literature (much in large print), newsletters for adults and children free by mail, loan library of large print books, and information on visual aids.

National Association of Elementary School Principals
1615 Duke St.
Alexandria, VA 22314-3483
703-684-3345
Serves as an advocate for children and youth in grades pre-K through 8, through award-winning publications, national

327

and regional meetings, and continuing representation before Congress, the executive branch, the news media, and joint efforts with its 51 state and District of Columbia affiliates.

National Association of the Deaf

814 Thayer Ave.
Silver Spring, MD 20910
301-587-1788 (voice)
301-587-1789 (TDD)
301-587-1791 fax
Mission is to ensure that a comprehensive, coordinated system of services is accessible to all persons with hearing impairments in America, enabling them to achieve their maximum potential through increased independence, productivity, and integration into the community.

National Black Child Development Institute

1463 Rhode Island Ave. NW
Washington, DC 20005
202-387-1281
Works to improve the lives of black children and youth through direct services and public education.

National Braille Association, Inc.

1290 University Ave.
Rochester, NY 14607
716-473-0900
Mission is to assist transcribers and narrators in the development and improvement of skills and techniques required for the production of reading materials for individuals who are print handicapped.

National Captioning Institute

5203 Leesburg Pike
Falls Church, VA 22041
800-533-WORD (voice)
800-321-TDDS (TDD)

Maintains a national closed-captioned television service for the entertainment industry to provide deaf and hearing-impaired people with the words accompanying news, drama, comedy, and special events programs.

National Center for Clinical Infant Programs

2000 14th St. N., Ste. 380
Arlington, VA 22201
703-528-4300
Mission is to facilitate optimal health, mental health, and development through preventive clinical approaches in the earliest years of life; to provide a forum for exchange of information emanating from clinical infant and early childhood programs; to stimulate and coordinate research; to encourage the training of personnel; and to foster the development of information and public policy in this important and growing field.

National Center for Health Education

30 E. 29th St.
New York, NY 10016
212-689-1886
212-689-1728 fax
Goal is to improve the health of the American people through health education, particularly the health of children and their families through effective school-based health education programs and services.

National Center for Missing and Exploited Children

2101 Wilson Blvd., Ste. 550
Arlington, VA 22201
703-235-3900 (business office)
800-543-5678 (hotline)
Serves as a clearinghouse of information on missing and exploited children, gives technical assistance to citizens and law enforcement agencies, provides training

programs for law enforcement, distributes photographs and descriptions of missing children nationwide, coordinates child protection efforts with the private sector, networks with nonprofit service providers and state clearinghouses, and provides information and advice on effective state legislation to ensure the safety and protection of children.

National Council of Teachers of English

111 Kenyon Rd.
Urbana, IL 61801
217-328-3879
800-369-NCTE

Promotes the development of literacy and the use of language to construct personal and public worlds and to achieve full participation in society through the learning and teaching of both English and the related arts and sciences of language.

National Crime Prevention Council

1700 K St. NW, 2nd Floor
Washington, DC 20006
202-466-NCPC

Mission is to teach individuals of all ages how to reduce their risk of being victimized and to energize citizens to look beyond self-protection and involve themselves in neighborhood and community-wide actions that attack causes of crime.

National Indian Youth Council, Inc.

318 Elm St. SE
Albuquerque, NM 87102
505-247-2251
505-247-4251 fax

Native American advocacy group engaging in education and advocacy activities, research, and development; provides legal research and Indian voter survey project and employment assistance; published "Americans before Columbus," covering issues relevant to the Native American population.

National Organization for Victim Assistance

1757 Park Rd. NW
Washington, DC 20010
202-232-NOVA

Purposes are national advocacy for victims; direct services for victims of crime, providing 24-hour crisis counseling and follow-up assistance for victims; local program development to establish new programs and expand existing services to better meet the needs of crime victims; and membership communication on new ideas, programs, and knowledge in the field of victim assistance.

National Parent-Teacher Association

700 N. Rush St.
Chicago, IL 60611
312-787-0977

The country's largest child advocacy volunteer group seeking to unite home, school, and community to promote the education, health, and safety of children, youth, and families.

Parent Cooperative Preschools International

P.O. Box 90410
Indianapolis, IN 46290-0410
317-849-0992

Purposes are to strengthen and extend the parent cooperative movement and community appreciation of parent education for adults and preschool education for children; to promote desirable standards for the program, practices, and conditions in parent cooperatives and encourage continuing education for parents, teachers, and directors; to promote interchange of information and help among parent cooperatives, nursery schools, kindergartens, and other parent-sponsored preschool groups; to cooperate with family living, adult education, and early childhood education organizations in the interest of more effective service relationships with parents of young children; and to study legislation designed to further the health and well-being of children and families.

Parents' Choice Foundation
P.O. Box 185
Newton, MA 02168-0185
617-965-5913

A nonprofit service organization offering mothers and fathers information to help their children to keep learning when school lets out; publishes a quarterly review guide, *Parents' Choice Magazine*, and *What-Kids-Who-Don't-Like-to-Read-Like-to-Read*, a free list of books offered on TV and radio as a public service; and grants the Parents Choice Awards, which identify for parents the year's best in all media for children of different ages, backgrounds, skills, and interests.

Reading Is Fundamental, Inc.
Smithsonian Institution
600 Maryland Ave. SW, Rm. 500
Washington, DC 20560
202-287-3220

A national nonprofit organization whose purpose is to help young people discover the joy and acquire the habit of reading; works for national literacy by bringing books to children, by motivating them to read, and by helping parents play an active role in their children's development as readers.

Southern Association on Children under Six
P.O. Box 5403, Brady Sta.
Little Rock, AR 72215-5403
501-663-0353

Purposes are to work on behalf of young children and their families in regard to developmentally based early childhood care and education and to provide opportunities for the cooperation of individuals and groups in the South who are concerned with the well-being of young children.

Southwest Educational Development Laboratory
Office of Institutional Communications and Development
211 E. Seventh St.
Austin, TX 78701-3281
512-476-6861

Development, dissemination, training, and technical assistance for improvement in K–12 schooling, supported by evaluation and applied research, with particular emphasis on ensuring educational equity for children and youth who live in poverty; who are Hispanic, black, or another minority; or who have physical or mental exceptionalities. Program foci relevant to very young children include early childhood language development approaches, transitions from early childhood education to early elementary grades, coordinated education and social services in schools, and teacher training for early elementary math/science education LEP students and others. Catalog of products and services is available free of charge.

U.S. Committee for UNICEF
333 E. 38th St.
New York, NY 10016
212-686-5522

Created for educational and charitable purposes to increase awareness of the needs of children and to raise funds for UNICEF-assisted projects.

U.S. Section of International Board on Books for Young People
c/o IRA
800 Barksdale Rd.
Newark, DE 19714
302-731-1600, x29

Purposes are to encourage the provision of reading materials for young people throughout the world; to cooperate with such organizations as IBBY, whose objectives are similar to those of the U.S. board; and to facilitate the international exchange of information on aspects of books and reading encouragement.

World Around Songs, Inc.
5790 Highway 80 S.
Burnsville, NC 28714
704-675-5343
Promotes international understanding through singing.

World Organization for Early Childhood Education
Organisation Mondiale pour l'Éducation Préscolaire
1718 Connecticut Ave. NW, Ste. 500
Washington, DC 20009
312-237-2854

Works both nationally and internationally to promote optimum conditions for the well-being and development of all children, to help with any endeavor that improves the lives of children 0–8 years of age, and to support and publicize research that contributes to improving the lives of children and families and promotes peace in the world.

Young Audiences
115 E. 92nd St.
New York, NY 10128
212-831-8110
A national arts-in-education organization whose purpose is to help establish the arts as an essential part of all children's education.

Indexes

Name Index

This index lists all authors, editors, translators, narrators, singers, and other contributors who are included in the bibliographic entries. The names are arranged alphabetically and are followed by the entry number(s). Entry numbers preceded by a P are found in Appendix 1: Professional Resources.

Aardema, Verna, 1053
Abercrombie, Barbara, 180
Ackerman, Karen, 852
Adams, Pam, 76, 407, 674, 687, 994
Adoff, Arnold, 131, 162
Aesop, 11
Agard, John, 523
Agutter, Jerry, 586
Ahlberg, Allan, 90, 266, 342
Ahlberg, Janet, 90, 266, 342
Alexander, Martha, 135, 676, 1027
Alexander, Terry, 424, 631
Aliki, 245, 302, 997
Allen, Pamela, 1044
Allender, David, 822
Alsop, Peter, 473
Ambrose, Catherine, 816
Andersen, Hans Christian, 283, 770, 929, 978
Anderson, Lena, 159
Anderson, Marcella F., P14
Anderson, Peggy P., 934
Anno, Mitsumasa, 57–60
Anvi, Fran, 324
Apple, Margot, 826
Applebee, Arthur N., P26

Archambault, John, 102, 184, 410, 531, 571, 985
Arnold, Tedd, 644, 646
Aruego, Jose, 183, 414, 524, 600, 632, 1031, 1033, 1050
Asch, Frank, 79, 105, 152, 389–390, 411, 595, 686
Atkinson, Lisa, 452

Babbitt, Natalie, 848
Baer, Gene, 401, 930
Baghban, Marcia, P97
Baker, Mark, 417
Baker, Pamela J., 643
Ballingham, Pamela, 268
Ballingham, Tim, 268
Bang, Molly, 238, 910
Banish, Roslyn, 525
Banks, Kate, 36
Barber, Michael, 748
Barklem, Jill, 70
Barlin, Anne, 234
Barnes-Murphy, Rowan, 707
Barrett, Judith, 52, 209, 841
Barrett, Ron, 52, 209
Bartels, Joanie, 561

Subject Index

This index lists the annotated titles under specific subject headings. The headings are arranged alphabetically. All numbers refer to entry numbers.

Aardvarks
Arthur Sets Sail, 64
Arthur's Eyes, 65
Arthur's Thanksgiving, 67

Accidents
The Accident, 8
Walter's Tail, 995

Adventure
Arthur, 63
Brave Irene, 150–151
Builder of the Moon, 158
The Giant Jam Sandwich, 347
Klippity Klop, 516
Where the Wild Things Are, In the
   Night Kitchen, Outside over
   There, 1038
Where's Spot? 1039

Africa
A Country Far Away, 226
The Dancing Granny, 236
Jambo Means Hello, 495
Mufaro's Beautiful Daughters, 631
Not So Fast, Songololo, 679
Tricky Tortoise, 959

Why Mosquitoes Buzz in People's
   Ears, 1053

Afro-Americans
Baby Says, 81
The Black Snowman, 132
Corduroy, 221–222
Eat up, Gemma, 271
Jamaica's Find, 493
Nightfeathers, 670
Peter's Chair, 749
Sam, 809
Tell Me a Story, Mama, 905
The Trip, 960
We Keep a Store, 998

Aged
See Old age

Airplanes
Airplanes, 15
Flying, 319
Redbird, 791

Alcoholism
I Wish Daddy Didn't Drink So
   Much, 455

Animation

Anteaters

Ants

Art

Artists

Autumn

See Fall

Feet
See also Anatomy
Feet! 303
Sounds My Feet Make, 854

Finger play
Finger Plays for Nursery & Kindergarten, 305
Finger Rhymes, 306
Hand Rhymes, 380–381
Music for Little People, 633
Piggies, 756
Round and Round the Garden, 802

Finger-sucking
Donald Says Thumbs Down, 256

Fire engines
Fire Engine Shapes, 307

Firefighters
Fire Fighters A to Z, 308

Fish
Big Al, 118
Fish Eyes, 314
Fish Is Fish, 316
Lend Me Your Wings, 523
Swimmy, 888
What's in the Deep Blue Sea? 1016

Fishing
Fish for Supper, 315
The Tale of Mr. Jeremy Fisher, 891

Fleas
The Napping House, 660–661

Flight
First Flight, 310
Flying, 319

Flowers
Planting a Rainbow, 759

Folk and fairy tales
Aesop's Fables, 11
The Baby's Story Book, 94
Baby's Storytime (Stories to Remember), 95
Beauty and the Beast, 107
Beauty & the Beast (Stories to Remember), 108
The Bremen Town Musicians, 154
A Child's First Book of Nursery Tales, 189
Classic Children's Tales, 203
The Clown of God, 210
The Cobweb Curtain, 211
The Dancing Granny, 236
Dawn, 238
Deep in the Forest, 242
The Emperor and the Kite, 282
The Emperor & the Nightingale, 283
The Empty Pot, 284
Foolish Rabbit's Big Mistake, 320
A Frog Prince, 340
The Giant's Toe, 348
Goldilocks and the Three Bears, 360
Hansel and Gretel, 384–385
Heckedy Peg, 402
The Helen Oxenbury Nursery Story Book, 404
Henny Penny, 408
Holiday Fairy Tales, 420
Hot Hippo, 424
How the Camel Got His Hump & How the Rhinoceros Got His Skin, 430
It Could Always Be Worse, 484
Jack and the Beanstalk, 489
Jackie Torrence, 492
Johnny Appleseed, 499
Journey Cake, Ho! 500
A Journey to Paradise, 501
Little Fingerling, 538
The Little Red Hen, 544
The Magic Porridge Pot, 570
The Man Who Kept House, 576
Many Moons, 577
The Mitten, 601
The Mud Pony, 630
Mufaro's Beautiful Daughters, 631

Halloween
Apples and Pumpkins, 61
Dinosaurs' Halloween, 250
A Halloween Mask for Monster, 379
*The Little Old Lady Who Was Not
    Afraid of Anything,* 542
The Magic Pumpkin, 571
The Pumpkin Blanket, 772
Teeny Tiny, 902–903
The Trip, 960

Hand games
See Finger play

Handicapped
See Disabled

Hands
See also Anatomy
Hands, 382
Hanimals, 383
Here Are My Hands, 410
My Hands Can, 648

Hanukkah
All about Hanukkah, 21
Hanukkah, 386

Hats
Caps for Sale, 168
Martin's Hats, 580
Whose Hat? 1049
The Witch's Hat, 1060

Health
Circle Around, 197
Humpty Dumpty's Magazine, 436

Hearing
Crash! Bang! Boom! 227
I Hear, 446

Hearing Impaired
See Deafness

Helpfulness
Herman the Helper, 414

Hiding
See Camouflage

Hills
See Mountains

Hippopotamuses
George and Martha, 344
Hot Hippo, 424

Holidays
See also Christmas; Easter; Halloween;
    Hanukkah; Mother's Day; Passover;
    Thanksgiving Day
Celebrations, 177
Classroom Holidays, 204
Holiday Fairy Tales, 420
Thanksgiving Treat, 913

Homes
See Houses

Honesty
The Empty Pot, 284
Jamaica's Find, 493

Horses
The Mud Pony, 630
With the Wind, 1061

Hospitals
The Emergency Room, 280
Eric Needs Stitches, 285
In the Hospital, 473

Houses
A Chair for My Mother, 178
Frederick, 327
Homes, 421
How a House Is Built, 427
In Our House, 471
Let's Look All Around the House, 527
The Little House, 541

Human body
See Anatomy

Sounds

Space and spaceships

Spain

Spanish language

Spiders

Sports

Age/Category Index

This index groups the annotated titles by age and category. Titles are arranged alphabetically within each grouping. All numbers refer to entry numbers.

INFANT: Concept/Counting/Alphabet

Animal Sounds, 49
Babies, 73
Baby's First Words, 92
First Things First, 313
Gobble, Growl Grunt, 356
Growing, 374
Happy Baby, 387
Homes, 421
I Went Walking, 454
Is It Red? Is It Yellow? Is It Blue? 481
Moo Baa La La La, 605
More First Words, 609
A Peaceable Kingdom, 735
Rain, 780
Spot's Toys, 862
Stop Go, 873
Ten, Nine Eight, 910
What Can You Do? 1005
What Is It? 1013

INFANT: Informational

Baby Inside, 80
The Baby's Book of Babies, 88
Baby's First Christmas, 91
Baby's First Year, 93

Jungle Sounds, 504
The Me Book, 589
My Day, 641
What Do Toddlers Do? 1007
What Does Baby See? 1009

INFANT: Participation and manipulative

Bunny Rattle, 160
Doggies, 255
Let's Look All Around the House, 527
My Daddy, 640
Pat the Bunny, 730
Touch Me Book, 950
Transitions 2, 955
Wally Whale and His Friends, 994

INFANT: Poetry/Nursery rhymes/Songs

All Small, 29
Baby Can Too, 77
Baby Songs, 84
Baby Songs by Hap and Martha
  Palmer, 85
The Baby's Bedtime Book, 86
Baby's Bedtime (Stories to
  Remember), 87

INFANT: Story

INFANT: Wordless

TODDLER: Concept/Counting/Alphabet

TODDLER: Folklore/Folktales/Fairy tales

TODDLER: Informational

TODDLER: Participation and manipulative

TODDLER: Periodicals

TODDLER: Poetry/Nursery rhymes/Songs

TODDLER: Story

TODDLER: Wordless

PRESCHOOL: Concept/Counting/ Alphabet

PRESCHOOL: Folklore/Folktales/Fairy tales

PRESCHOOL: Story

PRESCHOOL: Wordless

KINDERGARTEN: Concept/Counting/Alphabet

KINDERGARTEN: Story

KINDERGARTEN: Wordless

Age/Purchase Priority Index

This index groups the annotated titles by age and by purchase priority. Titles are arranged alphabetically within each grouping. All numbers refer to entry numbers.

INFANT: Purchase Priority [3]

TODDLER: Purchase Priority [1]

TODDLER: Purchase Priority [2]

TODDLER: Purchase Priority [3]

PRESCHOOL: Purchase Priority [1]

PRESCHOOL: Purchase Priority [2]

PRESCHOOL: Purchase Priority [3]

KINDERGARTEN: Purchase Priority [1]

Format Index

This index lists nonprint materials by format. Titles are arranged alphabetically under each format. All numbers refer to entry numbers.

Compact disc

Filmstrip

Filmstrip with audiocassette

Record

Software